U0964164

高等院校基于工作过程的校企合作系列教材

国际贸易单证操作实务
（第二版）

International Business Documents Practice
(Second Edition)

主　　编　辜晓康　赵　崎
副 主 编　张李丹　蒲新蓉
企业顾问　范　俊　郭　漫
校　　阅　李阳梅　杨熙玲

对外经济贸易大学出版社
中国·北京

图书在版编目（CIP）数据

国际贸易单证操作实务 ：汉、英 / 辜晓康，赵崎主编. --2 版. --北京：对外经济贸易大学出版社，2024.8. –(高等院校基于工作过程的校企合作系列教材). --ISBN 978-7-5663-2618-8

Ⅰ. F740.44

中国国家版本馆 CIP 数据核字第 2024V8P655 号

国际贸易单证操作实务（第二版）

International Business Documents Practice (Second Edition)

辜晓康　赵　崎　主编

责任编辑： 邱　悦

出版发行：对外经济贸易大学出版社

社　　址：北京市朝阳区惠新东街 10 号

网　　址：www.uibep.com

资源网址：www.uibepresources.com

邮政编码：100029

邮购电话：010－64492338

发行部电话：010－64492342

E-mail：uibep@126.com

成品尺寸：185mm×260mm

印　　张：20.25

字　　数：468 千字

ISBN 978-7-5663-2618-8

印　　刷：三河市少明印务有限公司

版　　次：2024 年 8 月北京第 2 版

印　　次：2024 年 8 月第 1 次印刷

定　　价：69.00 元

出版说明

党的二十大擘画了以中国式现代化推进中华民族伟大复兴的宏伟蓝图，发出了为全面建设社会主义现代化国家、全面推进中华民族伟大复兴而团结奋斗的伟大号召。习近平总书记在党的二十大报告中强调，要“推进职普融通、产教融合、科教融汇”，为我国未来职业教育的发展指明了方向。报告指出，“教育、科技、人才是全面建设社会主义现代化国家的基础性、战略性支撑”，而我们与之相对应的课程开发方式和课程内容的改革模式是“与行业企业共同开发紧密结合生产实际的实训教材，并确保优质教材进课堂”。“高等院校基于工作过程的校企合作系列教材”正是对外经济贸易大学出版社在高等职业教育课程建设领域的最新研究成果。

本系列教材适用于全国高等院校**应用型本科**商务英语专业和国际经济与贸易、贸易经济、国际商务、工商管理、市场营销等经济与贸易类和工商管理类专业的学生；同时适用于全国**高职高专院校**商务英语、应用英语、旅游英语等语言类专业以及国际贸易实务、国际经济与贸易、国际商务等财经商贸大类专业的学生。

本系列教材主要呈现以下特点：

1. 体现“基于工作过程”

在我国高等职业教育新一轮课程改革中，我们学习、引进并发展了德国职业教育的一种新的课程模式——基于工作过程的课程模式。该模式指“为完成一件工作任务并获得工作成果而进行的一个完整的工作程序”建立起来的课程体系。

2. 突出“校企合作”

课程体系的“校企合作”以教师和企业人员参与为主体，是“校企合作，工学结合”的人才培养模式发展的必然产物，旨在提高学生的综合能力，尤其是实践能力和就业能力，实现学校教学与工作实践的零距离。

“高等院校基于工作过程的校企合作系列教材”的课程方案与传统的课程方案相比，打破了高等职业教育学科系统化的课程体系，在分析典型职业活动工作过程的前提下，按照工作过程中的需要来设计课程，以突出工作过程在课程框架中的主线地位，整合优化了理论知识与实践活动。在教材编写过程中，教师结合自身的教学实践、调研论证和外贸专家对工作岗位的实际要求来安排课程结构和内容，而这形成了具有特色的基于工作过程的校企合作系列教材体系。

本套教材涵盖三大模块：语言技能类、专业英语类和专业知识类。作者都是本专业的“双师型”教师，不仅具有丰富的语言教学经验，而且具备企业第一线的工作经历，还主持或参与过多项国家或省市级相关科研项目。他们为本套教材的编写质量提供了有力的保证。

本系列教材包括：

语言技能类

商务英语听说
实用商务英语口语教程（第三版）
国际商务英语口语实训（第二版）
致用商务英语阅读（上册）
致用商务英语阅读（下册）
新编商务英语应用文写作
实用商务英语写作教程（第二版）
商务英语函电
外贸函电与单证实训教程（第二版）
商务翻译实务（第三版）
经贸英语口译实训教程（第二版）
英语语法实训教程

专业英语类

会展实务英语（第三版）
商务礼仪实务英语（第二版）
外事接待实务英语（第三版）
中英文酒店服务实训教程
旅游实务英语多模态教程
中英文导游实训教程
涉外酒店前厅服务技能实训教程

专业知识类

外贸跟单实务（第二版）
外贸单证实务
国际贸易单证操作实务（第二版）
进出口报关实务（第二版）
报检实务（第二版）
国际市场营销实务
涉外企业管理实务（英文版）
生产物流运作实务
集装箱运输实务
国际贸易实务（双语版）
商务英语谈判
国际结算（英文版）

值得注意的是，本系列教材不是封闭的，它随着教学模式和课程设置的变化，将不断推出新的内容，以丰富整个体系。

同时，本套教材均配有 PPT 课件等立体化教学资源，供教师教学参考（下载网址：http://www.uibepresources.com）。

对外经济贸易大学出版社
2024 年 1 月

前　言

习近平总书记在党的二十大报告中指出，要实施科教兴国战略，强化现代化建设人才支撑，为我们搞好大学课堂教学指明了方向。大学教材也必须顺应我国经济社会发展的需要，与时俱进，紧贴工作实际，为学习者提供够用、实用、好用的能够学以致用的好教材。

近六年来，本书得到了广大高校外向型专业师生的较高认可，令人十分欣慰。在第二版里，我们仍保留了取材于国际贸易实际的案例和习题，训练量充足（教学可根据需要取舍），难易呈梯度，制单能力训练分为初级、中级直至高级三个层次（供教学取舍），业务涉及陆海空运输方式，结算方式多样化，课件讲解精细精准，内涵丰富的贸易实践经验，作业示范准确无误等。

随着我国对外贸易管理机制的较大调整和国际贸易环境的巨大变化，报检报关已在一体化窗口操作，大大简化了填制报检报关单据的工作，自主报关甚至已不需要填写报关单。在是否保留报检报关这两章内容上，我们到进出口企业和国际物流企业做了深入调查，经过认真思考和讨论，决定还是保留这两章，但内容根据现在的工作实际做出重大修改，原因是如果企业采用代理报检报关，还是需要草填报检报关单据，否则与代理单位沟通就十分困难了。或者反过来，我们的学习者在代理报检报关单位工作中，也需要掌握必要的填写报检报关单据的知识和技能，才能给予中小微进出口企业有效帮助。另外，尽管绝大部分西方发达国家已取消了对我国输入产品的普惠制关税优惠，但仍有三个发达国家在给予我国普惠制优惠。我们的一些学习者也很有可能进入跨国公司被派往东南亚或其他地区做贸易，也会用到普惠制产地证书，所以我们保留了普惠制 FORM A 证书的讲解和训练。

我们本次对教材部分章节做出重大修改的工作中，赵崎老师在酷暑天里不辞辛劳，根据我国报检报关制度发生的重大调整和变化，对报检报关两章内容做了重大修改，详细介绍了我国一体化窗口报检报关的操作要领，同时也根据西方发达国家对我国普惠制关税优惠发生的政策变化，以及我国积极发展与东盟各国的贸易往来的客观现实，对原产地证书这一章内容做了重大的补充，增加了 RCEP 原产地证书和 Form E 证书的精细精彩讲解。利用这次再版机会，辜晓康老师也对全书曾经存在的错漏之处一一做了修改和更正。

为了帮助老师们提高教学成效，也为了一些自学的朋友们学习方便，我们把训练习题的参考答案都放在了课件里（课件下载网址：www.uibepresources.com）。在此，我们真诚地呼吁学习者不要在没有独立完成训练作业之前就去参看答案，更不要在学习中走“捷径”抄袭答案。

最后，我们热切希望本书能继续成为应用型本科和高职外向型专业师生的教学好帮手，能继续成为在岗外贸业务员学习和提高自己的国际贸易业务操作技能的好帮手。

编　者

2023 年 8 月

目　　录

项目一

课 程 导 入

国际贸易单证（International Business Documents）是国际贸易中广泛使用的各种单据、文件和证书的统称。进出口企业凭借各种单证来处理进出口货物的交付分销、仓储运输、检验检疫、报关清关、货运保险、收付结汇等环节的工作。可以说，单证工作贯穿了整个国际贸易的过程，其工作量之大，涉及范围之广，协调性之强，时间要求之严格，毋庸置疑。

学习目标

［知识目标］ 了解单证工作的基本要求和流转程序，熟悉单证工作依据的标准，掌握单证的分类。

［能力目标］ 能根据单证流转程序管理单据。

学习内容

一、国际贸易单证工作的地位

（一）国际贸易单证是合同履行的必要手段和证明

在各个外贸环节中，单证的运用真实地反映了国际贸易合同履行的进展情况和相关方的责任、权利和义务的发生、转移和终止。国际贸易中买卖双方处于不同的国家或地区，在绝大多数情况下，商品和货币不能进行直接交换而需以单证作为交换的手段。在象征性交货情况下，卖方交单意味着交付了货物，而买方付款则是以得到物权凭证的相关单据为前提，贸易合同的履行是通过单证和货款对流来实现的。

（二）国际贸易单证是结算工作的重要工具

单据代表着货物，掌握了单据就等于掌握了货物所有权。通过单据转移，达到了货物转移的目的。例如，在信用证这样的结算方式下，卖方交单意味着交货，买方则通过付款赎单获取货物，买卖双方的结算不是以货物本身作为依据，取而代之的是凭单据买卖完成结算。故而，单据和货物对流的原则已然成为国际贸易商品买卖和货款支付的一般原则。在整个国际贸易中，单证的质量为及时安全收汇提供了保障。

（三）国际贸易单证是解决争端的必要依据

当发生贸易纠纷时，国际贸易单证又常常是处理争议、解决索赔的依据和法律文件。例如，货物在运输途中受损，货方向保险公司提出索赔，保险单就是索赔的凭证；在计算赔偿额时发票是赔偿的依据。

（四）国际贸易单证是外贸企业经营管理水平的集中反映

单证工作服务于国际贸易全过程，是外贸企业经营管理水平的集中反映。贸易合同的内容、信用证条款、货源衔接、审证改证、交单议付等业务管理的问题，都会在单证工作中反映出来。由此可见，正确、完整、及时地缮制单证，确保单证的质量是衡量一家外贸企业经营管理水平高低的重要指标。

（五）国际贸易单证的质量彰显外贸企业的企业形象和素质，影响企业经济效益

简洁、清晰、完整的单证体现了外贸企业高水平的业务素质，塑造、完善了企业的良好形象。反之，杂乱、粗陋、充满不符点的单证不仅有损企业形象，更严重的是会给企业造成无法挽回的经济损失，影响企业的经济效益。

二、出口单证的流转程序

本书以信用证结算方式下 Cost Insurance and Freight（CIF）出口合同，海运方式、产地商检、异地报关的业务为例，说明出口业务的单证流转程序。图例如下：

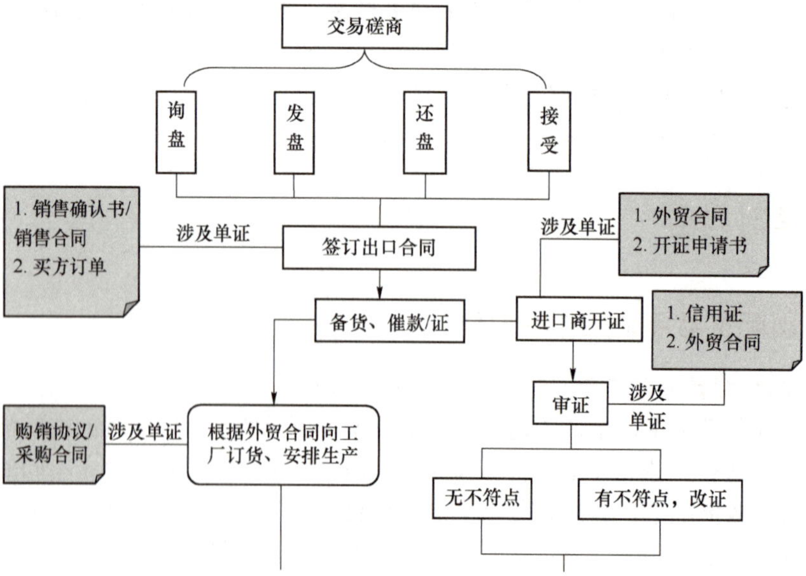

图 1-1　出口业务单证流转程序图

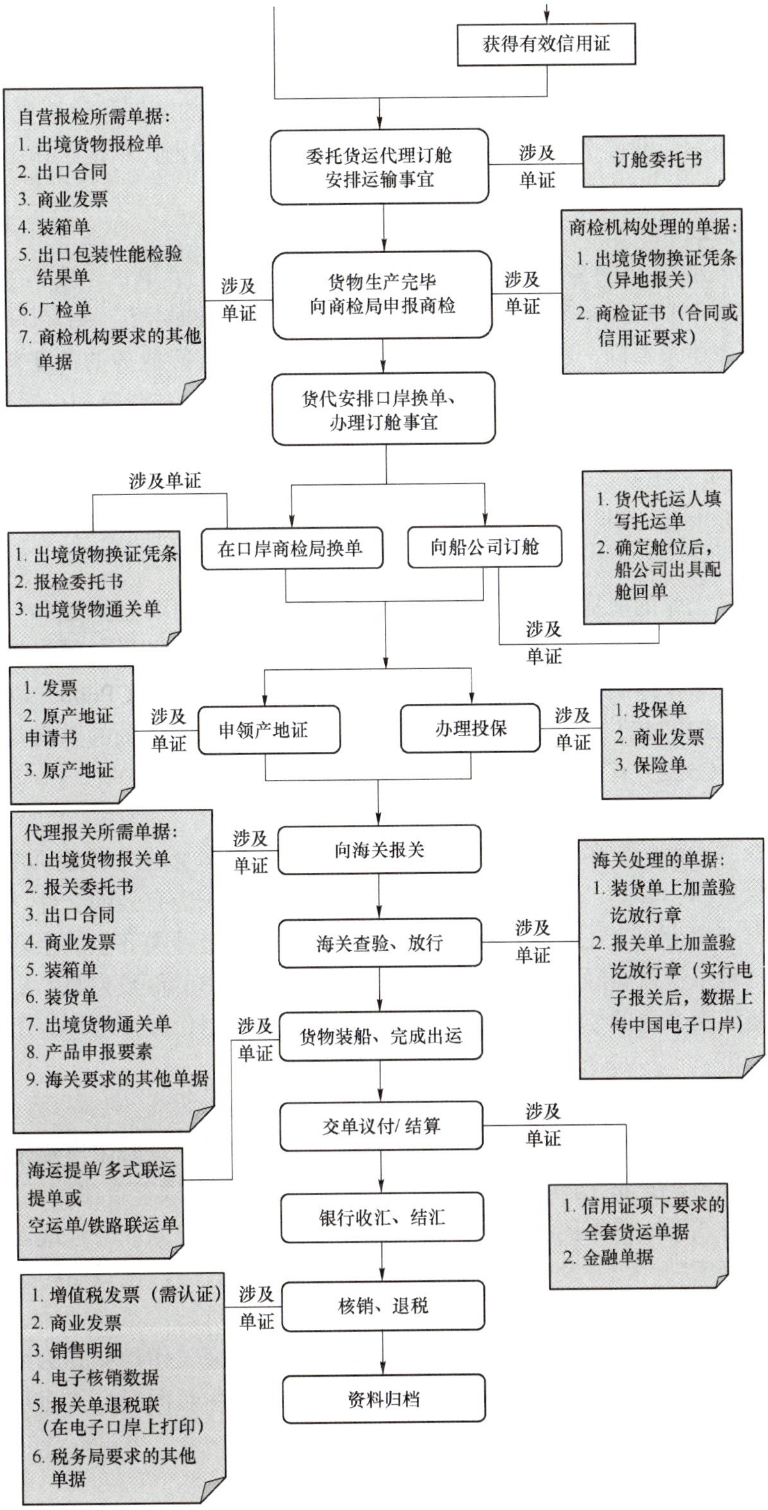

图 1-1　出口业务单证流转程序图（续）

三、单证工作的要求

在外贸实际工作中，特别是以信用证方式结算，对单证的缮制和审核要求极其严格，必须符合有关国际商业惯例、法令法规以及实际货物出货细则，单证工作必须遵循以下原则：

（一）四一致

所谓“四一致”，指的是单证一致、单单一致、单同一致、单货一致。在信用证结算方式下，单证工作要确保单证相符、单单一致，方能安全及时结汇。汇付和托收结算方式下，单证工作要求单同一致、单单一致，保证收汇。从实际业务的角度来看，要求单证完全代表实际发运的货物，即为单货一致，以确保合同的顺利履行和今后贸易的开展，同时也为外贸企业赢得良好的口碑和信誉。

（二）五要求

所谓“五要求”，即制单工作要求正确、完整、及时、整洁和简明。

1. 正确

正确是单证工作的前提和基础。一是要求各种单据要做到以上提及的“四一致”，数字和文字正确，二是要求各种单证必须符合有关国际贸易惯例和进口国有关法令法规。信用证结算方式下，缮制的单据要与《跟单信用证统一惯例》（UCP600）以及《国际标准银行实务》（ISBP745）有关条款相符；在托收结算方式下，缮制的单据要符合《托收统一规则》（URC522）有关条款的规定。

2. 完整

完整包含三方面的完备：（1）内容完整：每一种单据本身的内容必须齐全，包括其格式、项目、数据、签章、文字等必须齐全，否则不构成一份有效的文件。（2）种类完整：银行在办理议付或者托收时，一般都要求外贸企业提交种类齐全的全套货运单据，如果遗漏某一种单据就会导致拒付，从而无法顺利结汇。（3）份数完整：出口商必须按照信用证或者买卖合同的要求，如数提交规定的正副本单据份数，不可有所短缺，否则亦会影响到结汇。

3. 及时

单证的及时性体现在及时出单与及时交单两个方面。（1）及时出单是指各种单证的出单日期必须合理，在信用证结算方式下，单据的出单日期必须符合信用证的有关规定。非信用证结算方式下，单据的出单日期应按照国际贸易惯例、商业习惯或者买卖合同要求的合理日期来缮制。（2）及时交单是指在信用证结算方式下，出口商必须在信用证规定的交单期内向银行完成交单，逾期交单将会遭到银行拒付。

整个外贸业务流程环环相扣，以各种单证为纽带，单证工作贯穿其始终。任何一个环节中出现单证不及时的疏忽，不仅会对该环节的工作产生负面影响，而且还会导致连锁反应，造成不良后果，甚至是无法弥补的损失。

4. 整洁

单证工作的内在质量体现在制单的正确性和完整性上，单证工作的外显质量则体现在单证的整洁性上。单证格式的设计应尽量标准化、规范化，布局合理；缮制的内容应排列整齐、美观。单证工作的整洁性在一定程度上体现了外贸单证员的业务素养，反映了外贸公司的业务水平。

5. 简明

单证的内容应当力求简明扼要，以利于提高单证工作的效率，切记不要加列不必要的内容，以免画蛇添足、弄巧成拙。

四、制单和审单依据的标准

单证工作中制单和审单的主要依据有外贸合同、信用证、相关商品的实际原始资料、相关国际贸易惯例以及国内相关部门的规定等。

在信用证结算方式下，制单和审单的主要依据是商品的实际原始资料、信用证、《跟单信用证统一惯例》(UCP600)和《国际标准银行实务》(ISBP745)。在托收结算方式下，制单和审单的主要依据是商品的实际原始资料、外贸合同和《托收统一规则》(URC522)。在汇付结算方式下，制单和审单的主要依据是商品的实际原始资料和外贸合同。

五、单据的分类

根据不同的角度，国际贸易单证可做如下分类：

（一）国际惯例对单据的分类

1.《托收统一规则》（URC522）的分类

（1）金融单据（Financial Documents）：汇票（Draft/Bill of Exchange）、本票（Demand Draft）、支票（Check/Cheque）。

（2）商业单据（Commercial Documents）：商业发票（Commercial Invoice）、包装单据（Packing Documents）、保险单据（Insurance Documents）。

2.《跟单信用证统一惯例》（UCP600）的分类

（1）运输单据（Transport Documents）：包括海运提单（Ocean Bill of Lading (B/L)）、非转让海运单（Seaway Bill）、租船合约提单（Chartered B/L）、多式联运提单（Combined B/L）、航空运单（Air Waybill）、国际铁路联运单/承运货物收据（Railway Bill/Cargo Receipt）、邮包收据（Parcel Receipt）、运输代理人的运输单据（Agent B/L）。

（2）保险单据（Insurance Documents）：包括保险单（Insurance Policy）、保险凭证（Insurance Certificate）、承保证明（Risk Note）、预约保单（Open Policy）、保险批单（Insurance Endorsement）、联合保单（Combined Insurance Policy）。

（3）商业发票（Commercial Invoice）。

（4）其他单据（Other Documents）：包括包装单据、各种证明书等附属单据。其中，各种证明书包括了官方单据（Official Documents）：商检证书（Inspection Certificate）、产地证（Certificate of Origin）、普惠制产地证（Generalized System of Preferences Certificate of Origin Form A, GSP Form A）、海关发票（Customs Invoice）、领事发票（Consular Invoice）、领事产地证（Consular Certificate of Origin）、许可证（License）、配额（Quota）等单据；及其他证明（Other Certificates）：受益人证明/声明（Beneficiary's Certificate/Statement/Declaration）、电抄/启运电报（Copy of Cable/Fax/Shipping Advice）、船籍证明

（Certificate of Vessel's Nationality）、船龄证明（Seaworthy Certificate of Vessel）、航运路线证明（Itinerary Certificate）、船长/大副收据（Master's Receipt/Mate's Receipt）、运费收据（Freight Receipt）、邮包收据（Parcel Receipt）、传真传输报告（Fax Transmission Report）、生产商检验报告（Manufacturer's Certificate）等各类证明。

3. UN/EDIFACT 分类

《联合国/行政、商业和运输电子数据交换条例》（United Nations/Electronic Data Interchange for Administration, Commerce and Transport）是由联合国制定的国际标准，其主要工作目的是简化国际贸易单证并服务于贸易单证标准化；消除由于贸易数据元表述不一而产生的贸易双方的误解和差错；便于大范围地在贸易伙伴之间交换信息。根据联合国这一电子商务标准，国际商务单证划分为九大类，即生产单证、订购单证、销售单证、银行单证、保险单证、运输单证、货运代理服务单证、出口单证、进口和转口单证。

（二）按国际商务单证的用途分类

1. 结算类单据：结汇所需的各种单据，包括上述分类中的各种单据，在此不再赘述。

2. 非结算单据：包括货物订舱委托书/货运单、出口货物订舱配舱回单、装货单（S/O）、出/入境货物报检单、出境货物换证凭条、出/入境货物通关单、出/入境货物报关单、投保单等单据。

（三）按国际商务单证的方向分类

按国际贸易方向划分，单证可分为进口单证（买方单证）和出口单证（卖方单证）。

（四）按国际商务单证的形式分类

纸质单证和电子单证。根据《国际贸易术语解释通则》（International Rules for the Interpretation of Trade Terms, INCOTERMS2010）解释，纸质单证和电子单证具有同等法律效力。

操作能力训练

思考题：

S1-1　国际贸易的流程与单据流转程序之间有何关系？

操作题：

C1-1　用文字（非图表）列出国际贸易单证工作的流转程序。

C1-2　自行查阅并打印《跟单信用证统一惯例》（UCP600）和《国际标准银行实务》（ISBP745）。

C1-3　分小组讨论国际贸易的主要结算方式；弄清楚自营报检报关与代理报检报关的区别。

C1-4　探索学习下一项目，并独立阅读附录里的阅读分析信用证 C2-1，并尝试翻译其主要条款。

模块一

信用证阅读与分析

以信用证方式结算的国际贸易，其审证、制单和审单工作都离不开对信用证的正确理解和分析。实际上，外贸企业的一个外销业务员在拿到国外开来的信用证时，首先就要对信用证进行认真细致的阅读和分析。

项目二

阅读分析信用证

学习目标

[知识目标] 掌握信用证的结构，熟悉信用证条款含义，了解信用证业务流程。
[能力目标] 能独立快速阅读信用证，并正确理解其条款。

项目描述

这是一份 Society for Worldwide Interbank Financial Telecommunications（SWIFT）电开信用证及其条款翻译件。在实际工作中，来证并无翻译，需要业务员自己理解。电开信用证为目前信用证业务中最常见的信用证格式。本信用证由汇丰银行香港分行开出，以广东鸿艺贸易有限公司为受益人，商品为工艺品。

2015 MAY 23 14：49：12　　Logical Terminal SWPP
MT　S700　　Issue of a Documentary Credit　　Page 00002
电开证格式 700　　开立跟单信用证
Func SWIFT MSGACK DWS7651 Auth OK, key B30407186423644D, BKCHCNBJ SHBCHKHH
环银电协（环球银行金融电讯协会）信用证
Record875803

Basic Header　F　01 BKCHCNBJA400　1274　311389
Application Header　0 700 1411 050523 HSBCHKHHDHKH 0760　552387 050523　1411 N
报头

THE HONG KONG AND SHANGHAI
BANKING CORPORATION LIMITED
HONG KONG
（ALL HK OFFICES AND HEAD OFFICE）
开证行：汇丰银行 香港各办事处及总部

User Header	Service Code	103:
	Bank Priority	113:
	Msg User Ref.	108: 143090658
	Info. From CI	115:

Sequence of Total: *27 : 1/1
电文页次
Form of Doc. Credit *40 A : IRREVOCABLE
跟单信用证形式 不可撤销
Doc. Credit Number *20 : DC NPH182503
跟单信用证号码 DC NPH182503
Date of Issue *31C : 150523
开证日期 2015 年 5 月 23 日
Expiry *31D : Date 150804 Place CHINA
信用证有效期及到期地点 日期：2015 年 8 月 4 日 地点：中国
Applicant *50 : FUNDINS TORONTO, CANADA
信用证申请人 56 TOWER STREET, TORONTO, CANADA
加拿大多伦多 Fundins 公司
加拿大多伦多托尔大街 56 号
Beneficiary *59 : GUANGDONG WHOLE ARTS TRADING COMPANY
信用证受益人 FINANCE BUILDING 35—39
NO. 7 ZHONGSHAN ROAD, GUANGZHOU, CHINA
广东鸿艺贸易有限公司
中国广州中山路 7 号金融大厦 35—39 楼
Amount *32B : Currency USD Amount 38,963.80
信用证金额 币种 美元 金额 38 963.80
Pos./Neg. Tol. （5） 39A : 05/05
金额上下浮动允许的最大范围： 上下浮动 5%
Available with/by *41A : ANY BANK
指定的交单银行及 BY NEGOTIATION
信用证的兑付方式 自由议付
Drafts at... 42C : SIGHT FOR FULL INVOICE OF GOODS

汇票付款期限　即期汇票付款，金额为货物的发票全额

Drawee 42A : ISSUING BANK

汇票受票人/付款人　开证行

Partial Shipments 43P : ALLOWED

分批装运条款　允许分批装运

Transshipment 43T : ALLOWED

转运条款　允许转船

Loading in Charge 44A : ANY PORT IN CHINA

装船、发运和接收监管的地点　中国任意港口

For Transport to... 44B : TORONTO, CANADA

货物发运的最终目的地　加拿大多伦多港

Latest Date of Shipment 44C : 150731

最迟装运期　2015年7月31日

Description of Goods 45A : CIF INCOTERMS®2010 TORONTO, CANADA

货物描述　CIF 加拿大多伦多　适用惯例为 INCOTERMS®2010

1）20,000 PCS OF CORN BASKET AT USD1.40/PC
AS PER PURCHASE ORDER NO. 7980/05/FK
2万个玉米篮子，每个1.40美元，根据第7980/05/FK号订单

2）12,182 PCS OF RATTAN BASKET AT USD 0.90/PC
AS PER PURCHASE ORDER NO. 7990/05/FK
12 182个藤编篮子，每个0.90美元，按7990/05/FK号订单

Documents Required 46A :

单据要求

+ SIGNED COMMERCIAL INVOICE IN TRIPLICAT CONSIGNED TO FUNDINS TORONTO, CANADA AND CERTIFYING THAT GOODS ARE IN CONFORMITY WITH THOSE DESCRIBED IN PROFORMA INVOICE NO. E-11 13001/6 DATED FEB. 21, 2015.

签字商业发票一式三份，抬头人为加拿大多伦多 FUNDINS 公司，证实货物与2015年2月21日出具的第 E-11 13001/6 号形式发票中的描述一致。

+ PACKING LIST IN TRIPLICATE SHOWING NET WEIGHT, GROSS WEIGHT AND MEASUREMENT PER PACKAGE.

装箱单一式三份，注明每件包装的净重、毛重和体积。

+ FULL SET OF CLEAN ON BOARD OCEAN BILLS OF LADING MADE OUT TO ORDER BLANK ENDORSED MARKED FREIGHT PREPAID AND NOTIFY APPLICANT WITH FULL ADDRESS.

全套清洁已装船海运提单，抬头为凭指示，并作空白背书，标明运费预付，并通知开证申请人，同时载明详细地址。

+ INSURANCE POLICY OR CERTIFICATE BLANK ENDORSED FOR FULL CIF VALUE PLUS

10 PERCENT COVERING W.A. AND SRCC INCLUDING W/W CLAUSE AS PER CIC. CLAIMS, IF ANY, WILL BE PAYABLE AT DESTINATION IN CURRENCY OF DRAFT.

保险单或保险凭证，空白背书，按 CIF 价的 110%依据中国保险条款投保仓至仓水渍险和罢工、暴动、民变险，如有索赔，按汇票币制在目的港赔付。

+ CERTIFICATE OF ORIGIN.

原产地证书。

+ BENEFICIARY'S CERTIFICATE CERTIFYING THAT ONE SET OF SHIPPING DOCUMENTS HAS BEEN FAXED TO APPLICANT WITHIN 2 DAYS AFTER SHIPMENT.

受益人证明，证实一套装运单据已在装船后 2 天内传真给申请人。

+ COPY OF TELEX/FAX SENT BY BENEFICIARY TO APPLICANT ON OR BEFORE B/L ON BOARD DATE CONTAINING ALL SHIPMENT DETAILS INCLUDING AMOUNT, GROSS WEIGHT, NET WEIGHT, CARTONS NO., VESSEL NAME AND B/L NO., NO. OF THIS L/C AND RELEVANT S/C TO BE MENTIONED.

一份由受益人在提单装运日当天或之前发送给开证申请人的电传或传真，内容为说明装船详情，包括金额、毛重、净重、箱数、船名、提单号、信用证号和相关的销售合同号

Additional Cond. 47A :

附加条款

+ SHIPMENT MUST BE EFFECTED THROUGH "ROCKWOOD SHENZHEN" CHINA AND B/L TO EVIDENCE THIS EFFECT IS REQUIRED.

货物装运须由中国“ROCKWOOD 深圳”公司承担，且须在提单中证实此点。

+ 5 PERCENT MORE OR LESS IN QUANTITY OF EACH ITEM ACCEPTABLE.

允许每种货物的数量增减 5%。

+ BILL OF LADING MUST SHOW ACTUAL NAME OF PORT OF LOADING.

提单须载明装运港的具体名称。

+ A DISCREPANCY FEE OF HKD 400.00 OR EQUIVALENT CHARGES PLUS ALL RELEVANT CABLE CHARGES WILL BE DEDUCTED FROM THE REIMBURSEMENT CLAIM FOR EACH PRESENTATION OF DISCREPANT DOCUMENTS UNDER THIS DC. NOT WITHSTANDING ANY INSTRUCTIONS TO THE COUNTRARY. THESE CHARGES SHALL BE FOR THE ACCOUNT OF BENEFICIARY.

400 港元或等值的不符点费用加上全部相关的电报费将从本跟单信用证项下每次提交的，含有不符点单据的索偿款中扣除。即使存在相反的指示，此项费用将由受益人承担。

WE WILL COLLECT FROM THE BENEFICIARY AN ADDITIONAL FEE EQUIVALENT TO HKD 200.00 PER MONTH OR PART THEREOF IF THE DOCUMENTS REMAIN UNACCEPTED/UNPAID DUE TO DISCREPANCY FOR MORE THAN 1 MONTH AFTER OUR RECEIPT.

如果我行（开证行）接收到的单据因存在不符点不被接受或兑付超过了一个月，我行将每月或按实际天数向受益人收取相当于 200 港元或不超过该金额的额外费用。

+ DOCUMENTS TO BE PRESENTED WITHIN 15 DAYS AFTER THE SHIPMENT DATE BUT

WITHIN THE VALIDITY OF THE CREDIT.

所有单据必须在装船后 15 天之内提交议付，但不得超过信用证有效期。

+ NOTWITHSTANDING THE PROVISIONS OF UCP600. IF WE GIVE NOTICE OF REFUSAL OF DOCUMENTS PRESENTED UNDER THIS CREDIT, WE SHALL, HOWEVER, RETAIN THE RIGHT TO ACCEPT A WAIVER OF DISCREPANCIES FROM THE APPLICANT AND, SUBJECT TO SUCH WAIVER BEING ACCEPTABLE TO US, TO RELEASE DOCUMENTS AGAINST THAT WAIVER WITHOUT REFERENCE TO THE PRESENTER PROVIDED THAT NO WRITTEN INSTRUCTION TO THE CONTRARY HAVE BEEN RECEIVED BY US FROM THE PRESENTER BEFORE THE RELEASE OF THE DOCUMENTS. ANY SUCH RELEASE PRIOR TO RECEIPT OF CONTRARY INSTRUCTIONS SHALL NOT CONSTITUTE A FAILURE ON OUR PART TO HOLD THE DOCUMENTS AT THE PRESENTER'S RISK AND DISPOSAL, AND WE WILL HAVE NO LIABILITY TO THE PRESENTER IN RESPECT OF ANY SUCH RELEASE.

不考虑《跟单信用证统一惯例》（第 600 号）的规定，如果我行发出拒收此证项下单据的通知，我行将仍保留接受开证申请人对单据的不符点加以放弃的权利，只要这种放弃为我行所能接受。除非在放单之前收到来自交单人的相反的书面通知，我行将有权根据这种放弃在不征求交单人意见的情况下向开证申请人放单。在收到该相反的指示之前，放单将不构成我行为交单人的风险和指示持有单据之责任失职。对于此种放单，我行对交单人将不负任何责任。

+ EXCEPT SO FAR AS OTHERWISE EXPRESSLY STATED THIS DOCUMENTARY CREDIT IS SUBJECT TO UNIFORM CUSTOMS AND PRACTICE FOR DOCUMENTARY CREDITS (1993 REVISION) INTERNATIONAL CHAMBER OF COMMERCE PUBLICATION NO. 600.

除非另有明文规定，此跟单信用证遵照国际商会第 600 号出版物《跟单信用证统一惯例》（1993 年修订版）执行。

Details of Charges 银行费用	71B	: ALL CHARGES OUTSIDE COUNTRY OF ISSUE FOR ACCOUNT OF BENEFICIARY/EXPORTER 开证行所在国家以外的所有费用由受益人或出口商承担
Confirmation 保兑指示	*49	: WITHOUT 无保兑
Instructions 给 41A 条款中被指定银行的指示	78	: ON RECEIPT OF DOCUMENTS CONFORMING TO THE TERMS OF THIS DC AT OUR COUNTER, WE UNDERTAKE TO REIMBURSE YOU IN THE CURRENCY OF THIS CREDIT IN ACCORDANCE WITH YOUR PAYMENT INSTRUCTION AFTER DEDUCTING ALL RELATIVE REIMBURSING CHARGES INCURRED. 一旦收到符合此证要求的各项单据，我行在扣除所有相关索偿费用后，即刻按照你方的付款指示以此证项下的币种偿付你方。 DOCUMENTS MUST BE DISPATCHED BY COURIER IN ONE COVER TO HSBC ESD DIV. L5 HSBC BLDG MONG KOK 673 NATHAN RD. MONGKOK, KLN, HONG KONG.

	所有单据必须由快递公司一次送往以下地址：HSBC ESD DIV, L5 HSBC BLDG MONG KOK 673 NATHAN RD. MONGKOK, KLN, HONG KONG
Send to Rec. Info.	72 : BENEFICIARY'S TEL NO. 086-020-86479522 FAX NO. 086-020-86479518
附言	受益人电话号码：086-020-86479522　传真号码：086-020-86479518

操作要领

在制单前，我们必须快速、准确地理解信用证条款，从整体上掌握信用证的相关信息，方可保证单证制作的正确性。通常来讲，通知行和受益人在收到国外开来的信用证后，都要对信用证的条款要求做一番分析并填表。下例为受益人就上述汇丰银行开出的号码为 DC NPH182503 的 SWIFT 信用证进行填表分析。

SWIFT 电开信用证分析单

合同号：　　　　　　　　　　　　　　　　　　　　　　日期：

项目	代码	条款/项目性质（英文）	条款/项目性质（中文）	条款具体内容
信用证本身说明	27	SEQUENCE OF TOTAL	电文页次	1/1
	40A	FORM OF DOCUMENTARY CREDIT	跟单信用证性质	不可撤销
	40E	APPLICABLE RULES	适用的惯例	UCP600
	20	DC NUMBER	信用证号码	DC NPH182503
	31C	DATE OF ISSUE	开证日期	2015 年 5 月 23 日
	31D	DATE AND PLACE OF EXPIRY	信用证到期日和地点	2015 年 8 月 4 日在中国到期
	51a	APPLICANT BANK	信用证开证银行	THE HONG KONG AND SHANGHAI BANKING CORPORATION LIMITED HONG KONG (ALL HK OFFICES AND HEAD OFFICE)
	57a	ADVISE THROUGH BANK	通知行	根据实际业务填写通知行名称
	50	APPLICANT/OPENER	开证申请人	FUNDINS TORONTO, CANADA 56 TOWER STREET, TORONTO, CANADA
	59	BENEFICIARY	信用证受益人	GUANGDONG WHOLE ARTS TRADING COMPANY

（续表）

项目	代码	条款/项目性质（英文）	条款/项目性质（中文）	条款具体内容
金额	32B	CURRENCY CODE, AMOUNT	结算货币和金额	USD 38,963.80
	39A	Pos./Neg. Tol.（5）	金额允许浮动范围	允许金额上下浮动 5%
汇票条款	41a	AVAILABLE WITH... BY...	指定交单的银行和兑付方式/信用证种类	非限制议付或公开议付或自由议付
	42C	DRAFTS AT...	汇票的付款日期	即期
	42a	DRAWEE	汇票的受票人/付款人	开证行
运输条款	43P	PARTIAL SHIPMENTS	分批装运条款/规定	ALLOWED
	43T	TRANSSHIPMENT	转运条款/规定	ALLOWED
	44A	PORT OF LOADING/ AIRPORT DEPARTURE	装运港/启运机场	ANY PORT IN CHINA
	44B	PORT OF DISCHARGE/ DESTINATION	卸货港/目的地	TORONTO, CANADA
	44C	LATEST DATE OF SHIPMENT	最晚装运期	2015 年 7 月 31 日
商品条款	45A	DESCRIPTION OF GOODS AND/OR SERVICES	商品/货物描述	1）20 000 个玉米篮子，每个 1.40 美元 2）12 182 个藤编篮子，每个 0.90 美元 CIF TORONTO 适用 2010 通则
单据条款	46A	DOCUMENTS REQUIRED	提供给银行的单据要求	+ 签字商业发票一式三份，抬头人为加拿大多伦多 FUNDINS 公司，证实货物与 2015 年 2 月 21 日出具的第 E-11 13001/6 号形式发票中的描述一致 + 装箱单一式三份，注明每件包装的净重、毛重和体积 + 全套清洁已装船海运提单，抬头为凭指示，并作空白背书，标明运费预付，并通知开证申请人，同时载明详细地址 + 保险单或保险凭证，空白背书，按 CIF 价的 110% 依据中国保险条款投保仓至仓水渍险和罢工、暴动、民变险，如有索赔，按汇票币制在目的港赔付 + 原产地证书 + 受益人证明，证实一套装运单据已在装船后 2 天内传真给申请人 + 一份由受益人在提单装运日当天或之前发送给开证申请人的电传或传真，内容为说明装船详情，包括金额、毛重、净重、箱数、船名、提单号、信用证号和相关的销售合同号（其实就是需要提交装运通知）

（续表）

项目	代码	条款/项目性质（英文）	条款/项目性质（中文）	条款具体内容
附加条款	47A	ADDITIONAL CONDITIONS	附加/特别条款	+ 货物装运须由中国“ROCKWOOD 深圳”公司承担，提单上须证实此点 + 允许每种货物的数量增减 5% + 提单须载明装运港的具体名称 + 不符点扣费 400 港元，由受益人承担 + 单据保管费每月 200 港元 + 装船后 15 天之内交单议付 + 申请人接受不符点单据，开证行将放单，并不构成责任 + 信用证适用惯例：UCP600
交单条款	48	PERIOD FOR PRESENTATION	交单期限规定	装船后 15 天之内提交议付，但不得超过信用证有效期
保兑	49	CONFIRMATION INSTRUCTIONS	保兑指示	WITHOUT
费用条款	71B	CHARGES	费用分摊说明	开证行以外的所有费用由受益人承担
银行指示	78	INSTRUCTIONS	给指定银行的指示	+ 开证行承诺及时付款 + 所有单据必须由快递一次性寄送

相关知识

一、信用证分析

企业在收到信用证后，首先需要对信用证进行全面的仔细阅读，并对来证进行深入分析，方可确保后续的制单工作准确、高效。业务员应全面透彻地理解信用证，通常在收到来证后，会通过填写信用证分析单的方式，对来证内容进行梳理。因此，填写分析单是全面理解信用证的具体表现形式。关于单据内容，请参阅本项目后面的附件空白单据。

二、信用证知识

（一）信用证的基础知识

依据 UCP600 的解释，跟单信用证是指一项约定，不论其名称或描述如何，凡由一家银行依照客户的要求和指示或以自身的名义做出，在符合信用证条款的条件下，凭规定的单据（1）向第三者或其指定人付款或承兑并支付受益人出具的汇票；或（2）授权另一家银行进行该项付款或承兑并支付该汇票；或（3）授权另一家银行议付。

简单地说，信用证是开证银行应进口商（开证申请人）的要求和指示，开立以出口人为受益人的有条件的书面付款承诺书，并通过出口地的一家银行（通知行）送达。

（二）跟单信用证的开立方式

跟单信用证的开立方式主要有两种，即信开和电开。

1. 信开信用证

信开证是采用开证行印就的信函格式，由开证银行根据申请人指示填写信用证的各项条款内容，然后用快递方式传递到出口方所在地的银行予以通知和送达。这种形式开证目前已经较少使用。

2. 电开信用证

电开证是指开证行使用电报、电传或 SWIFT[①]系统等电信的方式将信用证条款传递给出口方所在地的通知行。

（三）跟单信用证的业务流程

现以即期跟单议付信用证为例，以图例方式说明跟单信用证的操作业务流程。

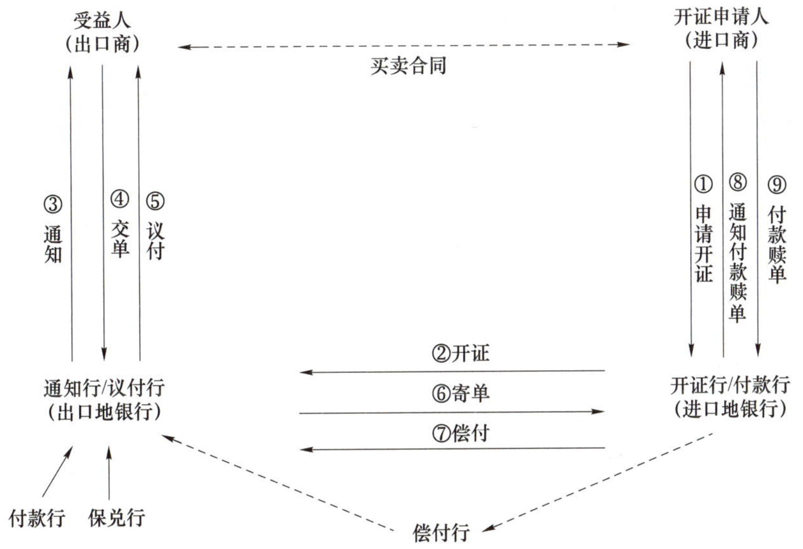

图 2-1　即期跟单议付信用证业务流程图

（四）跟单信用证结构内容

1. 对信用证本身的说明：包括开证行名称和地址、信用证类型、信用证号码、开证时间、信用证到期日和到期地点、开证申请人、受益人、通知行、议付行、付款行、货币和金额等内容。

2. 汇票条款：凡是需要使用汇票的信用证，一般都要规定汇票的出票人、受票人、付款期限、指定交单对象等内容。

① SWIFT（Society for Worldwide Interbank Financial Telecommunications）环球同业银行金融电讯协会，是国际银行同业间的国际合作组织，成立于 1973 年，目前全球大多数国家大多数银行已使用 SWIFT 系统，通过自动化国际金融电讯网办理成员银行间资金调拨、汇款结算、开立信用证、办理信用证项下的汇票业务和托收等业务。

3. 兑付方式的说明：信用证需要对该信用证项下的兑付方式：即期付款、延期付款、承兑还是议付或付款或提示等加以说明。

4. 运输条款：包括对装运港、目的港、分批、转运以及装运时间的说明。

5. 货物描述：包括货物名称、规格、数量、价格、贸易术语、包装、唛头等内容。

6. 单据条款：包括需要提交的单据名称、份数和对各种单据内容的具体要求。

7. 附加条款：包括银行间的费用划分、寄单要求、交单期限、不符点费用、偿付条款、背批条款、保兑条款等内容。

8. 责任文句和适用惯例：这两个条款也属于信用证本身的说明，通常位于信用证的末尾，包含银行保证付款的责任条款和信用证所遵循或适用的国际惯例。如果信用证中明确指出是按照《跟单信用证统一惯例》（UCP600）开立，因 UCP600 对开证行的责任已有明确规定，则开证行的责任文句可以不用再在信用证中单独列出。SWIFT 成员银行电开证也无须说明付款责任文句，因该协会章程里已统一规定开证行的付款责任，其成员银行必须遵守相关规则。

（五）SWIFT 电开信用证的固定结构

因 SWIFT 信用证具有快速、准确、简明、可靠等显著特点，故 SWIFT 信用证为目前各家银行最常使用的信用证。SWIFT 报文由各个项目（Field）组成，有其固定的格式和表示方法，具体表述如表 2-1 所示。

表 2-1　电开跟单信用证格式及条款代码解释（MT700）

M/O	Tag	Field Name	Content/Options
M	27	Sequence of Total 信用证的页数和页码（电文页次）	1n/1n
M	40A	Form of Documentary Credit 跟单信用证形式/性质（说明可否撤销，是否保兑或转让）	24x
M	20	Documentary Credit Number 信用证号码	16x
O	23	Reference to Pre-advice 预先通知号	16x
O	31C	Date of Issue 信用证的开证日期 SWIFT 用 6 位数表示年月日	6n
M	31D	Date and Place of Expiry 信用证到期日和到期地点	6n，29x
O	40E	Applicable Rules（信用证）适用惯例	1* 35x
O	51A	Applicant Bank 开证行	A or D
M	50	Applicant 信用证开证申请人名称和地址	4* 35x
M	59	Beneficiary 信用证受益人名称和地址	〔/34〕4*35x
M	32B	Currency Code, Amount 信用证结算货币及其金额	3a 15 number
O	39A	Percentage Credit Amount Tolerance 金额允许上下浮动的最大范围	2n/2n
O	39B	Maximum Credit Amount 信用证最高金额	13x
O	39C	Additional Amounts Covered 信用证项下的其他金额	4* 35x
M	41A	Available with... by... 指定银行（受款银行）及银行的支付方式，即议付、付款、提示或承兑	A or D

（续表）

M/O	Tag	Field Name	Content/Options
O	42C	Drafts at... 汇票的付款期限	3* 35x
O	42A	Drawee 或 Drawn on... 汇票的受票人/付款人	A or D
O	42M	Mixed Payment Details 综合支付方式	4* 35x
O	42P	Deferred Payment Details 延期支付方式	4* 35x
O	43P	Partial Shipments 分批装运	1* 35x
O	43T	Transshipment 转船	1* 35x
O	44A	Loading on Board/Dispatch/Taking in Charge at/From 装运港：装船、发送和货物接收监管的地点	1* 65x
O	44B	For Transportation to... 目的港/卸货港（货物发运的最终地）	1* 65x
O	44C	Latest Date of Shipment 最迟装船期	6n
O	44D	Shipment Period 装运期	6* 65x
O	45A	Description of Goods and/or Services 货物描述	100* 65x
O	46A	Documents Required 信用证要求提交银行的单据（单据要求/单据条款）	100* 65x
O	47A	Additional/Special Conditions 附加/特别条款	100* 65x
O	71B	Charges 银行费用条款	6* 35x
O	48	Period for Presentation 信用证规定的交单期限	4* 35x
M	49	Confirmation Instructions 保兑指示 CONFIRM: 请收报行加保兑 MAY ADD: 收报行可加保兑 WITHOUT: 收报行无需加保兑	7x
O	53A	Reimbursement Bank 偿付行	A or D
O	78	Instruction to the Paying/Accepting/Negotiating/Presenting Bank 对被指定银行的指示（通常包括了责任文句）	12* 65x
O	57A	"Advise Through" Bank 收电银行以外的通知行	A，B or D
O	72	Sender to Receiver Information 发报人对收报人的指示/附言（如信用证适用惯例）	6* 35x

注：表格第一栏目：M: Mandatory（必选项目）　O: Optional（可选/任意项目）

表格中第四栏为信用证中相应条款格式内容的说明：

n：只表示数字，例如"1n/1n"表示该栏的格式为"1 个数字/1 个数字"；

a：只表示字母，例如"52a"，该项目在一份报文中可能成为"52A"，在另一份报文中就可能成为"52B"；

Q：表示数字或字母；

x：表示 SWIFT 电讯中允许出现的任何一个字符（包括 10 个数字、26 个字母、有关标点符号、空格键、回车键和跳行键）；

：表示行数，例如"4 35x"表示该栏的格式为"4 行，每行最多 35 个字符"。

操作能力训练

思考题：

S2-1　三种常见的国际结算方式下货运单据的传递路径与风险控制点有哪些？

操作题：

C2-1　阅读理解下列信用证，并翻译相关条款。

FROM: INDUSTRIAL BANK OF JAPAN, LTD., HEAD OFFICE

TO: BANK OF CHINA, SHANGHAI BRANCH

SEQUENCE OF TOTAL:	27:	1/1
FORM OF DOC. CREDIT:	40A：	IRREVOCABLE
DOCU. CREDIT NO.:	20:	ILC136107800
DATE OF ISSUE:	31C:	151015
DATE AND PLACE OF EXP.:	31D:	151215 IN THE COUNTRY OF BENEFICIARY
APPLICABLE RULES:	40E:	THE LATEST VERSION
APPLICANT:	50:	YATO TRADING COMPANY, 1-3 MACHI KU STREET, OSAKA, JAPAN
BENEFICIARY:	59:	SHANGHAI DA SHENG CO., LTD. UNIT C 2/F JINGMAO TOWER, SHANGHAI, CHINA
CURRENCY CODE, AMOUNT:	32B:	USD21,240.00
AVAILABLE WITH/BY…	41D:	ANY BANK BY NEGOTIATION
DRAFTS AT…:	42C:	SIGHT FOR 100PCT INVOICE VALUE
DRAWEE:	42D:	THE INDUSTRIAL BANK OF JAPAN, LTD. HEAD OFFICE
PARTIAL SHIPMENT:	43P:	ALLOWED
TRANSSHIPMENT:	43T:	NOT ALLOWED
LOAD/DISPATCH/TAKING :	44A:	CHINESE PORTS
TRANSPORTATION TO…:	44B:	OSAKA/TOKYO
LATEST DATE OF SHIPMENT:	44C:	151130
DESCRIPTION OF GOODS/SERVICE:	45A:	4,000 PCS "DIAMOND" BRAND CLOCK ART NO. 791 AT USD5.31 PER PIECE CIF INCOTERMS®2010 OSAKA/TOKYO PACKED IN NEW CARTON AS PER P/O NO. YATO99-05 DATED SEP. 10, 2015
DOCUMENTS REQUIRED:	46A:	

IN 3 FOLD UNLESS OTHERWISE STIPULATED:

1. MANUALLY SIGNED COMMERCIAL INVOICE INDICATING THE COUNTRY OF ORIGIN AND THE NAME OF MANUFACTURER.
2. SIGNED PACKING LIST.
3. GSP CERTIFICATE OF ORIGIN FORM A.
4. BENEFICIARY'S CERTIFICATE STATING THAT ONE SET OF ORIGINAL SHIPPING DOCUMENTS INCLUDING ORIGINAL "FORM A" HAS BEEN SENT DIRECTLY TO THE APPLICANT.
5. COPY OF FAX FROM APPLICANT TO SUPPLIERS APPROVING THE SHIPPING SAMPLE.
6. INSURANCE POLICY OR CERTIFICATE ENDORSED IN BLANK FOR 110 PCT OF CIF VALUE, COVERING W.P.A RISK AND WAR RISK.
7. 2/3 PLUS ONE COPY OF CLEAN "ON BOARD" OCEAN BILLS OF LADING, MADE OUT TO ORDER AND BLANK ENDORSED MARKED "FREIGHT PREPAID" AND NOTIFY APPLICANT.

ADDITIONAL CONDITION: 47A:

1. ALL DRAFTS DRAWN HEREUNDER MUST BE MARKED "DRAWN UNDER INDUSTRIAL BANK OF JAPAN, LTD., HEAD OFFICE, CREDIT NO. ILC136107800 DATED OCT. 15, 2015" AND THE AMOUNT OF SUCH DRAFTS MUST BE ENDORSED ON THE REVERSE OF THIS CREDIT.
2. T/T REIMBURSEMENT IS NOT ACCEPTABLE.
3. ALL DOCUMENTS MUST BE SHOWING THE L/C NO.

DETAILS OF CHARGES	71B:	ALL BANKING CHARGES OUTSIDE JANPAN ARE FOR BENEFICIARY'S ACCOUNT
PRESENTAION PERIOD	48:	DOCUMENTS MUST BE PRESENTED WITHIN 10 DAYS AFTER THE DATE OF ISSUANCE OF THE TRANSPORT DOCUMENTS BUT WITHIN VALIDITY OF THE CREDIT
CONFIRMATION	49:	WITHOUT

SPECIAL INSTRUCTION TO THE ADVISING BANK:

ALL DOCUMENTS INCLUDING BENEFICIARY'S DRAFTS MUST BE SENT BY COURIER SERVICE DIRECTLY TO OUR HEAD OFFICE, MARUNOUCHI,
CHIYODA-U, TOKYO, JAPAN 100, ATTN. INTERNATIONAL BUSINESS DEPT.
IMPORT SECTION, IN ONE LOT. UPON OUR RECEIPT OF THE DRAFTS AND DOCUMENTS, WE SHALL MAKE PAYMENT AS INSTRUCTED BY YOU.

C2-2 阅读下列信用证，填写附录 **1** 里的信用证分析单二。

*KRUNG THAI BANK PUBLIC COMPANY LIMITED BANGKOK

USER HEADER	SERVICE CODE	103:
	BANK PRIORITY	113:
	MSG USER REF.	108:
	INFO. FROM CI	115:
SEQUENCE OF TOTAL	27:	1/1
FORM OF DOC.CREDIT	40A:	IRREVOCABLE
DOC. CREDIT NUMBER	20:	BL 120197
DATE OF ISSUE	31C:	160123
EXPIRY	31D:	DATE 160422 PLACE CHINA
APPLICANT BANK	51D:	KRUNG THAI BANK PCL., SUANMALI IBC.
APPLICANT	50:	METCH THAI CHEMICAL COMPANY LTD 45-7 MAITRICHITR RD., BANGKOK, THAILAND.
BENEFICIARY	59:	SINOCHEM GUANGDONG I&E CO. 58 ZHANQIAN ROAD, GUANGZHOU, CHINA
AMOUNT	32B:	CURRENCY USD AMOUNT 16,264.00
AVAILABLE WITH/BY	41D:	ANY BANK BY NEGOTIATION
DRAFT AT…	42C:	SIGHT
DRAWEE	42D:	KRUNG THAI BANK PCL., SUANMALI IBC
PARTIAL SHIPMENTS	43P:	PROHIBITED
TRANSSHIPMENT	43T:	ALLOWED
LOADING IN CHARGE	44A:	GUANGZHOU, CHINA
FOR TRANSPORT TO…	44B:	BANGKOK, THAILAND
LATEST DATE OF SHIP	44C:	160412
DESCRIPTION OF GOODS	45A:	42.80 MT LITHOPONE 30 PCT ARROW BRAND USD380.00 PER MT DETAILS AS PER PROFORMA INVOICE NO.01TH44GD176A3-032 DATED JAN. 22, 2016. C.I.F. BANGKOK, THAILAND INCOTERMS® 2010
DOCUMENTS REQUIRED	46:A	

+ SIGNED COMMERCIAL INVOICE IN 10 COPIES SHOWING SEPARATELY F.O.B. VALUE, FREIGHT CHARGE, INSURANCE PREMIUM, C.I.F. VALUE AND COUNTRY OF ORIGIN.

+ FULL SET OF CLEAN ON BOARD OCEAN BILLS OF LADING TO ORDER OF KRUNG THAI BANK PUBLIC COMPANY LIMITED MARKED FREIGHT PREPAID PLUS TWO NON-NEGOTIABLE COPIES, NOTIFY APPLICANT.

+ MARINE INSURANCE POLICY OR CERTIFICATE IN DUPLICATE, ENDORSED IN

BLANK, FOR FULL INVOICE VALUE PLUS 10% STATING CLAIM PAYABLE IN THAILAND COVERING INSTITUTE CARGO CLAUSES (A) AND WAR RISK.

+ PACKING LIST IN 5 COPIES.

+ CERTIFICATE OF ANALYSIS IN 5 COPIES SIGNED BY MANUFACTURERS.

+ ONE FULL SET OF NON-NEGOTIABLE SHIPPING DOCUMENTS MUST BE SENT TO THE APPLICANT BY AIR COURIER WITHIN 3 DAYS AFTER SHIPMENT AND BENEFICIARY'S CERTIFICATE TO THIS EFFECT IS REQUIRED.

+ BENEFICIARY'S CERTIFICATE CERTIFYING THAT ONE COPY EACH OF INVOICE, N/N B/L HAVE BEEN FAXED TO BUYER TO FAX NO.662-225 WITHIN 3 DAYS AFTER SHIPMENT.

ADDITIONAL CONDITION 47A:

+ ALL DOCUMENTS MENTION THIS L/C NO.

+ BOTH AMOUNT AND QUANTITY PLUS OR MINUS 5% ARE ACCEPTABLE.

+ IF ANY DISCREPANCY, WE SHALL DEDUCT USD50.00 BEING OUR FEE FROM THE PROCEEDS.

+ THE NAME, ADDRESS, TELEPHONE NO. OF SHIPPING AGENT IN BANGKOK MUST BE MENTIONED IN B/L.

DETAILS OF CHARGES	71B:	ALL BANK CHARGES OUTSIDE THAILAND INCLUDING COST OF WIRE AND REIMBURSEMENT CHARGES ARE FOR BENEFICIARY'S ACCOUNT.
CONFIRMATION	49:	WITHOUT
INSTRUCTIONS	78:	

+ UPON RECEIPT OF SHIPPING DOCUMENTS IN STRICT CONFORMITY WITH L/C TERMS, WE WILL COVER YOUR ACCOUNT AND LESS OUR COST OF WIRE IF ANY ACCORDING TO YOUR INSTRUCTION.

+ DRAFT AND DOCUMENTS TO BE SENT TO US BY COURIER SERVICE WITHIN 15 DAYS AFTER SHIPMENT MAILING ADDRESS SUANMALI IBC., 20 YUKHON 2 ROAD, POMPRAB, BANGKOK 10100, THAILAND.

+ THIS ADVICE THROUGH BANK OF CHINA GUANGDONG BRANCH IS OPERATIVE WITH NO CONFIRMATION TO FOLLOW AND SUBJECT TO ICC 2007 REVISION PUB 600.

SEND. TO REC. INFO.	72:	KINDLY ACKNOWLEDGE RECEIPT THIS CREDIT BY RETURN SWIFT WILL BE MUCH APPRECIATED

C2-3 阅读下列信用证，并回答相关问题。

APPLICATION HEADER	* BNP PARIBAS (CANADA) * MONTREAL

SEQUENCE OF TOTAL	27:	1/1
FORM OF DOC. CREDIT	40A:	IRREVOCABLE
DOC. CREDIT NUMBER	20:	63211020049
DATE OF ISSUE	31C:	150228
EXPIRY	31D:	DATE 150513 PLACE IN BENEFICIARY'S COUNTRY
APPLICANT	50:	ABLENDID DEVELOPMENT LTD P.O.BOX 7052 NEW TERMINAL, ALTA, VISTA MONTREAL, CANADA
BENEFICIARY	59:	SHUJIN TEXTILE AND LIGHT INDUSTRY CO. LTD. NO.10 RENMIN RD., CHENGDU, CHINA
AMOUNT	32B:	CURRENCY USD AMOUNT 48,300.00
AVAILABLE WITH/BY	41D:	ANY BANK BY NEGOTIATION
DRAFTS AT…	42C:	SIGHT
DRAWEE	42A:	BNP PARIBAS (CANADA) MONTREAL
PARTIAL SHIPMENTS	43P:	NOT ALLOWED
TRANSSHIPMENT	43T:	ALLOWED
PORT OF LOADING/ AIRPORT OF DEPARTURE	44E:	SHANGHAI
PORT OF DISCHARGE	44F:	MONTREAL
LATEST DATE OF SHIPMENT	44C:	150428
DESCRIPTION OF GOODS	45A:	SALES CONDITIONS: CIF MONTREAL, CANADA AS PER INCOTERMS®2010 S/C NO. F09CB05127 LADIES COTTON BLAZER (100% COTTON, 40S×20/140×60) AS PER P/O NO. 10056 DATED 150102 PACKED 50 PCS/CTN

STYLE NO.	PCS	USD/PC
50-201A	3,500	13.80

DOCUMENTS REQUIRED 46A:

+ SIGNED INVOICE IN DUPLICATE SHOWING BREAK DOWN OF THE AMOUNT AS FOLLOWS: FOB VALUE, FREIGHT CHARGES, PREMIUM.

+PACKING LIST IN DUPLICATE SHOWING QUANTITY, N.W. G.W AND MEA. OF EACH CARTON.

+ FULL SET OF CLEAN "ON BOARD" OCEAN BILLS OF LADING MADE OUT TO ORDER AND ENDORSED IN BLANK MARKED FREIGHT PREPAID AND NOTIFY

APPLICANT AND INDICATE THE FULL NAME, ADDRESS, TEL NO. AND FAX NO. OF THE AGENT AT THE DESTINATION.

+ INSURANCE POLICY IN DUPLICATE ENDORSED IN BLANK FOR 110% OF INVOICE VALUE COVERING ALL RISKS OF CIC OF PICC (01/01/1981).

+ GSP CERTIFICATE OF ORIGIN FORM A SHOWING THE NAME OF THE MANUFACTURER.

+SHIPPING ADVICE SHOWING THE NAME OF THE CARRYING VESSEL, DATE OF SHIPMENT, MARKS, QUANTITY, NET WEIGHT AND GROSS WEIGHT OF THE SHIPMENT TO THE APPLICANT WITHIN 1 DAY AFTER THE DATE OF SHIPMENT.

ADDITIONAL COND 47A:

+ IF DOCUMENTS PRESENTED ARE FOUND BY US NOT TO BE IN FULL COMPLIANCE WITH CREDIT TERMS, WE WILL ASSESS A CHARGE OF USD 55.00 PER SET OF DOCUMENTS.

+ 5 PCT MORE OR LESS IN AMOUNT AND QUANTITY IS ALLOWED.

+ ALL DOCUMENTS MUST INDICATE THE NAME OF ISSUING BANK, THE DATE OF THIS CREDIT AND CREDIT NO.

CHARGES	71B:	OUTSIDE CANADA BANK CHARGES TO BE BORNE BY THE BENEFICIARY AND OPENING BANK CHARGES TO BE BORNE BY THE APPLICANT
PERIOD FOR PRESENTATION	48:	WITHIN 15 DAYS AFTER THE DATE OF SHIPMENTE BUT WITHIN THE VALIDITY OF THIS CRDIT
CONFIRMATION	49:	WITHOUT
INSTRUCTIONS	78:	

+ WE SHALL COVER THE NEGOTIATING BANK AS PER THEIR INSTRUCTIONS.

+ FORWARD DOCUMENTS IN ONE LOT BY COURIER PREPAID TO BNP PARIBAS (CANADA) 1981 MCGILL COLLECE AVE. MONTREAL QC H3A 2W8 CANADA.

SEND. TO REC. INFO.	72:	THIS CREDIT IS SUBJECT TO UCP FOR DOCUMENTARY CREDIT 2007 REVISION ICC PUBLICATION 600 AND IS THE OPERATIVE INSTRUMENT

请从该信用证中找出下面的内容：

（1）开证人：

（2）受益人：

（3）信用证兑付方式：

（4）开证行：
（5）信用证金额：
（6）信用证号码：
（7）开证日期：
（8）信用证有效期及到期地点：
（9）汇票期限：
（10）装运港：
（11）目的港：
（12）装运期限：
（13）分批和装船的要求：
（14）商品数量和名称：
（15）订单号码及日期：
（16）贸易术语：
（17）要求单据及份数：
（18）交单期限：
（19）信用证特殊条款：
（20）适用惯例：

C2-4　阅读下列信用证，填写附录 1 里的电开信用证分析单一。

Copy received from SWIFT : Normal
Message output reference: 0646 030918BCITSHAXXX1534072086
Correspondent input reference: 1809 030917BARBINBBABAR572663543
-----------------------------------MESSAGE HEADER--------------------------------------
Swift Output: FIN 700 Issue of a Documentary Credit
Sender　　:　BARBINBBBAR
BANK OF BARODA
（INTERNATIONAL BUSINESS BR. VADODARA）
VADODARA (BARODA) IN
Receiver　　:　BCITCNSHXXX
INTESABCI S.P.A
(SHANGHAI BRANCH)
SHANGHAI CN
MUR　　　:　OBR/PLC/03/339
------------------------------------MESSAGE TEXT---
27:　Sequence of Total　　　1/1
40A: Form of Documentary Credit
IRREVOCABLE
20:　Documentary Credit Number

OBR/FLC/03/339

31C: Date of Issue

030917

31D: Date and Place of Expiry

031015 CHINA

51A: Applicant Bank BIC

BARBINBBBAR

BANK OF BARODA (INTERNATIONAL BUSINESS BR. VADODARA)

VADODARA (BARODA)　　IN

50: Applicant

CENTURY PHARMACENTICALS LTD.

406, WORLD TRADE CENTRE, SAYAJIGUNJ,

VADODARA-390 005(CUJARAT) INDIA

59: Beneficiary Name & Address

CHINA NORTH INDUSTRIES ZHANJIANG CORPORATION

6, HAI BIN NO.2 ROAD, ZHANJIANG, GUANGDONG, CHINA

32B: Currency Code, Amount

Currency:　　USD (US DOLLAR)

Amount:　　#82,000.00#

41D: Available With…By…- Name & Addr

ANY BANK

BY NEGOTIATION

42C: Drafts at…

180 DAYS USANCE FROM THE DATE OF B/L QUOTING THIS L/C NUMBER AND DATE.

42A: Drawee-BIC

BARBINBBBAR

BANK OF BARODA (INTERNATIONAL BUSINESS BR. VADODARA)

VADODARA (BARODA) IN

43P: Partial Shipments

NOT PERMITTED

43T: Transshipment

PERMITTED

44A: On Board/Disp/Taking Charge at/from

ANY CHINESE PORT (SEA)

44B: For Transportation to…

UNPT PORT, MUMBAI INDIA SEA PORT CIF BY SEA

44C: Latest Date of Shipment

030930

45A: Description of goods &/or services

Approx 2,000 KG ACTIVITY ERYTHROMYCIN THIOCYANATE AT RATE USD 4,200 PER ACTIVITY

46A: Documents Required

FOLLOWING DOCUMENTS IN ENGLISH IN DUPLICATE, UNLESS OTHERWISE SPECIFIED, ARE REQUIRED.

1. SIGNED COMMERCIAL INVOICES, IN TRIPLICATE, QUOTING IMPORT NOT INCLUDED IN NEGATIVE LIST OF EXPORT-IMPORT POLICY OF 2002—2007 AND CERTIFYING THAT THE GOODS ARE AS PER INDENT NO. AN03PDTEI-S DT, 04.9-03 OF ANANT AND COMPANY, MUMBAI.

2. CERTIFICATE OF CHINA ORIGIN ISSUED BY A CHAMBER OF COMMERCE.

3. FULL SET SIGNED CLEAN ON BOARD OCEAN BILLS OF LADING MADE OUT TO ORDER AND BLANK ENDORSED MARKED FREIGHT PREPAID AND CLAUSED NOTIFY BANK OF BARODA, INTERNATIONAL BUSINESS BRANCH, SURAJ PLAZA BLDG I. SAYAJIGUNJ, VADODARA-390 005, GUJIARAT, INDIA AND ALSO (APPLICANT) CENTURY PHARMACEUTICALS LTD., 406, WORLD TRADE CENTER, SAYAJIGUNJ, VADODARA-390 005, GUJARAT INDIA INDICATING LETTER OF CREDIT NUMBER AND DATE AND EVIDENCING CURRENT SHIPMENT OF MERCHANDISE STATED ABOVE.

4. MARINE INSURANCE POLICY COVERING INTER-ALIA TRANSIT (WAREHOUSE TO WAREHOUSE) CLAUSE PERTAINING TO CURRENT SHIPMENT/DISPATCH COVERED BY TRANSPORT DOCUMENTS CALLED FOR HEREIN UNTO ORDER AND BLANK ENDORSED FOR 10 PCT OVER INVOICE VALUE COVERING INSTITUTE CARGO CLAUSE “A”, INSTITUTE WAR CLAUSE (CARGO) AND INSTITUTE STRIKE CLAUSE (CARGO) WITH CLAIMS PAYABLE IN VADODARA, GUJARAT, INDIA.

5. CLASS CERTIFICATE CERTIFYING THAT SHIPMENT IS MADE BY SEA WORTHY VESSELS WHICH ARE NOT MORE THAN 25 YEARS OLD CLASSED LLOYDS’ 100 A1 ISSUED BY SHIPMENT COMPANY OR ITS AGENTS.

6. TEST CERTIFICATE/INSPECTION CERTIFICATE ISSUED BY BENEFICIARY SPECIFYING CONTENTS ARE AS PER INVOICE.

7. PACKING LIST WITH DETAILS AS PER INVOICE.

BILL OF LADING MUST BE DATED NOT LATER THAN 30-09-2003 NOR PRIOR TO THE DATE OF THIS CREDIT.

BILL OF EXCHANGE MUST BE DATED AND PRESENTED/NEGOTIATED NOT LATER

THAN 15-10-2003 AT THE COUNTERS OF ADVISING BANK. HOWEVER IT SHOULD BE NEGOTIATED/PRESENTED WITHIN 15 DAYS AFTER THE DATE OF EACH DISPATCH WITHIN VALIDITY OF THIS LETTER OF CREDIT.

WE HEREBY ENGAGE WITH THE DRAWERS, ENDORSERS, AND/OR BONA FIDE HOLDERS OF DRAFTS DRAWN UNDER AND IN COMPLIANCE WITH THE TERMS OF THIS CREDIT THAT SUCH DRAFTS SHALL BE DULY HONOURED ON PRESENTATION AND THAT DRAFT/S ACCEPTED WITH TERMS OF THIS CREDIT WILL BE DULY HONOURED AT MATURITY AND DELIVERY OF DOCUMENTS AS SPECIFIED ABOVE.

47A: Additional Condition

1. THE GROSS CIF VALUE OF THE GOODS BEFORE DEDUCTION OF AGENT'S COMMISSION, IF ANY, MUST NOT EXCEED THE CREDIT AMOUNT.

2. THIRD PARTY DOCUMENTS ARE NOT ACCEPTABLE/HOUSE BILL OF LADING NOT ACCEPTABLE.

3. ANY DOCUMENTS CALLED FOR HEREIN PRODUCED BY REPROGRAPHIC PROCESS/COMPUTERIZED SYSTEM ARE ACCEPTABLE PROVIDED ALL SUCH ORIGINAL DOCUMENTS ARE MANUALLY SIGNED.

4. TRANSPORT DOCUMENTS BEARING REFERENCE BY STAMP OR OTHERWISE TO COST ADDITIONAL TO THE FREIGHT CHARGES ARE NOT ACCEPTABLE EXCEPT MABARABITRE GOVERNMENT STAMP DUTY PAYABLE WITH EFFECT FROM MAY, 20, 1999 FOR IMPORT TAKING PLACE THROUGH THE PORTS SITUATED IN THE STATE OF MAHARSHTRA AS ALSO THE ADDITIONAL ADMINISTRATIVE FEE FOR THE ABOVE WORK.

5. SHIPPER MUST SEND ADDITIONAL SET OF NON-NEGOTIABLE DOCUMENTS TO THE OPENERS WITHIN 5 DAYS OF SHIPMENT OVER FAX. NO. 91 256 2226026 AND ONE SET BY AIR MAIL. FAX/AIRMAIL RECEIPT TO BE SUBMITTED FOR NEGOTIATION.

6. EVERY DRUM/TINS MUST HAVE LABEL BEARING THE PRODUCT NAME, BATCH NUMBER, DATE OF MANUFACTURER, GROSS WEIGHT, NET WEIGHT, NAME AND ADDRESS OF MANUFACTURER. A CERTIFICATE TO THIS EFFECT ALONGWITH SPECIMEN LABEL SHOULD BE PRESENTED FOR NEGOTIATION.

7. SHIPPING MARK–CENTURY PHARM

ERYTHROMYCIN THIOCYANACE

8. ALL CHARGES OTHER THAN THOSE OF THE ISSUING BANK ARE FOR THE BENEFICIARY'S ACCOUNT INCLUDING CHARGES FOR AMENDMENT TO L/C.

9. INVOICE IN EXCESS OF THE DRAFT AMOUNT ARE NOT ACCEPTABLE.

10. PRICE MENTIONED ABOVE IS INCLUSIVE OF INTEREST FOR 180 DAYS CREDIT. INVOICE SHOULD SHOW SPLIT-UP OF CIF VALUE AND INTEREST

CHARGES. SEPARATE DRAFTS NEED NOT BE PREPARED.

11. BILL OF LADING PRODUCED BY REPROGRAPHIC PROCESS/COMPUTERIZED SYSTEM NOT ACCEPTABLE UNLESS AUTHENTICATED OR MANUALLY SIGNED.

12. L/C TO BE FREELY NEGOTIABLE THROUGH ANY BANK IN CHINA.

13. THE MATERIAL SHIPPED SHOULD HAVE MIN. 78 PCT ERYTHROMYCIN A CONTENT AND ERYTHROMYCIN "B" NOT MORE THAN 4 PCT AND MICROBIOLOGICAL ASSAY ON THIS BASIS SHOULD BE BETWEEN 740–775 MCG/MG. A CERTIFICATE TO THIS EFFECT SHOULD BE SUBMITTED FOR NEGOTIATION.

14. INVOICE AND PACKING LIST MUST MENTION LC NUMBER, BATCH NUMBER MFG DATE, EXP DATE, NET WT IN KGS AND KGA, GROSS WT.

15. A DISCREPANCY FEE OF USD PER DISCREPANCY TO BE DEDUCTED FROM BENEFICIARY.

71B: Charges

ALL BANK CHARGES OUTSIDE INDIA ARE FOR BENEFICIARY'S ACCOUNT.

48: Period for Presentation

WITHIN 15 DAYS FROM THE DATE OF BILLS OF LADING.

49: Confirmation Instructions

WITHOUT

53A: Reimbursing Bank–BIC

BARBINBBBAR

BANK OF BARODA (INTERNATIONAL BUSINESS BR. VADODARA)

VADODARA (BARODA)

78: Instr to advs/Accptg/Negotg Bank

1 ON RECEIPT OF DOCUMENTS STRICTLY AS PER L/C TERMS, WE WILL REMIT THE PROCEEDS ON DUE DATE IN THE CURRENCY OF THIS L/C AS PER YOUR INSTRUCTIONS.

2 IF DOCUMENTS ARE PRESENTED WITH DISCREPANCIES AND ACCEPTED BY US, A DISCREPANCY FEE OF USD 50 OR EQUIVALENT FOR EACH SET OF SUCH DOCUMENTS IS FOR THE ACCOUNT OF BENEFICIARY AND WILL BE DEDUCTED FROM THE PROCEEDS.

3 ALL DOCUMENTS TO BE COURIERED IN ONE LOT TO BANK OF BARODA, VADODARA–390 005, GUJIARAT, INDIA.

67D: Advise Through Bank–Name & Addr

ANY BANK IN CHINA

72: Sender to Receiver Information PRC/EXCEPT AS OTHERWISE EXPRESSLY STATED THIS CREDIT IS SUBJECT TO THE UNIFORM CUSTOMS AND PRACTICE FOR DOCUMENTARY CREDITS (1993 REVISION) INTERNATIONAL CHAMBER OF COMMERCE, PUBLICATION NO. 500.

C2-5　探索学习下一项目，并根据附录 3 里的制单信用证 3-13-1，采用格式一单据，缮制符合要求的订舱委托书一份。

附录 1

表 2-2　SWIFT 电开信用证分析单一

合同号：　　　　　　　　　　　　　　　　　　　　日期：

项目	代码	条款/项目性质（英文）	条款/项目性质（中文）	条款具体内容
信用证本身说明	27	SEQUENCE OF TOTAL	电文页次	
	40A	FORM OF DOCMT CREDIT	跟单信用证性质	
	40E	APPLICABLE RULES	适用的惯例	
	20	DC NUMBER	信用证号码	
	31C	DATE OF ISSUE	开证日期	
	31D	DATE AND PLACE OF EXPIRY	信用证到期日和地点	
当事人	51A	APPLICANT BANK	信用证开证银行	
	57A	ADVISE THROUGH BANK	收电银行以外的通知行	
	50	APPLICANT/OPENER	开证申请人	
	59	BENEFICIARY	信用证受益人	
金额	32B	CURRENCY CODE, AMOUNT	结算货币和金额	
汇票条款	41A	AVAILABLE WITH... BY...	指定交单的银行和兑付方式/信用证种类	
	42C	DRAFTS AT...	汇票的付款日期	
	42A	DRAWEE	汇票的受票人/付款人	
运输条款	43P	PARTIAL SHIPMENTS	分批装运条款/规定	
	43T	TRANSSHIPMENT	转运条款/规定	
	44A	PORT OF LOADING/ AIRPORT DEPARTURE	装运港/启运机场	
	44B	PORT OF DISCHARGE/ DESTINATION	卸货港/目的地	
	44C	LATEST DATE OF SHIPMENT	最晚装运 g3 期	
商品条款	45A	DESCRIPTION OF GOODS AND/OR SERVICES	商品/货物描述	
单据条款	46A	DOCUMENTS REQUIRED	提供给银行的单据要求	
附加条款	47A	ADDITIONAL CONDITIONS	附加/特别条款	
交单条款	48	PERIOD FOR PRESENTATION	交单期限规定	
保兑	49	CONFIRMATION INSTRUCTIONS	保兑指示	
费用条款	71B	CHARGES	费用分摊说明	

表 2-3　信用证分析单二

合同号码：　　　　　　　　　　　　　　　　　　　　　　　　　　　　日期：

信用证本身说明	信用证种类		是否生效	□是 □否	密押/印鉴是否相符	□是 □否	是否保兑	□是 □否
	信用证号码		金额					
	开证日期		装运日期					
当事人	开证行			通知行				
	开证人			受益人				
	付款行			议付行				
汇票条款	出票人			付款期限	□即期	□远期		
				付款金额	□发票全额	□ 发票的百分之		
	收款人			出票依据				
	付款人							
货物描述	品名		规格/货号		贸易术语		唛头	
	数量		包装/件数		单价			
	合同/订单号		溢短装条款		总额			
装运条款	装运港		目的港		分批		转运	
	运输方式	□海运　□空运 □陆运　□其他			装运日期	最早 最晚		
单据条款	种类	份数	签字		主要内容/特别加注			
	发票		□盖章　□手签					
	装箱单		□盖章　□手签					
	提单	托运人			运费支付			
		抬头人			份数			
		通知人			特别加注			
	保险单	抬头人			份数			
		保险险别			赔付地点/币种			
		依据条款			保险加成			
	产地证	种类	□一般原产地证 □普惠制原产地证		签发机构		份数	
	检验证	种类	□品质证　□重量证 □其他证书		签发机构		份数	
	其他单据							
特殊条款								

模块二

信用证开立与审核

对于交易金额较大的贸易，通常还是采用信用证方式结算。进口方应该在出口方备货中或备货前依据双方签订的货物买卖合约条款，向其当地银行申请开立以卖方为受益人的信用证。当出口方收到由银行送达的信用证后，应当根据合约条款及时、审慎地对来证进行审核。如果发现来证有不符点，应及时用电文向信用证申请人（进口方）提出，要求其指示开证行对来证做相应的修改。

项目三

开立与审核信用证

学习目标

[知识目标] 熟悉申请开证的流程；熟悉审证的依据和步骤，掌握审证的要领。

[能力目标] 能根据外贸合同正确填写开证申请书；能根据外贸合同准确审核信用证，找出其中的问题条款并提出清晰的修改意见。

一、申请开立信用证

项目描述（案例情境描述）

2016 年 5 月 6 日，四川广皓进出口有限公司与意大利热那亚（Genova） HUT FURNITURE INDUSTRIES INC. 签订了购买家具的进口合同，公司的外贸业务员谢波根据进口合同的要求和其他相关业务信息填写开证申请书，并向招商银行四川省分行办理申请开证的手续。

附进口合同

PURCHASE CONFIRMATION

DATE: MAY 6, 2016

NO.: CNT0219

BUYERS: SICHUAN GUANGHAO IMP. & EXP. CO., LTD.

ADDRESS: 8/F, XIMAO BUILDING, NO.50 WUCHENG AVE. CHENGDU, SICHUAN, CHINA

TEL: 0086-28-86523300　　FAX: 0086-28-86523301

SELLERS: HUT FURNITURE INDUSTRIES INC.

ADDRESS: 153/155 BESANA BUILDING # 22066 MARIANO AVE. GENOVA, ITALY

TEL: 0039-1-32964550　　FAX: 0039-1-32964551

THIS CONFIRMATION IS MADE BY AND BETWEEN THE BUYER AND THE SELLER, WHEREBY THE BUYER AGREES TO BUY AND THE SELLER AGREES TO SELL THE UNDER-MENTIONED COMMODITY ACCORDING TO THE TERMS AND CONDITIONS STIPULATED BELOW:

DESCRIPTION OF GOODS	QUANTITY （PIECE）	UNIT PRICE （EUR）	AMOUNT （EUR）
		CFR GUANGZHOU	INCOTERMS 2010
COLZANI BRAND FURNITURE BED NO. B-D/206 SOFA NO. S-3/305 ARMCHAIR NO. C-2/105	 50 100 200	 450.00 510.00 180.00	 22,500.00 51,000.00 36,000.00
TOTAL	350		109,500.00
TOTAL VALUE （IN WORDS）	SAY EURO DOLLARS ONE HUNDRED AND NINE THOUSAND FIVE HUNDRED ONLY.		

PACKING: ALL FURNITURE PARTS TO BE PACKED IN FOAMED PLASTIC BOXES, ONE PIECE TO BE PACKED IN A CARTON, TOTAL 350 CARTONS.

SHIPMENT: DURING AUGUST, 2016 FROM GENOVA TO GUANGZHOU BY SEA WITH PARTIAL SHIPMENTS AND TRANSSHIPMENT NOT ALLOWED.

PAYMENT: IRREVOCABLE SIGHT L/C ISSUED BEFORE MAY 25, 2016.

DOCUMENTS:

(1) COMMERCIAL INVOICE SIGNED IN INK IN TRIPLICATE.

(2) PACKING LIST IN TRIPLICATE INDICATING QUANTITY OF GOODS, TOTAL GROSS AND NET WEIGHTS AND VOLUME OF THE SHIPMENT.

(3) FULL SET OF CLEAN ON BOARD OCEAN BILLS OF LADING MADE OUT TO ORDER OF SHIPPER AND BLANK ENDORSED MARKED FREIGHT PREPAID AND NOTIFY APPLICANT.

(4) CERTIFICATE OF ORIGIN IN DUPLICATE ISSUED BY THE AUTHORITIES.

(5) CERTIFICATION OF DEEP PROCESSING ISSUED BY THE SELLER.

(6) SHIPPING ADVICE ISSUED BY THE SELLER WITHIN 24 HOURS AFTER SHIPMENT NOTIFYING THE BUYER BY FAX INDICATING THE NAME OF THE GOODS, QUANTITY, GROSS WEIGHT, VOLUME, B/L NO., NAME OF VESSEL AND THE DATE OF SHIPMENT.

THIS CONFIRMATION IS MADE IN TWO ORIGINAL COPIES AND BECOMES VALID AFTER SIGNATURE, ONE COPY TO BE HELD BY EACH PARTY.

THE SELLER	THE BUYER
HUT FURNITURE INDUSTRIES INC.	SICHUAN GUANGHAO IM. & EX. CO., LTD.
Alessio	林皓

附其他业务信息：

1. 开证行：Bank of Communications, Sichuan Branch
2. 通知行：Banca Carige Head Office

操作要领

1. 申请书抬头（To）：确定开证行并填写其名称。

※本案例制单：　　制单操作

To: Bank of Communications, Sichuan Branch

2. 申请时间（Date）：填写开证申请日期。

※本案例制单：　　制单操作

Date: May 12, 2016

3. 开证申请人（Applicant）：填写开证申请人即合同项下买方的名称、地址和电话。

※本案例制单：

合同条款	制单操作
BUYERS: SICHUAN GUANGHAO IM. & EX. CO., LTD. ADDRESS: 8/F, XIMAO BUILDING, NO.50 WUCHENG AVE. CHENGDU, SICHUAN, CHINA TEL: 0086-28-86523300 FAX: 0086-28-86523301	Applicant: Sichuan Guanghao Imp. & Exp. Co., Ltd. Address: 8/F, Ximao Building, No.50 Wucheng Ave. Chengdu, Sichuan, China Telephone No.: 0086-28-86523300

4. 信用证号码、信用证有效期和交单地点（Expiry Date and Place）：信用证有效期一般为最晚装运期后 15 天；交单地点即为到期地点，一般主张在受益人所在国，对受益人有利。申请开证并不知信用证编号，此处信用证号码由开证行填写。

※本案例制单：　　制单操作

L/C No.:
Contract No.: CNT0219
Date and Place of Expiry of the Credit :
Sept.15, 2016 in Italy

5. 通知行（Advising Bank）：通知行的名称、地址和 SWIFT 号由开证行指定并填写。

6. 信用证开立方式：此栏填写指定的开证方式，采用信开或电开（即 SWIFT）形式开立。

※本案例制单：　　制单操作

Issue by teletransmission (the operative instruments)
Confirmation of the credit:
☒ not requested ☐ requested ☐ authorized if requested by beneficiary

7. 受益人（Beneficiary）：填写受益人即合同项下卖方的名称、地址和电话。

※本案例制单：　　合同条款　　　　　　　　　　　　　　　　　　　制单操作

合同条款	制单操作
SELLERS: HUT FURNITURE INDUSTRIES INC. ADDRESS: 153/155 BESANA BUILDING # 22066 MARIANO AVE. GENOVA, ITALY TEL: 0039-1-32964550 FAX: 0039-1-32964551	Beneficiary: Hut Furniture Industries Inc. Address:153/155 Besana Building # 22066 Mariano Ave. Genova, Italy Telephone No.: 0039-1-32964550

8. 信用证的类型（Form of Credit）：填写信用证的种类。

※本案例制单：　　　　　　　　　　　　　　　　　　　　　　　　　　制单操作

☒ Irrevocable documentary credit

☐ Irrevocable transferable documentary credit

9. 信用证金额大小写（Amount in figures and words）：按照合同金额填写。

※本案例制单：　　合同条款　　　　　　　　　　　　　　　　　　　制单操作

EUR109,500.00

TOTAL VALUE (IN WORDS)	SAY EURO DOLLARS ONE HUNDRED AND NINE THOUSAND FIVE HUNDRED ONLY.

Amount in figures and words

EUR109,500.00

SAY EURO DOLLARS ONE HUNDRED AND NINE THOUSAND FIVE HUNDRED ONLY

10. 货物描述（Description of Goods）：

※本案例制单：　　合同条款　　　　　　　　　　　　　　　　　　　制单操作

DESCRIPTION OF GOODS	UNIT PRICE (EUR)	AMOUNT (EUR)
COLZANI BRAND FURNITURE	CFR GUANGZHOU INCOTERMS® 2010	
BED NO. B-D/206	450.00	22,500.00
SOFA NO.S-3/305	510.00	51,000.00
ARMCHAIR NO.C-2/105	180.00	36,000.00

Description of goods, services or performance:

Colzani Brand Furniture

Bed No. B-D/206 at EUR450.00 per piece

Sofa No.S-3/305 at EUR510.00 per piece

Armchair No.C-2/105 at EUR180.00 per piece

CFR Guangzhou Incoterms® 2010

11. 指定银行和付款方式以及汇票条款：（1）在 Credit available with 后选择指定交单银行，并选择对应的付款方式。若不填写银行，则被视为任何银行。（2）如若需要出具汇票，则填写汇票金额，付款期限并填写付款人。

※本案例制单：　　制单操作

Credit available with ☐ issuing bank/☒any bank in beneficiary's country

☐ by sight payment　☒ by negotiation

☐ by acceptance　☐ by deferred payment

☐ by presentation

against the documents detailed herein and

☒ beneficiary's draft(s) for 100 %/☐___% of the invoice value at sight drawn on issuing bank

12. 分批和转运（Partial Shipments, Transshipment）：根据进口合同选择允许或者不允许。如若不填写，则被视为允许分批和允许转运。

※本案例制单：合同条款　　制单操作

合同条款	制单操作
SHIPMENT： DURING AUGUST, 2016 FROM GENOVA TO GUANGZHOU BY SEA WITH PARTIAL SHIPMENT AND TRANSSHIPMENT NOT ALLOWED	Partial shipments ☐ allowed ☒ not allowed Transshipment ☐allowed ☒ not allowed

13. 最晚装运时间以及装运港和目的港（Shipment to be made not later than..., Port of Loading, Port of Discharge）：根据合同填写最晚装运日期以及装运港、目的港信息。若装运港不能确定，可以笼统。

※本案例制单：　合同条款　　制单操作

合同条款	制单操作
SHIPMENT： DURING AUGUST, 2016 FROM GENOVA TO GUANGZHOU BY SEA WITH PARTIAL SHIPMENT AND TRANSSHIPMENT NOT ALLOWED	Shipment to be made not later than: August 31, 2016 Place of Taking in Charge/Dispatch from.../Place of Receipt: Port of Loading/Airport of Departure: Genova, Italy Port of Discharge/Airport of Destination: Guangzhou, China Place of Final Destination/for Transportation to.../Place of Delivery:

14. 价格术语（Terms of Price）：按照合同约定的贸易术语填写。

※本案例制单：合同条款　　制单操作

合同条款	制单操作
CFR GUANGZHOU　INCOTERMS® 2010	Terms of price: CFR Guangzhou　Incoterms® 2010

15. 单据条款（Documents Required）：根据进口合同的要求或实际需要选择受益人须向开证行提交的单据。本业务选择有：

☒ Signed Commercial Invoice indicating Contract No. CNT0219 and L/C No. in 4 copies.

☒ Full/☐_____set of original clean "on board" Bills of Lading made out ☒ to order ☐ to order of____________/and endorsed in blank by the shipper, marked "freight ☐ to collect ☒ prepaid" notifying: ☒ Applicant.

☒ Packing List/Weight List indicating quantity/gross and net weights of each package and packing conditions in 4 copies.

☒ Certificate of Origin issued by the authorities in duplicate.

☒ Beneficiary's certified copy of telex/fax dispatched to applicant within two working days after shipment advising shipping details including the name of the goods, quantity, gross weight, volume, B/L No., name of vessel and the date of shipment.

☒ Other documents, if any:

Certificate of deep processing issued by the seller in duplicate.

16. 特殊条款（Additional Instructions）：特殊条款一般包含费用条款、交单期限、交单的方式、溢短装条款以及对一些单据内容的补充要求等内容。

本业务项下为：

☒ All banking charges outside the issuing bank are for beneficiary's account.

☒ Documents to be presented within 15 days after the date of shipment but within the validity of the Credit.

☒ Third party as shipper is not acceptable. Short Form/Blank Back B/L is not acceptable. On Deck shipment is not allowed.

☐ Both quantity and amount ____% more or less are allowed.

☒ All documents to be forwarded in one cover by courier.

☐ Other terms, if any:

附开证申请书填制样例

开立信用证申请书 CREDIT APPLICATION

下表由申请人以英文填写，因表格字迹不清或词意含混或书/拼写错误而引起的一切后果由申请人承担。

To: Bank of Communications, Sichuan Branch　　Date: May 12, 2016

Applicant: Sichuan Guanghao Imp. & Exp. Co., Ltd. Address: 8/F, Ximao Building, No.50 Wucheng Ave. Chengdu, Sichuan, China Telephone No.: 0086-28-86523300	L/C No. Contract No. CNT0219 Date and Place of Expiry of the Credit: Sept.15, 2016 in Italy
Advising (if left in blank, any correspondent at your option) Issue by teletransmission (the operative instruments) Confirmation of the credit: ☒ not requested ☐ requested ☐ authorized if requested by beneficiary	Beneficiary: Hut Furniture Industries Inc. Address:153/155 Besana Building # 22066 Mariano Ave. Genova, Italy Telephone No.: 0039-1-32964550
☒ Irrevocable documentary credit ☐ Irrevocable transferable documentary credit	Amount in figures and words EUR109,500.00 SAY EURO DOLLARS ONE HUNDRED AND NINE THOUSAND FIVE HUNDRED ONLY

（续表）

<table>
<tr><td rowspan="5">Description of goods, services or performance:
Colzani Brand Furniture
Bed No. B-D/206 at EUR450.00 per piece
Sofa No. S-3/305 at EUR510.00 per piece
Armchair No. C-2/105 at EUR180.00 per piece
CFR Guangzhou　Incoterms® 2010</td><td>Credit available with ☐ issuing bank/☒ any bank in beneficiary's country
☐ by sight payment ☒ by negotiation ☐ by acceptance ☐ by deferred payment
☐ by presentation
against the documents detailed herein and
☒ beneficiary's draft(s) for __100__%/
☐_____% of the invoice value at sight drawn on issuing bank</td></tr>
<tr><td>Partial shipments ☐ allowed ☒ not allowed</td></tr>
<tr><td>Transshipment ☐ allowed ☒ not allowed
Shipment to be made not later than: August 31, 2016
Place of Taking in charge/Dispatch from…/Place of receipt:
Port of Loading/Airport of Departure: Genova, Italy</td></tr>
<tr><td>Port of Discharge/Airport of Destination: Guangzhou, China
Place of Final Destination/for Transportation to…/Place of Delivery:</td></tr>
<tr><td>Terms of price: CFR Guangzhou Incoterms® 2010</td></tr>
<tr><td colspan="2">Documents required (at least in duplicate unless otherwise specified): (marked with ×)
1. ☒ Signed Commercial Invoice indicating Contract No. CNT0219 and L/C No. in 4 copies.
2. Shipment to be effected by Sea from Port to Port:
☒ Full/☐_____set of original clean "on board" Bills of Lading made out ☒ to order ☐ to order of___________/and endorsed in blank by the shipper, marked "freight ☐ to collect ☒ prepaid" notifying: ☒ Applicant.
3. Shipment to be effected by Multimodal or Combined transport (covering at least two different modes of transport):
☐ Full set of original clean "On Board" Multimodal or Combined transport documents made out ☐ to order/☐ to order of ________________________ and endorsed in blank by the shipper marked "Freight ☐ prepaid/☐ to collect" and notify Applicant.
4. Shipment to be effected by Air
☐ Original Air Waybill showing "freight ☐ to collect ☐ prepaid" ☐ notifying applicant indicating freight amount and consigned to: ☐ Applicant ☐ ________________________
5. Shipment to be effected by Rail:
☐ Full set of Rail Waybill showing "freight ☐ to collect ☐ prepaid" ☐ notifying applicant indicating freight amount and consigned to: ☐ Applicant ☐ ____________________
6. ☐ Insurance Policy/Certificate blank endorsed for ____% of the invoice value showing claims payable in China in currency of the Credit covering:
7. ☒ Packing List/Weight List indicating quantity/gross and net weights of each package and packing conditions in 4 copies.</td></tr>
</table>

（续表）

8. ☐ Certificate of Quantity/Weight issued by:

indicating the actual surveyed quantity/weight of shipped goods as well as the packing condition.

9. ☐ Certificate of Quality issued by:

10. ☒ Certificate of Origin issued by the authorities in duplicate.

11. ☒ Beneficiary's certified copy of telex/fax dispatched to applicant within two working days after shipment advising shipping details including the name of the goods, quantity, gross weight, volume, B/L No., name of vessel and the date of shipment.

12. ☐ Beneficiary's letter certifying that one set of non-negotiable shipping documents have been sent to applicant directly by express mail immediately after shipment.

13. ☐ Article 10(c) &(f) of UCP600 are not applicable to the credit. Any subsequent amendment(s) to the credit will be considered as effective, if no objection is raised within seven days after its receipt. In case rejection is received, the advising bank is requested to advise us by telex immediately.

14. ☒ Other documents, if any :

☒ Certificate of deep processing issued by the seller in duplicate.

Additional instructions:

1. ☒ All banking charges outside the issuing bank are for beneficiary's account.

2. ☒ Documents to be presented within 15 days after the date of shipment but within the validity of the Credit.

3. ☒ Third party as shipper is not acceptable. Short Form/Blank Back B/L is not acceptable. On Deck shipment is not allowed.

4. ☐ Both quantity and amount ____% more or less are allowed.

5. ☒ All documents to be forwarded in one cover by courier.

6. ☐ Other terms, if any:

We request you to issue on our behalf and for our account your Irrevocable Credit in accordance with the above instructions (marked(×) where appropriate). This Credit will be subject to Current ICC Uniform Customs and Practice for Documentary Credits (as amended, modified or replace from time to time), insofar as they are applicable transacted by:

申请人（公章）	开证行（单位印章）
法定代表人（负责人）或授权代表	负责人或授权代表
林皓	
（签字或盖章）	（签字或盖章）

GUANGHAO IMP. & EXP. CO., LTD. SICHUAN
四川广皓进出口有限公司

相关知识

一、开证事宜

（一）进口开证的程序

填写开证申请书	进口商根据银行规定填写开证申请书，一般为一式三份。填写开证申请书应按照合同条款的具体规定，写明对信用证项下各项内容的具体要求。
⇩ 填写开证申请人承诺书	一般银行的开证申请书背面详细印就了开证申请人的承诺书，是开证申请人对开证行的行为声明，以明确双方的责任。
⇩ 提交外贸合同副本及相关附件	进口商（开证申请人）按照开证行的要求提交相关外贸合同的副本、进口许可证等相关文件。
⇩ 支付开证保证金	开证行对开证申请人的经营状况、收益状况、资信等企业情况以及开证文本的合法性审核通过后，要求申请人提供开证押金。保证金多以现金作押。保证金的多少和申请人的资信和销售盈利情况息息相关，高的甚至可以多达100%，低的只有百分之几，甚至免收保证金。除了现金，也可用其他动产或不动产作抵押。
⇩ 支付开证手续费	开证申请人在申请开证时需要按照银行的规定支付开证手续费，一般为开证金额的1.5‰。

（二）开证注意事项

1. 如若合同规定了开证时间的，申请人应于规定期限内申请开立信用证。

2. 信用证条款内容应按照外贸合同的条款来开立，同时还应明确规定各类单据的签发人（商业发票、保险单和运输单据除外），载明各单据应表述的内容。如若申请开证的条款与合同不符，被受益人审核发现后，申请人需向银行另付费用予以修改；若没有被出口人审核出来，则银行日后可以不符点单据为由，行使拒付的权利。

3. 通知行一般由开证行指定，如在外贸合同中出口商指定了通知行，则进口商在申请开证时应当予以说明，供开证行参考。

4. 不允许分批装运、转运或不接受第三者装运单据时，均应在信用证中表述出来，否则将被认为是允许分批装运、允许转运或接受第三方装运单据。

5. 合同中有溢短装条款的，在开立信用证时应当分别就总金额和货物总数量表明相同的溢短装比例，不可漏开。

6. 申请开证时，可以选择一些对申请人有利的条款。如果对方持有异议，可以再予修改。

操作能力训练

操作题：C3-1　根据附录 2 里的开证货物买卖合同，独立填写开立信用证申请书一份。

二、审核信用证

项目描述（案例情境描述）

2016 年 4 月 3 日，成都和润贸易有限公司和德国 JAMES BROWN & SONS INC.公司就小牛皮钱夹签订了销售确认书，4 月 10 日德国客户开来了信用证，成都和润贸易有限公司外贸业务员夏天根据销售确认书和实际的业务资料对来证进行仔细审核，梳理来证中的问题条款并提出修改意见。

附：销售确认书

SALES CONFIRMATION

Place: CHENGDU

Date: APRIL 03, 2016

The Seller: CHENGDU HERUN TRADING CO., LTD.
Address: 14TH FLOOR KINGSTAR MANSION,
676 JINLIN RD., CHENGDU, CHINA
TEL: (086) 28-62597480 FAX: (086)28-62597490

The Buyer: JAMES BROWN & SONS INC.
Address: D-4905 SPENGE/WESTF
BREMEN, GERMANY
TEL: (0049) 421-7709910 FAX: (0049) 421-7701100

Marks & Numbers	Commodity & Specifications	No. of Packages	Quantity (Piece)	Unit Price (US$)	Amount (US$)
J.B.S. HRWX16-10 BREMEN C/NO.1-100	Calf Leather Wallet in Black Color			CIFC3 BREMEN	
	Art No.P75506	50 CTNS	9,000 PCS	4.00/PCS	36,000.00
	Art No.P75507	50 CTNS	9,000 PCS	4.50/PCS	40,500.00
	TOTAL	100 CTNS	18,000 PCS		76,500.00
TOTAL CONTRACT VALUE: SAY US DOLLARS SEVENTY SIX THOUSAND FIVE HUNDRED ONLY					

PACKING: 10 PCS TO BE PACKED IN A BOX, 18 BOXES TO BE PACKED IN A CARTON. TOTAL: 100 CARTONS. 5% MORE OR LESS IN QUANTITY AND AMOUNT IS ALLOWED.

SHIPMENT: TO BE EFFECTED BY THE END OF MAY 2016 FROM SHANGHAI CHINA TO BREMEN GERMANY WITH PARTIAL SHIPMENTS AND TRANSSHIPMENT NOT ALLOWED.

PAYMENT: THE BUYER SHALL OPEN THROUGH A BANK ACCEPTABLE TO THE SELLER AN IRREVOCABLE LETTER OF CREDIT AT SIGHT TO REACH THE SELLER BEFORE APRIL 15, 2016 AND VALID FOR NEGOTIATION IN CHINA UNTIL THE 15TH DAY AFTER THE DATE OF SHIPMENT.

INSURANCE: THE SELLER SHALL COVER INSURANCE AGAINST WPA AND WAR RISK AND SRCC FOR 110% OF THE TOTAL INVOICE VALUE AS PER OR SUBJECT TO THE RELEVANT OCEAN MARINE CARGO CLAUSES OF PEOPLE'S INSURANCE COMPANY OF CHINA (P.I.C.C.) DATED 1/1/1981.

Confirmed by:

THE BUYER	**THE SELLER**
For and on behalf of	For and on behalf of
JAMES BROWN & SONS INC.	CHENGDU HERUN TRADING CO., LTD.
Paul Lockwood	张书梅
(signature)	(signature)

附：国外开来的信用证

APPLICATION HEADER	* WEST DEUTSCHE LANDES BANK
SEQUENCE OF TOTAL	27： 1/1
FORM OF DOC. CREDIT	40A: IRREVOCABLE
DOC. CREDIT NUMBER	20： 3-16509
DATE OF ISSUE	31C: 160410
EXPIRY	31D: DATE 160605 PLACE IN GERMANY
APPLICANT	50: JAMES BROWN & SONS INC. D-4950 SPENGE/WESTF, BREMEN, GERMANY
BENEFICIARY	59: CHENGDU HERUI TRADING CO, LTD. 14TH FLOOR KINGSTAR MANSION, 676 JINLIN RD., CHENGDU, CHINA
AMOUNT	32B: CURRENCY USD AMOUNT 76,500.00
AVAILABLE WITH/BY	41D: ANY BANK BY NEGOTIATION
DRAFTS AT…	42C: SIGHT
DRAWEE	42A: APPLICANT
PARTIAL SHIPMENTS	43P: NOT ALLOWED
TRANSSHIPMENT	43T: NOT ALLOWED
PORT OF LOADING	44E: SHANGHAI
PORT OF DISCHARGE	44F: BREMEN
LATEST DATE OF SHIP.	44C: 160510
DESCRIPTION OF GOODS	45A: CALF LEATHER WALLET IN BLACK COLOR AS PER P/O NO.10056 AND S/C NO.HRWX16-10 CIFC3 BREMEN SUBJECT TO INCOTERMS® 2010 PACKED 10 PCS/BOX AND 18 BOXES/CTN ART NO. P75506 9,000 PCS USD 4.50/PC ART NO. P75507 9,000 PCS USD 4.00/PC

DOCUMENTS REQUIRED	46A: + SINGED INVOICE IN DUPLICATE INDICATING BREAK DOWN OF THE AMOUNT OF COMMISSION AND CIF VALUE. + PACKING LIST IN DUPLICATE SHOWING QUANTITY, N.W., G.W. AND MEAS. OF EACH CARTON. + QUALITY CERTIFICATE IN DUPLICATE ISSUED BY THE PERSON AUTHORIZED BY APPLICANT. + FULL SET OF CLEAN "ON BOARD" OCEAN BILLS OF LADING MADE OUT TO ORDER AND ENDORSED IN BLANK MARKED FREIGHT TO COLLECT AND NOTIFY APPLICANT AND INDICATE THE FULL NAME AND ADDRESS OF SHIPPING AGENT AT THE DESTINATION. + INSURANCE POLICY IN DUPLICATE ENDORSED IN BLANK FOR 20% OVER INVOICE VALUE COVERING ALL RISKS AS PER CIC OF PICC (01/01/1981). + GSP CERTIFICATE OF ORIGIN FORM A ISSUED BY CCPIT STATING THE NAME OF THE MANUFACTURER. + SHIPPING ADVICE SHOWING THE NAME OF THE CARRYING VESSEL, DATE OF SHIPMENT, MARKS, QUANTITY, NET WEIGHT AND GROSS WEIGHT OF THE SHIPMENT TO THE APPLICANT WITH 1 DAY AFTER THE DATE OF SHIPMENT.
ADDITIONAL COND.	47A: + IF DOCUMENTS PRESENTED ARE FOUND NOT TO BE IN FULL COMPLIANCE WITH CREDIT TERMS, WE WILL ASSESS A FEE OF USD 55.00 PER SET OF DOCUMENTS. + ALL DOCUMENTS MUST INDICATE THE NAME OF ISSUING BANK, THE NUMBER AND DATE OF THIS CREDIT.
CHARGES	71B: CHARGES OUTSIDE GERMAN BANK TO BE BORNE BY BENEFICIARY.
PERIOD FOR PRESENTATION	48: WITHIN 5 DAYS AFTER DATE OF SHIPMENT, BUT WITHIN THE VALIDITY OF THIS CREDIT.
CONFIRMATION	49: WITHOUT
INSTRUCTIONS	78: + WE SHALL COVER THE NEGOTIATING BANK AS PER THEIR INSTRUCTIONS.

	+ DOCUMENTS IN ONE LOT FORWARDED BY COURIER TO WEST DEUTSCHE LANDES BANK 1981 MCGILL COLLECE AVE. BREMEN GERMANY.
SEND. TO REC. INFO.	72: THIS CREDIT IS AN OPERATIVE INSTRUMENT SUBJECT TO UCP FOR DOCUMENTARY CREDIT 2007 REVISION ICC PUBLICATION NO. 600.

操作要领

对照销售确认书各条款，且根据业务操作的可行性和信用证 UCP 的相关规定，夏天逐条审核了第 3-16509 号信用证，发现了如下不符点，并在公司的信用证审核记录里做了如下记录：

成都和润贸易有限公司

CHENGDU HERUN TRADING CO., LTD.

14TH FLOOR KINGSTAR MANSION, 676 JINLIN RD., CHENGDU, CHINA

审证记录

L/C No. 3-16509　　　　日期：2016 年 4 月 12 日

开证行：WEST DEUTSCHE LANDES BANK

S/C No. HRWX16-10

品名：CALF LEATHER WALLET

不符点	修改意见
1. 条款 31D：信用证到期日和到期地点不符	应改为 2016 年 6 月 15 日在中国到期

解释：来证规定的到期日应与合同规定的最晚装运期相隔 15 天，否则有可能造成受益人逾期交单。信用证到期地点即为交单地点，如果被规定在国外，受益人则将承担因投递方的责任延迟交单而被拒付的后果。

2. 条款 50：开证申请人的地址不符	应改为 D-4905 SPENGE/WESTF, BREMEN, GERMANY

解释：申请人或受益人的地址不符，将为受益人制单造成不符点，从而遭到银行拒付。

3. 条款 59：受益人名称不符	应将名称中的“HERUI”改为“HERUN”

解释：受益人或申请人名称不符，将造成受益人的单据出现不符点，从而遭到开证行拒付。

4. 条款 42A: 汇票的付款人为不符点	应将 APPLICANT 改为开证行或者开证行指定的付款行

解释：付款人若为开证申请人，开证行将不再承担第一性的付款责任，银行信用变为了商业信用，使信用证失去意义，受益人的收款权益将无法得到银行的保证。

5. 条款 44C：最晚装运日期不符	应将 2016 年 5 月 10 日改为 2016 年 5 月 31 日

解释：合同规定的装运期为 2016 年 5 月底之前，虽然来证规定的最晚装运日期也在 5 月份，但较 5 月份最晚日期大大提前了，有可能将会造成受益人无法按时交货。

6. 条款 45A：货物描述中合同号码不符	应将 HRWX15-10 改为 HRWX16-10

解释：来证合同号码与原始合同号码不符，受益人制作的单据始终存在不符点，将会遭到拒付。

7. 条款 45A：货物描述中两个货号的单价不符 应把 P75506 的改为 USD 4.00, P75506 的为 USD 4.50

解释：价格与原合同的不符，将造成不符点单据，遭到开证行拒付。

8. 条款 46A：品质证书由申请人授权人签发属“软条款”或“陷阱条款” 应改由第三方权威机构签发，如“...ISSUED BY CIQ”或“...ISSUED BY THE THIRD PARTY AUTHORIZED”

解释：品质证书由申请人或其派人签发，有可能造成受益人被动，将因无法提交合格的单据而遭拒付。

9. 条款 46A：提单条款要求运费到付不符 应将“FREIGHT COLLECT”改为“FREIGHT PREPAID”

解释：该业务采用的贸易术语是 CIF，应由出口方承担运费。否则，将跟国际惯例解释冲突。

10. 条款 46A：保险条款中投保加成不符 应将投保金额“120% OF...”改为“110% OF...”

解释：来证提高投保加成比例，受益人将多交保费，将增加受益人的成本。

11. 条款 46A：普惠制原产地证条款要求出单人为贸促会不符 应将“ISSUED BY CCPIT”修改为“ISSUED BY CIQ”或者笼统地表述成“ISSUED BY AUTHORITIES ”

解释：普惠制原产地证书在我国只能由商检机构签发，贸易促进委员会只签发一般原产地证书。

12. 条款 48：交单期限不符 应将“WITHIN 5 DAYS...”改为“WITHIN 15 DAYS...”

解释：装运后 5 日内向银行交单，时间太短促，极容易造成出口方逾期交单而遭拒付。

13. 来证缺少溢短装条款 应要求在信用证中加上“PERCENTAGE CREDIT AMOUNT TOLERANCE 39A : 05/05”，同时在附加条款 47A 中加上“5% MORE OR LESS IN QUANTITY AND AMOUNT OF GOODS IS ALLOWED”条款

解释：合同中有溢短装条款，出口方的交货数量和结算金额在规定的幅度内波动不属违反合约。如果来证删除该条款，出口人的权益将受到损害。应该允许数量和金额同比例增减。

审核人：夏天

相关知识

一、出口审核信用证

当前因单笔交易额或单笔出货金额较小，加之能操作信用证项下业务的人才匮乏，中小企业往往都愿意采用电汇或票汇的方式结算，其优点是手续简便、单据简单、资金流动快速。但在交易金额较大的情况下，尤其是大型企业的交易，还是需要采用信用更为可靠的信用证结算方式。出口方一旦收到进口商通过银行开来的信用证，须立即予以细致审核。

（一）审证依据

1. 外贸合同。信用证是依据外贸合同开立的，故而信用证的条款应与货物买卖合同的条款一致或相符。审核信用证的条款是否与合同条款相符，是外贸业务员收到信用证后首要的工作任务。

2. 国际惯例。跟单信用证统一惯例（简称 UCP）是指导国际结算各方行为的国际惯例，当前使用的惯例主要有 UCP500 和 UCP600。审核信用证时，应当根据国际惯例的相关条款规定来甄别和判断是否接受信用证中的某些条款。

3. 业务具体情况。对于外贸合同中未做规定的或无法根据国际惯例来做出判断时，业务员应根据贸易的实际业务情况来审核信用证，做出是否接受来证中某些条款的决定。

（二）审证原则

1. 审核后的信用证须不存在受益人不可控的因素（条款）。

2. 审核后的信用证没有可能引起歧义的条款存在。

3. 对于不会对结算造成影响的条款或拼写错误或语法错误不予审核和纠正。

4. 对于可能影响结算的轻微的、明显的拼写错误，如果仅有一两个，且没有其他不符点存在，则可不予提出修改，仅在制单时采取技术措施予以校正。

5. 对于来证中有利于受益人的条款，尽管可能与合同条款有出入，也不予提出修改。

（三）审证步骤

1. 熟悉外贸合同的条款。

2. 对照外贸合同，按照可操作原则逐条审核信用证各条款。

3. 列出信用证中的不符条款以及漏开条款。

4. 敦促开证申请人指示其开证行修改信用证。

（四）审证要点

1. 信用证的真伪与生效（Authenticity and Taking-effect）

由于 SWIFT 系统具有自动核押功能，故而以 SWIFT 开出的 MT700 格式的信用证无须担心其真实性。如果是信开信用证，则需通知行对开证行授权签名的真伪进行审核。如通知行被告知收到的信用证为预先通知信用证时，则一定要等到开证行随后寄来的信用证证实书后，该信用证才正式生效。因此，受益人审核的要点是，确保来证无限制生效的条款。

2. 信用证本身条款（Creit Terms）

（1）当事人（Parties Concerned）：受益人和申请人的名称及地址、电话及传真须准确无误。开证行的资信度不可太低，否则须要求申请人指示开证行在信用证中添加被指定银行，或保兑、或偿付、或支付。

（2）性质和种类（Nature and Type）：须确保来证是不可撤销信用证、接受议付信用证和付款信用证，审核是否加具保兑等。

（3）币别和金额（Currency and Amount）：信用证的币别和金额（大小写数额）必须与外贸合同相符。如若前期有预付货款或是含佣价，信用证金额也须是装运货物的全额价值。外贸合同有“溢短装”条款的，应审核来证是否允许交货数量增减的同时，也允许结算金额同比例增减。

（4）开证日期（Date of Issue）：一般不应过多晚于合同条款规定的开证日期。

（5）到期日和到期地（Date and Place of Expiry）：信用证的到期日即为信用证的有效期，一般与最晚装运期相隔 15 天。没载明有效期的信用证是无效信用证。若信用证没有明确有效期，但规定了付款、承兑或议付的截止日期，即为规定了信用证的到期日。一般规定的到期地点即为交单地，一般主张在出口地到期，以免除受益人承担邮程风险，以便保证受益人能够及时交单。

（6）交单期(Period for Presentation)：这是受益人向银行交单的日期规定。按 UCP600

第 14 条 C 款规定，受益人须于装运日后 21 个日历日内交单，但不得超过信用证的有效期。可接受的交单期为装运日后的 15 天内或 21 天内。来证若无规定交单期，信用证有效期就是最晚交单期。

（7）开证行付款保证的责任文句（Duty of Honor）：凡信用证须载明开证行的保证付款责任文句。否则，开证行可以不承担第一性的付款责任。但 SWIFT“环银电协”成员行的电开证即 MT700 格式的信用证有固定格式为 78 项，可以不必注明付款责任文句。

（8）所适用的惯例（Applicable Rules）：凡信用证须载明所适用的惯例。否则，一旦发生结算纠纷，将无规则可循。SWIFT 成员行的电开证即 MT700 格式的信用证有其固定格式为 40E 项。

（9）被指定银行（Named Banks）：根据开证行的资信度情况，审核是否指定了偿付（或保兑、提示、议付）银行，可否接受。一般被指定银行应是跨国大型银行。

3. 汇票条款（Draft）

（1）汇票期限（Draft at/Maturity）：按照外贸合同的规定注明汇票的付款期限，即期或远期。在远期付款的条款中，from 和 after 一样，都不包含提到的日期，计算日期从第二天开始。

（2）付款人（Drawee/Drawn on）：信用证项下汇票的付款人即为受票人，应是开证行或开证行指定的付款行。不接受开证申请人作为付款人。

（3）指定交单银行（Available with）：指定交单银行又为收款人或受款人。仅接受出口人当地银行作为交单银行，一般不宜接受境外银行作为交单银行。

（4）出票依据（Drawn Under）：如果来证有出票依据的条款，应审核是否跟本证信息相符。

4. 运输条款（Transportation）

（1）装运港和目的港（Ports of Loading and Discharge）：信用证中的装运港、目的港应与外贸合同的规定一致，交货地点应与价格条款一致。若合同规定了具体装运港口，应可以接受来证规定的装运港为笼统的。可以接受目的港有选择港。

（2）装运期（The Latest Date of Shipment）：装运期是指出口商将货物装上运往目的港/目的地的运输工具或交付给承运人的日期。通常信用证要规定一个最晚装运日期，如果没有规定，则最晚装运日期就是信用证的到期日。如果规定的装运期是月份，则以该月最后一天作为最晚装运期。需要注意的是，before 并不包含提到的日期，而 by 或 on or before 才包括了提到的日期；after 并不包含提到的日期，而 from 才包含了提到的日期。

（3）分批和转运（Partial Shipment and Transshipment）：该条款应与外贸合同条款一致。如果合同对分批和转运做了明确规定，但来证没有明确规定可否分批和转运，则视为允许分批和转运，是可以接受的。对于分期支付货款或分批装运，UCP600 第 32 条规定，如信用证规定在指定的时间段内分期付款或分期装运，任何一期没有按照信用证规定期限装运时，信用证对该期和以后各期均告失效。

5. 商品条款（Commodity Description）

需审核品名、货号、规格或品质、数量、单价及术语（价格术语后的目的港须与运输条款中的目的港一致）、包装种类、方法及唛头、货描中援引的合同号或订单号及其日期。

6. 单据条款（Documents Required）

仔细审核单据条款有无软条款的存在，份数规定是否合理（我国的官方单据正本只有一份）等。

（1）提单条款（Bill of Lading）

1）要求提交给银行的正本份数应全套提交给银行。

2）审核提单抬头（关键词 made out），不能接受“凭申请人指示”（to order of applicant）。

3）审核主运费支付规定，预付（freight prepaid）或到付（freight to collect）须与贸易术语解释的贸易双方责任和义务相符。

4）应该有被通知人（Notify Party）。若未规定，只有副本提单的通知人一栏可以打开证人。

（2）保险条款（Insurance）

1）根据贸易术语审核来证中是否应该规定保险条款。若是由买方办理保险的贸易术语，来证不应该规定受益人提交保险单据。

2）审核证内规定的险别是否与合同一致。若有增加险别，则应以不增加受益人费用为准。若未明确投保险别，则不必提出要求修改，受益人投保平安险即可。如果合同规定投保中国保险条款 CIC 的险种，但来证要求投保伦敦协会保险条款 ICC 相应的险种，可以接受，不必提出修改。

3）审核保险金额的规定是否与合同条款相一致，须注意来证所使用的介词和加成百分比率。若未明确投保加成比率，则不必提出修改，受益人加一成投保即可。

4）如果指定保险查勘代理人，应要求修改。因为我国保险公司规定，保险勘验代理人须由保险公司自主选择。

（3）其他（Others）

1）正本提单直寄客户（Original B/L Forward Opener）：若来证规定一份正本提单直接寄往申请人，不可接受。

2）客检条款（Document Issued by Opener）：不接受来证规定商品检验证书由开证申请人来人签发。

3）指装条款（Named Carriers）：不能接受仅指定一家承运人运载货物，至少应有三家被指定承运人。不接受指定转运船舶的条款。

4）审核信用证中涉及的各种业务号码是否正确。凡证内出现两次的号码，均需核对是否一致。

5）受益人能否提供信用证项下的单据。

6）信用证项下的单据在签发、细节或格式上是否由买方控制。

7）取得其他非受益人控制的单据的费用和风险（政府文件、各种证明）。

8）所交单据是否与合同或信用证其他内容相矛盾，证内内容不得相互冲突矛盾。

9）信用证对单据的特别要求能否办到。

10）单据加注内容（要求显示的内容）可否接受。

11）单据所要求使用的语言。

7. 银行费用条款（Banking Charges）

根据跟单信用证惯例规定，开证行费用应由开证申请人承担；被指定银行费用由指定银行承担。

但目前我国对外贸易的实际情况是，出口方银行费用由受益人承担，进口方银行费用由开证申请人承担。总之，不应接受开证行的费用也由受益人承担，应注意来证银行费用条款中的用词。

二、常见信用证软条款

软条款又称陷阱条款，即信用证中加的特殊条款，使受益人无法控制其执行情况。它赋予开证行或申请人单方面的主动权，使信用证项下的付款责任可随时因开证行或申请人的单方面行为而予以解除，从而变相地成为可撤销信用证或银行付款责任不明确的信用证。常见的情况如下：

1. 限制受益人装运的条款。信用证规定由申请人指定装载船只，或卸货港、被通知人、装运日期这些内容须日后经开证行以信用证修改书的方式确定并通知受益人，使得出口方不能按时实施货物装运。

2. 限制单据生效的条款。某单据须由特定的人（申请人指定或授权的人）签发或会签，并且其印鉴须与开证行的留样相符，以证明货物合格，或已经通关，或已收妥无误，或确认数量等。

3. 限制开证行付款责任的条款。

（1）货物到港后，由申请人或特定机构验货，并向开证行提供合格证明，开证行才付款；

（2）只有货物清关或获得由主管当局批准进口的相关文件后才付款；

（3）申请人在货物再出口得到货款后，开证行才承担付款责任；

（4）规定 80%即期付款，20%余款须凭开证申请人出具的证明付款；

（5）以货物收据作为结算单据。

4. 提单正本直接寄往客户收取或做电放提单。

5. 限制信用证生效的条款。规定信用证生效是有条件的，比如规定申请人获得当局进口许可，来证才予生效。

三、修改信用证

（一）改证的原则

受益人改证应该遵循既维护自身的合法利益，又不损害开证申请人正常利益的原则，具体可以按如下情况处理：

1. 对受益人有利，又不影响申请人利益的问题条款，不予修改。

2. 对受益人有利，但会严重影响到申请人利益的问题条款，一定要修改。

3. 对受益人不利，但在不增加或增加成本很少的情况下可以满足的问题条款，可以不修改。

4. 对受益人不利，增加成本较多的情况下，如果申请人愿意承担增加的费用，可以不修改，如果申请人不愿承担增加的费用，则一定要改。

5. 对受益人不利，会带来巨大的收汇风险的问题条款一定要修改。

（二）改证的路径和方法

受益人审证发现不符点后，应立即以传真方式向申请人提出明确具体的修改意见，要求其指示开证行做相应的修改。下图为修改信用证的路径示意图。

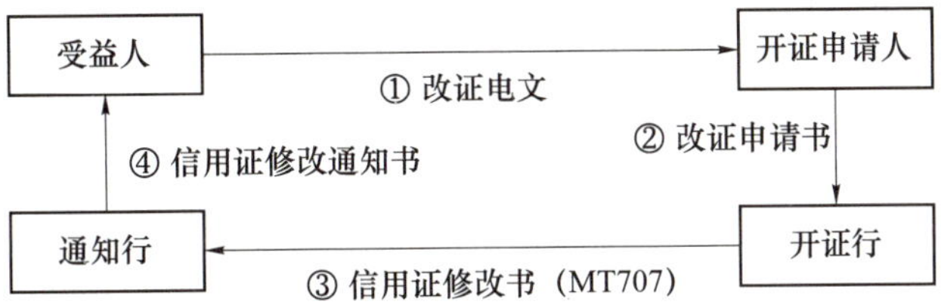

图 3-1　信用证改证路径

（三）接受改证的原则

受益人对信用证修改内容要么全部接受，要么全部拒绝；不得部分接受，部分拒绝。

操作能力训练

操作题：

C3-2　根据附录 2 里提供的审证资料一，独立审核相关信用证，指出其存在的不符点并提出修改意见。

C3-3　根据附录 2 里提供的审证材料二，独立审核相关信用证，指出其存在的不符点并提出修改意见。

C3-4　讨论和评讲后，根据附录 2 里的其余审证材料，逐一审核相关信用证，指出其存在的不符点并提出修改意见。

C3-5　探索学习核算合同价格和盈亏项目，根据附录 4（见本书第 311 页）里的报价核算题 15-1，尝试计算出口合同价。

附录 2　开立和审核信用证及其资料

C3-1　开证操作能力训练

C3-1.1　开证货物买卖合同

PURCHASE　CONFIRMATION

DATE: MAR.17, 2017

NO.: HX17-005

BUYER: CHENGDU HONGXIN BUILDING MATERIAL CO., LTD.

ADDRESS: 801-805 F8 MEIKAILONG MANSION NO. 35 HUAXI RD. CHENGDU, SICHUAN, CHINA

TEL: 0086-28-82244016　　　FAX: 0086-28-82244015

SELLER: WALES CERAMIC MARKETS CO., LTD.

ADDRESS: 1/F, JA BLDG., 69 CORPORTATION ROAD, CARDIFF, LIVERPOOL BF23, UK

TEL: 0044-151-3564202 FAX: 0044-151-3564203

THIS CONFIRMATION IS MADE BY AND BETWEEN THE BUYER AND THE SELLER, WHEREBY THE BUYER AGREES TO BUY AND THE SELLER AGREES TO SELL THE UNDER-MENTIONED COMMODITY ACCORDING TO THE TERMS AND CONDITIONS STIPULATED BELOW:

DESCRIPTION OF GOODS	QUANTITY（SET）	UNIT PRICE（GBP）	AMOUNT（GBP）
		FOB LIVERPOOL	INCOTERMS 2010
BATHROOM VANITY	180	106.00	19,080.00
STEAM SHOWER	420	210.00	88,200.00
TOTAL	600		107,280.00
TOTAL VALUE （IN WORDS）	SAY GREAT BRITAIN POUNDS ONE HUNDRED SEVEN THOUSAND TWO HUNDRED AND EIGHTY ONLY.		

PACKING: ONE SET TO BE PACKED IN FOAMED PLASTIC CASING PER WOODEN CASE, TOTAL 600 CASES.

SHIPMENT: FROM LIVERPOOL TO SHANGHAI BY SEA DURING MAY, 2017 WITH PARTIAL SHIPMENT AND TRANSSHIPMENT NOT ALLOWED.

PAYMENT: IRREVOCABLE SIGHT L/C ISSUED BEFORE MAR. 31, 2017

DOCUMENTS:

(7) SIGNED COMMERCIAL INVOICE IN FIVE COPIES.

(8) PACKING LIST IN FOUR COPIES INDICATING GROSS AND NET WEIGHTS OF EACH CASE.

(9) FULL SET OF CLEAN ON BOARD OCEAN BILL OF LADING MADE OUT TO ORDER OF SHIPPER AND BLANK ENDORSED MARKED FREIGHT TO COLLECT AND NOTIFY APPLICANT.

(10) CERTIFICATE OF ORIGIN IN DUPLICATE ISSUED BY THE AUTHORITIES.

(11) CERTIFICATE OF QUALITY.

(12) SHIPPING ADVICE ISSUED BY THE SELLER IN TIME BEFORE SHIPMENT NOTIFYING THE BUYER BY FAX THE NAME OF THE GOODS, QUANTITY, GROSS WEIGHT, VOLUME, B/L NO., NAME OF VESSEL AND THE DATE OF SHIPMENT.

THIS CONFIRMATION IS MADE IN TWO ORIGINAL COPIES AND BECOMES VALID AFTER SIGNATURE, ONE COPY TO BE HELD BY EACH PARTY.

THE BUYER
CHENGDU HONGXIN BUILDING MATERIAL CO., LTD.
楚潇

THE SELLER
WALES CERAMIC MARKETS CO., LTD.
GEORGE LEE

C3-1.2　开立信用证申请书格式一

不可撤销信用证申请书

APPLICATION FOR IRREVOCABLE DOCUMENTARY CREDIT

To:　　　　　　　　　　　　　　　　　　　　　　　　　　　　　　________ DATE:

Please establish by　☐SWIFT　☐brief cable　☐airmail an Irrevocable Credit as follows:

<table>
<tr><td>Advising Bank: (To be left for bank to fill in)</td><td>(20) Irrevocable Documentary Credit No.

(31D) Expiry Date and Place</td></tr>
<tr><td>(50) Applicant: (Full name & detailed address)</td><td>(59) Beneficiary: (Full name & detailed address)</td></tr>
<tr><td colspan="2">(32B) Currency code, Amount (In words and figures)

(39A) Quantity and Credit amount tolerance ______%</td></tr>
<tr><td colspan="2">(41A) Credit Available with ☐any bank ☐issuing bank ☐other (pl. Indicate)
By ☐Negotiation ☐Acceptance ☐Sight Payment ☐Presentation ☐Deferred Payment at</td></tr>
<tr><td colspan="2">(42C) Draft at ________for ______% of invoice value</td></tr>
<tr><td colspan="2">(42A) Drawn on ________________</td></tr>
<tr><td>(43P) Partial shipment ☐allowed ☐not allowed</td><td>(43T) Transshipment ☐allowed ☐not allowed</td></tr>
<tr><td>(44A) Loading on board from</td><td>(44B) For transportation to</td></tr>
<tr><td>(44E) Port of Loading</td><td>(44F) Port of Discharge</td></tr>
<tr><td colspan="2">(44C) Latest shipment date</td></tr>
<tr><td colspan="2">(45A) Description of goods or services</td></tr>
<tr><td colspan="2">Documents required: (marked with x)
☐ Signed commercial invoice in 1 original and 4 copies indicating this L/C No. and the contract No. ______
☐ FULL SET OF 3 ORIGINALS + 3 NON-NEGOTIABLE COPIES clean on board ocean Bills of Lading made out to order and blank endorsed marked “freight prepaid” and notify applicant.</td></tr>
<tr><td colspan="2">☐ Certificate of weight & quality in 1 original and 4 copies issued by independent surveyor.
☐ Certificate of ship’s tanks, pumps and pipes issued by any independent surveyor evidencing that the tanks, pumps and pipes are suitable to receive and carry the oil.
☐ Beneficiary’s certified copy of fax dispatched to applicant by Fax No.________within 3 working days after shipment.
Special terms and conditions:</td></tr>
<tr><td colspan="2">(47A) Additional conditions: (Marked with x)</td></tr>
<tr><td colspan="2">(71B) All banking charges and interest if any outside opening bank are for account of ☐beneficiary
☐ other (pl. Indicate)</td></tr>
<tr><td colspan="2">(48) Documents to be presented within _____days after the date of issuance of the transport document(s) but within the validity of the credit</td></tr>
</table>

法定代表人或被授权人:　　　　　　　　　　　　　　　　联系人（电话）：

C3-2 审证操作能力训练一

C3-2.1 审证合同

SALES CONFIRMATION

S/C No. : SPT-211
Place: Shanghai, China
Date: Jan. 8, 2006

The Seller: Shanghai Sporting Goods Imp. & Exp. Corp.
Address: 215 Huqiu Road, Shanghai, China

The buyer: Petrrco International Trading Co.
Address: 1,100 Sheppard Ave. East Suite 406
Willowdale Ontario, Canada M2K 2W2

We hereby confirm having sold to you the following goods on the terms and conditions as stated below:

Commodity & Specifications	Quantity	Unit Price	Amount
		CIF Vancouver	
SBW32 Basketball	2,000 pcs	USD16.95	USD33,900.00
GBW322 Football	2,000 pcs	USD21.33	USD42,660.00
Ervs Volleyball	1,000 pcs	USD12.15	USD12,150.00
		Total:	USD88,710.00
Total Contract Value: Say U.S. Dollars Eighty-eight Thousand Seven Hundred and Ten Only.			

PACKING: To be packed in cartons of 50 pcs each, total 100 cartons.

SHIPMENT: During March 2006 from Shanghai to Vancouver with partial shipment and transshipment permitted.

PAYMENT: The buyer shall open through a bank acceptable to the seller an irrevocable letter of credit at sight to reach the seller 30 days before the month of shipment and to be valid for negotiation in China until the 15th day after the date of shipment.

INSURANCE: To be covered by the seller for 110% of the invoice value against All Risks and War Risk as per C.I.C. dated Jan. 1, 1981.

REMARKS:

Confirmed by The Buyer (signature) The Seller (signature)

C3-2.2 审核信用证

33062 BOCSH CN
ROYAL BANK BCR
OUR L/C NO. PIT310
JANUARY 30, 2006

FROM:　THE ROYAL BANK OF CANADA, BRITISH, COLUMBIA INTERNATIONAL CENTER, 1055 WEST GEORGIA STREET, VANCOUVER, B.C. V6E 3P3

TO:　BANK OF CHINA, SHANGHAI BRANCH

BENEFICIARY:　SHANGHAI SPORTING GOODS IMP. & EXP. CORP.
251 HUQIU ROAD, SHANGHAI, CHINA

APPLICANT:　PETRRCO INTERNATIONAL TRADING CO.
1100 SHEPPARD AVENUE EAST SUITE 406
WILLOWDALE ONTARIO, CANADA M2K 2W2

FOR USD88,710.00 (SAY U.S. DOLLARS EIGHTY EIGHT THOUSAND SEVEN HUNDRED AND TEN ONLY) TO EXPIRE APRIL 15TH 2002 AT OUR COUNTER AVAILABLE BY NEGOTIATION OF YOUR DRAFTS AT 30 DAYS SIGHT FOR 100 PERCENT OF INVOICE VALUE DRAWN ON THE ROYAL BANK OF CANADA ACCOMPANIED BY FOLLOWING DOCUMENTS:

1. COMMERCIAL INVOICE IN QUADRUPLICATE INDICATING THE SALES CONFIRMATION NUMBER.

2. PACKING LIST/WEIGHT MEMO IN TRIPLICATE MENTIONING TOTAL NUMBER OF CARTONS, GROSS WIGHT AND MEASUREMENTS PER EXPORT CARTON.

3. 2/3 SET OF CLEAN "ON BOARD" OCEAN BILLS OF LADING MADE OUT TO ORDER MARKED "FREIGHT COLLECT" AND NOTIFY APPLICANT.

4. INSURANCE POLICY OR CERTIFICATE IN DUPLICATE ENDORSED IN BLANK COVERING OCEAN MARINE CARGO CLAUSE ALL RISKS AND WAR RISK FOR 100 PERCENT OF INVOICE VALUE AS PER CIC DATED 01/01/1981.

5. INSPECTION CERTIFICATE IN DUPLICATE ISSUED AND SIGNED BY AUTHORIZED PERSON OF APPLICANT WHOSE SIGNATURE MUST COMPLY WITH THAT HELD IN OUR BANK'S RECORD.

6. CERTIFICATE OF ORIGIN ISSUED BY CCPIT.

COVERING:

2,000 PCS GBW32 BASKETBALL USD16.95/PC 2,000 PCS GBW322 FOOTBALL USD21.33/PC 1,000 PCS ERVS VOLLEYBALL USD12.15/PC

TERMS OF SHIPMENT CIF VANCOUVER FROM SHANGHAI CHINA TO VANCOUVER O.C.P. EDMONTON CANADA DURING MARCH 2006 GOODS TO BE PACKED IN WOODEN CASES AND CONTAINER SHIPMENT PREFERABLE. TRANSSHIPMENT PERMITTED AND PARTIAL SHIPMENT PROHIBITED.

SHIPPING MARKS: PIT/EDMONTON/C/NO. 1-UP

ALL BANKING CHARGES INCLUDING REIMBURSEMENT COMMISSION OUTSIDE CANADA ARE FOR ACCOUNT OF BENEFICIARY.

DOCUMENTS TO BE PRESENTED WITHIN 3 DAYS AFTER THE DATE OF

ISSUANCE OF THE TRANSPORT DOCUMENTS BUT WITHIN THE VALIDITY OF THE CREDIT.

SPECIAL INSTRUCTIONS:

----- T.T. REIMBURSEMENT IS NOT ACCEPTABLE.

----- THIS CREDIT IS NOT TRANSFERABLE.

----- H.S. CODE NO. MUST BE SHOWN ON THE INVOICE AND PACKING LIST.

----- DOCUMENTS PRIOR TO THE ISSUANCE OF THIS CREDIT ARE NOT ACCEPTABLE.

----- CERTIFICATE OF ORIGIN MUST BEAR L/C NO.

----- A SET OF NON-NEGOTIABLE SHIPPING DOCUMENTS AND 1/3 ORIGINAL TRANSPORT DOCUMENT SHOULD BE SENT TO APPLICANT WITHIN 2 DAYS AFTER SHIPMENT AND THE COURIER RECEIPT MUST ACCOMPANY THE DOCUMENTS.

WE HEREBY ENGAGE WITH DRAWERS AND/OR BONA FIDE HOLDERS THAT DRAFTS DRAWN AND NEGOTIATED IN CONFORMITY WITH THE TERMS OF THIS CREDIT WILL BE DULY HONOURED ON PRESENTATION AND THAT DRAFTS ACCEPTED WITHIN THE TERMS OF THIS CREDIT WILL BE DULY HONOURED ON MATURITY.

THIS CREDIT IS ISSUED SUBJECT TO UNIFORM CUSTOMS AND PRACTICE FOR DOCUMENTARY CREDITS (1993 REVISION) ICC PUBLICATION NO. 500.

AUTHORISED SIGNATURES

C3-3 审证操作能力训练二

C3-3.1 审证合同

四川蜀韵丝绸进出口公司

SICHUAN SHUYUN SILK I/E CORP. LTD.

NO. 20 TAISHENG ROAD, CHENGDU, SICHUAN, CHINA

TEL: 0086-28-86523300 FAX: 0086-28-86523301

销售确认书 编号 NO.：CNT0219

SALES CONFIRMATION 日期 DATE: MAY 10, 2014

OUR REFERENCE：IT123JS

买方 BUYER： TAI HING LOONG SDN, BHD

地址 ADDRESS：7/F, SAILING BUILDING, NO. 50 AIDY STREET, KUALA LUMPUR, MALAYSIA

电话 TEL：0060-3-74236211 传真 FAX：0060-3-74236212

兹经买卖双方同意成交下列商品，订立条款如下：

THE UNDERSIGNED SELLER AND BUYER HAVE AGREED TO CLOSE THE FOLLOWING TRANSACTION ACCORDING TO THE TERMS AND CONDITIONS STIPULATED BELOW:

DESCRIPTION OF GOODS	QUANTITY	UNIT PRICE	AMOUNT
35% POLYESTER, 65% COTTON GREY GRASS LAWN	300,000 YARDS	CIF KELANG HKD3.00/YD	HKD900,000.00

包装 PACKING:　TO BE PACKED IN BALES OF 3,000 YARDS EACH.
5% MORE OR LESS BOTH IN QUANTITY AND AMOUNT ARE ALLOWED.

装运 SHIPMENT:　DURING JUNE/JULY, 2014 FROM GUANGZHOU TO KELANG BY SEA

付款条件 PAYMENT:　IRREVOCABLE SIGHT L/C

保险 INSURANCE:　TO BE EFFECTED BY THE SELLER COVERING ALL RISKS AND WAR RISK FOR 10% OVER THE INVOICE VALUE AS PER CIC OF PICC.

买方（签章）THE BUYER
TAI HING LOONG SDN, BHD
LEE XIANLIANG

卖方（签章）THE SELLER
四川蜀韵丝绸进出口公司
SICHUAN SHUYUN SILK I/E CORP. LTD.
林 星

C3-3.2　审核信用证

FROM BANGKOK BANK LTD., KUALA LUMPUR
DOCUMENTARY CREDIT NO.: 01/12345　　DATE: JUNE 12, 2014
ADVISING BANK: BANK OF CHINA, SICHUAN BRANCH
APPLICANT: TAI HING LOONG SDN, BHD.
7/F, SAILING BUILDING, NO.50 AIDY STREET, KUALA LUMPUR, MALAYSIA
BENEFICIARY: SICHUAN SHUYUN SILK I/E CORP. LTD.
NO. 22 TAISHENG ROAD, CHENGDU, SICHUAN, CHINA
AMOUNT: HKD 900,000.00 (HONGKONG DOLLARS NINE HUNDRED THOUSAND ONLY)
EXPIRY DATE: JUNE 15, 2014 IN CHINA FOR NEGOTIATION
DEAR SIRS:
WE HEREBY ISSUE THIS DOCUMENTARY CREDIT IN YOUR FAVOR, WHICH IS AVAILABLE BY NEGOTIATION OF YOUR DRAFT(S) IN DUPLICATE AT SIGHT DRAWN ON APPLICANT BEARING THE CLAUSE: “DRAWN UNDER L/C NO.

01/12345 OF BANGKOK BANK LTD., KUALA LUMPUR DATED JUNE 12, 2014" ACCOMPANIED BY THE FOLLOWING DOCUMENTS:

–SIGNED COMMERCIAL INVOICE IN QUADRUPLICATE COUNTER-SIGNED BY APPLICANT.

–FULL SET OF CLEAN ON BOARD OCEAN BILLS OF LADING MADE OUT TO ORDER, ENDORSED IN BLANK, MARKED "FREIGHT COLLECT" AND NOTIFY APPLICANT.

–MARINE INSURANCE POLICY OR CERTIFICATE FOR FULL INVOICE VALUE PLUS 50% WITH CLAIMS PAYABLE IN KELANG IN THE SAME CURRENCY AS THE DRAFT COVERING ALL RISKS AND WAR RISK FROM WAREHOUSE TO WAREHOUSE AS PER C.I.C. OF PICC DATED 01/01/1981.

–PACKING LIST IN QUADRUPLICATE.

–CERTIFICATE OF ORIGIN ISSUED BY THE CHAMMBER OF COMMERCE.

–COPY OF TELEX/FAX SENT BY BENEFICIARY TO APPLICANT ON OR BEFORE B/L ON BOARD DATE CONTAINING ALL SHIPMENT DETAILS INCLUDING AMOUNT, GROSS WEIGHT, NET WEIGHT, BALE NO./PACKAGE NO., VESSEL NAME AND B/L NO., NO. OF THIS L/C AND RELEVANT S/C TO BE MENTIONED.

COVERING:

300,000 YARDS OF 100% COTTON GREY GRASS LAWN AT USD3.00 PER YARD CIF KELANG AS PER BUYER'S ORDER NO. TH-108 DATED MAY 4, 2014.

SHIPMENT TO BE EFFECTED IN TWO EQUAL LOTS DURING MAY/JUNE, 2014 FROM CHINA PORT TO KELANG WITH PARTIAL SHIPMENTS ALLOWED AND TRANSSHIPMENT PROHIBITED.

ALL BANKING CHARGES OUTSIDE MALAYSIA ARE FOR THE ACCOUNT OF BENEFICIARY.

WE HEREBY ENGAGE WITH DRAWERS, ENDORSERS AND BONA FIDE HOLDERS THAT DRAFTS DRAWN AND NEGOTIATED IN CONFORMITY WITH THE TERMS OF THIS CREDIT WILL BE DULY HONORED ON PRESENTATION SUBJECT TO UCP500.

BANGKOK BANK LTD., KUALA LUMPUR (SIGNED)

C3-4 审证操作能力训练三

C3-4.1 审证合同

SALES CONFIRMATION **S/C No. YY-SWTSC102**

销售确认书 **DATE: Nov. 18, 2015 IN SHANGHAI**

The Seller: YONGYE NATIVE PRODUCE IMP. & EXP. CORP.

Address: No.18. DIAN CHI ROAD, SHANGHAI 201502, CHINA

The Buyer: S.W. TRADING CO., LTD.

Address: 283 WATER ROAD, ALPERTON, WEMBLEY, MIDDLESEX HAO 1HX U.K. ENGLAND

Shipping Marks	Commodity & Specification	Quantity	Unit Price (GBP)	Amount (GBP)
			CFR FELIXSTOWE	
S.W.T. 579734M FELIXSTOWE NO.1-UP	WHITE RABBIT BRAND PRESERVED VEGETABLES Art. No. GP04100 Art. No. GP04103 DOVE BRAND PRAWN CRACKERS Art. No. R213 Art. No. W673	 3,000 BAGS 3,000 BAGS 8,000 BAGS 7,000 BAGS	 1.95/BAG 1.65/BAG 0.78/BAG 0.70/BAG	 5,850.00 4,950.00 6,240.00 4,900.00
	TOTAL	21,000 BAGS		21,940.00
TOTAL CONTRACT VALUE: SAY GREAT BRITAIN POUNDS TWENTY ONE THOUSAND NINE HUNDRED AND FORTY ONLY				

PACKING:

For Art. No. GP04100 and Art. No. GP04103, 500g per bag, 20 bags to be packed in a carton, total 300 CTNS.

For Art. No. R213 and Art. No. W673, 240g per bag, 25 bags to be packed in a carton, total 600 CTNS.

PORT OF LOADING AND DESTINATION:

From Shanghai To Felixstowe port with partial shipments and transshipment allowed.

TIME OF SHIPMENT:　　Not later than Dec. 31st, 2015

TERMS OF PAYMENT:

The buyer shall open through a bank acceptable to the seller an irrevocable letter of credit at 30 days after sight to reach the seller 30 days before the month of shipment and to be valid for negotiation in China until the 15th day after the date of shipment.

INSURANCE:

To be covered by the Buyer.

Confirmed by:

THE BUYER	THE SELLER
S.W. TRADING CO., LTD.	YONGYE NATIVE PRODUCE IMP. & EXP. CORP.
Nathan	陆港
（signature）	（signature）

C3-4.2　审核信用证

LOGICAL TERMINAL P005

ISSUE OF A DOCUMENTARY CREDIT PAGE 00001

FUNC SWPR3
UMR 00342
MSGACK DWS765I AUTH OK, KEY B196051953B6ACD6, BKCHCNBJ YORKGB22 RECORD

Basic Header	F 01 BKCHCNBJA300 8191 216823		
Application Header	0 700 1650 981123 YORKBB22AXXX 3017 776134 981123 1810 N *YORKSHIRE BANK PLC		
User Header	Service Code 103: Bank Priority 113: Msg User Ref. 108: Info. from ci 115:		
Sequence of Total		*27:	1/1
Form of Doc. Credit		*40 A:	IRREVOCABLE
Doc. Credit Number		*20:	SWT-YYLC09
Date of Issue		*31C:	151123
Expiry		*31D:	Date 160115, AT OUR COUNTER
Applicant		*50:	S.W. TRADING CO., LTD. 238 WATER ROAD, ALPERTON, WEMBLEY, MIDDLESEX HAO 1HX U.K., ENGLAND
Beneficiary		*59:	YONGYE NATIVE PRODUCE IMP. & EXP. CORP. No. 18. DIAN CHI ROAD, SHANGHAI 201502, CHINA
Amount		*32 B:	CURRENCY USD AMOUNT 21,940.00
Available with/by		*41 D:	ANY BANK BY NEGOTIATION
Drafts at...		*42 C:	60 DAYS SIGHT QUOTING NO. AND DATE OF THIS LC AND NAME OF LC ISSUING BANK
Drawee		*42 D:	YORKSHIRE BANK PLC
Partial Shipments		*43 P:	ALLOWED
Transshipment		*43 T:	ALLOWED
Loading in Charge		*44 A:	SHANGHAI PORT CHINA
For Transport to...		*44 B:	FELIXSTOWE PORT UK
Latest Date of Ship		*44 C:	151231
Description of Goods		*45 A:	WHITE RABBIT BRAND PRESERVED VEGETABLES 3,000 BAGS ART. NO. GP04100 AT GBP1.95 PER BAG, 3,000 BAGS ART. NO. GP04103 AT GBP1.65 PER BAG. DOVE BRAND PRAWN CRACKERS 8,000

BAGS ART. NO. R213 AT GBP 0.70 PER BAG, 7,000 BAGS ART. NO. W673 AT GBP 0.78 PER BAG AS PER SALES CONTRACT NO. YY-SWT09 DATED NOV. 18, 2015 CFR FELIXSTOWE PACKED IN STANDARD EXPORT CARTONS SHIPPING MARKS: SWT/579734N/FELIXSTOWE/NO.1-UP

Documents Required *46 A:

+ SIGNED COMMERCIAL INVOICE IN TRIPLICATE SHOWING THIS L/C NUMBER.

+ SIGNED PACKING LIST IN DUPLICATE.

+ 2/3 OF MARINE BILLS OF LADING, CLEAN ON BOARD, MADE OUT TO THE ORDER OF SHIPPER, BLANK ENDORSED, AND MARKED "FREIGHT PREPAID" AND NOTIFY APPLICANT WITH FULL ADDRESS.

+ FULL SET OF MARINE INSURANCE POLICY OR CERTIFICATE, ENDORSED IN BLANK FOR 110 PERCENT OF FULL CIF VALUE, COVERING INSTITUTE CARGO CLAUSES (A) AND INSTITUTE WAR CLAUSES (CARGO), CLAIMS ARE TO BE PAID AT DESTINATION IN THE SAME CURRENCY OF THE DRAFTS.

+ ORIGINAL GSP FORM A.

+ INSPECTION CERTIFICATION ISSUED BY THE INSPECTORS APPROVED BY THE BUYER.

+ BENEFICIARY'S CERTIFICATE CERTIFYING THAT ONE ORIGINAL B/L AND ONE COPY COMMERCIAL INVOICE AND PACKING LIST RESPECTIVELY HAVE BEEN MAILED TO THE APPLICANT BY EMS WITHIN THREE WORKING DAYS AFTER BILL OF LADING DATE.

Additional Conditions *47 A:

1. PROCESSING OF DOCUMENTS WHICH DO NOT COMPLY WITH THE TERMS AND CONDITIONS OF THE LETTER OF CREDIT IS SUBJECT TO A SPECIAL DISCREPANCY HANDLING FEE OF GBP 35.00 OR EQUIVALENT PER SET OF DOCUMENTS PLUS RELATED CABLE CHARGES WHICH WILL BE DEDUCTED FROM ANY PROCEEDS.

2. ALL DOCUMENTS CALLED FOR UNDER THIS LETTER OF CREDIT, OTHER THAN THOSE WHICH THE CREDIT SPECIFICALLY STATES MAY BE COPIES, MUST CLEARLY BE MARKED "ORIGINAL" ON THEIR FACE.

3. ALL DOCUMENTS MUST BE IN ENGLISH.

4. BENEFICIARY'S STATEMENT CONFIRMING THEIR ACCEPTANCE OR NON-ACCEPTANCE OF THE AMENDMENT(S) MADE UNDER THIS CREDIT QUOTING THE RELEVANT AMENDMENT NUMBER, SUCH STATEMENT IS NOT REQUIRED IF THIS CREDIT HAS NOT BEEN AMENDED.

Details of Charges	*71 B:	ALL BANKING CHARGES ARE FOR ACCOUNT OF BENEFICIARY.
Presentation Period	*48:	WITHIN 5 DAYS AFTER SHIPMENT DATE
Confirmation	*49:	WITHOUT
Instructions	*78:	

1. EACH DRAWING TO BE ENDORSED ON THE REVERSE BY PRESENTING/NEG. BANK.
2. ALL DOCUMENTS MUST BE SENT TO US AT ARTNSWICK POINT, WAOE LANE, LEEOS LS2 8NG IN ONE COVER BY COURIER SERVICE.
3. UMR 00660 UPON RECEIPT OF FULL SET OF DOCUMENTS IN ORDER, WE SHALL REIMBURSE YOU IN ACCORDANCE WITH YOUR INSTRUCTIONS.

Send. to Rec. Info.	*72 :	SUBJECT TO U.C.P. (1993 REVISION) I.C.C. PUBLICATION NO. 600 THIS IS THE OPERATIVE INSTRUMENT, NO MAIL CONFIRMATION WILL FOLLOW.

Trailer Order is <MAC: > <PAC: > <ENC: > <CHK: > <TNG: > <PDE: >
MAC: 4DBC5FED CHK: 24C941CDE910

C3-5 审证操作能力训练四

C3-5.1 审证合同

SALES CONFIRMATION

S/C No.: FO-AL2015101

Date: 03-Jun-2015

The Seller: FORCEMAN INTERNATIONAL TRADING (SHANGHAI) CO., LTD.

Address: NO.1, LANE 170, YUEYANG ROAD, SHANGHAI 200031, P.R.C.

The Buyer: ALPHA TIRE IMPORTATION

Address: SERESFORD HOUSEBELLOZANNE ROAD ST. HELIER, JERSEY JE2 3JW, CHANNEL ISLANDS, U.S.A.

Item No.	Commodity	Unit	Qty	U/P (US$)	Amt. (US$)
				CIFC3 NEW YORK	
	PNEUMATIC RUBBER TIRES	PIECE	3,112	47.70	148,442.40
		TTL			148,442.40
大写合同金额：合计拾肆万捌千肆佰肆拾贰美元肆拾美分整					

PACKING: 每箱 8 件，共计 389 纸箱

SHIPMENT: 不晚于 2015 年 7 月 25 日自上海海运往纽约，允许分批装运，允许转运。

PAYMENT: 不可撤销保兑即期信用证，2015 年 6 月 15 日之前开到。

INSURANCE: 加成 10%投保一切险与战争险

REMARKS:

Confirmed by:

THE BUYER	THE SELLER
ALPHA TIRE IMPORTATION	FORCEMAN INTERNATIONAL TRADING (SHANGHAI) CO., LTD.
JAMES WHITE	杨伟国
MANAGER	MANAGER
(signature)	(signature)

C3-5.2　审核信用证

DBABANK

FORM OF DOC, CREDIT	*40A	:	IRREVOCABLE
DOC. CREDIT NUMBER	*20	:	N3 AMOLO00284
DATE OF ISSUE	31C	:	20150620
EXPIRY	*31D	:	DATE 20150810　PLACE U.S.A.
APPLICANT	*50	:	ALPHA TIRE IMPORTATION SERESFORD HOUSEBELLOZANNE ROAD, ST. HELIER, JERSEY JE2 3JW, CHANNEL ISLANDS, U.S.A.
BENEFICIARY	*59	:	FORCEMAN INTERNATIONAL TRADING（SHANGHAI） CO., LTD. NO.1, LANE 170, YUYAN ROAD, SHANGHAI 200031, P.R.C.
AMOUNT	*32B	:	CURRENCY USD AMOUNT148, 442.40 (SAY US DOLLARS ONE HUNDRED AND FORTY EIGHT THOUSAND FOUR HUNDRED AND FOUR TWO AND 40/100 ONLY)
AVAILABLE WITH/BY	*41D	:	ANY BANK BY NEGOTIATION
DRAFTS AT…	*42C	:	DRAFTS AT SIGHT FOR FULL INVOICE VALUE
DRAWEE	*42A	:	DBA BANK, NEW YORK, U.S.A.
PARTIAL SHIPMENTS	43P	:	PROHIBITED
TRANSSHIPMENT	43T	:	PERMITTED
LOADING IN CHARGE	44A	:	SHANGHAI
FOR TRANSPORT TO	44B	:	NEW YORK

LATEST DATE OF SHIP	44C	:	20150715
DESCRIPT. OF GOODS	45A	:	3121 PCS OF PNEUMATIC RUBBER TIRES CIFC5 NEW YORK
DETAILS OF CHARGES	71B	:	ALL CHARGES OUTSIDE THE USA ARE FOR ACCOUNT OF BENEFICIARY.
PRESENTATION PERIOD	48	:	WITHIN 2 DAYS AFTER SHIPMENT, BUT IN ANY EVENT WITHIN THE VALIDITY OF THE CREDIT.

Documents Require 78 B : + 2/3 SET OF BILL OF LADING CLEAN ON BOARD TO ORDER OF SHIPPER BLANK ENDORSED AND MARKED FREIGHT PREPAID AND 1/3 ORIGINAL BILL OF LADING SENT TO THE APPLICANT.

+ INSURANCE POLICY OR CERTIFICATE COVERING ALL RISKS AND WAR RISK AS PER ICC DATED 1/1/1982.

+ COMMERCIAL INVOICE IN 4 COPIES.

+ PACKING LIST.

Trailer (Order is <AUT:> <ENC:> <CHK:> <TNG:> <PDE:>...)

MAC:1CBB6271 CHK:76AF95AE1F59

C3-6 审证操作能力训练五

C3-6.1 审证合同

SALES CONFIRMATION

S/C No.: SH-IT2015001

Date: 03/Jun/2015

The Seller:	SHANGHAI TEXTILES IMP AND EXP CORPORATION.	The Buyer:	ITOCHU CORPORATION, OSAKA SECTION
Address:	27 ZHONGSHAN ROAD E, 1. SHANGHAI, CHINA	Address:	3-3-1, BUZENDA-CHO, SHIMONOSEKI OSAKA, JAPAN

Item No.	Commodity	Unit	Quantity	U/P (US$)	Amt (US$)
	CHINESE TOY PRODUCTS			FOB SHANGHAI	
1	REVOLVING BEAUTY SALON TWD001	PIECE	1,000	10.08	10,080.00
2	LOVELY CLOWNS TWD003	PIECE	800	8.70	6,960.00
	TTL				17,040.00
大写合同金额：合计美元壹万柒仟零肆拾元整					

PACKING: TWD001 十件装一纸箱，TWD003 八件装一纸箱，共 200 箱。

SHIPMENT: 不晚于 2015 年 7 月自上海海运往大阪（OSAKA），不允许分批装运，允许转运。

PAYMENT: 不可撤销的提单日后 30 天到期付款信用证，2015 年 6 月 15 日之前开到。

INSURANCE:　由买方办理。

REMARKS:

CONFIRMED BY:

THE BUYER	THE SELLER
ITOCHU CORPORATION	SHANGHAI TEXTILES IMP AND EXP CORPORATION
HAXIMODO	王媛
MANAGER	MANAGER
(signature)	(signature)

C3-6.2　审核信用证

KYOWA ASITAMA BANK, LTD.

FORM OF DOC, CREDIT	*40	: IRREVOCABLE
DOC, CREDIT NUMBER	*20	: LC-410-392216
DATE OF ISSUE	*31 C	: 20050610
EXPIRY	*31 D	: DATE 20150805 PLACE AT YOUR COUNTER
APPLICANT	*50	: ITOCHN CORPORATION, OSAKA SECTION 3-3-1, BUZENDA-CHO, SHIMONOSEKI, OSAKA, JAPAN
BENEFICIARY	*59	: SHANGHAI TEXTILES IMP AND EXP CORPORATION 27 ZHONGSHAN ROAD E, 1, SHANGHAI, CHINA
AMOUNT	*32 B	: CURRENCY USD AMOUNT 17,040.00
AVAILABLE WITH/BY	*41 D	: ANY BANK BY NEGOTIATION
DRAFTS AT...	*42 C	: DRAFTS AT 30 DAYS SIGHT FOR FULL INVOICE VALUE
DRAWEE	*42 A	: THE OPENER
PARTIAL SHIPMENTS	*43 P	: PERMITTED
TRANSSHIPMENT	*43 T	: PERMITTED
LOADING IN CHARGE	*44 A	: SHIPMENT FROM CHINESE PORT(S)
FOR TRANSPORT TO...	*44 B	: TO KOBE, JAPAN
LATEST DATE OF SHIP.	*44 C	: 20150730
DESCRIPTION OF GOODS	*45 A	: 1,800 PIECES OF CHINESE YOY PRODUCTS

ART NO.	QTY(PCS)	U/P(USD)
TWD001	1,000	10.08
TWD003	800	8.90

PRICE TERM　　: CIF OSAKA

DOCUMENTS REQUIRED *46 A :

1. COMMERCIAL INVOICE IN TRIPLICATE.

2. FULL SET OF CLEAN ON BOARD OCEAN BILLS OF LADING MADE OUT TO ORDER MARKED FREIGHT PREPAID AND NOTIFY APPLICANT.

3. INSURANCE POLICY OR CERTIFICATE IN DUPLICATE ENDORSED IN BLANK COVERING ALL RISKS AND WAR RISK FOR 140 PERCENT OF INVOICE VALUE SUBJECT TO C.I.C. DATED 1/1/1981.

4. CERTIFICATE OF INSPECTION ISSUED BY THE APPLICANT.

5. PACKING LISTS IN DUPLICATE SHOWING GROSS WEIGHT, NET WEIGHT, AND VOLUME OF EACH CASE.

TRAILER : ORDER IS <MAC:> <PAC:> <ENC:> <CHK:> <TN

C3-7 审证操作能力训练六

C3-7.1 审证合同

SALES CONFIRMATION

No. 2016BSC548AHT

The Buyer: Messrs Tomas & Brother Co., Ltd.
50,600 Detroit Ave.306, Westlake, Ohio 33415, USA
The Seller: Anhui Textiles Imp. & Exp. Corp.
No.658, Changjiang Road, Hefei, China

This is to confirm the transaction made by and between the Buyer and the Seller for the under-mentioned goods on the terms and conditions as set forth here below:

Name of Commodity: 100% Cotton Terry Tea Towels Art. No. K13009HA—A

Specification:	Checked designed in red, yellow, blue, green, purple and brown colors, 18” x 28”, 37.40g/doz.
Quantity:	4,000 dozens total with colors equally assorted.
Packing:	In cartons of 25 doz. each, one doz. in a polybag.
Unit Price:	USD 5.50 per doz. CIFC2 New York.
Total Amount:	USD 22,000.00 only.
Shipment:	From China port to New York during May, 2016. Partial shipments and transshipment are not allowed.
Payment:	The buyer shall open through a bank acceptable to the seller an irrevocable letter of credit at sight to reach the seller 30 days before the month of shipment and to remain valid for negotiation in China until the 15th day after the date of shipment.
Insurance:	To be covered by the seller for 110% of the invoice value against All Risks and SRCC as per the relevant ocean marine cargo clauses of

the People's Insurance Company of China dated 01/01/1981.

Shipping Marks: At Seller's option.

Remarks:

Buyer Seller

(Authorized Signature) (Authorized Signature)

This contract is done and signed at Hefei in China on the 18th day of March, 2016.

C3-7.2 审核信用证

ZCZC BDQ123QHD999

PS SDAAOC

HJ HOC

FROM: THE FIRST CITIZEN BANK OF NEW YORK, NEW YORK

ADVISING BANK: BANK OF CHINA

ANHUI BRANCH 313 CHANGJIANG MIDDLE ROAD ANHUI 230061 CHINA

WE HEREBY ISSUE THE DOCUMENTARY CREDIT IN YOUR FAVOUR. IT ENGAGES US IN ACCORDANCE WITH THE TERMS THEREOF. THE NUMBER AND THE DATE OF THE CREDIT AND THE NAME OF OUR BANK MUST BE QUOTED ON ALL DRAFTS REQUIRED. IF THE CREDIT IS AVAILABLE BY NEGOTIATION, EACH PRESENTATION MUST BE NOTED ON THE REVERSE OF THIS ADVICE BY THE BANK WHERE THE CREDIT IS AVAILABLE.

40A: FORM OF DOCUMENTARY CREDIT

IRREVOCABLE

20: DOCUMENTARY CREDIT NUMBER

2016LCC150487

31C: DATE OF ISSUE

MAR. 30, 2016

31D: DATE AND PLACE OF EXPIRY

MAY 31, 2016 AT OUR COUNTRY

50: APPLICANT

MESSRS TOMAS & BROTHER CO. LTD.

50600 DETRIOT AVE.306, WESTLAKE, OHIO 33415 USA

59: BENEFICIARY

ANHUI TEXTILES IMP. & EXP. CORP

NO. 658 CHANGJIANG ROAD, HEFEI, CHINA

32B: CURRENCY CODE, AMOUNT

USD22, 000.00 (SAY U.S. DOLLARS TWENTY TWO THOUSAND ONLY)

41D: AVAILABLE WITH…BY…

ANY BANK
NEGOTIATION

42C: DRAFT AT…
30 DAYS AFTER DATE OF B/L

42D: DRAWEE
MESSRS TOMAS & BROTHER CO., LTD.

43P: PARTIAL SHIPMENTS
PROHIBITED

43T: TRANSSHIPMENT
ALLOWED

44C: LATEST DATE OF SHIPMENT
15 MAY, 2016

45A: DESCRIPTION OF GOODS AND/OR SERVICES
100% COTTON TERRY TEA TOWELS
ART. NO. K23009HA—A

46A: DOCUMENTS REQUIRED
+BENEFICIARY'S SIGNED COMMERCIAL INVOICE IN DUPLICATE PLUS ONLY PHOTOCOPY.
+PACKING LIST IN DUPLICATE.
+FULL SET OF ORIGINAL CLEAN ON BOARD OCEAN BILLS OF LADING PLUS 1 N/N COPY MARKED FREIGHT COLLECT MADE OUT TO ORDER AND NOTIFY APPLICANT WITH NAME AND FULL ADDRESS.
+INSPECTION CERTIFICATE ISSUED BY APPLICANT CERTIFYING THAT GOODS HAVE BEEN INSPECTED BY THEM AND FOUND CONFORMING TO ALL POINTS.

47A: ADDITIONAL CONDITIONS:
+A FEE OF USD50.00 OR ITS EQUIVALENT WILL BE DEDUCTED FROM THE PROCEEDS OF EACH SET OF DISCREPANT DOCUMENTS, WHICH REQUIRE OUR OBTAINING ACCEPTANCE FROM APPLICANT.
+INSURANCE TO BE COVERED BY ULTIMATE BUYER.
+5 PERCENT MORE OR LESS BOTH IN CREDIT AMOUNT AND QUANTITY OF EACH ITEM ACCEPTABLE.

71B: CHARGES
ALL BANKING CHARGES OUTSIDE NEW YORK ARE FOR THE ACCOUNT OF BENEFICIARY.

48: PERIOD OF PRESENTATION
DOCUMENTS TO BE PRESENTED WITHIN 21 DAYS AFTER THE DATE OF SHIPMENT BUT WITHIN THE VALIDITY OF THE CREDIT.

49: CONFIRMATION INSTRUCTIONS
WITHOUT.

78: INSTRUCTIONS TO THE PAYING/ACCEPTING/NEGOTIATING BANK
+ UPON RECEIPT OF DOCUMENTS CONFORMING TO THE TERMS AND CONDITIONS OF THIS CREDIT, WE SHALL PAY THE PROCEEDS AS DESIGNATED.
+ NEGOTIATING BANK MUST FORWARD ALL DOCUMENTS TO US IN ONE LOT.
+ REIMBURSEMENT UNDER THIS L/C, IF APPLICABLE, IS SUBJECT TO ICC UNIFORM RULES FOR BANK TO BANK REIMBURSEMENTS.
THE FIRST CITIZEN BANK OF NEW YORK, NEW YORK.
(签章)

C3-8 审证操作能力训练七

C3-8.1 审证合同

上海闵华进出口有限公司

SHANGHAI MINHUA IMP./EXP. CO., LTD.

Rm. 9012 Union Building 1202, Zhongshan Road(N), Shanghai, China

销售确认书

SALES CONFIRMATION

The Buyer: FUJIDA TRADING CO., LTD.
Address: TOKYO FUJIDA BUILDING 11-2
FUJIDA 1-CHOME, CHIYODAKU
TOKYO 102, JAPAN

S/C No.: MH-FJDSC008
Place: Shanghai, China
Date : April 2nd, 2003
Our Ref.
Your Ref.

We hereby confirm having sold you the following goods on the terms and conditions as stated below:

Item No.	Commodity & Specifications	Unit	Quantity	Unit Price	Amount
	CHINESE CERAMIC			CIFC5 YOKOHAMA	
1	15PC TEA SET ART. NO. NF91115	SET	3,160	USD13.80	USD43,608.00
2	220PC CUP & SAUCER ART. NO. NC904	BOX	4,264	USD7.60	USD32,406.40
3	16PC KITCHENWARE ART. NO. NF10216/408	SET	2,104	USD11.50	USD24,196.00
4	20PC DINNER SET ART. NO. NH91120	SET	1,242	USD12.80	USD15,897.60
				TOTAL:	USD116,108.00

Total Contract Value: SAY U.S. DOLLARS ONE HUNDRED SIXTEEN THOUSAND ONE HUNDRED AND EIGHT ONLY.
More or Less Clause:

Packing:	NF91115	1 SET/BOX, 4 BOXES/CTN, 395CTNS/20'FCL.
		TOTAL 790CTNS IN TWO 20'FCL
	NC904	HALF DOZ./BOX, 8 BOXES/CTN, 533CTNS/20'FCL.
		TOTAL 533CTNS IN ONE 20'FCL
	NF10216/408	1 SET/COLAR BOX, 2 BOXES/CTN, 526CTNS/20'FCL.
		TOTAL 1052 CTNS IN TWO 20'FCL
	NH91120	1 SET/COLAR BOX, 2 BOXES/CTN, 621CTNS/20'FCL.
	TOTAL:	TOTAL 621CTNS IN ONE 20'FCL
		2996 CARTONS ONLY.

Port of Loading & Destination: FROM SHANGHAI TO YOKOHAMA, JAPAN

Shipment: TO BE EFFECTED BY THE SELLER DURING MAY 2003 WITH PARTIAL SHIPMENTS AND TRANSSHIPMENT PERMITTED.

Payment: BY IRREVOCABLE LETTER OF CREDIT AT 30 DAYS' SIGHT OPENED BY THE BUYER THROUGH A BANK ACCEPTABLE TO THE SELLER TO REACH THE SELLER BEFORE APRIL 25TH 2003 AND REMAIN VALID FOR NEGOTIATION IN SHANGHAI UNTIL THE 15TH DAY AFTER THE AFORESAID TIME OF SHIPMENT.

Insurance: TO BE COVERED BY THE SELLER FOR 110% OF TOTAL INVOICE VALUE AGAINST W.P.A., RISKS OF CLASH & BREAKAGE AND WAR RISK AS PER OR SUBJECT TO RELEVANT OCEAN MARINE CARGO CLAUSES OF THE PEOPLE'S INSURANCE COMPANY OF CHINA DATED 1/1/1981.

Remarks:

Confirmed by:

The Buyer	The Seller
	SHANGHAI MINHUA IMP./EXP. CO., LTD.
Authorized Signature(s)	唐建华 Authorized Signature(s)

C3-8.2 审核信用证

上海闵华进出口有限责任公司通过中国银行收到国外开来的信用证一份。请根据所签合同审核该信用证，指出存在的问题并提出理由，同时写一份传真要求修改信用证中的不符点。

THE FUKUOKA CITY BANK, LTD.

ORIGINAL

SWIFT FKCBJPJTFRA | International Division
TELEX NUMBER: 723205FKCITY J | 1-1 Hakataekimae 3-chome Hakata-ku
CABLE ADDRESS: FKCITYBANK | Fukuoka 812-91 Japan

Fukuoka, April 14th 2003

<table>
<tr><td>IRREVOCABLE DOCUMENTARY CREDIT</td><td>Credit Number: FJD-MHLC008</td></tr>
<tr><td>BENEFICIARY:
SHANGHAI MINHUA IMP. & EXP. CO., LTD.
RM. 9201 UNION BUILDING,
1202 ZHONGSHAN ROAD(N),
SHANGHAI, CHINA</td><td>APPLICANT:
FUJIDA TRADING CO., LTD.
TOKYO FUJIDA BUILDING,11-2
FUJIDA 1-CHOME, CHIYODAKU, TOKYO102,
JAPAN
TEL: 0081-03-5266576 FAX:0081-03-5266256</td></tr>
<tr><td>ADVISING BANK:
BANK OF CHINA
SHANGHAI BRANCH
50 HUQIU ROAD, SHANGHAI, CHINA</td><td>AMOUNT:
US$ 110,302.60 (SAY US DOLLARS ONE HUNDRED AND TEN THOUSAND THREE HUNDRED AND TWO POINT SIX ZERO ONLY)</td></tr>
<tr><td colspan="2">EXPIRY DATE AND PLACE: June 10th 2003 in Japan for negotiation</td></tr>
<tr><td colspan="2">Dear Sir(s),
We hereby issue the documentary credit which is available with any bank by negotiation of beneficiary's drafts at 30 days' sight for 95% of invoice price drawn on applicant being marked as drawn under this credit and accompanied by the following documents:
(1) Signed Commercial Invoice in five copies indicating L/C No. and Contract No.

(2) 2/3 set of clean on board ocean Bills of Lading made out to order and marked "Freight Prepaid" and notify applicant.

(3) Packing List in three copies
Covering: Chinese Ceramic 15pc Tea set Art. NO. 91115, 220pc Cup & Saucer Art. NO. NC904,16pc Kitchenware Art. NO. NY10216; and 20pc Dinner set Art. NO. NH91120 as per S/C No. MH-FJDSC008 CIFC5 Yokohama Japan Shipment from Shanghai China to Yokohama Japan dated not later than 31st May 2003 with partial shipments and transshipment prohibited.
Shipping marks: MH-FJDSC008/FUJIDA/YOKOHAMA/NO.1-UP

(4) GSP Form A in triplicate on separate form issued by Shanghai Inspection Bureau.

(5) Insurance Policy in duplicate issued by PICC covering All Risks and War Risk for total invoice value plus 110% as per relevant Ocean Marine Cargo Clauses dated 1/1/1981.
(6) Quality Report issued by applicant or the person named by applicant.</td></tr>
<tr><td colspan="2">Special Instructions:
(1) Drafts and documents to be presented within 15 days after the date of issuance of the transport documents, but within the credit validity.
(2) All banking charges outside Japan are for account of beneficiary.
(3) Shipment is limited to container.
(4) Cartons should be marked with contents, measurement, gross weight, color and these details must be expressed in the Packing List.</td></tr>
</table>

（续表）

<table>
<tr><td colspan="2">(5) Certificate stating that non-negotiable shipping documents including endorsed 1/3 original B/L must be airmailed to Fujida Trading Co., Ltd. within 2 days after shipment is effected.
(6) All documents presented for negotiation should bear the number of this credit.
(7) T. T. reimbursement is prohibited.
(8) Shipping advice must be sent to applicant over fax no. 0081-03-5266526 within 48 hours after shipment.
To negotiating bank:
Drafts and all documents must be airmailed directly to us in one lot.
Upon receipt of original documents in order, we shall remit proceeds of credit to your account as per your instructions.
We hereby engage with drawers, endorsers and bona fide holders that drafts drawn and negotiated in conformity with the terms of this credit will be duly honored on presentation and that drafts accepted within the terms of this credit will be duly honored at maturity.
The amount of each draft must be endorsed on the reverse of this credit by the negotiating bank.
This credit is subject to UCP 1993 revision ICC Publication 500.
No further confirmation will follow.

** BLANK SPACE HEREUNDER **</td></tr>
<tr><td>Yours faithfully,
THE FUKUOKA CITY BANK, LTD.
International Division
Y.J.
Authorized Signature</td><td>Advising Bank's notification
The advising bank is requested to notify the beneficiary without adding your confirmation unless otherwise stated.
BANK OF CHINA, SHANGHAI BRANCH
Shanghai 陈 洁
Place, date, name and signature of the advising bank</td></tr>
</table>

C3-9 审证操作能力训练八

C3-9.1 审证合同

SICHUAN TEXTILES I/E CO., LTD.

182, Jianghan Road, Chengdu, China

Tel: 86-28-86637138 Fax: 86-28-86633009

PROFORMA INVOICE

M/s. Borro Freres Ltd. No.: 575VGSL102

69 PUBLIC ROAD, ABIDJAN, IVORY COAST Date: Jan. 5, 2005

Tel: 96-35-6889693 Fax: 96-35-6889663

<table>
<tr><th>Art. No.</th><th>Commodity</th><th>Quantity</th><th>Unit Price</th><th>Amount</th></tr>
<tr><td></td><td>Office Furniture and Accessories</td><td></td><td>FOB China Port</td><td></td></tr>
<tr><td>305</td><td>Secretarial Chair Blue Color No.3</td><td>200 pcs</td><td>USD17.60/pc</td><td>USD3,520.00</td></tr>
<tr><td>601</td><td>Visitor Chair Blue Color No.3</td><td>350 pcs</td><td>USD8.63/pc</td><td>USD3,020.50</td></tr>
<tr><td>601</td><td>Visitor Chair Black Color No.6</td><td>500 pcs</td><td>USD8.63/pc</td><td>USD4,315.00</td></tr>
<tr><td>601A</td><td>Visitor Chair Black Color No.6</td><td>100 pcs</td><td>USD17.30/pc</td><td>USD1,730.00</td></tr>
<tr><td></td><td></td><td></td><td>Total FOB net:</td><td>USD12,585.50</td></tr>
<tr><td colspan="5">Total Value: Say U.S. Dollars Twelve Thousand Five Hundred and Eighty-five and Fifty Cents Only.
(in words)</td></tr>
</table>

Remarks: Sea Freight for 1×40'HQ to Abidjan Port, Ivory Coast US$5,400.00
On CFR Abidjan Port, Ivory Coast, US$17,985.50 (Say U.S. Dollars Seventeen Thousand Nine Hundred and Eighty-five Point Five Zero Only)

**No.601A comes with basket, single armrest, writing tablet and stronger steel frame.

**Shipment Time: If the L/C is issued before Jan. 10, 2005, shipment will be made before Feb. 10, 2005. Otherwise the shipment will be around Mar. 20, 2005.

**Payment: By L/C at sight to be opened to Bank of China, Sichuan Branch through an international bank to reach the seller 30 days before shipment stipulated herein.

**10% more or less in both total quantity and amount is acceptable.

Sichuan Textiles I/E Co., Ltd.

C3-9.2　审核信用证

------------------------------ Instance Type and Transmission ------------------------------

original received from SWIFT

Priority : Normal

Message Output Reference : 0730 050211SOGECN22AXXX0871111056

Correspondent Input Reference : 1610 050210SGCICIABAXXX7575629140

--------------------------------- Message Header ---

Swift Output : FIN 700 Issue of a Documentary Credit

Sender : SGCICIABXXX
SOCIETE GENERALE DE BANQUES EN COTE D'IVOIRE
ABIDJAN CI

Receiver : SOGECN22XXX
SOCIETE GENERALE
(GUANGZHOU BRANCH)
GUANGZHOU CN

------------------------------ Message Text ---

27: Sequence of total
1/1

40A: Form of Documentary Credit
IRREVOCABLE

20: Documentary Credit Number
00116CDI00000894

31C: Date of Issue
050210

31D: Date and Place of Expiry
050510 CHINA

17-02-2005

此信用证须与法国兴业银行有限公司
广州分行信用证通知函一起方可生效
我行编号：SGZ/ADV/050262

50:	Applicant
	BORRO FRERES
	69 PUBLIC ROAD, ABIDJAN, IVORY COAST
59:	Beneficiary–Name & Address
	SICHUAN TEXTILES I/E CO., LTD.
	NO.182 JIANGHAN ROAD, CHENGDU, CHINA
TEL:	86-28-86633009
32B:	Currency Code, Amount
	Currency : USD (US DOLLARS)
	Amount : #17,485.50#
39A:	Percentage Credit Amt. Tolerance
	10/10
39C:	Additional Amounts Covered
	INSURANCE IS COVERED BY BENEFICIARY
41A:	Available With… By… - BIC
	SOGECN22
	SOCIETE GENERALE (GUANGZHOU BRANCH)
	GUANGZHOU CN
	BY ACCEPTANCE
42C:	Drafts at…
	60 DAYS AFTER BILL OF LADING DATE
42A:	Drawee–BIC
	SOGECN22
	SOCIETE GENERALE
	(GUANGZHOU BRANCH)
	GUANGZHOU CN
43P:	Partial Shipments
	NOT ALLOWED
43T:	Transshipment
	NOT ALLOWED
44A:	On Board/Disp/Taking Charge at/from
	CHINA PORT
44B:	For Transportation to…
	ABIDJAN
45A:	Description of Goods &/or Services
	+ 200 PCS (+/- 10 PCT) SECRETARIAL CHAIR BLUE COLOR NO.3/305
	+ 350 PCS (+/- 10 PCT) VISITOR CHAIR BLUE COLOR NO.3/601
	+ 500 PCS (+/- 10 PCT) VISITOR CHAIR BLACK COLOR NO.6/601

+ 100 PCS (+/- 10 PCT) VISITOR CHAIR BLACK COLOR NO.6/601A
AS PER PROFORMA INVOICE NO.575VGBL102 DATED 05/01/05
VALUE CFR ABIDJAN

46A: Documents Required
+ 5/6 ORIGINAL COMMERCIAL INVOICE ONE OF THEM BEARING THE ORIGINAL SAFETY LABEL ISSUED BY BIVAC OR THEIR AFFILIATED COMPANIES OR AUTHORIZED AGENTS.
+ 2/3 ORIGINAL CLEAN ON BOARD MARINE BILL OF LADING ISSUED TO THE ORDER OF THE ISSUING BANK NOTIFY APPLICANT, MARKED "FREIGHT PREPAID" AND SHOWING THE L/C NO.
+ PACKING LIST.
+ BENEFICIARY'S SIGNED ATTESTATION CERTIFYING HAVING SENT DIRECTLY TO APPLICANT BY DHL COURIER 1/6 ORIGINAL COMMERCIAL INVOICE AND 1/3 ORIGINAL BILL OF LADING.

47A: Additional Conditions
+ DOCUMENTS HAVE TO BE SENT TO US BY DHL MAIL
+ GOODS HAVE TO BE CHECKED PRIOR TO SHIPMENT BY BUREAU VERITAS SHANGHAI
TEL: 86-21-58352011   FAX: 86-21-58354937
+ GOODS HAVE TO BE SHIPPED IN FULL 20' CONTAINERS
+ SHIPPING ADVICE MUST BE FAXED TO APPLICANT IN GOOD TIME OVER ITS FAX NO. 96-35-6889693
+ IN CASE OF NON-PRESENTATION OF DOCUMENTS WITHIN PRESENTATION PERIOD, APPLICANT WILL REQUEST FOR A LETTER OF GUARANTEE AT BENEFICIARY'S EXPENSES.
+ BILL OF LADING MUST BEAR THE BIVAC INT. NUMBER.

71B: Charges
BANK CHARGES OUTSIDE COTE D'IVOIRE ARE FOR BENEFICIARY'S ACCOUNT

48: Period for Presentation
WITHIN 30 DAYS AFTER SHIPMENT DATE, BUT WITHIN CREDIT VALIDITY

49: Confirmation Instructions
CONFIRMED

53A: Reimbursing Bank–BIC
SOGEUS33
SOCIETE GENERALE
NEW YORK, NY, US

78: Instr to Payg/Accptg/Negotg Bank

YOU ARE AUTHORIZED TO CLAIM REIMBURSEMENT FROM SOGEUS33 AT MATURITY.

57A: "Advise Through" Bank–BIC
/01545408091001
BKCHCNBJ570
BANK OF CHINA
（SICHUAN BRANCH）
CHENGDU CN

72: Sender to Receiver Information
THIS CREDIT IS SUBJECT TO UCP ICC
PUBLICATION 500, 1993 REVISION

For and on behalf of
SOCIETE GENERALE

张仕琨
……………………………………..
Authorized Signature(s)

-- Message Trailer --

{MAC:A460C63A}
{CHK:4D18BB8E35F0}
{DLM:}

C3-10 审证操作能力训练九

C3-10.1 审证合同

SALES CONFIRMATION

S/C No. : 02AG18184
Place: HEFEI, CHINA
Date: AUG. 25, 2002

The Seller:
ANHUI GARMENTS IMP. & EXP. CO., LTD.
Address: 436 CHANGJIANG ROAD (C)
HEFEI, ANHUI, CHINA

The buyer:
ABDULLA AL HOBASHI TRD. CO.
Address: P. O. BOX NO. 8545, DUBAI, U.A.E.
TEL: 97-14-2891025, FAX: 97-14-2891024

We hereby confirm having sold to you the following goods on the terms and conditions as stated below:

Commodity & Specifications	Quantity	Unit Price	Amount
100% COTTON STRIPE TOWEL ART. NO. AB96 SIZE: 30″ × 60″ COLOUR: STRIPE	4,500 DOZENS	CFRC1 HODEIDAH PORT USD4.90/DOZ	USD22,050.00
Total Contract Value: SAY U.S. DOLLARS TWENTY TWO THOUSAND AND FIFTY ONLY.			

Packing: TO BE PACKED IN BALES OF 20 DOZENS EACH, ONE DOZEN IN A POLYBAG.

Shipment: DURING NOVEMBER 2002 FROM CHINA PORT TO HODEIDAH, YEMEN WITH PARTIAL SHIPMENTS NOT ALLOWED AND TRANSSHIPMENT ALLOWED.

Payment: THE BUYER SHALL OPEN THROUGH A BANK ACCEPTABLE TO THE SELLER AN IRREVOCABLE L/C AT SIGHT TO REACH THE SELLER 30 DAYS BEFORE THE SHIPMENT VALID FOR NEGOTIATION IN CHINA UNTIL THE 15TH DAY AFTER THE DATE OF SHIPMENT.

Insurance: TO BE COVERED BY THE BUYER.

Remarks:

Confirmed by	The Buyer	The Seller
	×××	×××
	（signature）	（signature）

C3-10.2 审核信用证

Middle East Bank

TRADE FINANCE SERVICES

P.O. Box 5547, Dubai
United Arab Emirates
Tel: 97-14-274400, Fax: 97-14-271386
Telex: 46074 MEBBK EM
Cable: MEMAINBANK

ORIGINAL

<table>
<tr><td colspan="2">Page 1 of 5 of our Documentary Credit Number: MEB-LSS-0100837</td></tr>
<tr><td>Dispatch by: Mail</td><td>Date of Issue: 22/09/2002</td></tr>
<tr><td>IRREVOCABLE DOCUMENTARY CREDIT NO: MEB-LSS-0100837</td><td>Advising Banks No.</td></tr>
<tr><td>Advising Bank
BANK OF CHINA, ANHUI BRANCH,
155 CHANGJIANG ROAD, HEFEI,
ANHUI PROVINCE, CHINA.
POST CODE: 230061</td><td>Beneficiary's name and address
ANHUI GARMENTS IMP. &EXP. CO., LTD.
436 CHANGJIANG ROAD(C),
HEFEI, ANHUI, CHINA.</td></tr>
<tr><td>Applicant's name and address
ABDULLA AL HOBAISHI TRD CO.
P.O. BOX NO. 8545, DUBAI, U.A.E.
TEL 97-14-2891025, FAX 97-14-2891024</td><td>Expiry date: 20/11/2002 DD/MM/YYYY

Place for presentation: CHINA FOR PRESENTATION ONLY</td></tr>
</table>

（续表）

Credit available at the counters of MIDDLE EAST BANK, DUBAI. BY PAYMENT of beneficiary's draft Drawn on ourselves at SIGHT.	Amount in figures: NOT EXCEEDING USD22,050.00 Amount and currency in words: NOT EXCEEDING. Twenty two thousand fifty US DOLLARS only Shipment terms: CFR HODEIDAH, YEMEN
Partial shipments: ALLOWED	Transshipment: ALLOWED AT HONG KONG PORT ONLY
Shipment/Dispatch from ANY CHINESE PORT for transportation to HODEIDAH, YEMEN. Not later than 05/11/2002 DD/MM/YYYY	
Dear Sirs: We hereby establish our irrevocable documentary credit in favour of above beneficiary for the 100% invoice value of goods as detailed herein and to be accompanied by following documents at least in duplicate unless otherwise specified, covering shipment/delivery of the following:	
××× AUTHORISED SIGNATURE	××× AUTHORISED SIGNATURE

Page 2 of 5 of our Documentary Credit Number: MEB-LSS-0100837	
DESCRIPTION OF GOODS OR SERVICES: 4,500 DOZEN 100% COTTON MULTICOLOUR STRIPE TOWEL, ART NO. AB69, SIZE: 30×60″, WEIGHT: 175 GMS PER PIECE AT USD 4.90 PER DOZEN CFR HODEIDAH PORT, YEMEN. PACKING: ONE DOZEN IN A POLYBAG, FINALLY SUITABLE QUANTITY PER BALE ALL OTHER DETAILS ARE AS PER INDENT NO.8962/2001 OF M/S. AL HOOR TRADING CO. LLC, P.O.BOX NO.12500, DUBAI, U.A.E. AND BENEFICIARY'S S/C NO.01AG118148 SHIPPING MARKS: HOBISHI H.T.C./SANA'A/TEL.281114 HODEIDAH TEL. 246512 (MUST BE SHOWN ON PACKING LIST AND BILL OF LADING) END OF DESCRIPTION OF GOODS OR SERVICES.	
DOCUMENTS REQUIRED 1. Signed Commercial Invoices in 4 copies stating the name and address of the manufacturer/producer certifying the origin of goods and contents to be true and correct. 2. Full set of original Clean On Board Marine Bill of Lading issued to the order of Middle East Bank, Trade Finance Services, Dubai and marked freight prepaid and notify M/S. AL HUBAISHI TRADING CO, P.O. BOX 8753, SANA'A AL SALAM STREET, REPUBLIC OF YEMEN. The Bill of Lading must state (a) Name, Address and Telephone Number of the Carrying vessel's agent at the Port of Destination and (b) Name, Address and Telephone Number of the Carrier. 3. Certificate of Origin in duplicate issued by China Council for Promotion of International Trade, certifying that the goods are of CHINESE Origin, stating full name and address of Manufacturer/Producer of the goods and also name of the exporter and name of the Exporting Country.	
××× AUTHORISED SIGNATURE	××× AUTHORISED SIGNATURE

Page 3 of 5 of our Documentary Credit Number: MEB-LSS-0100837	
4. Insurance covered locally by applicant under Open Policy No. 22/0802/000849 of NORWICH UNION INSURANCE (GULF) LTD. with M/S. AL MULLA INSURANCE, P. O. BOX NO. 21075, DUBAI, U.A.E. FAX NO.2691717, DUBAI. Shipment advice quoting name of carrying vessel, date of shipment, number of packages, shipping marks, amount, Letter of Credit Number and Policy Number must be sent to (A) the above Insurance Company and (B) to the Applicant within 3 days from date of shipment by Fax. Copies of transmitted shipment advice accompanied by Fax transmission reports must accompany the documents. 5. Packing List in 4 copies under separate sets from invoice. 6. Certificate issued by the Carrier/Master or their agent certifying that the carrying vessel is allowed by YEMENI Authorities to call at YEMENI Ports and is not scheduled to call at any Israeli Port during its voyage to the HODEIDAH PORT, YEMEN. In case of shipment by sea by United Arab Shipping Company Line vessels, such certificate is not required. 7. Complete sets of non-negotiable shipping documents along with shipment sample must be sent to Applicant directly by speed post and a certificate to this effect from the beneficiary together with relevant speed post receipt must accompany the documents. 8. Shipment advice giving full details of shipment must be sent to Applicant by fax on their fax No. 9714-2291024 within 3 days from the date of shipment showing the name of carrying vessel, date of shipment, shipping marks, amount and L/C No. and a copy of such fax advice together with a copy of fax transmission report must accompany the documents. 9. One set of non-negotiable shipping documents along with shipment sample must be sent to M/s. Al Hoor Trading Co. LLC, P. O. Box No.12500, Dubai, U.A.E. Tel. No.2253090/2253338, Fax No.2253080 by Registered Airmail/Courier and a certificate to this effect from the beneficiary together with relevant Post/courier receipt must accompany the documents.	
××× AUTHORISED SIGNATURE	××× AUTHORISED SIGNATURE

Page 4 of 5 of our Documentary Credit Number: MEB-LSS-0100837
10. Shipment advice giving full details of shipment must be sent to Al Hoor Trading Co. LLC, Dubai over their Fax No.9714-2253080 and a copy of such fax advice together with a copy of fax transmission report must accompany the documents. 11. A copy each of Invoice, Packing List and Bill of Lading must be faxed to applicant on their Fax No. 009714-2291024 within 3 days from the date of shipment and a compliance certificate to this effect from beneficiary together with fax transmission reports must accompany the documents. SPECIAL INSTRUCTIONS 1. All documents must quote issuing bank name and L/C number. 2. All documents must be issued in English Language. 3. Bill of Lading must mention number of cartons and no need to mention the number of yards and the price.

（续表）

4. Documents must be presented within 15 days after the date of issuance of Bill of Lading but within the validity of this credit. 5. Side marks of the cartons to show proper description of goods such as item No., gross weight, net weight, quantity contents inside sizes, colors assortment and invoice to certify the same. 6. Shipment must be effected by APL vessels only and Bill of Lading must show the said liner as the Carrier. 7. Freight Forwarders Agents/Combined Bill of Lading is not acceptable. 8. Invoices and Bills of Lading must state the relevant Harmonized System (H.S.) Commodity Code Number(s). 9. Each carton/bale to show design number/article number and packing list to certify the same.

××× AUTHORISED SIGNATURE	××× AUTHORISED SIGNATURE

Page5 of 5 of our Documentary Credit Number: MEB-LSS-0100837
10. At the time of first presentation the Presenting Bank must deduct from payment to the Beneficiary Agent's Commission USD 220.50 payable to M/s. p.i. Hiranandani, Dubai, U.A.E. and claim reimbursement for the net amount only after such deduction which must be confirmed on presenting bank's schedule. 11. In the event shipment is effected in container(s), Bill of Lading must evidence the same and must also show the container number(s). DIRECTIONS TO ADVISING/PRESENTING BANK A. We undertake to honour the drafts drawn in conformity with terms and conditions of this Credit. B. The amount of each drawing must be endorsed on reverse of Page 1 of this Credit. C. The Presenting Bank must forward all documents in one lot to us by courier service at our address Middle East Bank, Trade Finance Service Dept., P.O. Box 5547, Dubai, U.A.E. D. Please quote our L/C reference number in all your communication and correspondence to us. E. A discrepancy handling fee of USD50—or its equivalent will be levied by us to beneficiary for each set of documents presented with discrepancy. F. All banking charges including communications/courier/postal charges and advising/presenting/ reimbursing bank charges are to beneficiary's account except L/C issuance charges. G. If documents are presented by any bank other than the advising bank, the presenting bank must confirm on its covering schedule that all charges of advising bank have been paid. H. In reimbursement, we shall remit the proceeds at beneficiary's cost as per the instructions to the presenting bank provided documents received by us are found in compliance with the Credit terms. I. Please advise this Credit to the beneficiary without adding your confirmation.
Except so far as otherwise expressly stated, this Credit is subject to Uniform Customs and Practice for Documentary Credit (1993 Revision) International Chamber of Commerce Publication No. 500. ==========================END OF LC====================

××× AUTHORISED SIGNATURE	××× AUTHORISED SIGNATURE

C3-2　审证记录单

（函头）

审证记录

L/C No.　　　　　　　　　　　　　　　　　　日期：　　　年　　月　　日

开证行：

S/C No.

品名：

不符点	修改意见

审核人：

模块三

装运单据制作

国际贸易在多数情况下是象征性交易，装运单据或货运单据(shipping documents)是实现国际贸易的重要核心手段和内容。一些非结算用的单据虽不属于货运单据，但由于其意义重大，也在我们的学习范围内。

项目四

缮制出口订舱委托书

订舱委托书的含义及作用

货运订舱委托书（Booking Note）是进出口企业（货主 Shipper）委托货运代理（Forwarding Agent/Forwarder）向承运人（Carrier）预订货运舱位（Shipping Space）的必要单据，货代据此填写托运单向承运人预订舱位或集装箱。虽然货主的订舱委托书是一份非结算单据，但它的内容正确与否将直接影响到日后承运人签发的运输单据正确与否，影响到货主能否顺利结算。因此，填写该单据的内容必须正确且充分。由于国际货物运输多为海运和空运，本项目重点学习海运和空运项下的订舱委托业务。

学习目标

［知识目标］熟悉进出口货物托运操作流程，掌握缮制出口货物订舱委托书的要领

［能力目标］能根据信用证条款和合同条款，正确缮制货运订舱委托书

一、缮制海运订舱委托书

项目描述（案例情境描述）

山东希望土产进出口公司联系青岛顺风物流总公司，希望通过后者联系船公司预订舱位，双方由此签订了货运代理协议。2015 年 6 月 28 日，山东希望土产进出口公司业务员唐欣（电话 65788877）根据信用证和合同（补充资料）中的运输和提单的相关条款和相关信息，缮制海运订舱委托书给青岛顺风物流总公司，办理货物托运手续。

附制单案例信用证

THE HONGKONG AND SHANGHAI BANKING CORPORATION
INCORPORATED IN HONGKONG WITH LIMITED LIABILITY
SHANGHAI OFFICE: 185 YUAN MING YUAN ROAD,
P. R. CHINA SHANGHAI 200000

香港上海汇丰银行有限公司
上海分行：中国上海
圆明园路 185 号
邮政编码：200000

OUR REF. EXP DC 007545

SHANDONG HOPE NATIVE PRODUCT I/E CORP.
62, GUANGXI ROAD, QINGDAO, CHINA

DATE 23 MAY, 2015

DEAR SIRS,

WE ADVISE HAVING RECEIVED THE FOLLOWING TELETRANSMISSION DATED 22 MAY 2015 FROM THE HONGKONG AND SHANGHAI BANKING CORP. LTD., DOWNING STREET, PENANG ISSUE OF AN IRREVOCABLE DOCUMENTARY CREDIT.

DC. NUMBER: PGH000348DC
DATE OF ISSUE: 21 MAY, 2015
EXPIRY DATE AND PLACE: 21 JULY 2015, CHINA
APPLICANT: SOO HUP SENG TRADING CO. SDN BHD.
165, 1ST FLOOR, VICTORIA STREET
10300 PENANG, MALAYSIA
BENEFICIARY: SHANDONG HOPE NATIVE PRODUCT I/E CORP.
62, GUANGXI ROAD, QINGDAO, CHINA
CCY/AMOUNT: HKD46,150.00
AVAILABLE BY NEGOTIATION
DRAFTS: AT SIGHT FOR FULL INVOICE VALUE OF GOODS DRAWN ON OURSELVES
PARTIAL SHIPMENTS: FORBIDDEN
TRANSSHIPMENT: PERMITTED
SHIPMENT FROM ANY PORT IN CHINA TO PENANG LATEST 06 JULY/2015
GOODS:
5M/TONS SHANDONG BLACK DATES HIGH QUALITY AT HKD9230 PER M/TON CIF PENANG INCOTERMS 2010 AS PER BUYER'S ORDER NO. SOO-6378

DOCUMENTS:

+ INVOICE IN TRIPLICATE.

+ FULL SET OF ORIGINAL CLEAN–ON BOARD–BILL(S) OF LADING MADE OUT TO SHIPPER'S ORDER AND ENDORSED IN BLANK AND MARKED "FREIGHT PREPAID" AND NOTIFY APPLICANT AND ISSUING BANK.

+ MARINE INSURANCE POLICY OR CERTIFICATE FOR FULL CIF VALUE PLUS 10 PERCENT COVERING OCEAN MARINE CARGO CLAUSES ALL RISKS (INCLUDING WAREHOUSE TO WAREHOUSE CLAUSES) AND WAR RISK CLAUSES (1/1/1981) OF THE PEOPLE'S INSURANCE COMPANY OF CHINA.

+ SIGNED WEIGHT LIST IN TRIPLICATE TO STATE THAT GOODS ARE PACKED IN 25KGS NET OR 26.2KGS GROSS PER CARTON REQUIRED.

+ QUALITY CERTIFICATE IN DUPLICATE ISSUED BY C.I.Q. (ENTRY-EXIT INSPECTION AND QUARANTINE OF CHINA).

SPECIAL CONDITIONS:

(1) DOCUMENTS PRIOR TO ISSUANCE OF THE CREDIT ARE NOT ACCEPTABLE.

(2) CERTIFICATE OF CHINESE ORIGIN IN TRIPLICATE ISSUED BY CHINA COUNCIL FOR THE PROMOTION OF INTERNATIONAL TRADE TO STATE THAT GOODS ARE OF SHANDONG/QINGDAO ORIGIN REQUIRED.

(3) DOCUMENTS TO EVIDENCE THAT ALL PACKAGES BEAR SHIPPING MARKS: SHS/PENANG/1-UP.

(4) DOCUMENTS TO EVIDENCE THAT PACKING IS DONE AS FOLLOWS:

IN CARDBOARD CARTONS OF 25KGS NET OR 26.2KGS GROSS PER CARTON.

(5) BENEFICIARY TO ADVISE OPENER BY TELEX/FAX ALL DETAILS OF SHIPMENT AND SUCH TELEX/FAX COPY TO ACCOMPANY DOCUMENTS.

(6) BENEFICIARY TO AIRMAIL DIRECTLY TO OPENER ONE SET OF NON-NEGOTIABLE DOCUMENTS IMMEDIATELY AFTER SHIPMENT AND A CERTIFICATE OF COMPLIANCE TO THIS EFFECT IS REQUIRED.

(7) PLUS OR MINUS 05 PERCENT IN BOTH QUANTITY AND AMOUNT ACCEPTABLE.

(8) A USD30.00 (EQUIVALENT) FEE SHOULD BE DEDUCTED FROM THE REIMBURSEMENT CLAIM FOR EACH PRESENTATION OF DISCREPANCY DOCUMENTS UNDER THIS DOCUMENTARY CREDIT NOT WITHSTANDING ANY INSTRUCTIONS TO THE CONTRARY, THIS CHARGE SHALL BE FOR THE ACCOUNT OF THE BENEFICIARY.

BANK TO BANK INFO:

(1) WE HEREBY ENGAGE WITH DRAWERS AND/OR BONA FIDE HOLDERS THAT DRAFTS DRAWN AND NEGOTIATED ON PRESENTATION, SO LONG AS THERE HAS BEEN STRICT COMPLIANCE WITH ALL TERMS AND CONDITIONS (INCLUDING SPECIAL CONDITIONS) OF

THIS CREDIT, SAVE TO THE EXTENT THAT THE SAME HAVE BEEN AMENDED IN WRITING AND SIGNED ON OUR BEHALF.
(2) DOCUMENTARY EVIDENCE WILL BE REQUIRED OF COMPLIANCE WITH ALL CONDITIONS OF THIS CREDIT.

NOTE: WE CANNOT MAKE ANY ALTERATIONS TO THIS CREDIT WITHOUT THE OPENER'S AUTHORITY. SHOULD ANY OF ITS TERMS AND CONDITIONS BE UNCLEAR OR UNACCEPTABLE, THE BENEFICIARY OF THIS CREDIT MUST CONTACT THE OPENER DIRECTLY. WE SHALL INSIST ON STRICT COMPLIANCE WITH ALL THE TERMS AND CONDITIONS OF THIS CREDIT UNLESS AND UNTIL THEY HAVE BEEN FORMALY AMENDED IN WRITING SIGNED ON OUR BEHALF. THE BENEFICIARY OF THIS CREDIT IS NOT ENTITLED TO RELY ON COMMUNICATIONS OR DISCUSSIONS WITH US, THE ADVISING BANK OF THE OPENER AS IN ANY WAY AMENDING THIS CREDIT.

CHARGES:
ALL BANKING CHARGES OUTSIDE MALAYSIA INCLUDING ADVISING, NEGOTIATING COMMISSION AND REIMBURSING BANK'S FEES ARE FOR APPLICANT'S ACCOUNT.
PERIOD FOR PRESENTATION: DOCUMENTS TO BE PRESENTED WITHIN 15 DAYS AFTER THE ISSUANCE OF THE SHIPPING DOCUMENTS BUT WITHIN THE VALIDITY OF THE CREDIT.
CONFIRMATION: WITHOUT
DIRECTIONS TO ADVISING BANK:
+ YOUR CHARGES ARE FOR APPLICANT'S ACCOUNT.
DIRECTIONS TO NEGOTIATING BANK:
+ THE AMOUNT OF EACH NEGOTIATION MUST BE ENDORSED BELOW.
+ DOCUMENTS MUST BE DESPATCHED BY REGISTERED AIRMAIL IN ONE COVER.

REIMBURSEMENT INSTRUCTION:
ON RECEIPT OF DOCUMENTS CONFORMING TO THE TERMS OF THIS DOCUMENTARY CREDIT, WE UNDERTAKE TO REIMBURSE YOU IN THE CURRENCY OF THIS CREDIT IN ACCORDANCE WITH YOUR INSTRUCTIONS. NEGOTIATING BANK'S DISCOUNT AND/OR INTEREST, IF ANY, PRIOR TO REIMBURSEMENT BY US ARE FOR ACCOUNT OF BENEFICIARY.
THIS CREDIT IS SUBJECT TO UCP ICC PUB NO.500 AND IS AN OPERATIVE CREDIT INSTRUMENT AND NO MAIL CONFIRMATION TO FOLLOW.

COL HKD46,150.00

附制单补充资料：

1. Container No. EISU2628205
2. GR. WT: 5,240kg; NET WT: 5,000 kg
3. Measurements: 13.427CBM (55×45×30 cm×200 carrons=14.850 CBM)
4. Shipped per m/v Victoria V.306 on July 5, 2015. B/L No.CCFASH1820960
5. 黑枣 HS 编码：0813403000020

操作要领

海运订舱委托书可以是一份供货代订舱和报关用的综合信息单据，各公司的格式不尽相同，但主要内容一致，各栏目的填制要求如下：

1. 发货人：本栏目填写托运人的名称和地址，在信用证结算方式下，填写受益人名称和地址，在汇款或托收结算方式下，一般填写外贸合同卖方的名称和地址。

※本案例制单：　来证条款　　　　制单操作

经营单位 （发货人）	山东希望土产进出口总公司 SHANGDONG HOPE NATIVE PRODUCT I/E CORP. 62, GUANGXI ROAD, QINGDAO, CHINA

2. 收货人：本格式本栏目不填写（除非单据格式中无抬头栏，只有收货人一栏），只有当进口方要求海运单（Sea Waybill）时才填写实名和地址，因为海运提单（ocean bill of lading）大多为指示提单，都采用抬头格式。提单的抬头，信用证结算方式下，须严格按照信用证中提单条款的相关规定填写；汇款或托收结算方式下，按照外贸合同中的相关规定填写。

※本案例制单：　来证条款　　　　制单操作

MADE OUT TO SHIPPER'S ORDER

收货人	

3. 发票号码：本栏目填写业务项下的商业发票号码，为报关提供信息。

※本案例制单：　　　　制单操作

发票号	BP13SHS02INV1051

4. 信用证号码：本栏目填写业务项下的信用证号码，为报关提供信息。

※本案例制单：　　　　制单操作

L/C 号码	PGH000348DC

5. 合同号码：本栏目填写业务项下的合同号码，为报关提供信息。

※本案例制单：

制单操作

合同号	ORDER NO.SOO-6378

6. 总金额：本栏目根据合同或信用证填写总金额，为报关提供信息。

※本案例制单：　来证条款

CCY/AMOUNT:　HKD46,150.00

制单操作

总金额	HKD46,150.00

7. 支付方式：本栏目根据外销合同中的支付方式填写，为报关提供信息。

※本案例制单：

制单操作

支付方式	L/C AT SIGHT

8. 贸易国别（地区）：本栏目填写信用证申请人或外销合同中买方所在国家（地区），即贸易中付款方的国家或地区，为报关提供信息。

※本案例制单：

制单操作

贸易国别（地区）	马来西亚

9. 贸易性质（方式）：本栏目填写与实际情况一致的海关规范贸易方式，须填写全称，为报关提供信息。常见的贸易方式有：一般贸易、进料加工贸易、来料加工贸易、易货贸易、补偿贸易等 90 多种贸易方式。本业务为一般贸易。

※本案例制单：

制单操作

贸易性质（方式）	一般贸易

10. 销售国别（地区）：本栏目填写货物实际销往的国家（地区），即最终目的港所在国家或地区，为报关提供信息。本业务的货物实际销往马来西亚。

※本案例制单：

制单操作

销售国别（地区）	马来西亚

11. 运输方式：本栏目填写实际的运输方式，为报关提供信息。本业务为海运。

※本案例制单：

制单操作

运输方式	海运

12. 出口口岸：本栏目填写实际的出口海关关区名，为报关提供信息。本业务为青岛海关口岸。

※本案例制单：　　　　　　　　　　　　　　　　　　　　　　　　制单操作

出口口岸	青岛海关

13. 装运港：本栏目根据信用证或合同填写启运港名称。注意：如若信用证或合同中只是笼统地说明装运港为中国任意港口，在制单时必须填写具体的装运港名称，其后最好加打 CHINA。

※本案例制单：　来证条款　　　　　　　　　　　　　　　　　　　制单操作

SHIPMENT FROM ANY PORT IN CHINA TO PENANG

装运港	QINGDAO, CHINA

14. 目的港：本栏目根据信用证或合同填写目的港名称。注意：如若信用证或合同中只是笼统地说明目的港为任意港口，在制单时必须填写明确具体的目的港英文名称。若有选择港，则应照打。

※本案例制单：　来证条款　　　　　　　　　　　　　　　　　　　制单操作

SHIPMENT FROM ANY PORT IN CHINA TO PENANG

目的港	PENANG

15. 提单或承运人收据：本栏目所有内容均应严格按照信用证对运输单据的要求进行填写。

（1）抬头人：信用证结算方式下，严格按照信用证中提单条款中对抬头的相关规定填写，汇款或托收结算方式下，一般填写 TO ORDER，或按外贸合同中的相关规定填写。

※本案例制单：来证条款　　　　　　　　　　　　　　　　　　　制单操作

MADE OUT TO SHIPPER'S ORDER

抬头人	TO SHIPPER'S ORDER

（2）可否分批：按照信用证上的运输条款要求填写。如果信用证上没有具体规定，按照 UCP600 解释，默认为允许。此信息主要为供承运人配载时选择使用。

※本案例制单：　来证条款　　　　　　　　　　　　　　　　　　　制单操作

PARTIAL SHIPMENTS: FORBIDDEN

可否分批	否

（3）可否转运：按照信用证上的要求填写。如果信用证上没有具体规定，按照 UCP600 解释，默认为允许。此信息主要是为供承运人配载时选择使用。

※本案例制单：　来证条款　　　　　　　　　　　　　　　　　　　制单操作

TRANSSHIPMENT: PERMITTED

可否转运	允许

（4）装运期：本栏目按照信用证的规定填写最晚装运日期，其他结算方式按合同规定填写。同时注意结合实际备货情况，可在后面的声明事项栏目中填写希望预订的具体船期。

※本案例制单：　来证条款　　　　　　　　　　　　　　　　　　　　　　制单操作

SHIPMENT FROM ANY PORT IN CHINA TO PENANG LATEST 06 JULY/2015

装运期	6-JUL-15

（5）有效期限：本栏目填写信用证的到期日，仅供出口人自己备注参考，并非必填。

※本案例制单：　来证条款　　　　　　　　　　　　　　　　　　　　　　制单操作

EXPIRY DATE AND PLACE: 21 JULY 2015-CHINA

有效期	21-JUL-15 CHINA

（6）被通知人：本栏目填写货物到达目的港时船代及时发送到货通知的收件人。信用证结算方式下，严格按照信用证中提单条款的 NOTIFY 后相关规定填写，须填写联系电话和传真号码。

其他结算方式下，一般填写进口商名称、地址、联系电话和传真，或按外贸合同中的相关规定填写。

※本案例制单：　来证条款　　　　　　　　　　　　　　　　　　　　　　制单操作

NOTIFY APPLICANT AND ISSUING BANK

被通知人	1. SOO HUP SENG TRADING CO. SDN BHD. 165 1ST FLOOR, VICTORIA STREET, 10300 PENANG MALAYSIA TEL: 60-4-2509730　FAX: 60-4-2509729 2. THE HONGKONG AND SHANGHAI BANKING CORP LTD., DOWNING STREET, PENANG TEL: 60-4-2517522　FAX: 60-4-2517520

（7）运费：本栏目只需填写运费支付方式。在 CFR、CIF、CPT、CIP 贸易术语下，根据信用证选择填写运费预付（freight prepaid）或已付（paid）；在 FOB、FAS 或 FCA 贸易术语下，选填运费到付（freight to collect）。若信用证规定提单显示具体的运费金额，则本栏照填付费方式，在提单注明栏要求船方在提单上显示运费金额。

※本案例制单：　来证条款　　　　　　　　　　　　　　　　　　　　　　制单操作

MARKED “FREIGHT PREPAID”

运费	☐ 已付 ☑ 预付 ☐ 到付

（8）提单份数：本栏目按照信用证要求填写。

※本案例制单：　来证条款　　　　　　　　　　　　　　　　　　　　　　制单操作

FULL SET OF ORIGINAL CLEAN–ON BOARD－BILL(S) OF LADING

提单份数：正本　3　　副本　3

（9）需要在提单上注明：本栏目填写信用证条款对于提单的额外加注（extra notations）要求。凡是需要船方照抄写的，用英文，注意时态改用一般现在时或现在完成时；凡是要求船方显示仅船方知道的内容，用中文表达，以免误解。

※本案例制单： 来证条款	制单操作
MARKED "FREIGHT PREPAID" DOCUMENTS TO EVIDENCE THAT ALL PACKAGES BEAR SHIPPING MARKS: SHS/PENANG/1-UP DOCUMENTS TO EVIDENCE THAT PACKING IS DONE AS FOLLOWS: IN CARDBOARD CARTONS OF 25KGS NET OR 26.2KGS GROSS PER CARTON	需要在提单上注明： 1. FREIGHT PREPAID 2. ALL PACKAGES BEAR SHIPPING MARKS: SHS/PENANG/1-UP 3. PACKING IS DONE AS FOLLOWS: IN CARDBOARD CARTONS OF 25KGS NET OR 26.2KGS GROSS PER CARTON 4. 目的港船务代理人的名称、地址及联系电话

16. 标记唛码：本栏目根据信用证或合同规定填写唛头，与发票一致。若系出口人自行设计唛头，需按国际标准唛头缮制。包装件数可开口填 UP, 也可填具体数字。若散货无唛头，应填写“N/M”。

※本案例制单： 来证条款	制单操作
DOCUMENTS TO EVIDENCE THAT ALL PACKAGES BEAR SHIPPING MARKS: SHS/PENANG/1-UP	标记唛码 SHS PENANG 1-UP

17. 货名规格及货号、海关编码：本栏目填写与信用证相符的货物英文名称或不会引起歧义的统称品名。同时，正确填写中文品名和该货物的 HS 商品协调编码或称海关税则号，此后一项主要是为委托货代报关提供信息。

※本案例制单： 来证条款	制单操作
5M/TONS SHANDONG BLACK DATES HIGH QUALITY	货名规格及货号、海关编码 SHANDONG BLACK DATES 山东黑枣 HS 编码：0813403000020

18. 包装方式及包装件数：本栏目根据合同或信用证填写具体的包装件数和商品报关数量。

※本案例制单： 来证条款	制单操作
SIGNED WEIGHT LIST IN TRIPLICATE TO STATE THAT GOODS ARE PACKED IN 25KGS NET OR 26.2KGS GROSS PER CARTON REQUIRED.	包装方式及包装件数 5,000 KG 25KG/CTN 200 CTNS 55×45×30 CM/CTN

19. 毛重/净重（公斤）：本栏目根据货物的实际情况填写，重量单位必须为千克。净重并非必填。

※本案例制单：

制单操作

毛重/净重（千克）
5,240/5,000

20. 成交条件：本栏目根据合同或信用证填写成交的贸易术语及总价，主要为报关提供信息。

※本案例制单： 来证条款

CCY/AMOUNT: HKD 46,150.00
5M/TONS SHANDONG BLACK DATES HIGH QUALITY AT HKD 9,230 PER M/TON CIF PENANG INCOTERMS 2010

制单操作

成交条件	
单价	总价
币别：HKD	
CIF PENANG 9.230/KG	46,150.00

21. 总体积：本栏目根据货物的实际发运情况填写。体积单位用立方米，精确到小数点后三位。须注明外包装的长宽高尺寸（单位为厘米），主要便于货代和承运人核对。

※本案例制单：

制单操作

55×45×30 cm

总体积	14.850	立方米

22. 备注与注意事项：本栏目填写提醒货代或承运人的有关特别包装、预订集装箱、运输与提货/送货的一些特别注意事项。一般来说，这些事项并不显示在提单上。

※本案例制单：

制单操作

备注与注意事项	1. 货物包装为：IN CARDBOARD CARTONS 2. 预订集装箱：20’ × 1 FCL 3. 物资进栈：派送，门到门 仓库地址：青岛广西路 62 号 联系人：唐欣 联系电话：65788877

附订舱委托书制单样例

<table>
<tr><td colspan="3" rowspan="3">出口货物明细单
订舱委托书</td><td colspan="2">发票号</td><td colspan="2">BP13SHS02INV1051</td><td colspan="2">外运公司编号</td><td colspan="2"></td></tr>
<tr><td colspan="2">L/C 号码</td><td colspan="2">PGH000348DC</td><td colspan="2">合同号</td><td colspan="2">ORDER NO. SOO-6378</td></tr>
<tr><td colspan="2">总金额</td><td colspan="2">HKD 46,150.00</td><td colspan="2">支付方式</td><td colspan="2">L/C AT SIGHT</td></tr>
<tr><td colspan="3">公司编号：×××　　日期：2015.6.28</td><td colspan="2">贸易国别（地区）</td><td colspan="2">马来西亚</td><td colspan="2">贸易性质（方式）</td><td colspan="2">一般贸易</td></tr>
<tr><td colspan="2">经营单位（发货人）</td><td>山东希望土产进出口总公司
SHANDONG HOPE NATIVE PRODUCT I/E CORP.
62, GUANGXI ROAD, QINGDAO, CHINA</td><td colspan="2">销售国别（地区）</td><td colspan="2">马来西亚</td><td colspan="2">运输方式</td><td colspan="2">海运</td></tr>
<tr><td colspan="2" rowspan="2">收货人</td><td rowspan="2"></td><td colspan="2">出口口岸</td><td colspan="2">青岛海关</td><td colspan="2" rowspan="2">目的港</td><td colspan="2" rowspan="2">PENANG</td></tr>
<tr><td colspan="2">装运港</td><td colspan="2">QINGDAO, CHINA</td></tr>
<tr><td rowspan="2">提单或承运人收据</td><td>抬头人</td><td>TO SHIPPER'S ORDER</td><td>可否分批</td><td>否</td><td>可否转运</td><td>允许</td><td>装运期</td><td>6-JUL-15</td><td>有效期</td><td>21-JUL-15 CHINA</td></tr>
<tr><td>被通知人</td><td colspan="9">1. SOO HUP SENG TRADING CO. SDN BHD.
165 1ST FLOOR, VICTORIA STREET,
10300 PENANG MALAYSIA
TEL: 60-4-2509730　FAX: 60-4-2509729
2. THE HONGKONG AND SHANGHAI BANKING CORP. LTD.,
DOWNING STREET, PENANG
TEL: 60-4-2517522　FAX: 60-4-2517520</td></tr>
<tr><td rowspan="2">提单或承运人收据</td><td>运费</td><td>☐ 已付　☑ 预付
☐ 到付</td><td colspan="5">提单份数：正本　3　　副本　3</td><td>车号</td><td colspan="2"></td></tr>
<tr><td colspan="10">需要在提单上额外注明：
1. FREIGHT PREPAID
2. ALL PACKAGES BEAR SHIPPING MARKS:
SHS/PENANG/1-UP
3. PACKING IS DONE AS FOLLOWS:
IN CARDBOARD CARTONS OF 25KGS NET OR 26.2KGS GROSS PER CARTON
4. 目的港船务代理人的名称、地址及联系电话</td></tr>
</table>

（续表）

<table>
<tr><td rowspan="3">标记唛码</td><td rowspan="3" colspan="2">货名规格及货号、海关编码</td><td rowspan="3">包装方式及
包装件数</td><td rowspan="3">毛重/净重
（千克）</td><td colspan="3">成交条件</td></tr>
<tr><td>单价</td><td colspan="2">总价</td></tr>
<tr><td colspan="3">币别：HKD</td></tr>
<tr><td>SHS
PENANG
1-UP</td><td colspan="2">SHANDONG BLACK DATES
山东黑枣
HS 编码：0813403000020

总计：</td><td>5,000 KG
25KG/CTN
200 CTNS

200CTN</td><td>5,240/5,000

55×45×30 CM/CTN</td><td>CIF
PENANG
9.230/KG</td><td colspan="2">46,150.00</td></tr>
<tr><td rowspan="8">备注与注意事项</td><td colspan="2" rowspan="8">1. 货物包装为：IN CARDBOARD CARTONS
2. 预订集装箱：20’ × 1 FCL
3. 物资进栈：派送，门到门
仓库地址：青岛广西路 62 号
联系人：唐欣
联系电话：65788877
SHANDONG HOPE NATIVE PRODUCT CORP.
山东希望土产进出口总公司</td><td>总体积</td><td colspan="4">14.850 立方米</td></tr>
<tr><td>船名和航次</td><td colspan="4"></td></tr>
<tr><td>提单号</td><td colspan="4"></td></tr>
<tr><td>提单日期</td><td colspan="4"></td></tr>
<tr><td>海关编号</td><td colspan="4"></td></tr>
<tr><td>海关放行日期</td><td colspan="4"></td></tr>
<tr><td>业务员</td><td colspan="4">唐欣</td></tr>
<tr><td>制单员</td><td>唐欣</td><td>审核</td><td colspan="2">×××</td></tr>
</table>

二、缮制空运订舱委托书

项目描述（案例情境描述）

成都市蜀鑫土产进出口公司向法国 OLIVIER FOODS CO., LTD. 出口一批盐渍松茸，双方于 2016 年 9 月 10 日签订了外销合同。蜀鑫土产进出口公司委托成都德诚国际货代有限公司办理货物空运事宜，外销合同与业务信息明细如下：

（一）外销合同

成都市蜀鑫土产进出口公司

CHENGDU SHUXIN NATIVE PRODUCE IMP. & EXP. CORP.

A-1502 YUNMAO MANSION NO.102 XIYULONG STREET QINGYANG DISTRICT, CHENGDU, CHINA

TEL: 0086-28-86632066　　FAX: 0086-28-86632065

成交确认书
SALES CONFIRMATION

编号（No.）：C-S185
日期（Date）：SEPT. 10, 2016

买方：
Buyer:　OLIVIER FOODS CO., LTD
Add:　AUTOROUTE B26Y.3 ST MAURICE-05700, PARIS, FRANCE
TEL: 0033-1-47256094　　FAX: 0033-1-47256095

兹经买卖双方同意成交下列商品订立条款如下：

The undersigned seller and buyer have agreed to close the following transactions according to the terms and conditions stipulated below:

唛头 Marks & No.	品名规格 Description of Goods	数量 Quantity	单价 Unit Price	总价 Amount
O.F. C-S185 PARIS C/NO. 1-150	SALTED MATSUTAKE MUSHROOM	900KGS	CPT PARIS CHARLES DE GAULLES AIRPORT	
			EUR32.00/KG	EUR28,800.00
合约总值 TOTAL VALUE	SAY EUROS TWENTY EIGHT THOUSAND EIGHT HUNDRED ONLY			

1. 包装 PACKING：GOODS TO BE PACKED 1KG/BAG, 6 BAGS TO A CARTON, TOTAL 150 CTNS.

2. 装运期 TIME OF SHIPMENT: DURING SEPT. 2016

3. 装运口岸和目的地 LOADING PORT AND DESTINATION: FROM CHENGDU CHINA TO PARIS FRANCE BY AIR.

4. 付款条件 TERMS OF PAYMENT: THE BUYER SHALL PAY 50% OF THE SALES PROCEEDS IN ADVANCE BY T/T TO REACH THE SELLER 5 DAYS BEFORE THE DELIVERY DATE AND THE BALANCE 50% IS TO BE PAID AGAINST COPY AIR WAYBILL.

PAYEE: CHENGDU SHUXIN NATIVE PRODUCE IMP. & EXP. CORP.

A/C NO. 2056638500107 WITH BANK OF CHINA, SICHUAN BRANCH SWIFT: BOCDB008

5. 单据要求 DOCUMENTS REQUIRED:

+ COMMERICAL INVOICE

+ PACKING LIST

+ GSP FORM A

THIS SALE CONFIRMATION IS MADE IN TWO ORIGINAL COPIES AND BECOMES VALID AFTER SIGNATURE, ONE COPY OF WHICH IS TO BE HELD BY EACH PARTY.

SIGNED BY: 卖方 买方

THE SELLER THE BUYER

FRANCOIS OLIVIER

（二）业务信息明细

1. 商品 HS 编码：2003909020
2. 外包装资料：每箱净重 6KGS，每箱毛重 6.5KGS，纸箱尺码 35CM×30CM×30CM
3. 出口商商检注册登记号：5100821006
4. 出口商食品卫生许可证号：5100/23047
5. 出口商统一社会信用代码：9151010608852131F
6. 航空公司承载反馈航班号：CA875
7. 航班日期：2016 年 9 月 28 日
8. 货运代理公司：成都德诚国际货运代理有限公司

统一社会信用代码 915101067022501009

附空运订舱委托书制单样例

托运人/地址 Shipper/Address CHENGDU SHUXIN NATIVE PRODUCE IMP. & EXP. CORP. A-1502 YUNMAO MANSION NO.102 XIYULONG STREET QINGYANG DISTRICT, CHENGDU, CHINA	**空运货物托运单** **成都德诚国际货运代理有限公司** **CHENGDU DECHENG INTERNATIONAL FORWARDING & AGENCY CO., LTD**
收货人/地址 Consignee/Address OLIVIER FOODS CO., LTD AUTOROUTE B26Y.3 ST MAURICE-05700 PARIS FRANCE	托运单号码：XY2015-36 联系人：张凌 TEL: 028-75881100 FAX: 028-75881102
并通知 Also Notify OLIVIER FOODS CO., LTD AUTOROUTE B26Y.3 ST MAURICE-05700 PARIS FRANCE TEL：0033-1-47256094 FAX: 0033-1-47256095	

航空公司 Carrier	航班/日期 Flight/Day	ADD: 成都市双流区航空大道 258 号
	BY SEP. 30, 2016	

始发地 Place/Airport of Departure	目的地 Place/Airport of Destination	空运单号 Air Waybill No.
CTU 成都双流国际机场	CDG 巴黎戴高乐机场	

唛头及号码 Marks and Numbers	件 数 No. of Packages	货品名称 Description of Goods	毛重（KGS）KGS	体积（M^3）MEAS
O.F. C-S185 PARIS NO./C 1-150	150 CTNS	SALTED MATSUTAKE MUSHROOM	975KGS	4.725M^3 35×30×30CM/CTN

随货文件 Accompany Documents	运输条款 Transit Term
☑ Invoice ☑ Packing List ☐ C/O ☑ Form A ☐ Others	☐ FCA ☑ CPT ☐ CIP ☐ DAT ☐ DAP ☐ DDP
报关方式 Customs Clearance ☐ 自行报关 Self-Customs Clearance ☑ 委托报关 Assigned 申报金额 Amount USD32,486.40	保险 Cargo Insurance ☐ 要求 Required ☑ 未要求 Not Required 保险金额 Insured Value

（续表）

<table>
<tr>
<td>运费确认 Freight Confirm

空运费率 Fright Rates　本地费用 Local Charges
☑预付 Prepaid　☑预付 Prepaid
□到付 Collect　□到付 Collect</td>
<td>托运人声明:
1. 非危险品声明，并承担一切相关不实行为责任后果。
2. 我公司/本人确认以上所填各项均正确，属实，货物符合国家海关及承运人的有关规定，我公司/本人愿对此负责。
3. 本公司/本人同意遵守国际运输公约的有关规定。
4. 如发生收货人拒提货物之事，本公司/本人愿承担所有由此产生的费用包括：运费、地面费用、清关费及仓租等。
5. 如收货人拒付运费（在运费到付时），本公司/本人愿在 5 日内付清全部运费及有关费用。</td>
</tr>
<tr>
<td>特别事项 Special Requirement
1. 提货地址
成都市双流区百家东二街 20 号
2. 请避免重压</td>
<td rowspan="2">托运人签字盖章：
Stamp and Signature of the Shipper

日期　2016 年 9 月 21 日
Date</td>
</tr>
<tr>
<td>托运联系人：
Contact Person：程栋
TEL：（028）86632066
E-MAIL:</td>
</tr>
</table>

几点说明：

1. 航空公司一栏，除非指定，一般在订舱时不应填写。

2. 航班和日期栏，订舱时并不知晓，除非指定，一般只能填写最晚装运日期。

3. 体积一栏，必须注明外包装的长宽高，以厘米为单位。

4. 随货文件一栏，应严格按买卖双方约定或买方要求提供的文件，填写齐全。除了随货提供，卖方还应另寄一套给买方。

相关知识

制单工作同审单工作一样，是国际贸易单证工作中的主体工作，主要是对各种装运单据进行缮制和签署。出口制单工作要求做到：单证相符，单单一致，单货一致，单约一致。尽管信用证项下的开证行只考虑前两项决定是否付款，但如果后两项没做到，结算后仍可能招致进口方索赔。

制单的主要依据有：

1. 买卖合约。非信用证结算制单以此为依据；信用证项下制单时一些信用证未涉及的细节也须参照合同或订单的条款。

2. 信用证。凡是信用证项下的单据，必须严格按来证条款缮制。

3. 出仓单或提货单。有关商品的数量、规格、包装、件数、毛净重和尺码等，均须以此为准。

4. 生产商或供货方提供的原始资料。工厂的装箱单，包装方法、花色或尺码搭配等，部分信息与出仓单相同。

5. 业务部门的必要资料和特别要求。例如买方指定唛头、运输特殊做法、船运信息、保险费用和赔付代理信息、款额收付安排、许可证号码等。

制单规程和方法：制单须遵循必要的操作规程，才可收到事半功倍的效果。现将制单“五步法”推荐如下：

1.“核”。先将货物的出仓单或提货单与信用证和买卖合约核对，弄清楚货、证是否相符，发现问题须与有关环节联系解决。

2.“算”。单据中有很多数字需要计算，例如货物的毛净重、体积、各种金额、佣金等，应在制单前准确计算出来。

3.“配”。根据信用证的要求，把出口本批货物所需的各种空白单据按所需份数配置在制单操作文件夹内，既可防止漏制，还能提高制单工作效率。

4.“制”。完成了前三项工作后，可以开始制单。通常从缮制发票和装箱单开始，因为发票是一切单据的中心，记载的内容比较全面。

5.“审”。单据制妥后，制单员应自审一遍，再送审单员复审。应尽量把出现的差错发现并更正在自审环节中。

进出口货物托运操作程序

1. 货物海运托运程序

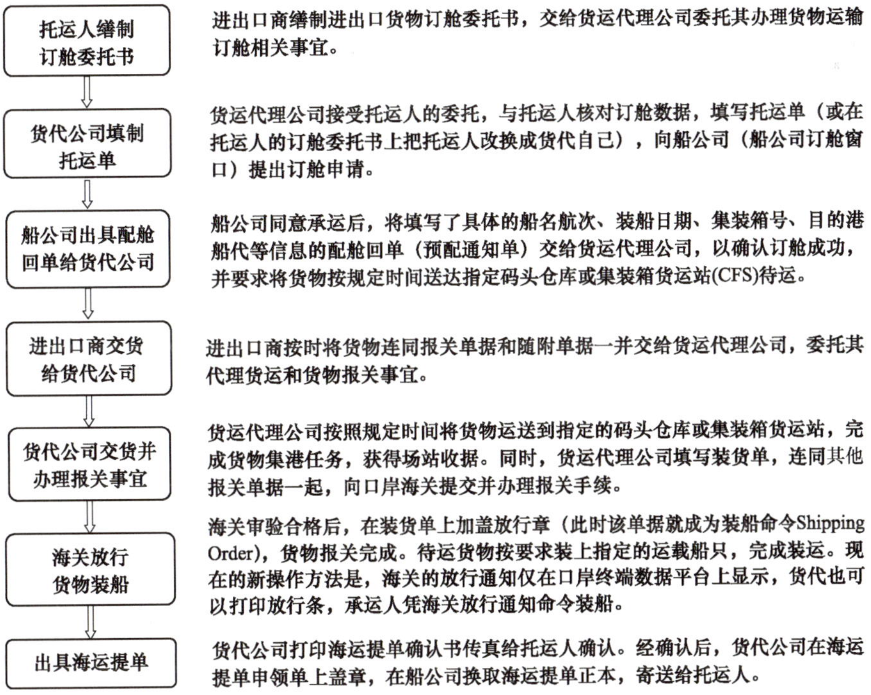

2. 出口货物空运订舱委托流程

订舱委托 预配舱位	外贸公司缮制出口货物订舱委托书给货运代理公司，货运代理公司据此填写托运单给航空公司，办理货物出口订舱托运手续，进行订舱确认。
机场货站收运货物	货代公司对外贸公司送进仓的货物进行必要的清点和核对，进行包装称重和丈量，严格按照航空公司的要求检查货物包装等是否符合航空运输的规定。货代交货或通知货主交货到机场货运站。
货代公司代理报关	货运代理公司代理外贸公司办理货物的报关手续。海关放行后，货运代理公司领取集装器装货。
出库装货 签发航空运单	货运代理公司将装载于集装器里的货物交航空公司验收，并填制该货物的总运单交航空公司签发航空运单，如有随机文件，也一并交航空公司验收。

操作能力训练

思考题：

S4-1　订舱委托书和大副收据与海运提单的关系是什么？

操作题：

C4-1　根据附录 3.1 里提供的制单信用证 3-13-2（见本书第 230 页），用格式二单据，独立缮制符合要求的订舱委托书。

C4-2　讨论和评讲后，根据附录 3.1 里的其余制单信用证（见本书第 230 页），用相对应的格式，逐一缮制订舱单。

C4-3　探索学习下一项目，并根据模块三附录 3.1 里的制单信用证 3-13-1（见本书第 230 页），用发票格式一，缮制符合要求的商业发票。

C4-4　独立学习 ISBP（2013 最新版本）和 UCP600 中关于商业发票的条款。

项目五

缮制商业发票

商业发票的含义及作用

商业发票（Commercial Invoice）是出口方向进口方出具的凭证，以向买方收取货款的发货清单，也是卖方对一笔交易的全面说明，早在报检报关时就需提供。在国际贸易中，它具有如下作用或功能：

1. 销售作用：它是卖方向买方发送货物的凭证；也是买方凭以收货和销售的依据。
2. 财务作用：它是买卖双方收付货款和记账的凭证。双方财务人员需要发票确定收、付货款并记账。在不使用汇票结算的汇付方式中，发票可代替汇票作为结算货款的依据。
3. 清关作用：它是买卖双方办理报关、清关、计征或计缴关税的凭证。
4. 中心作用：它是全套出口单据的核心，其余单据均需参照它缮制。
5. 索赔理赔作用：它是货运保险投保、索赔、理赔和价值证明的重要凭据。

学习目标

［知识目标］了解发票的分类，掌握商业发票的功能或作用，掌握缮制商业发票的要领。
［能力目标］能正确缮制信用证项下的商业发票和非信用证项下的商业发票。

项目描述（案例情境描述）

山东希望土产进出口公司向马来西亚出口一批山东黑枣，进口方通过银行开来信用证。出口方经审核无误后，开始缮制来证要求提供的全套单据。本次业务为缮制商业发票，信用证参考项目四。

操作要领（缮制商业发票各栏的填制要求）

缮制发票及其他单据仅用英文，一般使用大写，是因为可以省去复杂的打字手法，能提高打字速度。当然也可用小写缮制，但每行首字母、专有名词首字母和缩略语必须大写。

发票或商业发票并无统一格式，但为了规范起见，国际商会还是推荐了标准格式。本案采用了这一推荐格式的发票。

1. 文件名称（Title of Document）：Invoice 可理解为除了形式发票（Proforma Invoice）和临时发票（Provisional Invoice）以外的其他形式的任何发票。但 Commercial Invoice 只能涵盖 Invoice，不能提交其他形式的发票。

※本案例制单：来证条款　　　　制单操作

DOCUMENTS:
+ INVOICE IN TRIPLICATE

商业发票
Commercial Invoice

由于来证要求 invoice，缮制提交给银行的单据名称即可为 invoice，也可为 commercial invoice。

2. 出单人（Issuer, From, Exporter, Seller）：此栏应填写信用证受益人名称和地址，除非来证另有规定，可转让信用证除外。若非信用证结算，则填写合同的卖方。此栏的地址中可以不提供电话号码和传真号码。提供的号码也可与信用证上的不一致。邮编错误不属不符点*。名称占一行打完，地址不可与名称同行，须合理分行缮制。

※本案例制单：来证条款　　　　制单操作

BENEFICIARY: SHANDONG HOPE NATIVE PRODUCT I/E CORP.
62，GUANGXI ROAD, QINGDAO, CHINA

1.出口商 Exporter
SHANDONG HOPE NATIVE PRODUCT I/E CORP.
62, GUANGXI ROAD, QINGDAO, CHINA

3. 发票抬头/受票人（To, Importer, Buyer）：抬头（Addressee/Beneficiary）即为接受单据的一方或为受益方。此栏必须为信用证申请人，除非来证另有规定。填写名称和详细地址。若非信用证结算，则填写合同的买方。名称一行打完，地址不可与名称同行，须合理分行缮制。若来证规定：

“Invoice made out in name of applicant. Applicant: By order of XYZ Bank for account of ABC Co.”，发票抬头应照打“By...XYZ Bank...ABC Co.”，也可只做 ABC Co. 即可。

※本案例制单：来证条款　　　　制单操作

APPLICANT: SOO HUP SENG TRADING CO. SDN BHD.
165，1ST FLOOR, VICTORIA STREET
10300 PENANG，MALAYSIA

2.进口商 Importer
SOO HUP SENG TRADING CO. SDN BHD.
165 1ST FLOOR, VICTORIA STREET,
10300 PENANG MALAYSIA

4. 运输事项（Transport Details）：发票上应显示运输路线和方式，如 From Shenzhen to Liverpool by sea (by air, by rail, by parcel)；为了日后便于确定货物的承运人或发货批次，还应加上具体运载工具名称和航次、航班号或卡车号等，如...by s.s. “Daqing” V.205

(by Flight No.xxx, by Wagon No. xxx)。

必须显示具体港口。若来证规定港口笼统为 From any port in China to Canada port，单据上须打具体装运港口+China to 具体卸货港+Canada，此卸货港应与价格术语目的港一致。如果国外目的港有重名，则须注明国别。

若来证有选择港口，如 Liverpool/London，制单时应照打。若承运人通知航线上有转运港，则须在目的港后加以注明。如 Per s/s “Red Star” V.302 from Qingdao to London via/with transshipment (W/T) at Rotterdam。如果在目的港卸货后需要转运至内陆地区，则应注明 in transit to（内陆城市）。

※本案例制单：来证条款　　　　制单操作

TRANSSHIPMENT: PERMITTED
SHIPMENT FROM ANY PORT IN CHINA TO PENANG LATEST 06 JULY / 2015

3.运输事项 Transport Details
SHIPPED BY M/V "VICTORIA" FROM QINGDAO, CHINA TO PENANG

5. 发票号码（Invoice No.）：为便于管理，发票的编号一般源自合同号，应能传递操作部门、买方、单据类别、年代和序号等信息，与合同号的区别在于单据类别代码，例如合同号为 13SHS02SC1061。也可使用银行统一的编制方法，信用证项下使用 BP 开头，托收项下使用 OC 号。

※本案例制单：来证条款　　　　制单操作

4.发票日期和发票号 Invoice Date and No.
BP15SHS02INV1051　JUNE 28, 2015

6. 发票日期（Invoice Date）：出票日期早于或等于所有装运单据日期。为了给装运前的单据操作留出足够的时间，发票日期最好较提单装运期早 7–10 天。若信用证没有相反规定，银行可接受出具日期早于开证日期的发票。本案来证有明确反对条款。

※本案例制单：来证条款　　　　制单操作

SPECIAL CONDITIONS:
1) DOCUMENTS PRIOR TO ISSUANCE OF THE CREDIT ARE NOT ACCEPTABLE.

4.发票日期和发票号 Invoice Date and No.
BP15SHS02INV1051　JUNE 28, 2015

7. 合同号和信用证号（S/C No., L/C No.）：为了便于管理和提高工作效率，合同号和信用证号是发票的重要参考号码，应予显示。若无合同号，也可显示订单号或其他合同性质的单据编号，但应注明单据名称。若一票有多个合同号，最好分别打发票，因报关单上只能一份合同一单。

※本案例制单：来证条款　　　　制单操作

5.合同号 Contract No.	6.信用证号 L/C No.
ORDER NO. S00-6378	PGH000348DC

8. 原产地说明（Country/Region of Origin）：为了发挥发票的清关功能，须显示货物的原产地国名或地区名。如果发票格式上没有显示原产地的专门栏，则须在发票货物描述下的空白处或自由处置区显示这样的语句：All the goods named above are of China origin。

※本案例制单：来证条款　　　　　　　　　　　　　　　　　　　　　　　　　　　制单操作

7. 原产地国 Country/Region of Origin
CHINA

9. 贸易方式（Trade Mode）：此栏在一般的发票格式中并不多见，国际商会推荐使用也是便于清关所用，应准确填写。常见的售定贸易或卖断价格贸易被称为一般贸易。

※本案例制单：来证条款　　　　　　　　　　　　　　　　　　　　　　　　　　　制单操作

8. 贸易方式 Trade Mode
GENERAL

10. 交货和支付条款（Terms of Delivery and Payment）：交货条件即为贸易术语或价格术语，可在此栏显示，也可显示在下面的价格上方。如果来证有术语来源，制单时须照打。事实上，由于当前两个贸易术语解释通则并行使用，不注明术语来源是很容易发生纠纷而无法得到解决的。因此在业务中，合同上和单据上都应注明价格术语来源，或注明 This price term is subject to Incoterms ××××语句。

为体现财务功能，发票上应显示支付方式和支付日期，如 T/T, D/P at sight, L/C at sight 或 L/C at ×× days after ×××等，便于买卖双方财务管理。

※本案例制单：来证条款　　　　　　　　　　　　　　　　　　　　　　　　　　　制单操作

DRAFTS: AT SIGHT FOR
CIF PENANG INCOTERMS 2010 AS PER

9. 交货和付款条款 Terms of Delivery and Payment
BY L/C AT SIGHT
CIF PENANG INCOTERMS 2010

11. 运输标志（Shipping Marks）：运输标志的俗称为唛头，单据上的唛头应与信用证里的唛头一致，来证规定的细节必须照样显示。若来证唛头里的包装总数是 NO.1-UP，制单时可照写，或写具体数量，如 NO. 1-200。反之，若来证唛头已经明确了具体包装数量，则制单不能写 NO.1-UP。若来证没有唛头条款，则应按国际标准唛头缮制。只有散装货物和一些裸装货物本身就没有运输标志，制单时才显示 N/M（即 No Marks）。

实际上，唛头下方还可以显示内陆转运信息（in transit to 内陆城市）以及集装箱号码。需要说明的是，集装箱号码是订舱后才从承运人处获得的。在订舱环节缮制发票时是不可能获得集装箱编号的。如果需缮制的唛头较多，可以另加页缮制，并附在发票后。

※本案例制单：来证条款　　　　　　　　　　　　　　　　　　　　　　　　　　　制单操作

3) DOCUMENTS TO EVIDENCE THAT ALL PACKAGES BEAR SHIPPING MARKS: SHS / PENANG / 1-UP
4. Container No. EISU2628205

10. 运输标志和集装箱号
Shipment Marks; Container No.
SHS
PENANG
1-UP
CONTAINER NO.　25 KGS
EISU2628205　SAY TW

12. 货物描述和包装数量（Description of Goods, Number and Kind of Package）：货物描述应与信用证商品条款规定的相符（CORRESPONDING），而不是像照镜子那样完全相同（SAME 或 IDENTICAL）。缮制基本原则是：可以比信用证描述得丰富、详细，譬如分列各款货物细节，而其他单据则可以比信用证描述得更概括，外延更大。如信用证中描述有 DETAILS AS PER CONTRACT NO. ×××/PROFORMA INVOICE NO. ×××，则必须在发票的货物描述中照抄，即便发票中已经显示了作为参考号的合同号码或形式发票号码，也应如此。为便于清关，还应注明商品协调编码（H.S. CODE NO.），或称海关税则号。

填写货物描述，方法是把信用证的商品条款中的品名和文字描述提取出来，品名独占一行，把货物的数量、价格、包装、唛头等内容填写到发票的相关栏目里。散装货物须注明 IN BULK。

包装种类和数量在此栏仅显示小写即可或放到下面跟大写一起说明。包装种类有两个以上的，在分别描述后，包装件数总数单位要用 PACKAGES。如 25 cartons

40 bales

TTL 65 packages

※本案例制单：来证条款　　　　制单操作

GOODS:
5M/TONS SHANDONG BLACK DATES HIGH QUALITY AT HKD9230 PER M/TON
CIF PENANG INCOTERMS 2010 AS PER BUYER'S ORDER NO. SOO-6378

11. 包装类型及件数；商品编码；商品描述
Number and kind of Packages; Commodity No.; Commodity Description

SHANDONG BLACK DATES
HIGH QUALITY AS PER
BUYER'S ORDER NO. SOO-6378

13. 数量（Quantity）：商品数量仍属于货物描述的项目。数量须显示商品的正常数量，即数量的单位须与计价数量单位一致。譬如 1 000 打衬衫的单价为 EUR 20/DOZ, 则发票上记载的数量必须为 1 000DOZ, 而不能是 12 000PCS。

信用证中的数量、单价和金额三者中，ABOUT 修饰哪一项，该项才可有 10%的容差，并不是全部都同比例增减。以信用证方式结算，在大宗货物不以包装单位（BALE, CARTON, DRUM）和个体计数（PIECE, DOZEN）等表示数量时，允许货物有 5% 的溢短装。但并不意味着允许支取金额可以超过信用证金额；短装 5% 可以相应短支，不属不符点。

※本案例制单：来证条款　　　　制单操作

GOODS:
5M/TONS SHANDONG BLACK DATES HIGH QUALITY AT HKD9230 PER M/TON
CIF PENANG INCOTERMS 2010 AS PER BUYER'S ORDER NO. SOO-6378

12. 数量 Quantity	13. 单价 Unit Price	14. 金额 Amount
	CIF PENANG INCOTERMS 2010	
5 M/T	HKD9230.00	HKD46,150.00

14. 单价和金额（Unit Price, Amount）：商品价格和金额也属于货物描述的项目。信用证货物描述中的价格术语（PRICE TERMS）同样属于货物描述的一部分，要显示在发票中，并且价格术语的来源要与信用证相符。如来证规定 CIF HONGKONG INCOTERMS 2010，不能写成 INCOTERMS 2020，或仅写成 CIF HONGKONG, 或 CIF HONGKONG INCOTERMS。

如果信用证要求发票标明单价，则必须照办，即使通过总金额除以总量就能够得出平均单价也须如此。使用的币别须与信用证的一致，不得另外折算；金额须保留两位小数。

发票金额不得超过信用证规定的最大金额。如有溢短装，按允许的浮动范围增减。信用证项下，about 应理解为允许 10% 容差，非件杂货和不以包装为计量单位的大宗货物可自动享有 5% 溢短装。数量、单价和金额须显示在同一行。

信用证要求发票显示折扣或扣减，发票必须照做。发票还可以显示信用证未规定的涉及预付款或折扣及佣金等的扣减额。如果来证金额为已扣除佣金的净价 USD 30,118.50，发票上应显示含佣全价，并显示扣佣过程。这时，发票总额大于信用证金额，银行也是可以接受的，只要银行未对超额部分进行承兑或议付。例：

FOBC3 Shanghai USD 31,050.00
Less 3% Commission USD 931.50
FOB net USD 30,118.50

如果来证要求分列（breakdown or split of amount）FOB 价、运费、保费、佣金等，则须照办。例：

CIF ROTERDAM USD 20,500.00
LESS FREIGHT USD 2,200.00
PREMIUM USD 1,040.00
FOB USD 17,240.00

如系分批发货，一个批次的发票如果照抄信用证的全部货物描述及金额，然后再列明该批次装运的货物和金额，也是可以接受的。当然，也可以仅列本批次装运的货物细节。

※本案例制单：来证条款

GOODS:
5M/TONS SHANDONG BLACK DATES HIGH QUALITY AT HKD9230 PER M/TON
CIF PENANG INCOTERMS 2010 AS PER BUYER'S ORDER NO. SOO-6378

制单操作

12. 数量 Quantity	13. 单价 Unit Price	14. 金额 Amount
	CIF PENANG INCOTERMS 2010	
5 M/T	HKD9,230.00	HKD46,150.00

15. 金额大写（Amount in Words）：大写金额必须用文字表示，币别不能用代码，末尾须有 ONLY 字样。金额大写有零头的表示方法如下：USD816.75

1）Say U.S. Dollars eight hundred and sixteen and cents seventy-five only.

2）Say U.S. Dollars eight hundred and sixteen point seven five only.

3）Say U.S. Dollars eight hundred and sixteen and 75/100 or 75% only.

※本案例制单：来证条款

CCY / AMOUNT: HKD46, 150.00
AVAILABLE

制单操作

15. 总值（用数字和文字表示）Total Amount (in figure and word)

SAY H. K. DOLLARS FORTY-SIX THOUSAND ONE HUNDRED AND FIFTY ONLY.

16. 其他内容（Other Contents）：为体现发票的中心单据地位，发票上如果没有专门列出包装栏，则还须在空白处显示货物的外包装方法和包装件数的大小写，其大写末尾要有 ONLY 字样。如果来证包装条款里对包装材料有限制性定语，则须照打。如果货物是以重量计价的，还应显示总的毛净重；如果货物是以面积或体积计价的，还应显示总的面积或体积尺码，尽管可能信用证同时要求了 PACKING LIST, CERTIFICATE OF ORIGIN 等单据。

※本案例制单：来证条款　　　　制单操作

来证条款	制单操作
4) DOCUMENTS TO EVIDENCE THAT PACKING IN CARDBOARD CARTONS OF 25KGS NET OR	25 KGS NET PER CARTON SAY TWO HUNDRED (200) CARDBOARD CARTONS ONLY. TOTAL G. W. 5240. 00KGS　TOTAL N. W. 5000. 00KGS

17. 加注内容（Extra Notations）：在信用证项下，发票上还须在自由处置区（Free Disposal Zone）显示信用证要求额外注明的文句或内容。缮制发票时，应格外注意单据条款里和附加或特别条款里带有关键词 invoice 和 all documents 的条款对制单有些什么特别的或额外的要求。填写加注语句时，应注意改变动词的时态。

※本案例制单：来证条款　　　　制单操作

来证条款	制单操作
3) DOCUMENTS TO EVIDENCE THAT ALL PACKAGES BEAR SHIPPING MARKS: SHS / PENANG / 1-UP 4) DOCUMENTS TO EVIDENCE THAT PACKING IS DONE AS FOLLOWS: IN CARDBOARD CARTONS OF 25KGS NET OR 26.2KGS GROSS PER CARTON	Free Disposal Zone IT IS EVIDENCED THAT ALL PACKAGES BEAR SHIPPING MARKS: SHS/PENANG/1-UP PACKING IS DONE AS FOLLOWS: IN CARDBOARD CARTONS OF 25KGS NET EACH OR 26. 2KGS GROSS PER CARTON

本例来证在特别条款中的第 3 款和第 4 款里，都要求单据上要显示所操作的内容。这里的 documents 应理解为 all documents。

18. 签署（Signature）：发票无须签字。但信用证有签字要求，或发票上用了 certify 一词，则出单人应在正本上予以签字，可用图章。对 Manually Signed Invoice 或 Signed in ink 的要求，则必须手签。如来证规定："Facsimile signatures are acceptable only on duplicate of invoice." 模式印章只能用于副本发票上，正本发票必须手签（按签字式样制成的图章属于模式签字）。证实发票（Certified Invoice）必须签字，如果发票上印就了 E. & O.E.，则必须划掉。签署内容为出单人名称和授权人签字。

※本案例制单：来证条款　　　　制单操作

来证条款	制单操作
DOCUMENTS: + INVOICE IN TRIPLICATE	16. 出口商签章 Exporter's Stamp and Signature

19. 发票份数（Copies）：向银行交单时，务必备齐信用证要求的足量份数提交给银行。ONE INVOICE 或 INVOICE IN ONE COPY, 系正本。INVOICE IN 4 COPIES, 至少一份正本。ONE COPY OF INVOICE, 系一份副本，最好提交正本。如果只要求副本，来证则要明确规定。

没有签字的发票，应在其表面盖上 ORIGINAL（正本）印章或 COPY（副本）印章，以示单据的正副本区别。在校学习制单，交单份数应在单据外下方予以说明，表示完全理解。

※本案例制单：来证条款　　　　制单操作

来证条款	制单操作	
DOCUMENTS: + INVOICE IN TRIPLICATE	5000. 00KGS ORIGINAL	交单份数：一正两副

附商业发票制单样例

商业发票

Commercial Invoice

1. 出口商 Exporter SHANDONG HOPE NATIVE PRODUCT I/E CORP. 62, GUANGXI ROAD, QINGDAO, CHINA	4. 发票日期和发票号 Invoice Date and No. BP15SHS02INV1051 JUNE 28, 2015 5. 合同号 Contract No. ORDER NO.S00-6378 6. 信用证号 L/C No. PGH000348DC
2. 进口商 Importer SOO HUP SENG TRADING CO. SDN BHD. 165 1ST FLOOR, VICTORIA STREET, 10300 PENANG MALAYSIA	7. 原产地国 Country/Region of Origin CHINA 8. 贸易方式 Trade Mode GENERAL
3. 运输事项 Transport Details SHIPPED BY M/V "VICTORIA" FROM QINGDAO, CHINA TO PENANG	9. 交货和付款条款 Terms of Delivery and Payment BY L/C AT SIGHT

10. 运输标志和集装箱号 Shipment Marks; Container No.	11. 包装类型及件数；商品编码；商品描述 Number and Kind of Packages; Commodity No.; Commodity Description	12. 数量 Quantity	13. 单价 Unit Price	14. 金额 Amount
SHS PENANG 1-UP CONTAINER NO. EISU2628205	SHANDONG BLACK DATES HIGH QUALITY AS PER BUYER'S ORDER NO.SOO-6378 H.S.CODE NO. 0813403000020 25 KGS NET PER CARTON SAY TWO HUNDRED (200) CARDBOARD CARTONS ONLY. TOTAL G.W.5,240.00KGS TOTAL N.W.5,000.00KGS	CIP PENANG INCOTERMS 2010 5 M/T	HKD 9,230.00	KD 46,150.00

ORIGINAL

15. 总值（用数字和文字表示）Total Amount (in figure and word)

SAY H.K. DOLLARS FORTY-SIX THOUSAND ONE HUNDRED AND FIFTY ONLY.

Free Disposal Zone IT IS EVIDENCED THAT ALL PACKAGES BEAR SHIPPING MARKS: SHS/PENANG/1-UP PACKING IS DONE AS FOLLOWS: IN CARDBOARD CARTONS OF 25KGS NET EACH OR 26.2KGS GROSS PER CARTON	16. 出口商签章 Exporter's Stamp and Signature

交单份数：一正两副

相关知识

国际贸易中，发票的种类较多，除了商业发票，主要还有以下几种：

一、海关发票（Customs Invoice）

海关发票是根据某些进口国海关的规定，由出口商填制的一种由进口国海关统一制定并提供的特定格式的发票，其基本内容与普通商业发票类似，核心内容是证明商品的成本价值（Cost/Value of Goods）和证明商品的原生产国（Country of Origin），主要用于：

1. 进口国海关核定货物原产国和价值，以确定采用不同的国别政策，并计征进口关税款额。
2. 进口国海关据以判断是否有倾销行为，并确定是否征收反倾销税。
3. 进口国海关据以进行进口统计，便于政府制定国别贸易政策。
4. 进口商凭以向其海关办理进口报关和纳税等手续。

属于海关发票的单据名称较多，国外来证常见的海关发票名称有：

Customs Invoice

Appropriate Certified Customs Invoice

Invoice and Combined Certificate of Value and Origin

Certified Invoice in accordance with ×××（进口国名称）Customs Regulations

Signed Certificate of Value and Origin in Appropriate Form

Special Customs Invoice

二、领事发票（Consular Invoice）

领事发票是一些进口国驻出口国的领事馆提供并有领事签证的一种特别印就的发票，用于证明出口货物的原产地详细情况，防止外国商品可能出现的低价倾销，同时也可作为计征进口关税的依据。领事发票有其固定的格式，有些进口国也在商业发票上做领事签证。出口方填写并提交这种发票后，获取时需缴纳不低的签证费，且获取时间常常无法确定。如果进口方有此要求，一般都应婉拒，向其提供我国签发的原产地证书即可。

三、联合发票（Combined Invoice）

这是一种仅对港澳地区出口货物时习惯使用的发票，其内容集商业发票、装箱单、产地证和保险单信息为一体。

四、证实发票（Certified Invoice）

凡是在商业发票上使用了 certify 一词，就可称为证实发票。在这种发票上不得使用 E.&O.E.（错漏当查）字样。若发票上印就了该字样，则须划掉。证实发票必须签字。

五、厂商发票（Manufacturer's Invoice）

进口国为了确定出口商有无倾销行为，以便为了进行海关估价、核税和确定是否征收反倾销税，要求由货物的生产厂商出具销售货物的凭证。该发票上用本国货币计算货物的价格和价值，用来证明出口国国内市场的出厂价。

六、临时/形式发票（Provisional Invoice/Proforma Invoice）

这种被称为发票的单据尽管记载了商业发票所具有的所有信息，但并不能作为发票用于银行结算之用。出口商出具此单据仅供进口商向其本国政府申请外汇或许可证之用，所列的价格对进出口商均无最终约束力，它仅为一张估价单或意向书。如果双方在其上面签字认可，则可作为简式合约。

操作能力训练

思考题：

S5-1　商业发票的几个功能或作用是如何通过制单体现出来的，应承载哪些基本信息？

操作题：

C5-1　根据附录 3.1 里提供的制单信用证 3-13-2（见本书第 230 页），用发票格式二，独立缮制符合要求的商业发票。

C5-2　讨论和评讲后，根据附录 3.1 里的其余制单信用证（见本书第 230 页），采用相对应的发票格式，逐一缮制符合要求的商业发票。

C5-3　探索学习下一项目，并根据附录 3.1 里的制单信用证 3-13-1（见本书第 230 页），缮制符合要求的包装单据一份。

C5-4　独立学习 ISBP（2013 最新版本）和 UCP600 中关于包装单据的条款。

项目六

缮制包装单据

包装单据的含义及作用

包装单据（Packing Documents）是指一切记载或描述商品包装情况的单据。它既是商业发票的补充，又是一份独立文件，主要用于方便进口商对货物进行清点、仓储、运输、分销和转移单据等商业活动，商检和海关查验核对货物，以及办理索赔理赔公证之用。

学习目标

［知识目标］了解包装单据的分类，掌握包装单据的地位和作用，熟悉 UCP600 和 ISBP 中关于商品包装单据的条款，掌握缮制包装单据的要领。

［能力目标］能正确缮制信用证项下的包装单据和非信用证项下的包装单据。

项目描述（案例情境描述）

山东希望土产进出口公司向马来西亚出口一批山东黑枣，进口方通过银行开来信用证。出口方经审核无误后，开始缮制来证要求提供的全套单据。本次业务为缮制包装单据。

操作要领（缮制包装单据各栏的填制要求）

包装单据并无统一格式，但必须能够让其发挥出专门单据的功能。为了规范起见，国际商会还是推荐了标准格式。本案采用了这一推荐格式的包装单据，即装箱单。

1. 文件名称（Title of Document）：缮制向银行提交的包装单据名称必须与买方开来的信用证要求严格一致。如果来证要求提交 Weight Memo，就不能提交 Weight List。

※本案例制单：　来证条款　　　　　　　　　　　　　　　　　制单操作

+ WEIGHT LIST IN TRIPLICATE TO
AND EXP COMMODITY INSPECTI

重量单
Weight List
3.装箱单日期和

2. 出单人（Issuer, From, Exporter, Seller）：此栏应与发票一致，填写信用证受益人名称和地址，除非来证另有规定，可转让信用证除外。若非信用证结算，则填写合同的卖方。事实上，银行也可接受没有显示发货人（特别是不显示地址）的包装单据，尤其是当信用证要求提交中性包装单（Neutral Packing List）时，不能显示发货人、单据签发人和产地。因为这样可以更方便进口方转移单据，而不会暴露供货方的信息，从而保护自己的商业利益。如果包装单据上注明了出口方和地址，买方在转移单据时通常还需要另外出单，或遮盖出口方信息复印单据。同样道理，包装单据上不显示货物单价和金额，也不必显示运输细节或路线。

※本案例制单：　来证条款　　　　　　　　　　　　　　　　　制单操作

1.出口商 Exporter
SHANDONG HOPE NATIVE PRODUCT I/E CORP.
62, GUANGXI ROAD, QINGDAO, CHINA

3. 抬头人（To, Importer, Buyer）：此栏应与发票一致，填写信用证申请人名称和地址。若非信用证结算，则填写合同的买方。事实上，银行也可接受没有显示抬头人的包装单据，因为包装单据是发票的补充或附属单据，通常与发票同时使用。再者，这样可以更方便单据多次转移，而不暴露前手（中间卖方）的信息，从而保护最终卖方自己的商业利益。

※本案例制单：　来证条款　　　　　　　　　　　　　　　　　制单操作

2.进口商 Importer
SOO HUP SENG TRADING CO. SDN BHD.
165 1ST FLOOR, VICTORIA STREET,
10300 PENANG MALAYSIA

4. 单据号码和日期（No. and Date）：每种单据都必须显示自己的日期和编号，包装单据可以有自己的日期和编号。为便于管理，包装单据的号码和日期一般都与发票的保持一致。

※本案例制单：　来证条款　　　　　　　　　　　　　　　　　制单操作

3.装箱单日期和号码 Packing List Date and No.
BP13SHS02INV1051　JUNE 28, 2015

5. 合同号和信用证号(S/C No., L/C No.)：为了便于管理和提高工作效率，包装单据上也可以显示合同号和信用证号，应与发票上的一致。

※本案例制单：　来证条款　　　　　　　　　　　　　　　　制单操作

4.合同号 Contract No.	5.信用证号 L/C No.
ORDER NO. S00-6378	PGH000348DC

6. 发票日期和号码（Invoice Date and No.）：发票日期和号码在此仅为参考号，主要是为了在包装单据和日期与发票不一致时，能方便管理，提高工作效率。

※本案例制单：　来证条款　　　　　　　　　　　　　　　　制单操作

6.发票日期和发票号 Invoice Date and No.
BP15SHS02INV1051　JUNE 28, 2015

7. 运输标志（Shipping Marks）：包装单据的运输标志须与发票上的唛头一致。缮制方法参照发票里的制单要求。

※本案例制单：　来证条款　　　　　　　　　　　　　　　　制单操作

3) DOCUMENTS TO EVIDENCE THAT ALL PACKAGES BEAR SHIPPING MARKS: SHS / PENANG / 1-UP

7.运输标志和集装箱号
Shipment Marks: Container No.

SHS　　　　　　SHAND
PENANG　　　　1 — 2
1 —UP
　　　　　　　　25KG N
CONTAINER NO.　　TTL: T
EISU2628205

8. 货物描述和包装数量（Description of Goods, Number and Kind of Package）：此栏的货物描述不必像发票那样全面，可用货名统称，但不得引起歧义，一般都使用跟发票一致的品名。散装货物须注明 IN BULK。如果一票货有多个品种的，应分列各款货物的细节，譬如货号及其商品数量，并与发票一致。一般来说，还应在货号前注明该款货的外包装序号或序号段及包装数量和种类。这些数据应放在同一行。如果有两种以上的包装种类，显示方法按发票里的要求操作。

※本案例制单：　来证条款　　　　　　　　　　　　　　　　制单操作

r No.　8.包装类型及件数；商品编码；商品描述
Number and kind of Packages; Commodity No.;
Commodity Description

SHANDONG BLACK DATES　　　TARE WEIGHT
1 - 200　200CTN　　5 M/T　　240KG

9. 毛重、净重和体积（Gross Weight, Net Weight and Measurement）：这些栏目里的数据应显示商品或各品种的毛重、净重和体积和全部货物的合计总数据。如果货物数量单位是重量，还应显示皮重。重量单位为千克（kg），保留两位小数；体积单位为立方米（M^3/CBM），各品种保留四位小数，合计总体积保留三位小数。所有数据都须与发票保持一致。

※本案例制单：　　来证条款　　　　　　　　　　　　　　　　　　　　　　　　制单操作

编码； ckages; modity	9. 毛重kg Gross Weight	10. 净重kg Net Weight	11. 体积M³ Cubic Meters
TARE WEIGHT 240kG	5,240.00	5,000.00	14.850

10. 包装方法和外包装数量（Packing and Packages）：包装单据内容必须充分体现包装单据功能和信用证的特殊要求，应能显示详细的装箱细节，发挥专业单据功能。因此，除了显示前述信息外，譬如不同货号的外包装编号和包装数量，各货号总的毛重、净重、皮重和体积，还应显示货物的详细的包装方法，包括内包装（小包装）的细节。

包装单据还须显示外包装数量的大小写，该信息不容修改且须与发票保持一致。

※本案例制单：　　来证条款　　　　　　　　　　　　　　　　　　　　　　　　制单操作

25KG NET PER CARTON LINED WITH POLYBAG WITH SMALL HOLES

NO.　　TTL: TWO HUNDRED (200) CARDBOARD CARTONS ONLY.

11. 各品种单件包装的信息（Message of Each Item and Package）：为体现专业单据的功能，包装单据还需显示各货号每个外包装的毛重、净重和体积。这些信息既可单独分列，也可放在分列的各品种总的毛重、净重和体积前面，用斜线区别开。两种具体方法如下：

（1）在单据空白处单独分列

EACH ITEM/PACKAGE:	G.W.	N.W.	MEAS.
ITEM 1	××××kg	××××kg	×××.×××m³
ITEM 2	××××kg	××××kg	×××.×××m³

（2）在各品种的细节描述中显示（在分总毛净重和体积前面或上面显示单件信息）

商品 COMM/ITEM	数量 QTY	毛重 G.W. (kg)	净重 N.W. (kg)	体积 MEAS. (m³)
COMM				
ITEM 1	×××	@××/××××	@××/××××	@××/××××
ITEM 2	×××	@××/××××	@××/××××	@××/××××

※本案例制单：　　来证条款　　　　　　　　　　　　　　　　　　　　　　　　制单操作

EACH ITEM / PACKAGE:	G.W.	N.W.	MEASUREMENT
SHANDONG BLACK DATES	26.2KG	25.0KG	0.07425M³

为了便于进口方精准计算派去码头仓库接货的货车数量（货车大小不等）以及计算租用仓库堆放货物的面积，为对方提供优质服务，需要在单个包装尺码的上面或下面括

号注明外包装的长宽高尺寸。

12. 声明（Declaration）：包装单据名称如果冠以重量单（WEIGHT LIST）或重量证明（CERTIFICATE OF WEIGHT），还应加注以下的声明句子："WE CERTIFY THAT THE ABOVE WEIGHTS OR CONTENTS ARE TRUE AND CORRECT."。

※本案例制单：　　来证条款　　　　制单操作

WE CERTIFY THAT THE ABOVE WEIGHTS OR CONTENTS ARE TRUE AND CORRECT.

13. 加注内容（Extra Notations）：如果来证要求包装单据上额外注明一些文句或内容，须按要求在自由处置区（Free Disposal Zone）显示。缮制包装单据时，应格外注意单据条款里和附加或特别条款里带有关键词 packing 和 all documents 的条款对制单有些什么特别的或额外的要求。填写加注语句时，应注意改变动词的时态。

※本案例制单：　　来证条款　　　　制单操作

来证条款：

COMMODITY INSPECTION BUREAU OF THE PEOPLE'S REPUBLIC OF CHINA TO STATE THAT GOODS ARE PACKED IN 25KGS NET OR 26.2KGS GROSS PER CARTON REQUIRED.

3) DOCUMENTS TO EVIDENCE THAT ALL PACKAGES BEAR SHIPPING MARKS: SHS/PENANG/1-UP

4) DOCUMENTS TO EVIDENCE THAT PACKING IS DONE AS FOLLOWS:
IN CARDBOARD CARTONS OF 25KGS NET OR 26.2KGS GROSS PER CARTON

制单操作：

IT IS STATED THAT GOODS ARE PACKED IN 25KGS NET OR 26. 2KGS GROSS PER CARTON.

ORIGINAL

Free Disposal Zone

IT IS EVIDENCED THAT ALL PACKAGES BEAR SHIPPING MARKS: SHS/PENANG/1-UP

PACKING IS DONE AS FOLLOWS:
IN CARDBOARD CARTONS OF 25KGS NET EACH OR 26. 2KGS GROSS PER CARTON

14. 签署（Signature）：包装单据无须签字，特别是当来证要求中性包装（Neutral packing）或规定中性包装单（"in white paper" or "in plain"）时。只有当来证要求签字，则须按信用证要求签字。如果单据名称冠以重量证明（CERTIFICATE OF WEIGHT），或凡是用了 certificate 或 certify 一词，单据须经出单人签字且加注日期，才符合信用证相关的规定。签字方法与发票相同。

※本案例制单：　　来证条款　　　　制单操作

来证条款：

+ SIGNED WEIGHT LIST IN TRIPLICATE I

制单操作：

12. 出口商签章　Exporter's Stamp and Signature

SHANDONG HOPE NATIVE PRODUCT I/E CORP.

×××

15. 单据份数（Copies）：向银行交单时，务必备齐信用证要求的足量份数提交给银行，其中至少一份正本。在校学习制单，交单份数应在单据外下方予以说明，表示对条款完全理解。

※本案例制单：　　来证条款　　　　制单操作

来证条款：

+ SIGNED WEIGHT LIST IN TRIPLICATE I

制单操作：

交单份数：一正两副

附重量单制单样例

重　量　单
Weight List

1. 出口商 Exporter SHANDONG HOPE NATIVE PRODUCT I/E CORP. 62, GUANGXI ROAD, QINGDAO, CHINA	3. 装箱单日期和号码 Packing List Date and No. BP13SHS02INV1051　JUNE 28, 2015
2. 进口商 Importer SOO HUP SENG TRADING CO. SDN BHD. 165 1ST FLOOR, VICTORIA STREET, 10300 PENANG MALAYSIA	4. 合同号 Contract No. ORDER NO.S00-6378 5. 信用证号 L/C No. PGH000348DC 6. 发票日期和发票号 Invoice Date and No. BP15SHS02INV1051　JUNE 28, 2015

7. 运输标志和集装箱号 Shipment Marks; Container No.	8. 包装类型及件数；商品编码；商品描述 Number and Kind of Packages; Commodity No.; Commodity Description	9. 毛重 kg Gross Weight	10. 净重 kg Net Weight	11. 体积 m³ Cubic Meters
SHS PENANG 1-UP	SHANDONG BLACK DATES　TARE WEIGHT 1 - 200　200CTN　5 M/T　240kg	5,240.00	5,000.00	14.850

25KG NET PER CARTON LINED WITH POLYBAG WITH SMALL HOLES

TTL：TWO HUNDRED (200) CARDBOARD CARTONS ONLY.

CONTAINER NO.
EISU2628205

EACH ITEM/PACKAGE：	G.W.	N.W.	MEASUREMENT
SHANDONG BLACK DATES	26.2kg	25.0kg	0.074,25m³

WE CERTIFY THAT THE ABOVE WEIGHTS OR CONTENTS ARE TRUE AND CORRECT.
IT IS STATED THAT GOODS ARE PACKED IN 25KGS NET OR 26.2KGS GROSS PER CARTON.

ORIGINAL

Free Disposal Zone IT IS EVIDENCED THAT ALL PACKAGES BEAR SHIPPING MARKS: SHS/PENANG/1-UP PACKING IS DONE AS FOLLOWS： IN CARDBOARD CARTONS OF 25KGS NET EACH OR 26.2KGS GROSS PER CARTON	12. 出口商签章　Exporter's Stamp and Signature SHANDONG HOPE NATIVE PRODUCT I/E CORP. ×××

交单份数：一正两副

相关知识

在国际贸易中，常见的包装单据有如下几种，最常见的当然是装箱单：

1. 重量单/重量证明（Weight List/Weight Certificate），用于记录以重量为单位的货物包装情况。

2. 磅码单（Weight Memo），用于包装方法并不统一，或外包装重量各异的货物包装详情描述，逐件列明。

3. 尺码单（Measurement List），用于以面积、体积等为单位的货物包装详情记录。

4. 装箱单（Packing List），用于记录以个数为单位的件杂货物或以包装为单位的货物包装情况。

5. 规格单/花色搭配单（Specification List/Assortment List），用以侧重说明包装货物的规格、型号、花色搭配等情况。

6. 包装明细单/包装提要（Packing Specification/Packing Summary），用途与装箱单差不多。

操作能力训练

思考题：

S6-1 包装单据是怎样发挥出自身功能的，应承载哪些基本信息？

操作题：

C6-1 独立学习 ISBP（2013 最新版本）和 UCP600 中关于包装单据的条款。

C6-2 根据附录 3.1 里提供的制单信用证 3-13-2（见本书第 230 页），用包装单据格式二，独立缮制符合要求的包装单据。

C6-3 讨论和评讲后，根据附录 3.1 里的其余制单信用证（见本书第 230 页），用相对应的单据格式，逐一缮制符合要求的包装单据。

C6-4 探索学习下一项目，并根据附录 3.1 里的制单信用证 3-13-1（见本书第 230 页），缮制符合要求的报检单。

项目七

缮制出境货物报检单

报检单的作用

报检单是我国进出口货物报关前向海关申报货物和运载工具检验检疫的必要单据。虽然它不是银行结算单据，但报检单填写准确与否直接关系到货物能否按时、顺利通关和装运。同时，由海关签发的检验证书还是索赔理赔的依据之一。

进出口企业可以自理报检，也可委托第三方（货代公司）报检。

学习目标

［知识目标］熟悉报检流程，熟悉各种商检证书以及通关单据的用途，掌握报检时限规定。

［能力目标］能根据具体信用证/合同条款，实际的货物资料，准确缮制出境货物报检单以及正确填报报检委托书。

项目描述（案例情境描述）

2015年6月29日，山东希望土产进出口公司外贸单证员唐欣收到青岛顺风物流公司的通知：

"已按照贵公司要求订妥舱位，2015年7月5日船期，船名VICTORIA，航次866S，1个20英尺集装箱整箱。"

黑枣HS编码0813403000020，监管条件A/B[①]，即需要进行出境货物检验检疫申报，

① 监管条件：A：入境货物通关单；B：出境货物通关单。

检验检疫类别为 P/Q，R/S[①]，属于法定检验检疫商品。所以唐欣根据商业发票、重量单和信用证的相关检验条款的要求（自行查看信用证），于 6 月 29 日向青岛海关申报商检。本次业务为缮制出口货物报检单，该单据属于非结算单据。

附制单补充资料：

（1）山东希望土产进出口公司报检登记注册号：3700745016

（2）黑枣供货工厂卫生注册证号：3700/16088

（3）Container No. EISU2628205

（4）黑枣 HS 编码：0813403000020

操作要领

（一）出境货物报检单各栏目的填制要求

目前报检采用的软件系统一般为榕基软件或九城软件，通过登录电子报检系统填报出境货物报检单，具体各栏目填制要求如下：

1. 编号：该编号无须填写，是由系统自动生成的 15 位报检号。

2. 报检单位：填写自理/代理报检单位的中文全称，并加盖与名称一致的公章。

※本案例制单：

制单操作

报检单位（加盖公章）： 山东希望土产进出口公司

3. 报检单位登记号：填写自理/代理报检单位在检验检疫机构备案登记/注册登记的 10 位数代码。

※本案例制单：

制单操作

报检单位登记号： 3700745016

4. 报检日期：检验检疫机构实际受理的报检日期。直通式报检为系统通过机审自动生成正式报检号的日期。非直通式是受理报检的日期，而非申请人制作报检单据的日期。

※本案例制单：

制单操作

报检日期： 2015 年 6 月 29 日

5. 联系人和电话：填写报检人员的姓名以及联系电话。

※本案例制单：

制单操作

联系人： 唐欣 电话：0532-32564800

6. 发货人：填写外销合同中卖方的全称（中英文）。

※本案例制单：

制单操作

发货人	（中文）	山东希望土产进出口公司
	（外文）	SHANDONG HOPE NATIVE PRODUCT I/E CORP.

① 检验检疫类别：P：进境动植物、动植物产品检疫；Q：出境动植物、动植物产品检疫；R：进口食品卫生监督检查；S：出口食品卫生监督检查。

7. 收货人：填写外销合同的买方。没有相应翻译名称的，中文栏输入“***”。

※本案例制单：　　　　制单操作

收货人	（中文）	***
	（外文）	SOO HUP SENG TRADING CO. SDN BHD.

8. 货物中英文名称：填写货物的具体中文名称，不能笼统地输入货物的大类名称。填写准确的英文名称，须和外销合同、发票一致，且与中文货物名称相符。

※本案例制单：　发票项目描述　　　　制单操作

11.包装类型及件数；商品编码；商品描述 Number and kind of Packages; Commodity No.; Commodity Description
SHANDONG BLACK DATES

货物名称(中/外文)
山东黑枣 SHANDONG BLACK DATES

9. H.S. 编码：填写有效的 13 位数 H.S. 编码（以当年海关公布的商品税则编码分类为准）。H.S. 编码应与货物相对应，并与报关时的 H.S. 编码一致（商品编码由 10 至 13 位数组成，只有当商品需要检验检疫时，比如法定检验商品和进口商有商检要求的，商品编号才采用 13 位数）。

※本案例制单：　　　　制单操作

H.S.编码
0813403000020

10. 产地：填写具体准确的产地，应具体到县市、区级，并能明确区分不同的检验检疫机构辖区。

※本案例制单：　　　　制单操作

产地
青岛

11. 数/重量：根据包装单据填写相应的数量和重量。与法定第一计量单位对应的数量或重量必须填写，并且不得改动法定第一计量单位。如法定第一计量单位是“米”，则不得填入“码”。本业务项下商品的法定第一计量单位为“千克”。

※本案例制单：包装单项目描述　　　　制单操作

10.净重 kg Net Weight
5,000.00

数/重量
5 000 千克

12. 货物总值：按照发票、合同的货物总值填写。

※本案例制单：　发票项目描述　　　　制单操作

14.金额 Amount
HKD46,150.00

货物总值
46,150.00 港元

13. 包装种类/数量：填入货物实际运输包装的种类及数量。包装种类必须明确具体，不能只填箱、袋等笼统类别。要明确是哪种质地，箱是木箱、纸箱还是其他箱；袋是麻袋、编织袋还是其他袋。有两种以上包装的，应添加辅助包装；同时有木质包装和其他包装的，应将非木质包装填入为辅助包装。

※本案例制单：　　制单操作

包装种类及数量
200 纸箱

14. 运输工具名称号码：填写运输工具名称。报检时如已确定运输工具名称号码的，可直接填入名称和号码；若未确定运输工具的名称及号码时，可以笼统地填制运输方式总称，如填报“水路运输”或“船舶”“飞机”等。

※本案例制单：　　制单操作

运输工具名称号码	M/V "VICTORIA"

15. 贸易方式：填写与实际情况一致的贸易方式，如一般贸易、来料加工、进料加工、补偿贸易等。特殊贸易方式的，必须准确、完整填写，如退运货物、保税区进出境、仓储货物等。

※本案例制单：　　制单操作

贸易方式	一般贸易

16. 货物存放地点：本栏关系到是否属于接受报检的检验检疫机构受理该批货物报检和对其实施检验检疫的区域，应按货物实际的具体存放地点填制（可具体到街道，不能采用类似“本公司仓库”等表达方式）。

※本案例制单：　　制单操作

货物存放地点	青岛市广西路 62 号

17. 合同号：填写对外贸易合同、订单的号码。企业未签订合同的，应在此注明无合同及原因，如“长期客户无合同”。

※本案例制单：　　制单操作

合同号	S00-6378

18. 信用证号：以信用证方式结算的，填写准确的信用证号码。以其他方式结汇的，填写具体的结汇方式。

※本案例制单：　　制单操作

信用证号	PGH000348DC

19. 用途：选择准确的产品用途。共有九个选项：种用或繁殖、食用、奶用、观赏或演艺、伴侣动物、试验、药用、饲用、其他。

※本案例制单：　　制单操作

用途	食用

20. 发货日期：若在订舱后报检，填写承运人通知的确定的装载运输工具的日期。若在订舱前报检，则填写信用证或合同规定的最晚装运日期。否则按实际开船日或起飞

日填写。

※本案例制单：　　制单操作

发货日期	2015.07.05

21. 输往国家（地区）：填写该批货物最终的目的国家或地区。输往保税区或加工区的，直接填入保税区或加工区。

※本案例制单：　　制单操作

输往国家(地区)	马来西亚

22. 许可证/审批号：属于两证管理、检疫注册登记、备案以及其他许可证、审批管理的，输入相应的证书号码。无许可证或审批文件的出境货物本栏目免于填报。本业务项下商品为食品，海关对食品企业实施备案管理，故而本业务项下该栏目应输入食品生产企业的备案证明编号。

※本案例制单：　　制单操作

许可证 / 审批号	3700/16088

23. 启运地：填写装运本批货物的运输工具的启运地点，填写装载本批货物的运输工具出境所经过的口岸名称或该口岸所在城市名称。

※本案例制单：　　制单操作

启运地	青岛

24. 到达口岸：填写输往国家的具体口岸。输往保税区或加工区的，直接填写保税区或加工区名称。

※本案例制单：　　制单操作

到达口岸	槟城（马来西亚）

25. 生产单位注册号：填写生产单位在海关注册登记的10位数代码。如发货人和生产单位不一致时，不得填写发货人的登记代码。暂未登记的可填“***”；对特殊情况确实无法填写生产单位备案登记代码的，如市场采购、伴侣动物、个人携带物等，应填写特殊单位代码（四位局机构代码+000000），并注明原因。

※本案例制单：　　制单操作

生产单位注册号	3700745016

26. 集装箱规格、数量及号码：以集装箱装运的货物，填写准确的集装箱信息。集装箱号码报检时未确定的，可在“号码”一栏记载“***”。拼箱的，应在号码栏注明“拼箱”。填写集装箱号码时，多个集装箱号码以“/”分隔。属非集装箱装载的（包括散货入仓），本栏记载“***”。

※本案例制单：　　制单操作

集装箱规格、数量及号码	20' x 1　EISU2628205

27. 合同、信用证订立的检验检疫条款或特殊要求：填写合同、信用证中与检验检疫有关的特殊要求或检验检疫机构要求在此栏填写的内容。如没有特殊要求，记载“***”。

※本案例制单： 来证条款 制单操作

3) DOCUMENTS TO EVIDENCE THAT ALL PACKAGES BEAR SHIPPING MARKS: SHS / PENANG / 1-UP
4) DOCUMENTS TO EVIDENCE THAT PACKING IS DONE AS FOLLOWS:
IN CARDBOARD CARTONS OF 25KGS NET OR 26.2KGS GROSS PER CARTON

合同、信用证订立的检验检疫条款或特殊要求
请在品质证书中加注： IT IS EVIDENCED THAT ALL PACKAGES BEAR SHIPPING MARKS: SHS/PENANG/1-UP PACKING IS DONE AS FOLLOWS: IN CARDBOARD CARTONS OF 25KGS NET OR 26.2KGS GROSS PER CARTON

28. 标记及号码：根据实际合同、发票等填写，如果没有唛头的，填写“N/M”，不可以留空。

※本案例制单： 发票项目描述 制单操作

10. 运输标志和集装箱号 Shipment Marks; Container No.
SHS PENANG 1-UP

标 记 及 号 码
SHS PENANG 1-UP

29. 随附单据（划“√”或补填）：选择检验检疫机构要求提交的单据。

※本案例制单： 制单操作

随附单据（划“✓”或补填）	
☑合同	☑包装性能结果单
☑信用证	☐许可/审批文件
☑发票	☐
☐换证凭单	☐
☑装箱单	☐
☑厂检单	☐

30. 需要证单名称（划“√”或补填）：根据信用证或买方具体要求，勾选所需单证名称。

※本案例制单： 制单操作

需要证单名称（划“✓”或补填）			
☑品质证书	_1_正_2_副	☐动物卫生证书	__正__副
☐重量证书	__正__副	☐植物检疫证书	__正__副
☐数量证书	__正__副	☐熏蒸/消毒证书	__正__副
☐兽医卫生证书	__正__副	☐出境货物换证凭单	__正__副
☐健康证书	__正__副	☐出境货物通关单	__正__副
☐卫生证书	__正__副	☐	

31. 检验检疫费用：本栏目由检验检疫机构计费人员核定费用后填写。

32. 报检人郑重声明：本栏目由报检人员签署名字，必须手签。

※本案例制单：

制单操作

报检人郑重声明：
　1. 本人被授权报检。
　2. 上列填写内容正确属实，货物无伪造或冒用他人的厂名、标志、认证标志，并承担货物质量责任。
　　　　　　　　　　签名：唐欣

33. 领取证单：本栏目由报检人员在领取证单时填写领证日期和领证人签名（手签）。

附出境货物报检单制单样例：

	中华人民共和国海关 出境货物检验检疫申请				583000002069835
报检单位（加盖公章）：	山东希望土产进出口公司			*编　号	583000002069835
报检单位登记号：3700745016	联系人：唐欣	电话：0532-32564800		报检日期：2015 年 6 月 29 日	
发货人（中文）	山东希望土产进出口公司				
发货人（外文）	SHANDONG HOPE NATIVE PRODUCT I/E CORP.				
收货人（中文）	***				
收货人（外文）	SOO HUP SENG TRADING CO. SDN BHD.				
货物名称（中/外文）	H.S. 编码	产地	数/重量	货物总值	包装种类及数量
山东黑枣 SHANDONG BLACK DATES	0813403000020	青岛	5,000 千克	46,150.00 港元	200 纸箱
运输工具名称号码	M/V “VICTORIA”	贸易方式	一般贸易	货物存放地点	青岛市广西路 62 号
合同号	S00-6378	信用证号	PGH000348DC	用途	食用
发货日期	2015.07.05	输往国家（地区）	马来西亚	许可证 / 审批号	3700/16088
启运地	青岛	到达口岸	槟城（马来西亚）	生产单位注册号	3700745016
集装箱规格、数量及号码	20’ x 1　EISU2628205				

（续表）

<table>
<tr><td>合同、信用证订立的检验检疫条款或特殊要求</td><td>标 记 及 号 码</td><td colspan="2">随附单据（划“✓”或补填）</td></tr>
<tr><td>请在品质证书中加注：
IT IS EVIDENCED THAT ALL PACKAGES BEAR SHIPPING MARKS: SHS/PENANG/1-UP

PACKING IS DONE AS FOLLOWS:
IN CARDBOARD CARTONS OF 25KGS NET OR 26.2KGS GROSS PER CARTON</td><td>SHS
PENANG
1-UP</td><td>☑合同
☑信用证
☑发票
☐换证凭单
☑装箱单
☑厂检单</td><td>☑包装性能结果单
☐许可/审批文件
☐
☐
☐</td></tr>
</table>

<table>
<tr><td colspan="2">需要证单名称（划“✓”或补填）</td><td colspan="2">*检验检疫费</td></tr>
<tr><td rowspan="3">☑品质证书 _1_正_2_副
☐重量证书 __正__副
☐数量证书 __正__副
☐兽医卫生证书 __正__副
☐健康证书 __正__副
☐卫生证书 __正__副
☐动物卫生证书 __正__副</td><td rowspan="3">☐植物检疫证书 __正__副
☐熏蒸/消毒证书 __正__副
☐出境货物换证凭单 __正__副
☐出境货物检验检疫工作联系单 __正__副

☑电子底账</td><td>总金额（人民币元）</td><td></td></tr>
<tr><td>计费人</td><td></td></tr>
<tr><td>收费人</td><td></td></tr>
</table>

<table>
<tr><td rowspan="3">报检人郑重声明：
1. 本人被授权报检。
2. 上列填写内容正确属实，货物无伪造或冒用他人的厂名、标志、认证标志，并承担货物质量责任。
签名：<u>唐欣</u></td><td colspan="2">领 取 证 单</td></tr>
<tr><td>日期</td><td></td></tr>
<tr><td>签名</td><td></td></tr>
<tr><td>注：有“*”号栏由出入境检验检疫机关填写</td><td colspan="2">◆国家出入境检验检疫局制</td></tr>
<tr><td></td><td colspan="2">[1-2 (2000.1.1)]</td></tr>
</table>

（二）品质证书的缮制要点

本业务项下商品山东黑枣属于法定检验货物，出口商除了按照法律法规的规定如实申报出口检验检疫外，按照信用证相关条款的规定，还需要向检验检疫机构申请签发《品质证书》，在上述的报检单中已经表达了这种意愿，并在所需证单中勾选了该证书。

《品质证书》是由检验检疫机构签发的官方单据，由检验检疫机构根据检验检疫法规和报检人的具体要求填制。附品质证书制单样例。

中华人民共和国出入境检验检疫

ENTRY-EXIT INSPECTION AND QUARANTINE OF THE PEOPLE'S REPUBLIC OF CHINA

编　号 No.: 3700256410

品质证书

QUALITY CERTIFICATE

发货人
Consignor　SHANDONG HOPE NATIVE PRODUCT I/E CORP.

收货人
Consignee　SOO HUP SENG TRADING CO. SDN BHD.

品名
Description of Goods　SHANDONG BLACK DATES

报检数量/重量
Quantity/Weight Declared　5,000KGS

包装种类及数量
Number and Type of Packages　200 CTNS

运输工具
Means of Conveyance　BY SEA

标记及号码
Mark & No.

SHS
PENANG
1-UP

RESULTS OF INSPECTION:

THE CHEMICAL ADDICTIVES ARE NOT FOUND IN THE SAMPLES WHICH ARE DRAWN FROM THE WHOLE LOT OF GOODS (LOT NO. 15–50).

CONCLUSION: THE ABOVE RESULTS OF INSPECTION ARE IN CONFORMITY WITH THE REQUIREMENTS OF STANDARD Q/GNF002S FOR THE GOODS.

IT IS EVIDENCED THAT ALL PACKAGES BEAR SHIPPING MARKS: SHS/PENANG/1-UP, PACKING IS DONE AS FOLLOWS: IN CARDBOARD CARTONS OF 25KGS NET OR 26.2KGS GROSS PER CARTON.

印章　签证地点 Place of Issue QINGDAO, CHINA　签证日期 Date of Issue JULY 3, 2015

Official Stamp

授权签字人 Authorized Officer 周宏明　签　名 Signature 周宏明　（手签）

相关知识

一、一般出入境货物报检知识

（一）报检的含义

出入境商品报检是指进出口商品的收发货人或其代理人根据《中华人民共和国进出口商品检验法》及其实施条例等有关法律、行政法规的规定，在检验检疫机构规定的地点和期限内向出入境检验检疫机构申请对其进出口商品实施法定检验的程序。

（二）报检的范围与时限

1. 报检的范围

国家出入境检验检疫部门对进出口商品实施法定检验检疫的范围：

（1）列入《出入境检验检疫机构实施检验检疫的进出境商品目录》（简称《检验检疫商品目录》）。

（2）《中华人民共和国食品卫生法（试行）》规定，应实施卫生检验检疫的进出口食品。

（3）《中华人民共和国进出境动植物检疫法》规定，应实施检疫的进出口动植物及其产品。

（4）危险货物的包装容器、危险货物运输设备和工具的安全技术条件的性能和使用鉴定。

（5）装运易腐烂变质食品、冷冻品的船舱、货仓、车厢和集装箱等运载工具。

（6）国家其他有关法律、法规和有关国际条约规定须经出入境检验检疫机构检验的进出口商品、物品、动植物等。

2. 报检的时限和地点

出境货物最迟应在出口报关或装运前 7 天报检，对于个别检验检疫周期较长的货物，应留有相应的检验检疫时间。需要隔离检疫的出境动物在出境前 60 天预报，隔离前 7 天报检。法定检验检疫货物，除去活动物在口岸检验检疫外，其他货物原则上在产地进行检验检疫。

入境的一般货物或运输工具及人员，应在入境前或入境时向入境口岸、指定的或到达地的检验检疫机构报检；输入微生物、人体组织、生物制品、血液及其制品或种畜、禽及其精液、胚胎、受精卵的，应在入境前 30 天报检；输入其他动物的，应在入境前 15 天报检；输入植物、种子、种苗及其他繁殖材料的，应在入境前 7 天报检。入境卸货有破损或短缺的商品、大宗散装商品、易腐烂变质商品、废旧品，在卸货口岸检验检疫机构报检，其他入境货物，在入境前或入境时向报关地的检验检疫机构报检。

（三）报检的一般程序

我国实行先检验检疫，后通关放行的检验制度。出入境报检流程如图 7-1 所示：

报检/申报（报检单位）	报检单位按有关法律等规定向检验检疫机构报检或申报。第一步进行电子申报，机审无误后进行第二步人工交单，检验检疫工作人员审核无误后方可受理报检。
抽样/采样（检验检疫人员）	检验检疫人员对报检货物进行检验检疫，判定其是否符合有关强制性标准、合同或进口国官方机构的有关规定。
检验检疫（检验检疫人员）	检验检疫人员对报检货物进行现场抽（采）样品，而后进行相关检验。
卫生除害处理（检验检疫人员）	检验检疫人员按照相关法律及其实施条例的规定，对有关出入境货物、动植物、运输工具、交通工具等实施出入境卫生除害处理。
计收费（相关工作人员）	检验检疫机构工作人员依据有关规定受理报检企业计费并收取费用。
签证放行	检验检疫机构对检验检疫合格的出入境货物签发通关单，作为通关依据；对检验检疫不合格的出入境货物出具不合格通知书。对入境货物经除害处理或检验检疫后签发入境货物通关单或入境货物检验检疫证明；不合格的签发检验检疫证书，供有关方面对外索赔。

图 7-1　出入境报检流程

（四）电子申报流程

涉检的出境货物可向海关业务主管部门进行出境检验检疫数据申请。出境检验检疫申请审核通过之后即电子底账，可以在出口报关单申报时被调用。目前大多数企业都是通过“中国国际贸易单一窗口（http://new.singlewindow.cn）”进行申报。

具体操作步骤如下所示：

Step 1：登录“中国国际贸易单一窗口”

Step 2：点击进入“货物申报—出口整合申报—出境检验检疫申请”。

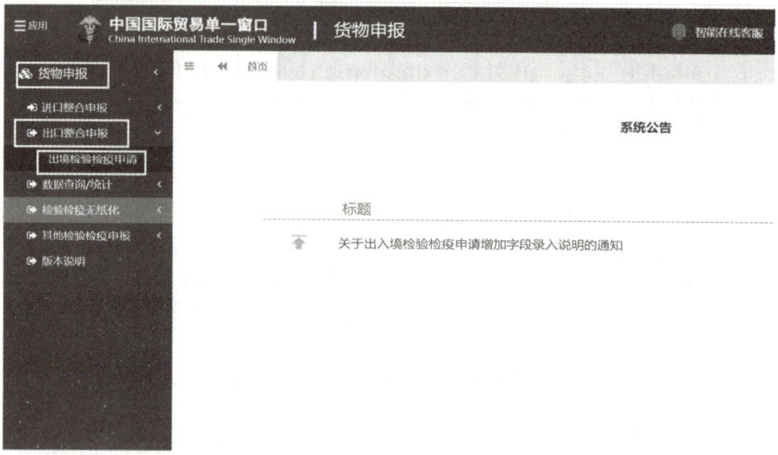

Step 3：逐项录入“基本信息、商品信息、集装箱信息”等内容。录入后，确认无误，保存后点击“申报”。

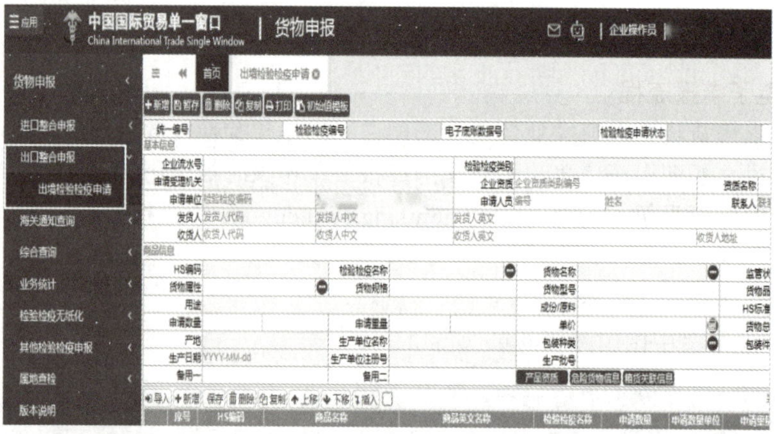

Step 4：点击进入“货物申报—报检无纸化—电子单据申报”，上传报检所需随附单据。

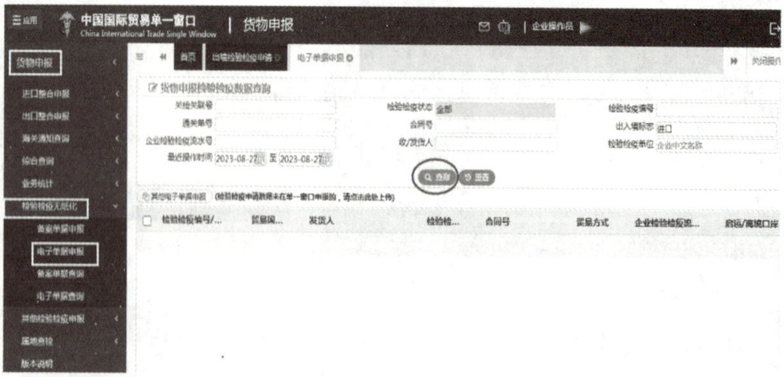

（备注：点击“报检无纸化—电子单据申报”，右侧默认显示查询界面，输入相应的

查询条件并点击【查询】蓝色按钮，系统会显示符合条件的数据，选择相应的“报检号/关检关联号”链接，方能进入电子单据录入界面。）

Step 5：点击进入“货物申报—数据查询/统计—检验检疫申请数据查询”，可查询到检验检疫的申报状态，也可打印检验检疫申报单。

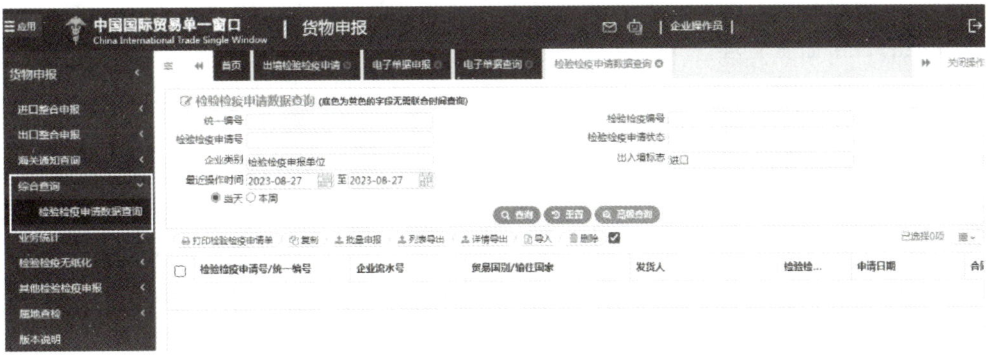

二、我国的检验检疫机构及其主要工作内容

2018 年 4 月 20 日起，原中国出入境检验检疫部门正式并入中国海关。关检业务的全面融合将检验检疫作业全面融入全国通关一体化整体框架和流程中，实现了“统一申报单证、统一作业系统、统一风险研判、统一指令下达、统一现场执法”。海关和国检融合后，原出入境检验检疫的组织结构也产生了新的改变。

（一）海关总署内的检验检疫业务司局如图 7-2 所示

有关出入境检验检疫地方组织机构，关检融合后，国家原质检总局在全国各省（自治区、直辖市）所设的直属出入境检验检疫局、海陆空口岸以及货物集散地的分支局和办事处，分别并入海关及隶属海关，履行相应的检验检疫职能。

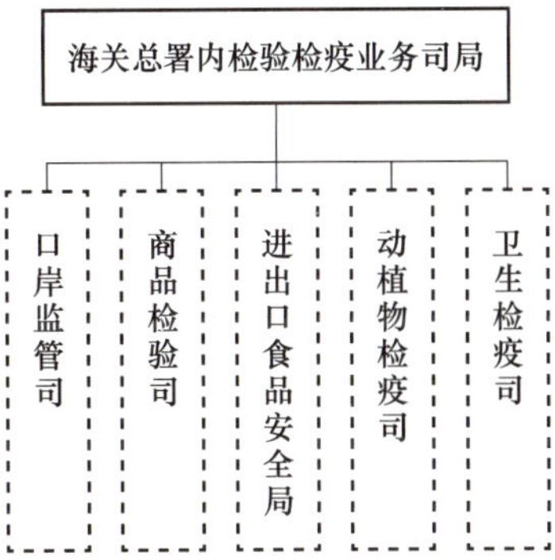

图 7-2　海关总署内检验检疫业务司局分布图

（二）主要工作内容

1. 法定检验检疫：法定检验检疫又称强制性检验检疫，是指根据《中华人民共和国进出口商品检验法》及其实施条例、《中华人民共和国进出境动植物检疫法》及其实施条例、《中华人民共和国卫生法》及其实施细则、《中华人民共和国食品安全法》及其他有

关法律法规的规定，海关依法对出入境人员、货物、运输工具、集装箱及其他法定检验检疫物（统称法定检验检疫对象）实施检验、检疫、鉴定等检验检疫业务。法定检验检疫涉及进出口商品检验（包含出口商品运输包装检验）、出入境动植物检疫和国境卫生检疫。

2. 进出口食品安全管理：即对进出口食品的安全、卫生、质量以及食品添加剂、食品容器、包装材料、食品用工具及设备进行检验监督管理，组织实施对进出口食品及其生产单位的日常监督管理。

3. 进出口鉴定业务：包括对出口危险货物运输包装进行性能和使用鉴定，对货物装载和残损进行鉴定，对外商投资财产进行鉴定。

4. 开展国际合作：比如承担世界贸易组织/技术性贸易壁垒协定（World Trade Organisation/Technical Barriers to Trade, WTO/TBT）和《实施卫生与植物卫生措施协议》（Agreement on the Application of Sanitary and Phytosanitary Measures, SPS）的咨询业务；承担与国际组织在标准与一致化以及检验检疫领域的联络工作；负责对外签订政府部门间的检验检疫合作协议、认证认可合作协议、检验检疫协议执行议定书等，并组织实施。

5. 其他工作内容：如产地证签证与管理；质量体系认可、实验室认可；口岸通关管理等工作。

三、官方或权威机构出具的常见检验单据种类

根据不同的检验检疫要求，我国的检验检疫机构签发不同的检验检疫证书、凭单、监管类证单、报告单和记录报告等证单，种类繁多，常见的证书如下：

1. 出入境检验检疫品质证书
2. 出入境检验检疫数量检验证书
3. 出入境检验检疫植物检疫证书
4. 出入境检验检疫动物卫生证书
5. 出入境检验检疫卫生证书
6. 出入境检验检疫熏蒸/消毒证书
7. 出境货物运输包装性能鉴定结果单
8. 包装检验证书
9. 残损鉴定证书
10. 温度检验证书
11. 船舶检验证书
12. 货载衡量检验证书

四、委托报检需随附的单据

1. 对外贸易合同、销售确认书或订单；
2. 商业发票；
3. 包装单据；
4. 厂检单，实施卫生注册及质量许可证管理的货物还应提供出入境检验检疫机构签发的卫生注册/质量许可证副本，并在报检单上注明卫生注册证号或质量许可证号；

5.《出境货物运输包装性能检验结果单》（正本），法定检验检疫的出境货物，报检时必须提供；

6. 出口危险货物时，必须提供《出境货物运输包装性能检验结果单》（正本）和《出境危险货物运输包装使用鉴定结果单》（正本）；

7. 按照检验检疫的要求，提供其他的相关特殊单据；

8. 报检委托书。

操作能力训练

思考题：

S7-1　某进出口企业出口货物 10 吨，由产地海关对货物进行了检验检疫。检验检疫合格后，海关按出口企业申报时提出的申请出具了相关的品质证书。此时，出口企业接到买方追加 1 吨货物，并要求同前 10 吨货物一同装运的来函。考虑到所追加的 1 吨货物和原来的货物品质以及各项指标完全一致，出口企业认为无须再向海关进行出口检验检疫申报，直接委托报关行向海关申报 11 吨货物的出口。该企业的操作是否妥当？

操作题：

C7-1　根据制单附录 3.1 里提供的制单信用证 3-13-4（见本书第 230 页），独立缮制符合要求的出境货物报检单。

C7-2　探索学习下一项目，并根据制单附录 3.1 里提供的制单信用证 3-13-1（见本书第 230 页），独立尝试缮制符合要求的出境货物报关单。

项目八

缮制出口货物报关单

报关单的作用

报关是进出口业务中的一个重要环节，它是指进出口货物收发货人、进出境运输工具负责人、进出境物品的所有人或者他们的代理人向海关办理货物、物品或运输工具进出境手续及行管海关事务的过程。报关应在订舱后进行。

出入境货物报关单由海关总署规定统一格式和填制规范，由进出口货物收发货人或其代理人填制，对进出口货物的真实情况做电子或书面申明并提交海关办理进出口货物申报手续的法律文书，是海关依法监管货物进出口、征收关税、进行海关统计及其他事务的重要凭证。

学习目标

［知识目标］掌握报关单的填制方法，熟悉出入境货物报关的程序、报关分类和时限要求，理解商品协调编码与海关税则号的关系，了解各种代码查询表和各类报关单据。

［能力目标］能根据合同或信用证正确缮制出口货物报关单。

项目描述（案例情境描述）

2015 年 7 月 4 号，山东希望土产进出口公司委托青岛顺风物流总公司代为办理出口报关手续，由青岛顺风物流总公司报关人员根据山东希望土产进出口公司提供的外贸合同、商业发票、重量单、报关委托书、出境货物通关单以及出口货物的相关资料，如货物申报要素等，向海关进行电子申报。本次业务为缮制出口报关单，该单据属于非结算单据。

附制单补充资料：

（1）山东希望土产进出口公司海关注册登记号：4200139852

（2）青岛顺风物流总公司海关注册登记号：4200287660

（3）Container No. EISU2628205

（4）黑枣 HS 编码：0813403000020

（5）运费：HKD1 300.00

（6）保费：HKD730.00

（7）杂费：CNY162.00

操作要领

1. 预录入编号：本栏目填报预录入报关单的编号，预录入编号规则由接受申报的海关决定。

2. 海关编号：本栏目填报海关接受申报时给予报关单的编号，一份报关单对应一个海关编号。报关单海关编号为 18 位数，其中第 1—4 位为接受申报海关的编号（海关规定的《关区代码表》中相应海关代码），第 5—8 位为海关接受申报的公历年份，第 9 位为进出口标志（“1”为进口，“0”为出口；集中申报清单“I”为进口，“E”为出口），后 9 位为顺序编号。网上申报时自动生成编号。

※本案例制单：

制单操作

海关编号：420020150354782201

3. 境内发货人：本栏目填报在海关注册的对外签订并执行进出口贸易合同的中国境内法人、其他组织或个人的名称及编码。编码可选填 18 位数法人和其他组织统一社会信用代码或 10 位数海关注册编码任一项。

※本案例制单：

制单操作

收发货人　山东希望土产进出口公司
4200139852

4. 出境关别：本栏目应根据货物实际进出境的口岸海关，填报海关规定的《关区代码表》中相应口岸海关的名称及代码。特殊情况填报要求如下：

（1）进口转关运输货物应填报货物进境地海关名称及代码，出口转关运输货物应填报货物出境地海关名称及代码。按转关运输方式监管的跨关区深加工结转货物，出口报关单填报转出地海关名称及代码，进口报关单填报转入地海关名称及代码。

（2）在不同海关特殊监管区域或保税监管场所之间调拨、转让的货物，填报对方特殊监管区域或保税监管场所所在的海关名称及代码。

（3）其他无实际进出境的货物，填报接受申报的海关名称及代码。

※本案例制单：

制单操作

出口口岸
青岛海关 4200

5. 进口日期/出口日期：进口日期填报运载进口货物的运输工具申报进境的日期。出口日期指运载出口货物的运输工具办结出境手续的日期，本栏目供海关签发打印报关单证明联用，在申报时免予填报。无实际进出境的报关单填报海关接受申报的日期。本栏目为 8 位数字，顺序为年（4 位）、月（2 位）、日（2 位）。

※本案例制单：

制单操作

出口日期
20150705

6. 申报日期：申报日期指海关接受进出口货物收发货人、受委托的报关企业申报数据的日期。以电子数据报关单方式申报的，申报日期为海关计算机系统接受申报数据时记录的日期。以纸质报关单方式申报的，申报日期为海关接受纸质报关单并对报关单进行登记处理的日期。申报日期为 8 位数字，顺序为年（4 位）、月（2 位）、日（2 位）。本栏目在申报时免予填报。

※本案例制单：

制单操作

申报日期
20150702

7. 备案号：本栏目填报进出口货物收发货人、消费使用单位、生产销售单位在海关办理加工贸易合同备案或征、减、免税备案审批等手续时，海关核发的《加工贸易手册》《征免税证明》或其他备案审批文件的编号。一份报关单只允许填报一个备案号。具体填报要求如下：

（1）消费使用单位填报已知的进口货物在境内的最终消费、使用单位的名称，包括：

–自行从境外进口货物的单位；

–委托进出口企业进口货物的单位。

（2）生产销售单位填报出口货物在境内的生产或销售单位的名称，包括：

–自行出口货物的单位；

–委托进出口企业出口货物的单位。

本栏目可选填 18 位法人和其他组织统一社会信用代码或 10 位数海关注册编码或 9 位数组织机构代码任一项。没有代码的应填报“NO”。

（3）有 10 位数海关注册编码或 18 位数法人和其他组织统一社会信用代码或加工企业编码的消费使用单位/生产销售单位，本栏目应填报其中文名称及编码；没有编码的应填报其中文名称。

使用《加工贸易手册》管理的货物，消费使用单位/生产销售单位应与《加工贸易手册》的“加工企业”一致；减免税货物报关单的消费使用单位/生产销售单位应与《中华人民共和国海关进出口货物征免税证明》（以下简称《征免税证明》）的“减免税申请人”一致。

※本案例制单：

制单操作

备案号
***

8. 境外收货人：本栏目填写境外收货企业英文名称，如有检验检疫等特殊需要的，在英文名称后填报该企业或自然人除英文外的其他外文名称。为已互认 AEO 企业[①]的，同时填报 AEO 编码。

※本案例制单：

制单操作

境外收货人 SOO HUP SENG TRADING CO.

9. 运输方式：运输方式包括实际运输方式和海关规定的特殊运输方式。前者指货物实际出入境的运输方式，按出入境所使用的运输工具分类；后者指货物无实际进出境的运输方式，按货物在境内的流向分类。本栏目应根据货物实际出入境的运输方式或货物在境内流向的类别，按照海关规定的《运输方式代码表》选择填报相应的运输方式。具体的实际运输方式如下：水路运输、公路运输、铁路运输、航空运输、邮件运输和其他运输。

（1）特殊情况填报要求如下：

–非邮件方式进出境的快递货物，按实际运输方式填报；

–进出境旅客随身携带的货物，按旅客所乘运输工具填报；

–进口转关运输货物，按载运货物抵达进境地的运输工具填报；出口转关运输货物，按载运货物驶离出境地的运输工具填报；

–不复运出（入）境而留在境内（外）销售的进出境展览品、留赠转卖物品等，填报“其他运输”（代码 9）。

（2）无实际进出境货物在境内流转时填报要求如下：

–境内非保税区运入保税区货物和保税区退区货物，填报“非保税区”（代码 0）；

–保税区运往境内非保税区货物，填报“保税区”（代码 7）；

–境内存入出口监管仓库和出口监管仓库退仓货物，填报“监管仓库”（代码 1）；

–保税仓库转内销货物，填报“保税仓库”（代码 8）；

–从境内保税物流中心外运入中心或从中心运往境内中心外的货物，填报“物流中心”（代码 W）；

–从境内保税物流园区外运入园区或从园区内运往境内园区外的货物，填报“物流园区”（代码 X）；

–保税港区、综合保税区、出口加工区、珠澳跨境工业区（珠海园区）、中哈霍尔果斯边境合作区（中方配套区）等特殊区域与境内（区外）（非特殊区域、保税监管场所）之间进出的货物，区内、区外企业应根据实际运输方式分别填报，“保税港区/综合保税区”（代码 Y），“出口加工区”（代码 Z）；

① AEO（Authorized Economic Operation），即以任何一种方式参与货物国际流通，并被海关当局认定符合世界海关组织或相应供应链安全标准的一方，包括生产商、进口商、出口商、报关行、承运商、理货人、中间商、口岸和机场、货站经营者、综合经营者、仓储业经营者和分销商。中国海关已与 14 个经济体的 42 个国家和地区实现互认。

–境内运入深港西部通道港方口岸区的货物，填报“边境特殊海关作业区”（代码 H）；

–经横琴新区和平潭综合实验区（以下简称综合试验区）二线指定申报通道运往境内区外或从境内经二线制定申报通道进入综合试验区的货物，以及综合试验区内按选择性征收关税申报的货物，填报“综合试验区”（代码 T）；

–其他境内流转货物，填报“其他运输”（代码 9），包括特殊监管区域内货物之间的流转、调拨货物，特殊监管区域、保税监管场所之间相互流转货物，特殊监管区域外的加工贸易余料结转、深加工结转、内销等货物。

※本案例制单：

制单操作

运输方式
水路运输 2

10. 运输工具名称即航次号：本栏目填报载运货物进出境的运输工具名称或编号。填报内容应与运输部门向海关申报的舱单（载货清单）所列相应内容一致。以直接在出境地或采用区域通关一体化通关模式办理报关手续为例，具体填报要求如下：

–水路运输：填报船舶编号（来往港澳小型船舶为监管簿编号）或者船舶英文名称；

–公路运输：启用公路舱单前，填报该跨境运输车辆的国内行驶车牌号，启用公路舱单后，免予填报；

–铁路运输：填报车厢编号或交接单号；

–航空运输：填报航班号；

–邮件运输：填报邮政包裹单号；

–其他运输：填报具体运输方式名称，例如：管道、驮畜等。

※本案例制单：

制单操作

运输工具名称
M/V “VICTORIA”

11. 提运单号：本栏目填报出口货物提单或运单的编号。一份报关单只允许填报一份提单或运单号，一票货物对应多份提单或运单时，应分单填报。以直接在出境地或采用区域通关一体化通关模式办理报关手续为例，具体说明填报要求：

–水路运输：填报进出口提单号。如有分提单的，填报进出口提单号+“*”+分提单号；

–公路运输：启用公路舱单前，免予填报；启用公路舱单后，填报进出口总运单号；

–铁路运输：填报运单号；

–航空运输：填报总运单号+“_”+分运单号，无分运单的填报总运单号；

–邮件运输：填报邮运包裹单号。

※本案例制单：

制单操作

提运单号　CCFASH18 20960

12. 生产销售单位：本栏目填报出口货物在境内的生产或销售单位的名称，包括：

–自行出口货物的单位；

–委托进出口企业出口货物的单位。

本栏目可选填 18 位法人和其他组织统一社会信用代码或 10 位数海关注册编码或 9

位数组织机构代码任一项。

※本案例制单：

制单操作

生产销售单位 （4200139852）
山东希望土产进出口公司

13. 监管方式：监管方式是以国际贸易中进出口货物的交易方式为基础，结合海关对进出口货物的征税、统计及监管条件综合设定的海关对进出口货物的管理方式。本栏目应根据实际对外贸易情况按海关规定的《监管方式代码表》选择填报相应的监管方式简称及代码。一份报关单只允许填报一种监管方式。不同贸易方式的货物应填制相应的报关单。

※本案例制单：

制单操作

监管方式 （0110）
一般贸易

14. 征免性质：本栏目应根据实际情况按海关规定的《征免性质代码表》选择填报相应的征免性质简称及代码，持有海关核发的《征免税证明》的，应按照《征免税证明》中批注的征免性质填报。一份报关单只允许填报一种征免性质。

※本案例制单：

制单操作

征免性质 （101）
一般征税

15. 许可证号：本栏目填报国家给予特殊监管的货物的进出口业务批准的许可证编号，是批准文件的编号。我国常见的有以下几种许可证：进（出）口许可证、两用物项和技术进（出）口许可证、两用物项和技术出口许可证（定向）、纺织品临时出口许可证。一份报关单只允许填报一个许可证号。

※本案例制单：

制单操作

许可证号 ***

16. 合同协议号：本栏目填报进出口货物合同（包括协议或订单）编号。未发生商业性交易的免予填报。不同合同的出口货物，不能填写在同一份报关单上。

※本案例制单：

制单操作

合同协议号 ORDER NO. S00-6378

17. 贸易国（地区）：本栏目填报对外贸易中与境内企业签订贸易合同的外方所属的国家（地区）。未发生商业性交易的填报货物所有权拥有者所属的国家（地区）。本栏目应按海关规定的《国别（地区）代码表》选择填报相应的贸易国（地区）或贸易国（地区）中文名称及代码。

※本案例制单：

制单操作

贸易国（地区） （MYS）
马来西亚

18. 运抵国（地区）：运抵国（地区）填报出口货物离开我国关境直接运抵或者在运输中转国（地区）未发生任何商业性交易的情况下最后运抵的国家（地区）。本栏目应按海关规定的《国别（地区）代码表》选择填报相应的运抵国（地区）中文名称及代码。

※本案例制单：

制单操作

运抵国（地区）（MYS）
马来西亚

19. 指运港：指运港填报出口货物运往境外的最终目的港；最终目的港不可预知的，按尽可能预知的目的港填报。本栏目应根据实际情况按海关规定的《港口代码表》选择填报相应的港口中文名称及代码。指运港在《港口代码表》中无港口中文名称及代码的，可选择填报相应的国家中文名称或代码。

※本案例制单：

制单操作

指运港　（MYS099　）
槟城（马来西亚）

20. 离境口岸：本栏目应填写跨境运输工具离开境内的第一个口岸的名称和口岸代码。

※本案例制单：

制单操作

离境口岸　（370101）
青岛

21. 包装种类：本栏目应根据进出口货物的实际外包装种类，即运输包装，如果有其他辅助包装以及植物性铺垫材料，按海关规定的《包装种类代码表》选择填报相应的包装种类和代码。

※本案例制单：

制单操作

包装种类　（2）
纸箱

22. 件数：本栏目填报有外包装的进出口货物的实际件数。本栏目不得填报为零，散装货物填报为“1”。特殊情况填报要求如下：

-舱单件数为集装箱的，填报集装箱个数；

-舱单件数为托盘的，填报托盘数。

※本案例制单：

制单操作

件数
200

23. 毛重（千克）：本栏目填报进出口货物及其包装材料的重量之和，计量单位为千克，不足一千克的填报为“1”。

※本案例制单：

制单操作

毛重（千克）
5 240

24. 净重（千克）：本栏目填报进出口货物的毛重减去外包装材料后的重量，即货物本身的实际重量，计量单位为千克，不足一千克的填报为“1”。

※本案例制单：

制单操作

净重（千克）
5 000

25. 成交方式：本栏目应根据进出口货物实际成交价格条款，按海关规定的《成交方式代码表》选择填报相应的成交方式代码。

※本案例制单：

制单操作

成交方式（1）
CIF

26. 运费：本栏目填报出口货物运至我国境内输出地点装载后的运输费用。运费可按运费单价、总价或运费率三种方式之一填报，注明运费标记并按海关规定的《货币代码表》选择填报相应的币种代码。

-运费标记“1”表示运费率；

-运费标记“2”表示每吨货物的运费单价；

-运费标记“3”表示运费总价。

※本案例制单：

制单操作

运费
110/1300/3

27. 保费：本栏目填报出口货物运至我国境内输出地点装载后的保险费用。保费可按保险费总价或保险费率两种方式之一填报，注明保险费标记并按海关规定的《货币代码表》选择填报相应的币种代码。

-保险费标记“1”表示保险费率；

-保险费标记“3”表示保险费总价。

※本案例制单：

制单操作

保费
110/730/3

28. 杂费：本栏目填报成交价格以外的、按照《中华人民共和国进出口关税条例》相关规定应计入完税价格或应从完税价格中扣除的费用。可按杂费总价或杂费率两种方式之一填报，注明杂费标记并按海关规定的《货币代码表》选择填报相应的币种代码。应计入完税价格的杂费填报为正值或正率，应从完税价格中扣除的杂费填报为负值或负率。

-杂费标记“1”表示杂费率；

-杂费标记“3”表示杂费总价。

※本案例制单：

制单操作

杂费
110/142/3

29. 随附单证及编号：本栏目根据海关规定的《监管证件代码表》选择填报除第 15 栏规定的许可证件以外的其他进出口许可证件或监管证件代码及编号。本栏目分为随附单证代码和随附单证编号两栏，其中代码栏应按海关规定的《监管证件代码表》选择填报相应证件代码，比如 A 或 B；编号栏应填报证件编号，即申报检验检疫的电子底账编号，也是报检单的编号。如随附出境货物检验检疫申报的，应填写“B”，加上出境货物检验检疫申报单的编号。

※本案例制单：

制单操作

随附单证及编号　B　583000002069835

30. 标记唛码及备注：本栏目填报要求如下：

-标记唛码中除图形以外的文字、数，无标记唛码的填报 N/M；

-集装箱标箱数及号码；

-监管方式为“暂时进出货物”（2600）和“展览品”（2700）时，如果为复运出境货物，在本栏内填报“复运出境”；

-跨境电子商务出口货物，在本栏目内填报“跨境电子商务”；

-申报时其他必须说明的事项。

※本案例制单：

制单操作

标记唛头及备注	
SHS PENANG 1-UP	集装箱标箱数及号码:EISU2628205

31. 项号：本栏目分两行填报及打印。第一行填报报关单中的商品顺序编号；第二行专用于加工贸易、减免税等已备案、审批的货物，填报和打印该项货物在《加工贸易手册》或《征免税证明》等备案、审批单证中的顺序编号。

※本案例制单：

制单操作

项号
1

32. 商品编号：本栏目填报的商品编号由 13 位数字组成。前 8 位数为《中华人民共和国进出口税则》确定的全球通用的等效的进出口货物的税则号列，同时也是《中华人民共和国海关统计商品目录》确定的商品编码，第 9、10 位数为符合海关监管要求的附加或延伸的子目录编号，第 11–13 位为检验检疫附加编号（若无检验检疫要求则不填写）。

※本案例制单：

制单操作

商品编码
0813403000020

33. 商品名称及规格型号：本栏目分两行填报及打印。第一行填报进出口货物规范的中文商品名称，第二行按照“商品规范申报（申报要素）—商品要素申报”要求的内容进行填报。

※本案例制单：

制单操作

商品名称及规格型号
山东黑枣 25千克/箱 无品牌 制作方法：干枣

34. 数量及单位：本栏目分三行填报及打印。

-第一行应按进出口货物的法定第一计量单位填报数量及单位，法定计量单位以《中华人民共和国海关统计商品目录》中的计量单位为准。

-凡列明有法定第二计量单位的，应在第二行按照法定第二计量单位填报数量及单位。无法定第二计量单位的，本栏目第二行为空。

-成交计量单位及数量应填报并打印在第三行。

※本案例制单：

制单操作

数量及单位
5 000千克 5公吨

35. 单价/总价/币制：本栏目分三行进行填报，第一行填报单价，第二行填报总价，第三行填报币制。总价=单价×成交数量 单价=总价÷成交数量。

※本案例制单：

制单操作

单价/总价/币制
9.2300 46 150.00 港元110

36. 原产国（地区）：原产国（地区）应依据《中华人民共和国进出口货物原产地条例》《中华人民共和国海关关于执行〈非优惠原产地规则中实质性改变标准〉的规定》以及海关总署关于各项优惠贸易协定原产地管理规章规定的原产地确定标准填报。

※本案例制单：

制单操作

原产国（地区）
中国 （CHN）

37. 最终目的国（地区）：最终目的国（地区）填报已知的出口货物的最终实际消费、使用或进一步加工制造国家（地区）。不经过第三国（地区）转运的直接运输货物，以运抵国（地区）为最终目的国（地区）；经过第三国（地区）转运的货物，以最后运往国（地区）为最终目的国（地区）。

※本案例制单：

制单操作

最终目的国（地区）
马来西亚 （MYS）

38. 境内货源地：填报出口货物在国内的产地或原始发货地。出口货物产地难以确定的，填报最早发运该出口货物的单位所在地。本栏目按海关规定的《国内地区代码表》选择填报相应的国内地区名称及代码。

※本案例制单：

制单操作

境内货源地
青岛其他

39. 征免：本栏目应按照海关核发的《征免税证明》或有关政策规定，对报关单所列每项商品选择海关规定的《征减免税方式代码表》中相应的征减免税方式填报。

※本案例制单：

制单操作

征免
照章

40. 特殊关系确认：本栏目根据《中华人民共和国海关审定进出口货物完税价格办法》（以下简称《审价办法》）第十六条，填报确认进出口行为中买卖双方是否存在特殊

关系，有下列情形之一的，应当认为买卖双方存在特殊关系，在本栏目应填报“是”，反之则填报“否”。

（1）买卖双方为同一家族成员的；

（2）买卖双方互为商业上的高级职员或者董事的；

（3）一方直接或者间接地受另一方控制的；

（4）买卖双方都直接或者间接地受第三方控制的；

（5）买卖双方共同直接或者间接地控制第三方的；

（6）一方直接或者间接地拥有、控制或者持有对方5%以上（含5%）公开发行的有表决权的股票或者股份的；

（7）一方是另一方的雇员、高级职员或者董事的；

（8）买卖双方是同一合伙企业的成员的。

买卖双方在经营上相互有联系，一方是另一方的独家代理、独家经销或者独家受让人，如果符合前款的规定，也应当视为存在特殊关系。

※本案例制单：

制单操作

特殊关系确认：　否

41. 价格影响确认：本栏目根据《审价办法》第十七条，填报确认进出口行为中买卖双方存在的特殊关系是否影响成交价格，纳税义务人如不能证明其成交价格与同时或者大约同时发生的下列任何一款价格相近的，应当视为特殊关系对进出口货物的成交价格产生影响，在本栏目应填报“是”，反之则填报“否”。

（1）向境内无特殊关系的买方出售的相同或者类似进出口货物的成交价格；

（2）按照《审价办法》倒扣价格估价方法的规定所确定的相同或者类似进出口货物的完税价格；

（3）按照《审价办法》计算价格估价方法的规定所确定的相同或者类似进出口货物的完税价格。

※本案例制单：

制单操作

价格影响确认：否

42. 支付特许权使用费确认：本栏目根据《审价办法》第十三条，填报确认进出口行为中买方是否存在向卖方或者有关方直接或者间接支付特许权使用费。特许权使用费是指进出口货物的买方为取得知识产权权利人及权利人有效授权人关于专利权、商标权、专有技术权、著作权、分销权或者销售权的许可或者转让而支付的费用。如果进出口行为中买方存在向卖方或者有关方直接或者间接支付特许权使用费的，在本栏目应填报“是”，反之则填报“否”。

※本案例制单：

制单操作

支付特许权使用费：否

43. 自报自缴费：本栏目是针对是否属于自理报关设置，属于自理报关的，应填报“是”，属于代理报关的，应填报“否”。

※本案例制单：

制单操作

自报自缴：　否

44. 报关人员，报关人员证号，电话：本栏目用于记录录入操作人员在海关备案的姓名、编码和联系电话，并加盖申报单位印章。

45. 申报单位：本栏目用于记录录入单位名称，自理报关的，填报进出口企业的名称及统一社会信用代码；委托代理报关的，填报报关企业的名称及统一社会信用代码。

46. 海关批注及签章：本栏目供海关作业时签注。

附出口报关单制单样例

中华人民共和国出口货物报关单

预入录编号：　　海关编号：420020150354782201　　页码/页数：

境内发货人　(4200139852) 山东希望土产进出口公司	出境关别　(4200) 青岛海关	出口日期　20150705	申报日期　20150702	备案号 ***
境外收货人 SOO HUP SENG TRADING CO.	运输方式（2） 水路运输	运输工具名称及航次号 M/V "VICTORIA"	提运单号　CCFASH1820960	
生产销售单位　(4200139852) 山东希望土产进出口公司	监管方式（0110） 一般贸易	征免性质　(101) 一般征税	许可证号 ***	
合同协议号　ORDER NO. S00-6378	贸易国（地区）(MYS) 马来西亚	运抵国（地区）(MYS) 马来西亚	指运港　(MYS099　) 槟城（马来西亚）	离境口岸　(370101) 青岛

包装种类	件数	毛重（千克）	净重（千克）	成交方式（1）	运费	保费	杂费
(2) 纸箱	200	5 240	5 000	CIF	110/1300/3	110/730/3	110/142/3

随附单证及编号　B　583000002069835

标记唛头及备注
SHS
PENANG
1-UP　　集装箱标箱数及号码:EISU2628205

项号	商品编码	商品名称及规格型号	数量及单位	单价/总价/币制	原产国（地区）	最终目的国（地区）	境内货源地	征免
1	081340300002	山东黑枣 25千克/箱 无品牌 制作方法：干枣	5 000千克 5公吨	9.2300 46 150.00 港元110	中国　(CHN)	马来西亚（MYS）	青岛其他	照章

特殊关系确认：否		价格影响确认：否	支付特许权使用费：否	自报自缴：否
报关人员　唐欣	报关人员证号　x x x	电话　65788877	兹声明对以上内容承担如实申报、依法纳税法律责任 申报单位（签章）	海关批注及签章
申报单位	山东希望土产进出口公司			

相关知识

一、出入境货物报关的程序

《中华人民共和国海关法》（以下简称《海关法》）规定的一般报关程序，适用于一般进出口货物、进出境物品和进出境运输工具的报关。报关程序一般由四个环节组成。

（一）进出口申报

1. 准备申报单证

申报单证可以分为主要单证、随附单证两大类。主要单证就是报关单。报关单是由报关员按照海关规定格式填制的申报单。随附单证包括基本单证、特殊单证和预备单证。

基本单证是指进出口货物的运货单据和商业单据，主要有进口提货单据、出口装货单据、商业发票、装箱单等。

特殊单证主要是指进出口许可证件、加工贸易登记手册、特定减免税证明、作为特殊货物出入境证明的原进口货物报关单证、出口收汇核销单、原产地证明书等。

预备单证主要是指贸易合同、进出口企业的有关证明文件等。这些单证，海关在审单、征税时可能需要调阅或者收取备案。

特别注意：实际业务中，一般出口报关具体需要准备如下单证：商业发票、装箱单、报关单、报关委托书、装货单以及其他海关需要单证。

2. 确认货物

进口货物的收货人向海关申报前，因确定货物的品名、规格、型号、归类等需要，可以向海关提出查看货物或者提取货样的书面申请。海关审核同意的，派员到场监管。

查看货物或提取货样时，海关开具取样记录和取样清单。提取货样的货物及动植物以及产品以及其他须依法提供检疫证明的，应当按照国家的有关法律规定，在取得主管部门签发的书面批准证明后提取。提取货样后，到场监管的海关官员与进口货物的收货人在取样记录和取样清单上签字确认。

3. 申报

我国采取电子数据申报，海关有需要时可以提交纸质报关单。

目前大多数企业登录中国国际贸易单一窗口标准版进行进出口报关申报。

申报的流程如下（以出口报关申报为例）：

Step 1：登录中国国际贸易单一窗口。

Step 2：选择“货物申报”中的“出口报关单整合申报”。

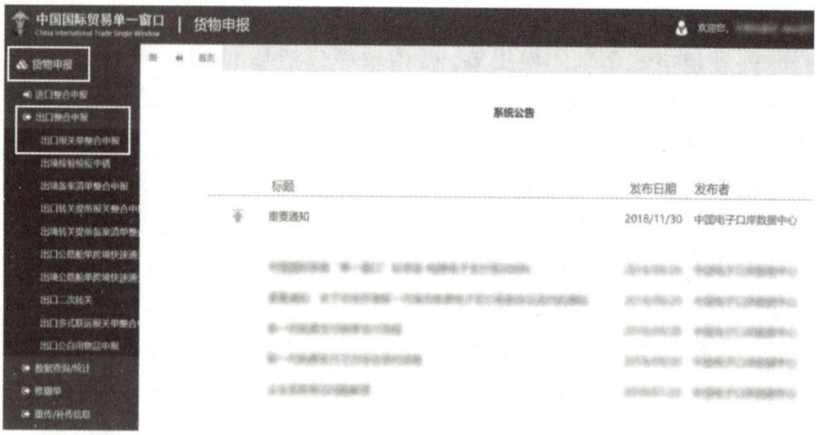

Step 3：逐项填报基本信息、商品信息、集装箱、随附单证、涉检信息等部分。

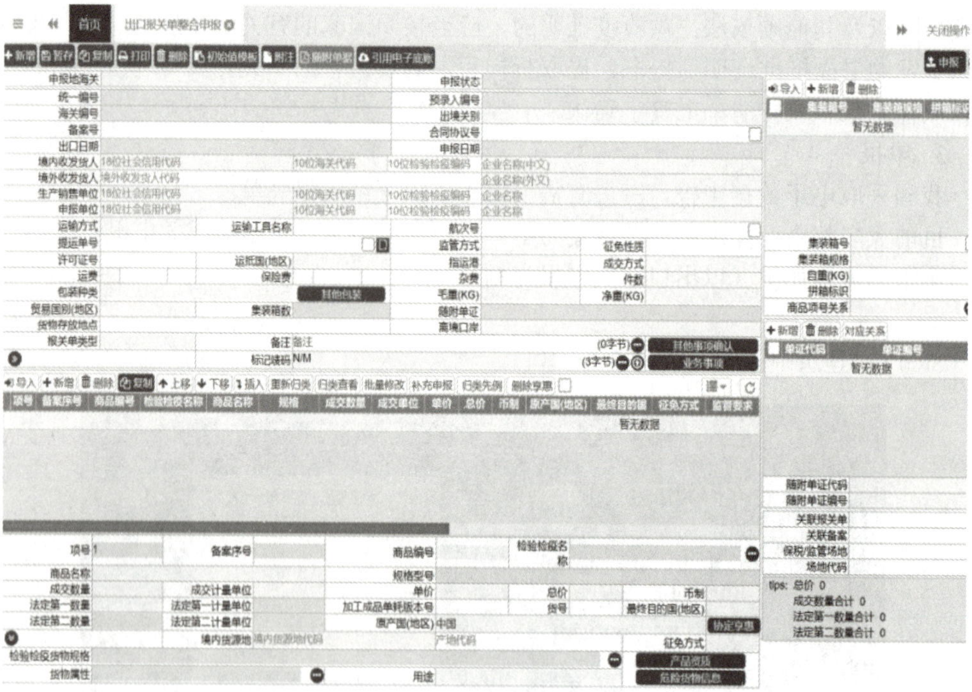

Step 4：暂存填报信息，检查无误，点击“申报”。

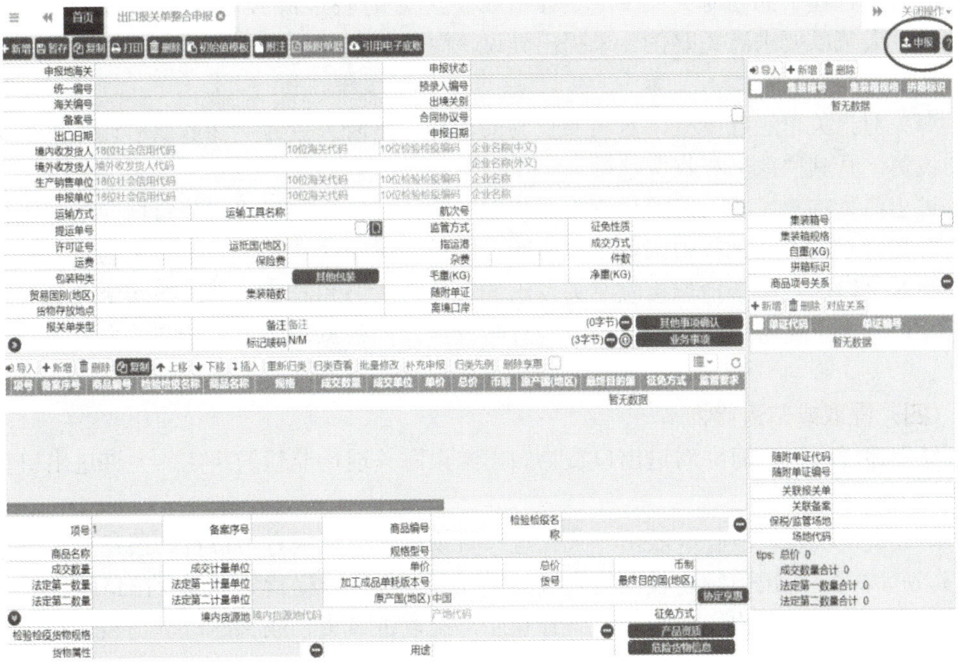

（二）海关查验

《海关法》规定进出口货物还应当接受查验。海关查验是指海关依法确定进出境货物的性质、价格、数量、原产地、货物状况等是否与报关单上已申报的内容相符，对货物进行实际检查的行政行为。

1. 检查地点

一般在货物所在的海关监管区内查验，特殊情况下，经当事人申请，海关同意，也可以在海关监管区外进行查验。

2. 查验时间

当海关决定查验时，将查验的决定以书面通知的形式通知进出口货物收发货人及其代理人，约定查验的时间。查验时间一般约定在海关正常工作时间。但有一些进出口业务繁忙的口岸，海关也可能应进出口货物收发货人或其代理人的请求，在海关正常工作时间以外安排查验作业。

3. 查验方式

-彻底查验。彻底查验即对货物逐件开箱、开包查验，对货物所有情况逐一与报关单详细核对。

-抽查。抽查即按一定比例或一定排序，对货物进行选择性的查验。

-外形查验。外形查验即对货物的包装、唛头进行核验，适用于大型机械设备、大宗原材料等不易搬运、移动，但堆放整齐、比较直观的货物。

-径行开验。径行开验是指海关在进出口货物收发货人或其代理人不在场的情况下，自行开拆货物进行查验。

4. 货物损坏赔偿

在查验过程中因为海关关员的责任造成被查验货物损坏的，进出口货物的收发货人或其代理人可以要求海关赔偿。未提出异议，海关不负赔偿责任。

（三）缴费纳税

海关对报关单进行审核，对需要查验的货物先由海关查验，然后核对计算机系统计算的税费，开具税款书和收费票据。

进出口货物收发货人或其代理人在规定时间内，持缴款书或收费票据向指定银行办理税费交付手续。在试行中国电子口岸网上缴税和付费的海关，进出口货物收发货人或其代理人可以通过电子口岸接收海关发出的税款缴款书和收费票据，在网上向签有协议的银行进行电子支付税费。一旦收到银行缴款成功的信息，即可报请海关办理货物放行手续。

（四）提取或装运货物

经上述过程后，海关对进出口货物做出结束海关现场监管的决定，允许进出口货物离开海关监管场所。

海关进出境现场放行一般由海关在进口货物提货凭证或者出口货物装货凭证上签盖“海关放行章”。进出口货物收发货人或其代理人签收进口提货凭证或者出口装货凭证，凭此到货物进境地或出境地的海关监管仓库，提取进口货物或将出口货物装运到运输工具上离境。

在实行“无纸通关”申报方式的海关，海关做出现场放行决定时，通过计算机系统将“海关放行”报文发送给进出口货物收发货人或其代理人和海关监管货物保管人。进出口货物收发货人或其代理人在计算机上自行打印海关通知放行的凭证，凭此提取进口货物或将出口货物装运到运输工具上离境。

二、报关分类和时限要求

1. 报关的分类

根据不同的角度，报关可以分为几种类型，如表 8-1 所示。

表 8-1　报关单分类

分类方式		说　明
报关对象	运输工具报关	即对货物或物品的载体报关，如船舶、车辆、航空器、驮畜等。进出境运输工具作为货物、人员及其携带物品的进出境载体，其报关主要是向海关直接交验随附的、符合国际商业运输惯例、能反映运输工具进出境合法性及其所承运货物、物品情况的合法证件、清单和其他运输单证，报关手续较为简单。
	货物报关	即为贸易性质的报关，包括一般进出口货物，保税货物，暂准进出境、特定减免税、过境、转运、通运的货物；还有特殊货物，如通过电缆、管道输送进出境的水、电等无形的货物，附着在货品载体上的软件等也属报关范围。进出境货物报关较为复杂，因此，海关根据对进出境货物的监管要求制定了一系列报关管理规范，并要求必须由具备一定的专业知识和技能且经海关核准的专业人员代表报关单位专门办理。

（续表）

分类方式		说明
报关对象	物品报关	即为非贸易性质的报关，包括行李物品、邮递物品和其他物品。自用物品按相关规定应以自用合理数量为限。进出境物品由于其非贸易性质，且一般限于自用、合理数量，报关手续也很简单。
按报关活动实施者	自理报关	进出口货物收发人自行办理报关手续称为自理报关。
	代理报关	代理报关指的是接受进出口货物收发货人的委托代理其办理报关手续的行为。
按报关目的	进境报关	海关对运输工具、货物、物品的进出境有不同的管理要求，根据进出境目的分别形成了一套进、出境报关手续。另外，需要转关的货物同样需要办理相应的报关手续。
	出境报关	

2. 报关的时限要求

《海关法》第 24 条规定，进口货物的收货人应当自运输工具申报进境之日起 14 日内，出口货物的发货人除海关特准外应当在货物运抵海关监管区后、装货的 24 小时以前，向海关申报。进口货物的收货人超过前款规定期限向海关申报的，由海关征收滞报金。申报最后一天为法定节假日的，顺延至节假日结束后的第一个工作日。滞报金按日征收，起征日为规定申报时限的次日，截止日为申报日，起征日与申报日均记入滞报时间。滞报金起征点为人民币 50 元。滞报金的日征收金额为进口货物完税价格的 0.5‰。

三、委托报关需随附的单据

1. 外贸合同
2. 商业发票
3. 装箱单
4. 代理报关委托书（扫描件）
5. 报关单

四、商品协调编码与海关税则号

（一）H.S. 编码协调制度

为使用统一的标准对商品进行管理，世界上产生了多种商品分类目录。国际上对商品分类的标准影响最大的、使用国家最多的当属海关合作理事会 1998 年实施的《商品名称与编码协调制度》（The Harmonized Commodity Description and Coding System，简称协调制度）。

商品编码，又称商品代码，或称商品代号、货号。它是赋予某种商品或某类商品的代表符号，可以由数字、字母和特殊标记组成。

按照 H.S. 编码的分类和编目，所有国际贸易商品按生产部门归类。共划分成 21 类（section），如：活动物，动物产品；植物产品；矿物品；化学工业及其相关工业制品；塑料及其制品；橡胶及其制品；纺织原料及纺织制品；艺术品；收藏品及古物等。在各类内，基本按同一起始原料和同一类型产品划分为 97 章（chapter）（其中第 77 章留空，为将来备用章），如纺织品类包括有棉织品、毛织品、丝织品、织品和化纤品五大类。在每一章内，按照从原料至成品的加工程度排列成各种商品，并按顺序编号，共4位数1 241个编码，通常称为税目号（heading No. 或 tariff No.）。税目号的前两位数字表示商品所在的章，后两位数字代表相关商品在该章内的税目编号。H.S. 编码对 1 241 个税目号中的 311 个税目未再细分，在用 6 位子目表示时，一级子目和二级子目均用“0”表示。如 H.S.OO.06.00 表示其他活动物。其他 930 个税目被进一步细分，这样共形成 5 019 个子目（或称商品组，subheading No.）。综上所述，《协调制度》对国际贸易商品分类情况为：21 类—97 章—1 241 税目—5 019 子目。显而易见，这种分类是非常便于查找使用的。

（二）我国海关进出口商品分类名录

我国的海关进出口商品分类名录是指根据海关征税和海关统计工作的需要，分别编制的《中华人民共和国海关进出口税则》和《中华人民共和国海关统计商品名录》。这两个分类目录品目号列均以《协调制度》为基础，结合我国国际货物买卖的实际情况编制而成。

世界海关组织 2017 版《商品名称及编码协调制度》已经发布。新版《协调制度》共有 242 组修订，主要关注环境保护、生态可持续发展、科学技术的新变化、国际贸易新业态的发展等方面，进一步明确了商品分类。根据《协调制度国际公约》对缔约国权利义务的规定，中国海关进出口税则和统计目录已于 2017 年 1 月 1 日起采用新的《协调制度》，并据此编制了 2017 年版《中华人民共和国海关进出口税则》和《中华人民共和国海关统计商品名录》。 2017 年《中华人民共和国海关统计商品名录》与《中华人民共和国海关进出口税则》结构基本相同，《商品名录》中的商品号列称为商品编号，为统计需要，每项商品编号后列出该商品的计量单位。2017 年《中华人民共和国海关进出口税则》中的商品号列称为税号，为征税需要，每项税号后列出了该商品的税率。2017 年版进口税则税目共计 8 547 个，税号的前 6 位数码与商品名称和《协调制度》完全一致，第 7、8 两位数码是根据我国关税、统计和贸易管理的需要细分的。

操作能力训练

思考题

S8-1　填写报关单为什么需要填写各种代码？

操作题

C8-1　根据附录 3.1 里提供的制单信用证 3-13-4（见本书第 230 页），独立缮制符合要求的报关单。

C8-2　探索学习下一项目，并根据附录 3.1 里提供的制单信用证 3-13-1（见本书第 230 页），独立尝试缮制符合要求的原产地证书。

C8-3　独立学习 ISBP（2013 最新版本）和 UCP600 中关于原产地证书的相关条款。

项目九

缮制货物原产地证书

货物原产地证明的地位及作用

原产地证明（Certificate of Origin）简称产地证，是各国根据相关的原产地规则签发的证明商品原产地，即货物的生产或制造地的一种具有法律效力的证明文件。简单讲，是商品进入国际贸易领域的"护照"，证明商品的经济国籍。同时，产地证在国际贸易中主要是供货物进口国的海关进行贸易统计、确定征收关税率和清关的重要文件，它属于"有价证券"。这份文件应在货物装运前办妥，但 RCEP 和 FORM E 证书可在货物装运后办理。

学习目标

[知识目标] 了解原产地证书的分类，掌握原产地证书的地位和作用，掌握缮制原产地证书的要领。

[能力目标] 能正确缮制信用证项下的原产地证书。

项目描述（案例情境描述）

山东希望土产进出口公司向马来西亚出口一批山东黑枣，进口方通过银行开来信用证。出口方经审核无误后，开始缮制来证要求提供的全套单据。本次业务为缮制原产地证书，向签发机关申请签发。信用证可参考项目四。

一、缮制普通原产地证书

普通原产地证书又称一般原产地证书，是一种最为常用的货物原产地证明。

操作要领（缮制普通原产地证书各栏的填制要求）

1. 证书编号（Certificate No.）：证书号码已由签发机关印就。出口人申领空白证书，须登记领取证书的编号。

※本案例制单：　来证条款　　制单操作

Certificate No.　××××

2. 出口商（Exporter）：此栏填写发货人/出口商（Consignor/Exporter）的名称和详细地址，一般应与发票的出票人一致；如果是可转让信用证，也可以是受益人或运输单据上托运人之外的另外一人。

※本案例制单：　来证条款　　制单操作

来证条款	制单操作
BENEFICIARY: SHANDONG HOPE NATIVE PRODUCT I/E CORP. 62，GUANGXI ROAD, QINGDAO, CHINA	1.出口商 Exporter SHANDONG HOPE NATIVE PRODUCT I/E CORP. 62, GUANGXI ROAD, QINGDAO, CHINA

3. 收货人（Consignee）：该栏须填写货物销售国的最终进口商。直接贸易的收货人应与发票抬头一致，不得与运输单据中的相矛盾。但是，如果运输单据抬头为TO ORDER、TO ORDER OF SHIPPER、TO ORDER OF ISSUING BANK、TO ISSUING BANK 等，产地证可以显示信用证的申请人或信用证中具名的另外一人（如提单的 NOTIFY PARTY）为收货人。

在转口贸易中或信用证已转让，填写提单条款中被通知的货物销售国一方或原证申请人；在最终进口商不明确的情况下，此栏显示为“TO WHOM IT MAY CONCERN”（特别是当信用证要求此栏留空时），两种皆须在最终进口商下面空一行，加打 via 转口商或第一受益人，写明其名称和地址。

若来证要求做成××客户的抬头，可在证书格式的左上角打上“TO M/S ×××CO.”，收货人栏仍填信用证申请人。若填写了第一受益人作为收货人，则第一受益人须在其当地更换原产地证书。

※本案例制单：　来证条款　　制单操作

来证条款	制单操作
APPLICANT: SOO HUP SENG TRADING CO. SDN BHD. 165，1st FLOOR, VICTORIA STREET 10300 PENANG，MALAYSIA	2. Consignee　(full name, address, country) SOO HUP SENG TRADING CO. SDN BHD. 165，1ST FLOOR, VICTORIA STREET 10300 PENANG，MALAYSIA

4. 运输方式和路线（Means of Transport and Route）：此栏须与发票和提单一致，但不必写船名和航次。为便于进口国海关查证，最好显示航运时间，如：DURING MM/YY 或 ON / AFTER （装船日期） BY SEA / VESSEL（船名和航次）FROM（装运港）TO

（卸货港）。装船日期为订舱后承运人通知所获得。

若遇转船，还须在目的港后加注 VIA 或 W/T at（转船港）；内陆转运则打 in transit to（目的地）。

※本案例制单：　来证条款　　　　　　　　　　　　　制单操作

来证条款	制单操作
TRANSSHIPMENT: PERMITTED SHIPMENT FROM ANY PORT IN CHINA TO PENANG LATEST 06 JULY, 2015	3. Means of transport and route FROM QINGDAO, CHINA TO PENANG, MALAYSIA BY SEA ON / AFTER JULY 5, 2015.

5. 目的地的国家或地区名称（Country/Region Destination）：此栏填写本批货物最终抵达目的地所属的国家或地区名称，应与最终收货人或最终目的港国别一致。

※本案例制单：　来证条款　　　　　　　　　　　　　制单操作

来证条款	制单操作
SHIPMENT FROM ANY PORT IN CHINA TO PENANG LATEST 06 JULY, 2015	4. Country/Region Of Destination MALAYSIA

6. 供签证机构使用栏（For Certifying Authority Use Only）：本栏为签证机构在签发后发证书、补发证书或加注其他声明时使用，证书申领单位应将此栏留空不填。

※本案例制单：　来证条款　　　　　　　　　　　　　制单操作

来证条款	制单操作
	5. For certifying authority use only

7. 运输标志（Marks Numbers of Packages）：须与发票和提单一致，最好不要简式填写，如：As per Invoice No.××或 As per B/L No.××。若散装或裸装货物的包装没有唛头，填写“N/M”即 NO MARKS，此栏不得留空。若唛头过多，可另附纸页。

※本案例制单：　来证条款　　　　　　　　　　　　　制单操作

来证条款	制单操作
ALL PACKAGES BEAR SHIPPING MARKS: SHS / PENANG / 1-UP	6. Marks and Numbers of Packages SHS PENANG 1-UP

8. 货物描述（Description of Goods）：本栏显示货物的品名和外包装件数大小写，或使用与信用证规定不相矛盾的不会引起歧义的货名统称，与箱单、保单和提单一致。散装货在品名下注明 in bulk。

※本案例制单：　来证条款　　　　　　　　　　　　　制单操作

来证条款	制单操作
GOODS: 5M/TONS SHANDONG BLACK DATES	7. Description of goods: number and kind of packages SHANDONG BLACK DATES SAY TWO HUNDRED(200) CARDBOARD CARTONS ONLY.

要求填写完品名和包装数量和种类后，或填写完加注内容后，在其下加打隔断符号，以避免任何添加。该栏空白处为自由处置区，用于填写信用证要求的或其他必要的加注内容。

※本案例制单：　来证条款　　　　　　　　　　　　　　　　　制单操作

来证条款
TO STATE THAT GOODS ARE OF SHANDONG / QINGDAO ORIGIN REQUIRED.
SPECIAL CONDITIONS: 3) DOCUMENTS TO EVIDENCE THAT ALL PACKAGES BEAR SHIPPING MARKS: SHS/PENANG/1-UP 4) DOCUMENTS TO EVIDENCE THAT PACKING IS DONE AS FOLLOWS: IN CARDBOARD CARTONS OF 25KGS NET OR 26.2KGS GROSS PER CARTON

制单操作
**************************** IT IS STATED THAT GOODS ARE OF SHANDONG ORIGIN. IT IS EVIDENCED THAT ALL PACKAGES BEAR SHIPPING MARKS: SHS/PENANG/1-UP PACKING IS DONE AS FOLLOWS: IN CARDBOARD CARTONS OF 25KGS NET OR 26.2KGS GROSS PER CARTON

9. 商品编码（H.S. Code）：本栏填写该商品的商品协调编码，要求与报关单一致。若同一证书包含有几种商品，则应将相应的税目号全部填写，此栏不得留空。

※本案例制单：　来证条款　　　　　　　　　　　　　　　　　制单操作

制单操作
8. H.S. Code 0813403000

10. 数量及重量（Quantity or Weight）：按发票商品的正常计量单位填写，即数量单位与计价的数量单位一致。若以重量为单位的货物，则填写商品的净重或毛重，须予注明。

※本案例制单：　来证条款　　　　　　　　　　　　　　　　　制单操作

来证条款	制单操作
GOODS: 5M/TONS SHANDONG BLACK DATES	9. Quantity or Weight N.W. 5 M/T

11. 发票号码及日期（Number and Date of Invoices）：此栏填写所申请出口货物的商业发票号码及日期。为避免对月份和日期的误解，月份一律不得用阿拉伯数字表示（包括第十二栏和十三栏的日期）。

※本案例制单：　来证条款　　　　　　　　　　　　　　　　　制单操作

制单操作
10. Number and date of invoices BP15SHS02INV1051 28-Jun-15

12. 出口商声明（Declaration by the Exporter）：本栏由申领证书的出口商签章（名称+签字），须注明声明地点及日期。日期不得早于第 10 栏日期，一般应为第 12 栏签证日期留足三个工作日。

※本案例制单：　来证条款　制单操作

11. SHANDONG HOPE NATIVE PRODUCT I/E CORP. ××× (STAMPED) QINGDAO, CHINA　　JULY 1, 2015 Place and date. signature and stamp of certifying authority

13. 签证机构证明（Certification）：本栏由签发机构签字并盖章（盖章不得压住签字），并填写签证日期和地点。根据我国现行管理体制，贸促会和海关都有权签发此证书，出口商不得填写此栏。该栏日期不得早于第 11 栏声明日期，也不得晚于提单日期。签字人员必须事先经海关备案。

如果信用证要求由受益人、出口商或制造商出具产地证，可由商会出具。反之不行。

来证要求由商会出具产地证，可在贸促会签发的普通产地证上加注："THE CCPIT IS THE CHAMBER OF COMMERCE FOR FOREIGN TRADE IN CHINA." 现在此句已印就在单据上。

如果信用证规定由"当地的""一流的""胜任的"等含混词语表示的出具人出具产地证，任何人出具均可，但不能由受益人出具。

若信用证未规定产地证签发人，出口商可自行签发，也可让贸促会或当地海关在自己出具的产地证上签章。这样可降低费用，又符合信用证的规定。

附原产地证书样例

ORIGIANL

1. Exporter (full name and address) SHANDONG HOPE NATIVE PRODUCT I/E CORP. 62, GUANGXI ROAD, QINGDAO, CHINA	Certificate No　.×××× **CERTIFICATE OF ORIGIN** **OF** **THE PEOPLE'S REPUBLIC OF CHINA**
2. Consignee (full name, address, country) SOO HUP SENG TRADING CO. SDN BHD. 165, 1ST FLOOR, VICTORIA STREET 10300 PENANG, MALAYSIA	
3. Means of transport and route FROM QINGDAO, CHINA TO PENANG, MALAYSIA BY SEA ON/AFTER JULY 5, 2015.	5. For certifying authority use only
4. Country/Region of Destination MALAYSIA	

（续表）

6. Marks and Numbers of Packages	7. Description of goods; number and kind of packages	8. H.S. Code	9. Quantity or Weight	10. Number and date of invoice
SHS PENANG 1-UP	SHANDONG BLACK DATES SAY TWO HUNDRED (200) CARDBOARD CARTONS ONLY. ********************************** IT IS STATED THAT GOODS ARE OF SHANDONG ORIGIN. IT IS EVIDENCED THAT ALL PACKAGES BEAR SHIPPING MARKS: SHS/PENANG/1-UP PACKING IS DONE AS FOLLOWS: IN CARDBOARD CARTONS OF 25KGS NET OR 26.2KGS GROSS PER CARTON	0813403000020	N.W. 5 M/T	BP15SHS02INV1051 28-Jun-15

11. **Declaration by the exporter**	12. **Certification**
The undersigned hereby declares that the above details and statements are true and correct; that all the goods were produced in China and that they comply with the Rules of Origin of the People's Republic of China SHANDONG HOPE NATIVE PRODUCT I/E CORP. ×××　　(STAMPED) QINGDAO, CHINA　　JULY 1, 2015 Place and date. signature and stamp of authorized authority	It is hereby certified that the declaration by the exporter is true and correct. Place and date. signature and stamp of certifying authority

二、缮制普惠制原产地证书

尽管多数发达国家已经取消了对我国的普惠制原产地制度，但仍有挪威、澳大利亚和新西兰三个发达国家保留了给予中国的普惠制关税优惠制度，同时，考虑到学习者可能到跨国公司就职被派往东南亚国家工作，仍有可能使用到普惠制原产地证书，本章保留了缮制普惠制证书 FORM A 的填写讲解。

普惠制原产地证书的填制与一般原产地证略有不同，现以 FORM A 为例，在此只针对不同点进行阐述（货物输往国改为挪威）。

1. 证书的名称（Title of Document）：在证头横线上方需显示签证国，国名须英文全称，不得简化，“Issued in THE PEOPLE’S REPUBLIC OF CHINA”（国内的证书已将此印就，无须再缮打）。

※本案例制单： 来证条款

制单操作

GENERALIZED SYSTEM OF PREFERENCES
CERTIFICATE OF ORIGIN
(COMBINED DECLARATION AND CERTIFICATE)
FORM A
ISSUED IN THE PEOPLE’S REPUBLIC OF CHINA
(COUNTRY)

2. 第 1 栏：出口商（Goods consigned from...）

此栏带有强制性，必须打上国名。出口商的名称、地址和国名须与发票上一致，应填明详细地址，包括街道名、门牌号码等。

※本案例制单： 来证条款

制单操作

1. Goods consigned from (Exporter’s business name, address, country)
SHANDONG HOPE NATIVE PRODUCT I/E CORP.
62, GUANGXI ROAD, QINGDAO, CHINA

3. 第 2 栏：收货人（Goods consigned to (Consignee’s name, address, country))

除欧盟 25 国、挪威外，此栏须填上给惠国最终收货人名称和地址、国名，不可填中间转口商的名称。欧盟 25 国、挪威对此栏是非强制性要求，若第 2 栏进口商国家和第 12 栏最终目的国都是欧盟国家，则可以与第 12 栏国家不同，也可以不填详细地址，只填写 To Order。其余缮制要领与一般原产地证收货人栏相同。

※本案例制单： 来证条款

制单操作

2. Goods consigned to (Consignee’s name, address, country)
TO ORDER

4. 运输方式和路线（Means of Transport and Route）：此栏须与发票和提单一致，但不必写船名和航次。为便于进口国海关查证，也可显示航运时间，如：DURING MM/YY 或 ON/AFTER（装船日期）BY SEA / VESSEL（船名和航次）FROM（装运港）TO（卸货港）。装船日期为订舱后承运人通知所获得。

若遇转船，还须在目的港后加注 VIA 或 W/T at （转船港）；内陆转运则打 in transit to（目的地）。

※本案例制单：来证条款

TRANSSHIPMENT: PERMITTED
SHIPMENT FROM ANY PORT IN CHINA
TO OSLO LATEST 06 JULY/2015

制单操作

3. Means of transport and route
FROM QINGDAO, CHINA TO OSLO, NORWAY
BY SEA ON/AFTER JULY 5, 2015.

5. 供签证机构使用栏（For Certifying Authority Use Only）：本栏出口人不填写。

6. 第 5 栏：商品顺序号（Item number）

此栏填写出货的品种数量。若同批出口货物有不同品种，则按不同品种分列“1”“2”“3”……以此类推。单项商品，此栏填“1”。

※本案例制单：　　来证条款　　　　制单操作

5. Item number 1

7. 第 8 栏：原产地标准（Origin Criterion）

此栏用字最少，但却是国外海关审核的核心项目。对含有进口成分的商品，因情况复杂，国外要求严格，极易弄错而造成退证查询，应认真审核、慎重填写。现将填写该栏原产地标准符号的一般规定说明如下：

（1）完全原产地商品，不含任何非原产成分，出口到所有给惠国，填写“P”；

（2）含有非原产成分的产品，出口到欧盟、挪威、瑞士和日本，填写“W”，其后加上出口产品的 H.S. 品目号。例如“W”42.02。条件为：① 产品列入了上述给惠国的“加工清单”，符合其加工条件；② 产品未列入“加工清单”，但产品生产过程中使用的非原产原材料和零部件经过充分的加工，产品的 H.S. 品目号不同于所用的原材料和零部件的 H.S. 品目号；

（3）含有非原产成分的产品，出口到加拿大，填写“F”。条件为：非原产成分的价值未超过产品出厂价的 40%；

（4）含有非原产成分的产品，出口到俄罗斯、乌克兰、白俄罗斯、哈萨克斯坦、捷克、斯洛伐克六国，填写“Y”，其后加上非原产成分价值占该产品 FOB 价格的百分比，例如“Y”38%。条件为：非原产成分的价值未超过产品 FOB 价的 50%；

（5）输往澳大利亚、新西兰的货物，此栏可以留空。

※本案例制单：　　来证条款　　　　制单操作

8. Origin Criterion (see notes overleaf) “P”

8. 第 11 栏：签证当局的证明（Certification）

此栏由签证机构签证人经审核后签名，盖签证印章（印章不得压住签名），填写签证地点和日期。此栏日期不得早于第 10 栏发票日期和第 12 栏申报日期，且不晚于提单（货物的装运）日期。

※本案例制单：　　来证条款　　　　制单操作

11. Certification It is hereby certified, on the basis of control carried out, that the declaration by the exporter is correct. Place and date, signature and stamp of certifying authority

9. 第 12 栏：出口商的声明（Declaration by the exporter）

该栏先填写出口国名（一般预先印就），进口国横线上填最终进口国，进口国必须与第三栏目的港的国别一致。另外，申请单位应授权专人在此栏手签，注明声明地点、日期，并加盖申请单位中英文印章。手签人笔迹必须在海关注册登记，并保持相对稳定。此栏日期不得早于第 10 栏发票日期。盖章应避免覆盖进口国名称和手签人姓名。本证书一律不得涂改，证书不得加盖校对章。

※本案例制单： 来证条款 制单操作

来证条款：

SHIPMENT FROM ANY PORT IN CHINA TO OSLO LATEST 06 JULY/ 2015

制单操作：

12. Declaration by the exporter
The undersigned hereby declares that the above details and statements are correct; that all the goods were produced in

CHINA
(country)

and that they comply with the origin requirements specified for those goods in the Generalized System of Preference for goods exported to

NORWAY
(importing country)

××× (STAMPED)

QINGDAO, CHINA JULY 1, 2015
Place and date, signature of authorized signatory

三、缮制 RCEP 原产地证书

为避免船期更改，提高办证效率，该证书和 FORM E（中国东盟自由贸易区优惠原产地证明书）均可在货物装运后一个月内办妥为有效。现将有关各栏目的填制要求介绍如下：

1. 货物运自（出口商名称、地址、国家）（Goods Consigned from (Exporter’s name, address and country)）：此栏目应填写已办理原产地证书申请人备案的中国境内（不含港澳台地区）出口商的名称、详细地址和国家。此栏不得填写两个或两个以上出口公司名称。

2. 货物运至（进口商/收货人名称、地址、国家）（Goods Consigned to (Importer’s/ Consignee’s name, address, country)）：此栏应填写 RCEP 成员方收货人名称、地址和国家。此栏不得填写非进口方公司信息。

3. 生产商名称、地址、国家（如已知）（Producer’s name, address and country (if known)）：此栏应填写货物生产商的名称、地址和国家。具体填制要求如下：

–如证书货物由多个生产商生产，此栏填写“SEE BOX 8”，同时应在第八栏每项货物描述后列明对应生产商的名称、地址、国家；

–出口商或生产商希望该信息保密的，可在本栏填写“CONFIDENTIAL”；

–如果不知道生产商，可在本栏填写“NOT AVAILABLE”。

4. 运输工具及路线（如已知）（Means of transport and route (if known)）：

–离港日期（Departure date）：此栏填写离港日期；

–船舶名称/航班号等（Vessel name/Aircraft flight number, etc.）：装运后申报的原产地证书，此栏必须填写具体运输工具名称及号码；出运前申报且具体运输工具名称及号码未知的原产地证书，此栏可填写“***”或“BY SEA”或“BY AIR”或其他运输方式；

–卸货口岸（Port of discharge）：填写 RCEP 成员方口岸。

5. 官方使用栏（For Official Use）：本栏目留空。

6. 项目编号（Item number）：在收货人、运输条件相同的情况下，如同批出口货物有不同品种，则可按不同品种分列“1、2、3、4……”，以此类推。

7. 包装唛头及编号（Marks and numbers on packages）：此栏目填写的唛头及包装编号应与发票、货物外包装上的唛头和包装编号一致。具体填写要求如下：

–如果货物没有唛头及包装编号，应填写“N/M”或“NO MARKS”或“NO MARKS AND NUMBERS”；

–如果有特殊唛头的，可在此栏填写“SEE ATTACHMENT”，并在证书背页贴唛（盖骑缝章）或 A4 白纸打印唛头（盖骑缝章）；

–CARTON LABEL 和下列描述文字 AS ADDRESS、AS PER INVOICE、AS PACKING LIST、AS B/L、AS BILL OF LADING、COLOR LABEL 等不能作为唛头。

8. 包装件数及种类；货物名称（Number and kind of packages; and description of goods）：具体填制要求如下：

–货物描述必须详细，以使对方验货的海关关员可以识别。货物描述应与清关发票一致，不同类型、型号的货物应分项列明；

–如果信用证、合同中品名笼统或拼写错误，应在括号内加注具体描述或正确品名；

–包装数量必须用英文或阿拉伯数字表示大小写，并表明货物具体包装种类。货物无包装的，应填明货物装运时的状态，如“NUDE CARGO”“IN BULK”“HANGING GARMENTS”等；

–信用证有具体要求，如要求填具合同号码、信用证号码等信息可填写在商品描述特殊条款栏。

9. 货物 6 位数 H.S. 编码（H.S. Code of the goods (6 digit-level)）：此栏填写第 8 栏每项货物名称对应的 6 位数 H.S. 编码。

10. 原产地标准（Origin Conferring Criterion）：具体填写要求如下：

–货物在一成员方完全获得或者生产，填写“WO”（注：WO 主要适用于农林牧渔产品、矿产品等未经加工生产的初级产品）；

–货物在一成员方完全使用原产材料生产，填写“PE”；

–货物在一成员方使用非原产材料生产，但符合货物特定原产地规则规定的税则归类改变、区域价值成分、制造加工工序或者其他要求的：

① 货物以税则归类改变标准获得 RCEP 项下原产资格的，此栏填写“CTC”；

② 货物以区域价值成分标准获得 RCEP 项下原产资格的，此栏填写“RVC”；

③ 货物以制造加工标准获得 RCEP 项下原产资格的，此栏填写“CR”；

–如果货物获得 RCEP 项下原产资格使用了“累积规则”条款或“微小含量”条款的，应在填写上述标准基础上增加填写“ACU”或“DMI”。

11. RCEP 项下原产国（地区）（RCEP Country of Origin）：此栏填写货物确定的 RCEP 项下原产国或地区。

12. 数量（毛重或其他计量单位下的数量），适用区域价值成分时应填写价格（FOB）(Quantity, gross weight or other measurement, and value (FOB) where RVC is applied)：

–此栏应填写货物的正常计量单位，如“PCS”“SETS”等。货物以重量计的则填毛重或净重，需要加注“G.W.”或“N.W.”；另外需注意：

–原产地标准采用区域价值成分标准时（包括“RVC”“RVC ACU”）应在此栏填写货物的 FOB 价格。涉及第三方的，FOB 价格可填写第三方发票金额或国内出口发票金额。如已知第三方发票金额的，一般应填写第三方发票金额，以避免金额与清关发票不一致导致进口方海关核查。

13. 发票编号及日期（Invoice number(s) and date of invoice(s)）：此栏填写发票号和发票日期，所填写的发票号码、日期应与货物在进口方海关清关使用的发票一致。注意事项如下：

–发票日期不能迟于第 4 栏离港日期和第 15、16 栏证书申请、签证日期；

–如使用第三方发票，此栏必须填写第三方发票号码和日期；

–若该份证书有多份发票，则需要在每一项货物对应的本栏打印发票号码和发票日期。申报多份发票的，货币单位和价格条款须保持一致。

14. 备注（Remarks）：具体填写要求如下：

–如果发票由第三方开具，应在此栏注明开具发票的公司名称、地址及所在国家或地区等第三方信息。

–若该份证书为背对背证书[①]，需在本栏目备注原始原产地证明信息，包括原始证明号码（ORIGINAL PROOF OF ORIGIN REF NO.）、原始证明签发日期（DATE OF ISSURANCE）、签发国（ISSUING COUNTRY）、首次出口的 RCEP 项下原产国（地区）（RCEP COUNTRY OF ORIGIN OF THE FIRST EXPORTING PARTY）、首次出口国的经核准出口商授权号（APPROVED EXPORTER AUTHORISATION CODE OF THE FIRST EXPORTING PARTY）；

–若该份证书为经过认证的真实副本，需要在本栏打印以下信息：“CERTIFIED TRUE COPY”和“THE DATE OF ISSUANCE：XXX.XX.XXXX”（如：JAN.0102022）。

–如合同或信用证对单证有加注信息要求的，应在本栏按要求备注具体信息，包括填写客户订单编号、信用证号码等。

15. 出口商或生产商声明（Declaration by the exporter or producer）：此栏填写申报地点、日期，申请人授权的专人在此栏签字。填写时注意以下几点：

–申报地点应与签证地点一致；

–进口国应为最终进口国且与卸货港的国别一致，进口国必须是 RCEP 成员方；

–申报日期应为实际申请日期。

16. 证明（Certification）：此栏填写签证机构签证地点、日期。签证人员在此栏签名，并在证书正本和交给申请人的副本上加盖原产地 ORIGIN 印章。签名和印章应清晰完整且不得重叠。

---

① RCEP 背对背原产地证明是中间缔约方针对已由原出口缔约方出具原产地证明的货物，再次分批分期灵活出具的原产地证明，相关货物在其他缔约方进口时仍然可以享受关税优惠待遇。该类证明适应现代国际物流的需要，有利于货物在成员国之间进行运输和物流分拆，极大地提高了企业在销售策略以及物流安排方面的灵活性。需要注意的是，背对背原产地证明的有效期不得超过初始原产地证明的有效期。

17. 其他标注

–背对背原产地证书：勾选“Back-to-back Certificate of Origin”；

–使用第三方发票：勾选“Third-party invoicing”；

–补发证书：勾选“ISSUED RETROACTIVELY”。

四、缮制中国—东盟自由贸易区 FORM E 产地证

在此只针对与 RCEP 证书不同点进行阐述。

1. 第 4 栏，官方使用（For Official Use）：不论是否给予优惠待遇，进口方海关必须在第 4 栏做出相应的标注 ☑。如给予优惠则在 Preferential Treatment Given 栏标识 ☑；如不给予优惠则在 Preferential Treatment Not Given (Please state reason/s) 栏标识 ☑ 并说明理由。

2. 第 7 栏，包装件数及种类；产品名称（包括相应数量及进口成员方 H.S. 编码）Number and type of packages, description of products (including quantity where appropriate and H.S. number in six digit code)。此栏目填写要求如下：

–包装件数大小写和种类，如果产品无包装，申报产品出运时的实际状态，如“NUDE CARGO”“IN BULK”。

–产品名称必须详细，以使验货的海关关员可以识别；

–H.S. 编码应与产品名称相符，填写 6 位数 H.S. 编码。例如 HS CODE: 5206.32。

3. 第 8 栏，原产地标准（Origin criteria）。关于本栏目的填写要求在 FORM E 证书的背页上有详细介绍，填法如下表：

是否含有进口成分	详　情	标准填写
无进口成分	农林牧副渔矿产品及初级制品、协议 PSR 清单[①]中仅适用完全获得标准的产品（完全获得）	“WO”
	仅使用中国和东盟成员国原材料生产的产品（完全生产）	“PE”
含进口成分	在 PSR 清单里（不含完全获得）的产品	“PSR”
	在 CTH 清单[②]里的产品	“CTH”
	未列入 PSR 清单，区域价值成分不少于货物离岸价格的 40%的产品。	中国—东盟累计成分的百分比

4. 第 10 栏，发票编号及日期（Numbers and date of invoices）。本栏目填写本业务项下发票的编号和日期。如使用的是第三方发票即中国大陆地区和进口方之外的公司开具

① PSR 清单：《中华人民共和国与东南亚国家联盟全面经济合作框架协议》项下 PSR 清单涉及产品太多，在此无法一一阐述。

② CTH 清单：进出口税则第 25、26、28、29（29.01、29.02 除外）、31（31.05 除外）、39（39.01、39.02、39.03、39.07、39.08 除外）、42-49、57-59、61、62、64、66-71、73-83、86、88、91-97 章项下货物，非原产材料加工后，发生 4 位级税则归类改变的产品。

的发票，应在第 13 栏勾选“第三方发票”栏目并填写第三方公司名称和国别。

5. 第 11 栏，出口商申明（Declaration by the exporter）。“出口商”可包括制造商或生产商。作为流动证明[①]时，“出口商”也包括中间方的出口商。

6. 第 13 栏，包含以下 4 个选项：

–补发（Issued Retroactively）：在特殊情况下，由于非主观故意的差错、疏忽或者其他合理原因，可按照中国—东盟自由贸易区原产地规则的规定补发原产地证书（Form E）。相应地在“补发”栏予以标注 ☑。

–展览（Exhibition）：当产品由出口方运至另一方展览并在展览期间或展览后销售给一方时，应在“展览”予以标注 ☑。展览的名称及地址应在第 2 栏中注明。

–流动证明（Movement Certificate）：作为流动证明时，应在“流动证明”栏予以标注 ☑。成员方的原始签证机构名称、签发日期以及原始原产地证书（Form E）证书的编号也应在第 13 栏中注明。

–第三方发票（Third Party Invoicing）：当发票是由第三国开具时，应在“第三方发票”予以标注 ☑。

相关知识

一、原产地证书的性质及作用

我国的原产地证书是证明中国出口货物符合《中华人民共和国出口货物原产地规则》，货物确系中华人民共和国原产的证明文件。原产地证书的主要作用在于证明货物的原产国，从而根据国别的不同，实行差别关税、分配和控制进口配额或者其他进口管制。该文件具有法律效力，被视为“有价证券”，是通关、结汇、进行贸易统计的重要文件。

对进口国而言，出口国签发的原产地证书的作用主要体现在以下五个方面：

1. 确定税率待遇的主要依据；
2. 进行贸易统计的重要依据；
3. 实施进口数量控制、反倾销、反补贴等外贸管理措施的依据；
4. 控制从特定国家进口货物，确定准予放行与否的依据；
5. 证明商品内在品质或结汇的依据。

二、原产地证的管理

（一）备案登记

申请单位在申请办理原产地证之前应向所在地签证机构办理备案手续，登录国际贸易单一窗口，选择“原产地”栏目进入到原产地综合服务平台，填写企业备案信息。申

① 流动证明：流动证明是指出口中间方根据第一个出口方所签发的原始原产地证书（Form E）签发的，用于证明所涉产品的原产地资格。流动证明本身也是有效的原产地证书，并且与原产地证书具有相同格式且相同的效力。只是流动证明并非由第一个出口方，而是由出口中间方的签证机构签发。

请单位的印章和申领人员的姓名应在备案时进行登记。申请单位如果是生产型企业还需通过中国国际贸易“单一窗口”平台进入原产地综合服务平台进行产品预审，按照要求申报产品 H.S. 编码、中英文名称、原材料情况、生产工序等相关信息（非生产型企业免于产品预审）。

（二）申请签证

申请单位应至少在货物装运前三天，向原产地证签发机关申请签证。

申请单位登录国际贸易单一窗口进行申领，以向海关申领为例说明申领程序如下：

Step 1：证书申报：填写进出口双方信息、运输细节、商品描述、使用的原产地标准等信息，应依据不同原产地证书的填制规范进行申报。

Step 2：证书签发：企业登录中国国际贸易“单一窗口”，查询可自助打印的原产地证书。对于尚未开通自助打印的原产地证书，企业须使用针式打印机在申领的空白证书上打印原产地证书，并加盖企业中英文印章、授权人员签字后，到签证海关现场办理证书签发手续(附上打印出来的原产地证书申请书和发票)。

三、原产地证书的分类

货物原产地证书的种类很多，按照不同的分类方法，可以将原产地证书分为以下几种：

（一）按用途分类

可以分为非优惠类原产地证书和优惠类原产地证书。

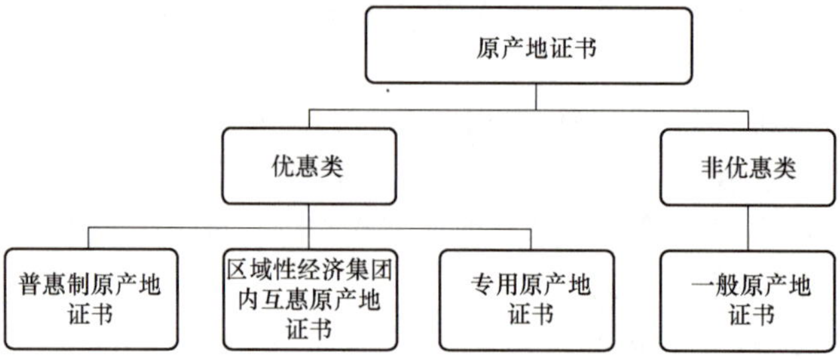

图 9-1　原产地证书的分类图

1. 非优惠类原产地证书：即为普通原产地证书（Certificate of Origin，简称 C/O），由中国国际贸易促进委员会（China Council for the Promotion of International Trade，CCPIT）或海关签发。

2. 优惠类原产地证书：优惠类原产地证书是国际贸易货物享受进口方差别关税待遇的必要凭证，也被称为“纸黄金”。该类证书目前由海关和贸促会分别签发。

（1）普惠制原产地证书（FORM A 证书）

该证书是发达国家给予发展中国家的一种关税优惠安排，是在普惠制下所签发的产地证书。所谓“普惠制”，是指发达国家单方面对从发展中国家输入的工业制成品或半制成品普遍给予优惠关税待遇的一种国际贸易制度。普惠制原产地证书上所列的商品只有符合有关给惠国的普惠制原产地规则才有资格享受减免关税待遇。之前共有 39 个国家给予中国普惠制待遇，但随着我国经济的不断发展，给惠国纷纷采取了“普惠制毕业”，该证书目前只对挪威、澳大利亚和新西兰三国签发了。

（2）区域性经济集团内互惠原产地证书

我国加入 WTO 后与许多国家达成了自由贸易协定，区域性经济集团内互惠原产地证书近年一直活跃在进出口业务中。以下介绍几种比较常见的区域性经济集团内互惠原产地证书。

–RCEP 原产地证书：RCEP 即区域全面经济伙伴关系（Regional Comprehensive Economic Partnership），由东盟十国发起，由中国、日本、韩国、澳大利亚、新西兰等与文莱、柬埔寨、印度尼西亚、老挝、马来西亚、菲律宾、新加坡、泰国、缅甸、越南（东盟十国）共计 15 个国家所构成的自由贸易协定。RCEP 旨在通过削减关税及非关税壁垒，建立统一市场的自由贸易协定。RCEP 是目前世界上最大的自贸区，其人口数量、经济体量、贸易总额约占全球总量的 30%。2022 年 1 月 1 日，区域全面经济伙伴关系协定（RCEP）正式生效。

在 RCEP 协定框架下，只有办理 RCEP 原产地证书，区域成员国之间才能享受关税优惠。按照协定，降税模式分为四种：（1）协定生效立即降为零；（2）过渡期降为零；（3）部分降税；（4）例外产品。总体而言，按照税目计算，RCEP 生效后将实现 90%以上货物贸易最终降为零关税。

–中国—东盟自由贸易区 FORM E 证书：中国—东盟自由贸易区原产地证书是根据《中华人民共和国与东南亚国家联盟全面经济合作框架协议》的要求签发的、在协定成员国之间就特定产品享受互惠减免关税待遇的官方证明文件，签证依据为《中国—东盟自由贸易区原产地规则》及其《签证操作程序》。东盟成员国为文莱、柬埔寨、印度尼西亚、老挝、马来西亚、缅甸、菲律宾、新加坡、泰国、越南。

–其他的区域性经济集团内互惠原产地证书还有中国—孟加拉国、印度、老挝、韩国和斯里兰卡《亚太贸易协定》框架下的 FORM B 证书、中国—巴基斯坦自由贸易区 FORM P 证书、中国—智利自由贸易区 FORM F 证书、中国—新加坡自由贸易区优惠原产地证书、中国—秘鲁自由贸易区优惠原产地证书、中国—瑞士自由贸易区优惠原产地证书、中国—冰岛自由贸易区优惠原产地证书、中国—格鲁吉亚自由贸易区优惠原产地证书、中国—毛里求斯自贸协定原产地证书、《亚洲—太平洋贸易协定》原产地证书（输韩国、印度）以及对中国港澳地区的 Closer Economic Partnership Agreement（CEPA）原产地证和对中国台湾的 Economic Cooperation Framework Agreement（ECFA）原产地证书等。

（3）专用原产地证书

此类证书是国际组织或国家根据整治和贸易措施的需要，针对某一特殊行业的特定产品规定的原产地证书。专用原产地证书上所列的产品均属某一特殊行业的某项特定产品，这些产品应符合特定的原产地规则。签证依据为中国政府与外国政府签订的双边协议规定。如《输欧盟农产品原产地证书》、原产地命名证书（《托考依葡萄酒原产地名称证书》《皇帝牌葡萄酒真实性证书》《奶酪制品证书》）《烟草真实性证书》《金珀利进程国际证书》《手工制品原产地证书》和《原产地标记证书》等。

（二）按签发人分类

可以分为领事产地证（Consular Certificate of Origin）[①]、厂商产地证（Manufacturer's Certificate of Origin）[②]、中国国际贸易促进委员会出具的产地证、海关出具的产地证。在实际业务中，因海关和贸促会的权威性、严格的缮制格式以及申领要求，进出口业务多采用海关和贸促会出具的产地证。

1. 海关签发的原产地证种类

海关可签发非优惠类的一般原产地证书，大多数优惠类原产地证书和一些专用原产地证书，签发的具体产地证种类如下图所示：

图 9-2　海关签发的原产地证书种类

2. 贸促会签发的原产地证书种类

贸促会可以签发非优惠类的一般原产地证书以及部分优惠类原产地证书。自 2009 年 8 月 1 日开始，贸促会可以签发《亚太自由贸易协定》《中国—新加坡自由贸易协定》《中国—新西兰自由贸易协定》《中国—秘鲁自由贸易协定》《中国—哥斯达黎加自由贸易协定》《海峡两岸经济合作框架协议》等协定项下的原产地证书，企业持有这些优惠原产地证书可享受 5%—50%的关税优惠，销往新加坡的产品可享受零关税优惠待遇。具体签发的原产地种类如下表：

---

① 是指应进口商要求，由进口国派驻出口国的使领馆签字或加注的产地证书。由于使领馆签字加注要收取一定的费用，会增加出口商的成本，办理加注也需要一定的时间，应尽量不采用该证书，或须提前预留相应的时间办理。

② 一般是由出口人自行签发的原产地证明书，在合同或信用证规定由商品的实际生产商签发产地证时出具。个别单位将产地证书联合在发票上或在发票上加注货物产地证明文句。

表 9-1　贸促会签发的原产地证书种类

类　别	种　类
非优惠类	一般原产地证书
优惠类	中国—哥斯达黎加自由贸易协定优惠原产地证书
	澳大利亚优惠原产地证书
	冰岛优惠原产地证书
	格鲁吉亚优惠原产地证书
	韩国优惠原产地证书
	海峡两岸优惠原产地证书
	秘鲁优惠原产地证书
	毛里求斯优惠原产地证书
	内地与港澳优惠原产地证书
	瑞士优惠原产地证书
	新西兰优惠原产地证书
	亚太优惠原产地证书
	智利优惠原产地证书
	新加坡优惠原产地证书
	巴基斯坦优惠原产地证书

操作能力训练

思考题

S9-1　为什么原产地证书的收货人一栏必须填最终进口商？

操作题

C9-1　根据附录 3.1 里提供的制单信用证 3-13-2（见本书第 230 页），用符合信用证要求的证书格式，独立缮制符合要求的货物原产地证书。

C9-2　讨论和评讲后，根据附录 3.1 里的其余制单信用证（见本书第 230 页），用恰当的格式，逐一缮制符合要求的原产地证书。

C9-3　探索学习下一项目，并根据附录 3.1 里的制单信用证 3-13-1（见本书第 230 页），用投保单格式一和保险单格式一，分别缮制符合要求的投保单和保险单。

C9-4　独立学习 ISBP（2013 最新版本）和 UCP600 中关于保险单据的相关条款。

项目十

缮制货运投保单和保险单据

出口货物在装上运载工具之前，出口人应为货物办理运输投保手续，并获得保险人出具的货物运输保险单据。本项目将学习填写货运投保单和缮制货运保险单。

学习目标

[知识目标] 了解货运投保的流程，了解货运保险的相关知识，掌握缮制投保单和保险单的要领。

[能力目标] 能根据信用证或合同要求，正确缮制投保单和保险单。

一、缮制投保单

货物装运前，出口人为货物办理运输保险，首先需要填写一份投保单，向当地一家保险公司进行投保。以信用证方式结算的，按信用证的要求填写投保单，以其他方式结算的，按合同要求填写。

项目描述（案例情境描述）

山东希望土产进出口公司向马来西亚出口一批山东黑枣，进口方通过银行开来信用证。出口方经审核无误后，开始缮制来证要求提供的全套单据。本次业务为缮制投保单，办理货运保险。

操作要领（缮制投保单各栏的填制要求）

投保单并无固定格式，但投保必要的基本内容都是一致的。

1. 保险人（Insurer/Underwriter）：此栏填写投保人选定的保险公司名称和地址（写明分公司即可）。一些投保单格式已印就了保险人，则不必再填写。若来证有指定保险人，则须照要求填写并向其投保。本例来证无此要求，则可任意选择一家保险人。

※本案例制单： 来证条款 制单操作

来证条款	制单操作
+ MARINE INSURANCE POLICY OR CERTIFICATE FOR FULL CIF VALUE PLUS 10 PERCENT	中保财产保险有限公司青岛市分公司

2. 被保险人（The Insured's Name）：此栏填写保险单的受益人。在信用证项下，来证若无其他要求，则填写信用证的受益人名称。以其他方式结算的，填写合同的卖方名称。

※本案例制单： 来证条款 制单操作

来证条款	制单操作
+ MARINE INSURANCE POLICY OR CERTIFICATE FOR FULL CIF VALUE PLUS 10 PERCENT	被保险人： The Insured's Name：SHANDONG HOPE NATIVE PRODUCT I/E CORP.

3. 发票号码（出口用）或合同号码（进口用）(Invoice No. or Contract No.)：由于保险单上需要显示发票号码，因此，在出口业务中，该栏填写商业发票的号码；在进口投保业务中，该栏填写进口合同的号码。同时，该栏要填上运输标记，并与商业发票和提单一致。

※本案例制单： 发票、来证条款 制单操作

发票、来证条款	制单操作
4.发票日期和发票号：Invoice Date and No. BP15SHS02INV1051 JUNE 28, 2015 SHIPPING MARKS: SHS/PENANG/1-UP	发票号码（出口用）或合同号码（进口用） Invoice No. or Contract No. BP15SHS02INV1051 SHIPPING MARKS: SHS PENANG 1-UP

4. 包装数量（Package Quantity）：此栏按要求填入商品的包装数量，并与发票和提单一致。如果是非件杂货物，还应填写商品的合同数量。如果信用证对包装种类有限制词，则应照写。

※本案例制单： 发票条款 制单操作

发票条款	制单操作
GOODS: 5M/TONS SHANDONG BLACK DATES SAY TWO HUNDRED (200) CARDBOARD CARTONS ONLY	包装数量 Quantity 5 M/T 200 CARDBOARD CARTONS

5. 保险货物项目（Description of Goods）：一般要求按发票品名填，如果发票品名繁多，本栏允许填写货物统称，但其统称不得与发票或信用证规定的品名相抵触或

引起歧义。

※本案例制单：　来证条款　　　　　　　　　　　　　　　　　　　制单操作

来证条款	制单操作
GOODS: 5M/TONS SHANDONG BLACK DATES	保险货物项目 Description of Goods SHANDONG BLACK DATES

6. 保险金额（Amount Insured）：保险金额又称投保金额，按 CIF 价值加成得到，采用进位取整的方法，如：USD1 658.03→USD1 659.00。信用证项下，按来证保险条款中的加成要求计算填写，其他方式结算的，按合同保险条款规定加成计算。若无具体加成要求，则按发票 CIF 或 CIP 总值加成 10% 计算投保金额，即按发票总额的 110% 投保。如果发票金额包含佣金，应按未扣除佣金前的金额计算保险金额。

如果发票显示的仅是总价值的一部分，比如已经部分预付货款，或部分价款以后支付，也必须按货物的总价值投保。若已扣除佣金，也应按未扣除前的毛总值投保（按含佣价计算投保金额）。

但发票金额显示有折扣须扣除时，保险金额按折扣后的金额加成投保，也可按未做折扣的金额计算投保。通常是采用“保佣不保折”的原则。

中国人保最高可接受发票价值的 200% 的保险金额。投保加成达到 20% 时，须事先经保险人同意。

※本案例制单：　来证条款　　　　　　　　　　　　　　　　　　　制单操作

来证条款	制单操作
CCY/AMOUNT: HKD 46,150.00 MARINE INSURANCE POLICY OR CERTIFICATE FOR FULL CIF VALUE PLUS 10 PERCENT	保险金额 Amount Insured HKD 50,765.00

7. 装载运输工具（Per Conveyance）：按订舱后承运人通知的运载工具名称填写。海运中，S.S.即 steamship 的缩写，M/V 即 motor vessel 的缩写。如有转船，而第二程船名已明确，亦应同时表示出来，两程船名用斜线分开。

若为陆运，则显示“BY TRAIN, BY TRUCK”；空运则显示“BY AIR, BY AREOPLANE”。若为多式运输，如先装火车，然后空运，最后以汽车转到最终目的地，则显示为“BY TRAIN/AIR/TRUCK”。

※本案例制单：　来证条款　　　　　　　　　　　　　　　　　　　制单操作

来证条款	制单操作
	装载运输工具　M/V “VICTORIA” Per Conveyance

8. 航次、航班或车号（Voy. No）：本栏填写海运货轮航次，或空运的航班号，或陆运的火车车卡号或汽车车牌号。按承运人通知填写。

※本案例制单：　来证条款　　　　　　　　　　　　　　　　　　　制单操作

来证条款	制单操作
	航次、航班或车号　V.306 Voy. No.

9. 开航日期（Slg. Date）：此栏填写承运人通知的未来的运输单据上所载明的实际装运日期。

※本案例制单：　　来证条款

制单操作

开航日期 JULY 5, 2015 Slg. Date

10. 起讫地点（From ××× to ×××）：此栏为运输路径，须填写具体的装运港/地和卸货港/地，须与发票和提单记载的一致，且符合信用证要求。如果货物在中途转船，则应注明转运港/地。若来证有选择港口，则应照填，用斜线隔开。

※本案例制单：　　来证条款

制单操作

SHIPMENT FROM ANY PORT IN CHINA TO PENANG

自 QINGDAO, CHINA From	至 PENANG To	转运地 W/Tat

11. 赔付地（Claim Payable at）：此栏填写明确具体的保险赔付地点，按信用证保险条款中要求的具体地点填写。若来证对赔付地点未予明确或笼统，则以目的港为赔付地点；若来证明确规定了赔付使用的货币，则应照填予以注明。否则，可以不特别注明赔付时使用的货币。

※本案例制单：　　来证条款

制单操作

赔款地 PENANG, MALAYSIA　IN HK$ Claim Payable at

12. 承保险别（Condition &/or Special Coverage）：本栏是投保单的核心内容，是将来确定理赔责任范围的主要依据，必须慎重填制，严格与信用证规定相符，即使信用证没有规定保险依据，投保单上也应说明该险别适用的条款文本名称及其生效日期。

※本案例制单：　　来证条款

MARINE INSURANCE POLICY OR CERTIFICATE FOR FULL CIF VALUE PLUS 10 PERCENT COVERING OCEAN MARINE CARGO CLAUSES ALL RISKS (INCLUDING WAREHOUSE TO WAREHOUSE CLAUSES) AND WAR RISK CLAUSES (1/1/1981) OF THE PEOPLE'S INSURANCE COMPANY OF CHINA.

制单操作

承保险别 Condition & / or Special Coverage: COVERING OCEAN MARINE CLAUSES ALL RISKS (INCLUDING WAREHOUSE TO WAREHOUSE CLAUSES) AND WAR RISK CLAUSES(1/1/1981) OF THE PEOPLE'S INSURANCE COMPANY OF CHINA.

13. 投保人签章及公司名称、电话、地址（Applicant's Signature and Co.'s Name, Add. And Tel. No.）：本栏填写投保人的基本信息，一般与第一栏的被保险人一致。联系方式应尽量详细，并需签字盖章。

※本案例制单：　　来证条款　　　　　　　　　　　　　　　　　　　　　制单操作

BENEFICIARY: SHANDONG HOPE NATIVE PRODUCT I/E CORP. 62, GUANGXI ROAD, QINGDAO, CHINA

投保人签章及公司名称、电话、地址： Applicant's Signature and Co.'s Name, Add. And Tel. No. 山东青岛希望土产进出口总公司 SHANDONG HOPE NATIVE PRODUCT I/E CORP. 中国青岛广西路 62 号 ×××　　电话：　65788877

14. 备注（Remarks）：本栏一般填写信用证规定在保险单据上需要加注的内容，同时要求保险公司在出具的保单上注明其在目的港的赔付代理人名称、地址和联系方式，便于保单持有人联系索赔。

※本案例制单：　　来证条款　　　　　　　　　　　　　　　　　　　　　制单操作

SPECIAL CONDITIONS: 3) DOCUMENTS TO EVIDENCE THAT ALL PACKAGES BEAR SHIPPING MARKS: SHS/PENANG/1-UP 4) DOCUMENTS TO EVIDENCE THAT PACKING IS DONE AS FOLLOWS: IN CARDBOARD CARTONS OF 25KGS NET OR 26.2KGS GROSS PER CARTON

备注： Remarks	保单上须注明 1. PACKING IS DONE AS FOLLOWS: IN CARDBOARD CARTONS OF 25KGS NET OR 26.2KGS GROSS PER CARTON. 2. ALL PACKAGES BEAR SHIPPING MARKS: SHS/PENANG/1-UP 3. 目的港的赔付代理人名称和地址

15. 投保日期（Date）：投保手续需要在货物离开出口仓库前办理。填写的投保日期应至少早于提单显示的装运日或货物接受监管日。

※本案例制单：　　来证条款　　　　　　　　　　　　　　　　　　　　　制单操作

SHIPMENT FROM ANY PORT IN CHINA TO PENANG LATEST 06 JULY, 2015

投保日期：　JULY 2, 2015 Date

附投保单样例

中保财产保险有限公司青岛分公司

The People's Insurance (Property) Company of China Ltd. , Qingdao Branch

进出口货物运输保险投保单

Application Form for I/E Marine Cargo Insurance

被保险人 The Insured' s Name	SHANDONG HOPE NATIVE PRODUCT I/E CORP.		
发票号码（出口用）或合同号码（进口用） Invoice No. or Contract No.	包装数量 Quantity	保险货物项目 Description of Goods	保险金额 Amount Insured
BP15SHS02INV1051 SHIPPING MARKS： SHS PENANG 1-UP	5 M/T 200 CARDBOARD CARTONS	SHANDONG BLACK DATES	HKD 50,765.00

装载运输工具 M/V "VICTORIA" 航次、航班或车号 V.306 开航日期 JULY 5, 2015
Per Conveyance Voy. No. Slg. Date
自 QINGDAO, CHINA 至 PENANG 转运地 赔款地 PENANG, MALAYSIA IN HK$
From To W/Tat Claim Payable at
承保险别： COVERING OCEAN MARINE CLAUSES ALL RISKS (INCLUDING WAREHOUSE TO WAREHOUSE CLAUSES) AND WAR RISK CLAUSES (1/1/1981) OF THE PEOPLE'S INSURANCE COMPANY OF CHINA.
Condition &/or Special Coverage

投保人签章及公司名称、电话、地址：

Applicant's Signature and Co.'s Name, Add. And Tel. No.
山东青岛希望土产进出口总公司
SHANDONG HOPE NATIVE PRODUCT I/E CORP.
中国青岛广西路 62 号
×××　电话：65788877

保单上须注明
备注： 1. PACKING IS DONE AS FOLLOWS:
Remarks IN CARDBOARD CARTONS OF 25KGS NET OR 26.2KGS GROSS PER CARTON.
2. ALL PACKAGES BEAR SHIPPING MARKS：SHS/PENANG/1-UP
3. 目的港的赔付代理人名称和地址　　投保日期：JULY 2, 2015
Date

保险公司填写：　　保单号：　　费率：

二、缮制保险单

办理货运投保后，在货物装运前，出口人还需要拿到由承保保险公司出具的，证明其承保货物运输保险的保险单或保险凭单。各公司印就的保险单据格式不尽相同，但其基本内容都是一致的。

项目描述（案例情境描述）

山东希望土产进出口公司向马来西亚出口一批山东黑枣，进口方通过银行开来信用证。出口方经审核无误后，开始缮制来证要求提供的全套单据。本次业务为缮制保险公司出具的保险单。

操作要领（缮制保险单的填制要求）

1. 保险单号次（Policy No.）、发票号码（Invoice No.）及单据名称（Title of Document）：保险单号次由保险公司编列。保单上须注明商业发票号。单据名称必须与信用证要求相符。若来证和投保时无特别要求，则可出具保险单或保险凭单。

※本案例制单：

制单操作

发票号码 Invoice No.　INV. NO. BP13SHS02INV1051	保险单号次 Policy No.　××××

海 洋 货 物 运 输 保 险 单 MARINE CARGO TRANSPORTATION INSURANCE POLICY

2. 被保险人（The Insured）及背书要求（Endorsement）：被保险人又称抬头（Addressee），为保单受益人（Beneficiary），是未来获得保险赔偿或有权转移单据的一方。此栏的填写方式较多，具体介绍如下：

（1）信用证在保险条款中未做规定时，通常都填写信用证受益人即出口人名称。此种情况都由受益人背书。若来证规定“BLANK ENDORSED”或未做具体背书规定，则一律由受益人做空白背书。

（2）若来证要求做成“to order”或“to the order”，被保险人栏应照打，并由受益人做空白背书。

（3）若来证要求做成“to order of bearer”，被保险人栏应照打，或在“to order of”其后注明受益人名称。这两种方式都由受益人做空白背书。

（4）若来证明确规定了被保险人为信用证受益人以外的第三方，保险单抬头则应照打该第三方名称。若来证规定抬头为“to the order of...Bank”，保险单抬头照打，受益人不做背书。

但这种情况也可把抬头做成先写受益人名称，其后填写“HELD TO THE ORDER OF...”字样。例如来证的保险条款规定：“INSURANCE POLICY ISSUED IN NEGOTIABLE FORM TO THE ORDER OF BANK OF OMAN LTD. (ISSUING BANK) FOR FULL CIF VALUE PLUS 10%...”

保险单抬头也可做成：“投保人名称+HELD TO THE ORDER OF BANK OF OMAN

LTD.”。这种情况由受益人做记名背书。背书的原则是：谁受益谁背书；凭谁指示，谁背书。

（5）在 FOB 和 CFR 价格条件下，若国外买方委托卖方代为办理保险，被保险人栏可做成“××（卖方）ON BEHALF OF ××（买方）”，并由卖方按此形式背书。

（6）若来证要求让渡给第三方，即规定“endorsed to order of ××”或“endorsed in favor of ××”，被保险人栏应显示受益人名称，然后由受益人照此做记名背书，并根据来证文字的不同情况，背书格式分别为：“To order of ××”“In favor of ××”或“Please pay to order of ××”“Please pay in favor of ××”“Please deliver to ××”“Claim if any, pay to...”等。

（7）若来证规定“Loss if any, pay to ××”，被保险人栏应为受益人，由受益人做空白背书，在索赔地栏目上注明“Pay to ××”。

空白背书格式（Blank endorsement）：在单据背面记录背书人信息。例：

XYZ Co. Ltd.
×××
July 22, 2016

记名/特别背书（Special endorsement）：记录被背书人和背书人双方的信息。例：

Please pay to... Bank
XYZ Co. Ltd.
×××
July 22, 2016

※本案例制单：

投保单条款	制单操作
被保险人： The Insured's Name：SHANDONG HOPE NATIVE PRODUCT I/E CORP.	被保险人： Insured's Name：SHANDONG HOPE NATIVE PRODUCT I/E CORP.
	背书：SHANDONG HOPE NATIVE PRODUCT I/E CORP. ××× JULY 8, 2015

3. 保险货物项目（Description of Goods）：此栏按发票品名填写，与提单一致。如果发票品名繁多，可填写统称，但其统称不得与发票或信用证规定品名相抵触或引起歧义。散装货物须注明 IN BULK。如果信用证规定有加注内容，一般填在此栏下方空白处。

※本案例制单：

来证条款	制单操作
GOODS: 5M/TONS SHANDONG BLACK DATES	保险货物项目 Descriptions of Goods
SPECIAL CONDITIONS: 3) DOCUMENTS TO EVIDENCE THAT ALL PACKAGES BEAR SHIPPING MARKS: SHS/PENANG/1-UP 4) DOCUMENTS TO EVIDENCE THAT PACKING IS DONE AS FOLLOWS: IN CARDBOARD CARTONS OF 25KGS NET OR 26.2KGS GROSS PER CARTON	SHANDONG BLACK DATES PACKING IS DONE AS FOLLOWS: IN CARDBOARD CARTONS OF 25KGS NET OR 26.2KGS GROSS PER CARTON. ALL PACKAGES BEAR SHIPPING MARKS: SHS/PENANG/1-UP

4. 包装、单位、数量（Packing, Unit, Quantity）：包装种类和件数须与发票和提单一致。有包装的件杂货物只注明包装件数（大、小写）；裸装货要注明本身件数；散装货要注明净重；有包装的非件杂货物，包装件数和计价装运数量都要显示。如果信用证对外包装种类有限制词，应照写。

※本案例制单：　发票条款　　　　　　　　　　　　　　　　制单操作

GOODS: 5M/TONS SHANDONG BLACK DATES SAY TWO HUNDRED (200) CARDBOARD CARTONS ONLY

包装 Parking　单位 Unit　数量 Quantity
5M/TONS TWO HUNDRED (200) CARDBOARD CARTONS ONLY

5. 保险金额（Amount Insured）：此栏金额按投保单保险金额填写，即严格按信用证或合同对保险加成的规定计算后填写，所使用货币与信用证的一致。若来证没有加成要求，则按发票 CIF 或 CIP 总值的 110% 计算填写。金额精确到小数点后两位。

转让信用证下，如果第一受益人未能更换单据，保险比例可能超过发票金额的 110%，是可以接受的。由于这种情况导致的单价、发票金额、发票抬头和出具人等与原信用证的不符不属于不符点。

※本案例制单：　来证条款　　　　　　　　　　　　　　　　制单操作

CCY/AMOUNT:　HKD46,150.00
MARINE INSURANCE POLICY OR CERTIFICATE FOR FULL CIF VALUE PLUS 10 PERCENT

保险金额 Amount Insured HKD 50,765.00

6. 承保险别（Condition &/or Special Coverage）：本栏按投保单要求填写，严格与信用证规定相符。为便于处理索赔，即使信用证没有规定，保险单上也应注明该险别适用的保险条款名称及其日期。

多投保信用证未规定的险别不是不符点。若信用证未规定投保险别，银行接受所提交的保险单据，并对漏保险别不负责任。受益人也可按最低限度对货物进行投保。

保险范围必须涵盖信用证规定的运输全程（此全程不是运输单据显示的运输全程）。比如信用证规定港至港，保险单显示的保险范围可以是从收货地至最终目的地。

※本案例制单：　投保单条款

承保险别 Condition &/or Special Coverage：COVERING OCEAN MARINE CLAUSES ALL RISKS (INCLUDING WAREHOUSE TO WAREHOUSE CLAUSES) AND WAR RISK CLAUSES (1/1/1981) OF THE PEOPLE'S INSURANCE COMPANY OF CHINA.

制单操作

承保险别 Condition	COVERING OCEAN MARINE CLAUSES ALL RISKS (INCLUDING WAREHOUSE TO WAREHOUSE CLAUSES) AND WAR RISK CLAUSES (1/1/1981) OF THE PEOPLE'S INSURANCE COMPANY OF CHINA.

7. 运输标记（Marks & Nos.）：填写商品的运输标记，须与发票和提单一致。若散装和裸装货物包装没有唛头，应填写 N/M。标记栏原则上应注明原唛头，但也可简式填写“As per Invoice No. ××”。

※本案例制单： 发票条款 制单操作

SHIPPING MARKS: SHS PENANG 1-UP

货物标记 Marks of Goods	SHS PENANG 1-UP

8. 保险总金额大写（Total Amount Insured）：保险金额须显示大写，须与小写一致。大写金额末尾须加 ONLY。

※本案例制单： 来证条款 制单操作

保 险 金 额： Total Amount Insured:	H.K. DOLLARS FIFTY THOUSAND SEVEN HUNDRED AND SIXTY-FIVE ONLY.

9. 保费（Premium）和费率（Rate）：为保守商业秘密，保险公司一般不在保险单上显示具体收费金额和保费率，而是在本栏分别显示 AS ARRANGED，保费也可显示为 AS PAID 或 PREPAID。除非信用证要求标明保费，则应填上具体金额数字。

※本案例制单： 来证条款 制单操作

保费 Premium	AS ARRANGED

10. 装载运输工具（Per Conveyance S.S.）：按投保单要求填写运输工具名称及航次。

※本案例制单： 来证条款 制单操作

运输工具 Per conveyance S. S	M/V “VICTORIA” V.306

11. 开航日期（Sailing on or about）：保单上可显示具体的起航日期，但为了避免特殊情况预定装运发生变化，此栏一般笼统地填为 AS PER B/L DATE 或 AS PER B/L。

※本案例制单： 来证条款 制单操作

开航日期 Slg. on or abt	AS PER B/L. DATE

12. 起讫地点（From... To...）：本栏按投保单填写具体港口，须与发票和提单记载的一致，且符合信用证要求。若货物需转船，应在目的港后加注转运港，即“Via ××或 W/T at ××”。例：“From Shanghai to London W/T at Hong Kong”，或“...to London via Hong Kong”。

若保险承保到内陆某地，应在目的港后注明。例：“From Shanghai to Marseilles and thence to Paris”或“...in transit to Paris”。

来证若有买方选择港口，例如“Option London/ Liverpool/ Manchester”，保单目的港应照打。

※本案例制单： 来证条款 制单操作

来证条款	制单操作
SHIPMENT FROM ANY PORT IN CHINA TO PENANG	起运港 目的港 From QINGDAO, CHINA To PENANG, MALAYSIA

13. 勘查理赔代理人（Agent）：根据中国人民保险公司《货损检验、理赔代理人名册》选择在目的地或目的港附近有关机构为货损检验、理赔代理人。保单上须注明其全称和详细地址，以便保单持有人联系查找。若当地没有合格的保险公司作为代理机构，可注明由当地法定检验机构代为检验。

※本案例制单： 来证条款 制单操作

来证条款	制单操作
	AGENT IN MALAYSIA: ××× ×× ×× ××

14. 赔付地点和赔付货币（Claim Payable at Place/in Currency Code）：此栏必须按信用证的规定填写具体港口或地点。若来证对赔付地点未做明确规定，则打上目的港。若来证规定不止一个目的港或赔付地，则应全部照打。若来证明确规定了赔付货币，应照打；若无规定，可以不打赔付币别。

若来证规定：“CLAIMS PAYABLE AT DESTINATION IN CURRENCY OF THE DRAFT/CREDIT.”这句话应显示在保单赔付地点上方，尽管保险单显示的币别是信用证的币别，并已注明赔付代理在进口国。

※本案例制单： 投保单要求 制单操作

投保单要求	制单操作
赔款地 PENANG, MALAYSIA IN HK$ Claim Payable at	赔款偿付地点 Claim Payable at / in PENANG, MALAYSIA IN HK$

15. 出单日期和地点（Place and Date of Issue）：保险单的签发地址应为保险人所在地。保险生效日期（除非特别声明，一般为签发日期）即为保险公司责任开始日期，必须早于或同于运输单据的装运日期。除非保单有条款声明其生效日期不晚于装运日期，则签发日期可晚于运输单据日期。

※本案例制单： 来证条款 制单操作

来证条款	制单操作
SHIPMENT FROM ANY PORT IN CHINA TO PENANG LATEST 06 JULY, 2015	日期 Date JULY 3, 2015 at QINGDAO

16. 保险人签章（Authorized Signature）：此处由签发保单的保险公司签字盖章。保险单的签署者，可以是保险公司 UNDERWRITER 或他们的代理人。本身要求会签生效者，保险单须会签。无签字，则无效。海上保险单只盖图章即可。

保险经纪人 BROKER 出具的 COVER NOTE 不能接受。但其作为保险公司的代理人，可以在保险经纪人的信笺上出具保险单据，并由保险公司签署，这样的保险单据可以接受。

保险单的正面标注效力超越其背面保险条款效力。

※本案例制单：　来证条款　制单操作

中保财产保险有限公司青岛分公司 THE PEOPLE'S INSURANCE (PROPERTY) COMPANY OF CHINA, LTD. QINGDAO BRANCH 张洪良

17. 其他条款（Other Terms）：如果信用证规定保险单不得显示免赔率 IRRESPECTIVE OF PERCENTAGE, I.O.P.，则不得显示 FRANCHISE / EXCESS。若保单本身未予显示，保单缮制时不再重复 IRRESPECTIVE OF PERCENTAGE 是完全可以的。

18. 份数（Copies）：保单一般一式两份，一正一副。同一运输的同一险种的保险一般提交一份保单，也可以提供多份。每一份保一定的百分比，每一份的保险人承担各自百分比的责任份额。在一份上注明各自比例。

附保险单样例

中保（财产）保险有限公司青岛分公司

The People's Insurance (Property) Company of China, Ltd., Qingdao Branch

发票号码　　保险单号次

Invoice No.　INV. NO.BP13SHS02INV1051　　Policy No.　××××

海 洋 货 物 运 输 保 险 单

MARINE CARGO TRANSPORTATION INSURANCE POLICY

被保险人：

The Insured: SHANDONG HOPE NATIVE PRODUCT I/E CORP.

中保财产保险有限公司（以下简称本公司）根据被保险人的要求，及其所缴付约定的保险费，按照本保险单承担的险别和背面所载条款与下列特别条款承保下列货物运输保险，特签发本保险单。

This policy of Insurance witnesses that The People's Insurance (Property) Company of China, Ltd. (hereinafter called "The Company"), at the request of the Insured and consideration of the premium paid by the Insured, undertakes to insure the under-mentioned goods in transportation subject to the condition of this Policy as per the Clauses printed overleaf and other special clauses attached hereon.

保险货物项目 Descriptions of Goods	包装　单位　数量 Parking　Unit　Quantity	保险金额 Amount Insured
SHANDONG BLACK DATES PACKING IS DONE AS FOLLOWS:	5M/TONS TWO HUNDRED (200) CARDBOARD CARTONS	HKD 50,765.00

（续表）

保险货物项目 Descriptions of Goods	包装 单位 数量 Parking Unit Quantity	保险金额 Amount Insured
IN CARDBOARD CARTONS OF 25KGS NET OR 26.2KGS GROSS PER CARTON. ALL PACKAGES BEAR SHIPPING MARKS: SHS/PENANG/1-UP	ONLY	

ORIGINAL

承保险别 COVERING OCEAN MARINE CLAUSES ALL RISKS

Condition (INCLUDING WAREHOUSE TO WAREHOUSE CLAUSES) AND WAR RISK CLAUSES (1/1/1981) OF THE PEOPLE'S INSURANCE COMPANY OF CHINA.

货物标记 Marks of Goods SHS PENANG 1-UP

总 保 险 金 额：

Total Amount Insured: H.K. DOLLARS FIFTY THOUSAND SEVEN HUNDRED AND SIXTY-FIVE ONLY.

保费 运输工具 开航日期

Premium AS ARRANGED Per conveyance S. S M/V "VICTORIA" V.306 Slg. on or abt AS PER B/L. DATE

起运港 目的港

From QINGDAO, CHINA To PENANG, MALAYSIA

所保货物，如发生本保险单项下可能引起索赔的损失或损坏，应立即通知本公司下述代理人查勘。如有索赔，应向本公司提交保险单正本（本保险单共有 2 份正本）及有关文件。如一份正本已用于索赔，其余正本则自动失效。

In the event of loss or damage which may result in a claim under this Policy, immediate notice must be given to the Company's Agent as mentioned hereunder. Claims, if any, one of the Original Policy which has been issued in **TWO** Original (s) together with the relevant documents shall be surrendered to the Company, if one of the Original Policy has been accomplished, the others to be void.

AGENT IN MALAYSIA：

××× ××

×× ××

中保财产保险有限公司青岛分公司

THE PEOPLE'S INSURANCE (PROPERTY) COMPANY OF CHINA, LTD.

QINGDAO BRANCH

张洪良

General Manager

The People's Insurance (Property) Company of China, Ltd Qingdao Branch

赔款偿付地点

Claim Payable at / in PENANG, MALAYSIA IN HK$

日期 在

Date JULY 3, 2015 at QINGDAO

地址：

Address：23 Dongfeng Road, Qingdao, China. Cable：42001 Qingdao

Tel：83234305 83217466-44 Telex：33128 PICCS CN

背书格式： SHANDONG HOPE NATIVE PRODUCT I/E CORP.

×××

JULY 8, 2015

相关知识

一、货运保险单的作用

保险单据（INSURANCE DOCUMENTS）既是保险公司对被保险人的承保证明，也是双方权利和义务的契约。被保货物或运载工具（标的物）在承保责任范围内遭受损失时，保险单是被保险人索赔的主要依据，也是保险公司理赔的主要根据。

二、保险单据的分类

1. 保险单（INSURANCE POLICY）：这是一种全式保险单，俗称大保单，是一种正规的保险合同，其表面除了载明被保险人（投保人）的名称、被保险货物（标的物）的名称、数量或重量、唛头、运输工具、保险的起讫地点、承保险别、保险金额、出单日期等项目外，还在保险单的背面列有保险人的责任范围，以及保险人与被保险人各自的权利、义务等方面的详细条款，它是最完整的保险单据。保险单可由被保险人背书，随物权的转移而转让，它是一份独立的保险单据。

2. 保险凭证（INSURANCE CERTIFICATE）：该单据又可称为保险凭单，俗称小保单。它有保险单正面的基本内容，但没有了保险单背面的保险条款，是一种简式保险合同，其法律效力等同于大保单。

3. 联合保险凭证（COMBINED INSURANCE CERTIFICATE）：该单据俗称承保证明（RISK NOTE），它是我国保险公司特别使用的一种更为简化的保险单据，由保险公司在出口公司提交的发票上加注保险编号、承保险别、保险金额、装载船只、开船日期等，并加盖保险公司印章即可。这种单据不能转让，主要用于我国出口港澳地区的货运保险。

4. 预约保险单（OPEN POLICY/OPEN COVER）：办理预约保险，通常是负责办理货运保险的进口商，为了避免在货物启运时，自己因出差或其他原因无法为货物办理货运保险而致货物漏保或脱保，提早在货物装运之前就到保险公司办理保险预约。

预约保险单上载明其编号、保险货物的范围、险别、保险费率、每批运输货物的最高保险金额以及保险费的结付、赔款处理等项目。一经保险人接到预约保单标的物的启运通知，该保单即刻自动生效。为了做到及时，作为投保人的进口方往往要求出口方及时地直接向预约保险公司发一份货物装运通知。

5. 保险批单（INSURANCE ENDORSEMENT）：该单据是指保险人签发的同意被保险人要求变更保险单内容的书面文件。它是保险人对投保人提出的补充或变更保险单的内容进行审核，同意后向投保人另出的一种凭证，注明保险人对保险单的补充或更改内容。

一般保险批单须粘贴在保险单上，并加盖骑缝章，作为保险单的一部分。保险批单是保险人与被保险人变更保险合同的证明文件，一经批改后，保险应按批改后的内容承担责任。结算银行接受保险批单，并以此单的条款为准。

三、常见的保险条款

（一）中国保险条例及其险别（China Insurance Clauses，简称 C.I.C.）

在中国，进出口货物运输最常用的保险条款是 C.I.C. 中国保险条款，该条款是由中国人民保险公司制订，中国人民银行及中国保险监督委员会审批，于 1981 年 1 月 1 日颁布实施的（我国海上货运保险条款最新版是 2009 版）。C.I.C.保险条款按运输方式来分，有海洋、陆上、航空和邮包运输四大类保险条款；对某些特殊商品，还配备有海运冷藏货物、陆运冷藏货物、海运散装桐油及活牲畜、家禽的海陆空运输保险条款，以上八种条款，投保人可按需选择投保。

中国保险条款的保险险别分为主险或基本险（Basic Risks）、一般附加险（General Additional Risks）和特殊附加险（Special Additional Risks）。其基本险别有平安险（Free From Particular Average, F.P.A.）、水渍险（With Particular Average, W.P.A.）和一切险（All Risks, A.R.）。

（二）伦敦保险协会货物保险条款（Institute Cargo Clauses，简称 I.C.C）

伦敦保险协会新修订的保险条款一共有六种（条款生效日期是 1982 年 1 月 1 日）：

（1）协会货物条款（A）[Institute Cargo Clauses A，简称 I.C.C.(A)]；

（2）协会货物条款（B）[Institute Cargo Clauses B，简称 I.C.C.(B)]；

（3）协会货物条款（C）[Institute Cargo Clauses C，简称 I.C.C.(C)]；

（4）协会战争险条款（货物）（Institute War Clauses-Cargo）；

（5）协会罢工险条款（货物）（Institute Strikes Clauses-Cargo）；

（6）恶意损坏条款（Malicious Damage Clause）。

以上六种保险条款中，前三种为主险或基本险，后三种则为附加险。值得注意的是，三种基本险 ICC(A)、ICC(B)、ICC(C)的承保责任范围是依次递减的，这与我国的保险条例是不一样的。其 A 险、B 险和 C 险的责任范围分别与我国的一切险、水渍险和平安险大致相对应。另外，其“战争险”和“罢工险”是可以作为独立险别投保的，这也不同于中国保险条款的规定。《协会货物保险条款》最新版本是 ICC2009 版，自 2009 年 1 月 1 日生效。

四、保险投保加成的规定

各国保险法及国际贸易惯例一般规定出口货物运输保险的保险金额在 CIF 货价基础上适当加成，加成率最低为 10%，这也是通常做法；也可与被保险人约定不同的加成率，但一般应不超过 30%。在我国，投保加成率一旦达到了 20%，投保人应事先征得保险人的同意。

五、保险金额和保险费的计算

保险金额又称投保金额，是货物发生损失后保险公司赔付的最高金额，又是保险公司计算收取其保险费的依据。

计算保险金额的公式为：保险金额=CIF 货价×（1+投保加成率），其结果保留整数，精确到小数点后两位；小数点以后采用向上进位方式，不管小数点后是几，都向上进一位。如果是 CFR 合同价，则应折算成 CIF 价，即 CIF=CFR/［1–（1+投保加成率）×保险费率］；如果是 FOB 合同价，则需先在 FOB 价中加入主运费，成为 CFR 价后，再折算成 CIF 价。

保险费为保险公司承保收取的费用，其计算公式为：保费= CIF 货价×（1+投保加成率）×保费费率。如果投保多种险别，计算保费时，需将所有险别的保费费率相加。

例：某商品出口报价 12 000 美元 FOB Shanghai，海运费为 300 美元，客户要求加一成投保一切险和战争险，保险费率分别为 1%和 0.63%，求保险金额和保险费。

1. 先算出 CIF 价：CIF 价=(FOB 价+海运费)/[1–(1+投保加成率)×保险费率]

=(12 000+300)/[1–110%×(1+0.63%)]=12 300/

(1–1.793)=15 510.72 美元

2. 计算保险金额：保险金额=15 510.72×(1+10%)=17 061.792 美元

进位取整，得 17 062.00 美元。

3. 计算保费：保险费=17 062×1.63%=278.11 美元。

六、投保需随附的单据

办理投保手续需随附下列单据：商业发票、包装单据、合同。

操作能力训练

思考题

S10-1　保险单据为什么要背书？背书的原则是什么？

操作题

C10-1　根据附录 3.1 里提供的制单信用证 3-13-2（见本书第 230 页），分别用投保单格式一和保险单格式一，独立缮制符合要求的投保单和保险单据。

C10-2　讨论和评讲后，根据附录 3.1 里的其余制单信用证（见本书第 230 页），分别用投保单格式二和保险单格式二，逐一缮制符合要求的投保单和保险单据。

C10-3　探索学习下一项目，并根据附录 3.1 里的制单信用证 3-13-1（见本书第 230 页），用提单格式一缮制符合要求的海运提单。

C10-4　独立学习 ISBP（2013 最新版本）和 UCP600 中关于运输单据的相关条款。

项目十一

缮制货物运输单据

出口货物装上出境运载工具后，承运人依据托运单（Booking Note-B/N）和船长/大副收据（Master's/Mate's Receipt-M/R）向托运人签发运输单据。如果托运单上有不准确之处，运输单据上就会出现不符点；若大副收据上有货物包装的不良记录，则提单为不清洁提单。在实际业务中，由货运代理公司根据货主（出口人）提供的订舱委托书初步填制海运提单，然后交予出口人审核，经确认无误后再通知承运人出具正式的海运提单。

学习目标

［知识目标］了解并掌握运输单据的性质、作用和种类，掌握缮制海运提单和航空运单的要领。

［能力目标］能正确缮制海运提单和航空运单。

一、缮制海运提单

项目描述（案例情境描述）

山东希望土产进出口公司向马来西亚出口一批山东黑枣，进口方通过银行开来信用证。出口方经审核无误后，开始缮制来证要求提供的全套单据。本次业务为货物装运后，缮制由承运人出具的海运提单。

详细资料请参阅项目四的信用证和订舱委托书。附目的港货运代理：

ASAHI LOGISTICS CO. LTD.

2F YOMIURI, YOUKOHAMA BLDG, 48-3YAMASHI, PENANG, MALAYSIA

TEL：60-4-2504312　FAX：60-4-2504311

操作要领

海运提单的格式各不相同，但主要内容一致，各栏目的填制要求如下：

1. 提单的名称、承运人名称和地址，以及提单号（Title of B/L, Name and Address of Carrier）：本栏目反映的是提单号码、承运人信息以及提单名称。若来证对承运人有所指定，则承运人名称必须与来证要求相符。多式联运提单（COMBINED TRANSPORT B/L）的性质与作用与海运提单（OCEAN BILL OF LADING）完全相同，如果提单中只反映了装运港和目的港的信息，而没有前段运输或后段运输信息，就证明这是一份单纯的港至港（PORT TO PORT）提单，即为海运提单。

※本案例制单：

制单操作

B/L NO.CCFASH1820960

CARRIER

COSCO

中国远洋运输（集团）总公司

CHINA OCEAN SHIPPING（GROUP）CO .

CABLE:COSCO BEIJING

TEL: 210740 CPC CN

ORIGINAL

Combined Transport B/L

2. 托运人/货主（Shipper）：本栏目填写托运人。在信用证结算方式下，填写受益人名称和地址；在汇付或托收结算方式下，一般填写外贸合同卖方的名称和地址。

※本案例制单：　　订舱委托书操作

经营单位(发货人)	山东希望土产进出口总公司 SHANDONG HOPE NATIVE PRODUCT I/E CORP. 62, GUANGXI ROAD, QINGDAO, CHINA

制单操作

Shipper SHANDONG HOPE NATIVE PRODUCT I/E CORP. 62, GUANGXI ROAD, QINGDAO, CHINA

3. 收货人/抬头（Consignee）：此栏通常填写抬头格式。信用证项下，严格按照信用证中提单条款的相关规定填写（按 Made out 后面的要求填写）；汇付或托收结算方式下，通常填写 to order，或按照外贸合同中的相关规定填写。

※本案例制单：　　订舱委托书操作

收货人	TO SHIPPER’S ORDER

制单操作

Consignee TO SHIPPER’S ORDER

4. 被通知人（Notify Party）：本栏目货物到达目的港时，船方代理及时发送到货通知给收件人，其联系方式须尽量详细，包括电话和传真号码。信用证项下，严格按照信用证中提单条款的 notify 相关规定填写，若被通知人为两方，则其中一方打在货物描述下方空白处或唛头下方空白处（Also Notify/The Second Notify Party）。汇付或托收结算方式下，一般填写进口商名称、地址、联系电话和传真号码，或按照外贸合同中的相关规定填写。

※本案例制单：　　订舱委托书操作

被通知人	1. SOO HUP SENG TRADING CO. SDN BHD. 165 1ST FLOOR, VICTORIA STREET, 10300 PENANG MALAYSIA TEL: 60-4-2509730 FAX: 60-4-2509729 2. THE HONGKONG AND SHANGHAI BANKING CORP. LTD., DOWNING STREET, PENANG TEL: 60-4-2517522 FAX: 60-4-2517520

制单操作

Notify Party
SOO HUP SENG TRADING CO. SDN BHD.
165 1ST FLOOR, VICTORIA STREET,
10300 PENANG MALAYSIA
TEL: 60-4-2509730 FAX: 60-4-2509729

Also Notify:
THE HONGKONG AND SHANGHAI
BANKING CORP. LTD.,
DOWNING STREET, PENANG
TEL: 60-4-2517522 FAX: 60-4-2517520

5. 前段运输（Pre-carriage by）：在多式联运的运输业务中，本栏目填写前段运输的信息，需填运输方式和车卡号、或航班号、或汽车自编号。本业务项下信用证要求提交海运提单，故本栏目留空不填。

※本案例制单：

制单操作

Pre-carriage by

6. 船名、航次（Vessel Name and Voyage）：本栏目根据实际订妥的船名航次填写。若有两程船，则需打出两程船的船名。如："RED STAR" / "VICTORY"。

※本案例制单：

制单操作

Ocean Vessel Voy. No.
M/V VICTORIA

7. 收货地（Place of Receipt）：本栏目仅供多式联运方式使用，填写承运人收货的具体地点。本业务项下信用证要求提交海运提单，故而本栏目留空不填。

※本案例制单：

制单操作

Place of Receipt

8. 装运港（Port of Loading）：本栏目填写具体的装运港信息，与商业发票一致。

※本案例制单：　　订舱委托书操作

装运港	QINGDAO

制单操作

Port of Loading
QINGDAO, CHINA

9. 卸货港（Port of Discharge）：本栏目填写具体的卸货港信息。卸货港/目的港是指运保费付至的港口，须列出具体名称，有时还需加注国别（地区）名称以避免重名港口。若有选择港，则须照打。

若经转船，应在卸货港后或唛头下方或货名空白处加注。如："London W/T at H.K." 或 "London via H.K."。

若卸货后须经内陆转运，则在上述位置加注："In transit to..." 或 "and thence to..."

对美加 Overland Common Points（O.C.P.）地区出口，应在唛头下方或货名栏空白处加注："O.C.P. ×××"（内陆城市名称），以享受运费优惠。

※本案例制单：　订舱委托书操作

制单操作

目 的 港	PENANG

Port of Discharge PENANG

10. 交货地点、最终目的地（Place of Delivery and Final Destination）：本栏目为多式联运方式下填写，本业务项下免于填写。

※本案例制单：

制单操作

Place of Delivery	*Final Destination	via

11. 集装箱号/封号（Container No./ Seal No.）：本栏目填写集装箱号和封号。

※本案例制单：

制单操作

Container No.
EISU2628205

12. 唛头及件号（Shipping Marks & Numbers）：本栏目按信用证或合同规定填写唛头，须与商业发票一致。若散装货或部分裸装货无唛头，应填写"N/M"。

※本案例制单：订舱委托书操作

制单操作

标记 唛码
SHS PENANG 1-UP

Seal No. Marks & No.
SHS PENANG 1-UP

13. 件数及货名（Number & Kind of Packages: Description of Goods）：本栏目填写货物的包装件数小写和货物的名称，可显示统称，但不得引起歧义。此栏空白处常用来显示来证要求的其他加注内容和目的港船务代理。大写栏可以显示外包装的数量，也可以显示集装箱数量，均需显示 only，如（SAY...ONLY）。

如果是散装货，须加注"In bulk"，无须大写。

如果是裸装货，应显示件数，如（20 units, 100 heads），并大写（...only）。

如果是两种以上的包装，应逐一列明件数和包装种类，加注合计及其大写，单位用 package。

例如：100 Cartons

50 Bales

150 Packages （Say one hundred and fifty packages only.）

※本案例制单： 订舱委托书操作 制单操作

需要在提单上注明：
1. FREIGHT PREPAID
2. ALL PACKAGES BEAR SHIPPING MARKS: SHS/PENANG/1-UP
3. PACKING IS DONE AS FOLLOWS: IN CARDBOARD CARTONS OF 25KGS NET OR 26.2KGS GROSS PER CARTON
4. 目的港货代的名称、地址及联系电话

货名规格及货号、海关编码
SHANDONG BLACK DATES 山东黑枣 HS 编码：0813403000020

包装方式及包装件数
5,000 KG 25KG/CTN 200 CTNS

No. &Kind of Packages; Description
SHANDONG BLACK DATES 200 CARTONS PACKING IS DONE AS FOLLOWS: IN CARDBOARD CARTONS OF 25 KGS NET OR 26.2KGS GROSS ALL PACKAGES BEAR SHIPPING MARKS: SHS/PENANG/1-UP FREIGHT PREPAID ASAHI LOGISTICS CO. LTD 2F YOMIURI YOUKOHAMA BLDG 48-3 YAMASHI PENANG MALAYSIA TEL: 60-4-2504312 FAX: 60-4-2504311

14. 毛重量和体积（Gross Weight and Measurement）：毛重以千克为单位，保留两位小数或四舍五入取整，只有净重的货物则须显示“N.W”；尺码以立方米为单位，保留小数后三位。

※本案例制单： 订舱委托书操作 制单操作

毛重/净重（千克）
5,240/5,000

总体积	14.850 立方米

Gross Weight	Measurement
5,240.00KG	14.850M³

15. 包装件数及集装箱件数大写（Total Number of Containers or Packages in Words）：本栏目填写外包装件数或集装箱个数的大写。若来证的包装条款对外包装有限制词，大写件数时须照写。

※本案例制单： 制单操作

TOTAL NUMBER OF CONTAINERS OR PACKAGES (IN WORDS)	TWO HUNDRED CARDBOARD CARTONS ONLY IN ONE 20’ CONTAINER.

16. 运费条款（Freight & Charges）：船方为保守商业秘密，运费栏一般不填具体金额，而填写 FREIGHT PREPAID/PAID，或 FREIGHT TO COLLECT，除非信用证有特别要求。本例在自由处置区已显示运费预付情况，故在此栏不必重复填写。

※本案例制单：

制单操作

Freight & Charges	Revenue Tons	Rate	Per	Prepaid	Collect

17. 运费支付总额和地点（Total Prepaid, Place at）：采用 CIF/CFR 交货条件，运费预付地（PREPAID AT）填写装运港，多式联运方式填货交承运人地。若采用 FOB 术语，在运费到付地（PAYABLE AT）填写卸货港，多式联运填承运人交货地。

※本案例制单：

制单操作

Ex. Rate	Prepaid at: QINGDAO	Payable at
	Total Prepaid AS ARRANGED	No. of Original B/L THREE (3)

18. 正本提单份数（Original No.）：正本提单份数须用大、小写显示。

※本案例制单：

制单操作

No. of Original B/L THREE (3)

19. 已装船信息（On Board the Vessel）：银行只接受“已装船”提单，并以此日期判断货物是否逾期装运。因此，提单须据实注明装船日期并加承运人简签。提单上没有印就“装船备忘录”的，应在提单空白处加注 Shipped on Board 或 On Board the Vessel，下方注明装船日期及承运人签名等字样。

※本案例制单：

制单操作

LADEN ON BOARD OF THE VESSEL
Date JULY 5, 2015 By
CHINA OCEAN SHIPPING AGENCY QINGDAO BRANCH
COSCO STANDARD FORM11 （TERMS CONTINUED ON BACK HEREOF）

20. 签发地点、日期（Issuing Place and Date）：本栏目填写提单的签发日期和地点，日期一般采用装运日期，也可晚于装运日期，银行并不以此日期判断是否按时装运。

※本案例制单：

制单操作

Place and Date of Issue: QINGDAO JULY 5, 2015

21. 承运人或船长签字或盖章（Signature of the Carrier/Master）：提单签署人只能是承运人或其授权代理/代表，或船长或其授权代理/代表。签字均需显示身份，其各种格式如下：

（1）由承运人自己签发提单如：　XYZ Shipping Co. Ltd.（船公司名称）

（签署）

As Carrier named above

（2）由船长签发提单如：　John Smith

（签署）

As Master of XYZ Shipping Co. Ltd.（船公司名称）

（3）代理人代表承运人签发提单（提单正面应表明承运人。例：Carrier, XYZ Shipping Co. Ltd.）

如：ABC Co. Ltd.（船代理名称）

（签署）

As agent for（或 on behalf of）the Carrier XYZ Shipping Co. Ltd. 或

As agent for（或 on behalf of）XYZ Shipping Co. Ltd. 或

As agent for（或 on behalf of）the Carrier named above 或

As agent for（或 on behalf of）the Carrier

（4）代理人代表船长签发提单

如：ABC Co. Ltd.　（代理人名称）

（签署）

As agent for（或 on behalf of）John Smith, Master

※本案例制单：　　　　　　　　　　　　　　　　　制单操作

Signed as the Carrier named above/as the Agent for the Carrier named above
CHINA OCEAN SHIPPING AGENCY QINGDAO BRANCH 王伟国 （STAMPED）

22. 背书（Endorsement）：提单通常做成“凭指示”抬头，是为了可以经背书转让。提单的背书一般是空白背书。抬头为 TO ORDER, TO SHIPPER'S ORDER, TO BEARER 等都被视为凭托运人指示，大多都由托运人做成空白背书（Endorsement in Blank）。若来证提单条款里要求转让权益，如 CONSIGNED/DELIVERED TO×××或 IN FAVOR OF ×××，即便抬头为 TO THE ORDER，则提单须做出与信用证要求相符的记名背书（Special Endorsement）。若提单抬头做成“凭××银行指示”（TO ORDER OF 具体银行名称），则出口人不做提单背书，提单的背书应由指定的银行做出。两种背书格式如下：

空白背书	记名背书
	DELIVERED TO ×××/IN FAVOR OF ×××（被背书人）
××××年××月××日 Co.（背书人）	××××年××月××日 Co.（背书人）
××××年××月××日（签字）	××××年××月××日（签字）
××××年××月××日（日期）	××××年××月××日（日期）

※本案例制单：

制单操作

提单背书格式：　SHANDONG HOPE NATIVE PRODUCT I/E CORP.

王伟国

JULY 9，2015

附海运提单制单样例

<table>
<tr><td colspan="2">Shipper
SHANDONG HOPE NATIVE PRODUCT I/E CORP.,
62, GUANGXI ROAD, QINGDAO, CHINA</td><td rowspan="5">B/L NO.CCFASH1820960
CARRIER
COSCO
中国远洋运输（集团）总公司
CHINA OCEAN SHIPPING（GROUP）CO.
CABLE: COSCO BEIJING
TEL: 210740 CPC CN
ORIGINAL
Combined Transport B/L</td></tr>
<tr><td colspan="2">Consignee
TO SHIPPER’S ORDER</td></tr>
<tr><td colspan="2">Notify Party
SOO HUP SENG TRADING CO. SDN BHD.
165 1ST FLOOR, VICTORIA STREET,
10300 PENANG MALAYSIA
TEL: 60-4-2509730 FAX: 60-4-2509729</td></tr>
<tr><td>Pre-carriage by</td><td>Place of Receipt</td></tr>
<tr><td>Ocean Vessel Voy. No.
M/V VICTORIA</td><td>Port of Loading
QINGDAO, CHINA</td></tr>
<tr><td>Port of Discharge
PENANG</td><td>Place of Delivery</td><td>*Final Destination　　via</td></tr>
</table>

<table>
<tr><td>Container No.</td><td>Seal No. Marks & No.</td><td>No. & Kind of Packages; Description</td><td>Gross Weight</td><td>Measurement</td></tr>
<tr><td>EISU2628205

Also notify:
THE HONG KONG AND SHANGHAI BANKING CORP. LTD.,
DOWNING STREET,
PENANG
TEL: 60-4-2517522
FAX: 60-4-2517520</td><td>SHS
PENANG
1-UP</td><td>SHANDONG BLACK DATES
200 CARTONS

PACKING IS DONE AS FOLLOWS:
IN CARDBOARD CARTONS OF 25 KGS NET OR 26.2KGS GROSS
ALL PACKAGES BEAR SHIPPING MARKS: SHS/PENANG/1-UP

AGENT AT DESTINATION:
ASAHI LOGISTICS CO. LTD.
2F YOMIURI YOUKOHAMA BLDG
48-3 YAMASHI PENANG MALAYSIA
TEL: 60-4-2504312
FAX: 60-4-2504311</td><td>5,240.00KG

FREIGHT PREPAID</td><td>14.850M³</td></tr>
<tr><td colspan="2">TOTAL NUMBER OF CONTAINERS OR PACKAGES （IN WORDS）</td><td colspan="3">TWO HUNDRED CARDBOARD CARTONS ONLY IN ONE 20’ CONTAINER.</td></tr>
</table>

<table>
<tr><td colspan="2">Freight & Charges</td><td>Revenue Tons</td><td>Rate</td><td>Per</td><td>Prepaid</td><td>Collect</td></tr>
<tr><td rowspan="2">Ex. Rate</td><td colspan="2">Prepaid at:
QINGDAO</td><td colspan="2">Payable at</td><td colspan="2">Place and Date of Issue:
QINGDAO　JULY 5, 2015</td></tr>
<tr><td colspan="2">Total Prepaid
AS ARRANGED</td><td colspan="2">No. of Original B/L
THREE　（3）</td><td colspan="2">Signed as the Carrier named above/as the Agent for the Carrier named above</td></tr>
</table>

（续表）

LADEN ON BOARD OF THE VESSEL Date JULY 5, 2015　　By CHINA OCEAN SHIPPING AGENCY QINGDAO BRANCH COSCO STANDARD FORM11　　(TERMS CONTINUED ON BACK HEREOF)	CHINA OCEAN SHIPPING AGENCY QINGDAO BRANCH 王伟国 （STAMPED）

提单背书格式：　SHANDONG HOPE NATIVE PRODUCT I/E CORP.

王伟国

JULY 9, 2015

二、缮制航空运单

项目描述（案例情境描述）

成都市蜀鑫土产进出口公司向法国 OLIVIER FOODS CO., LTD.出口一批盐渍松茸。蜀鑫土产进出口公司委托成都德诚国际货代有限公司办理货物空运事宜，并于 2016 年 9 月 21 日向货运代理公司传送了订舱委托书。本次操作为货物装运后，缮制由承运人出具的空运单。

详细资料请参阅项目四的空运订舱委托书。附业务信息明细：

1. 商品 HS 编码：2003909020
2. 外包装资料：每箱净重 6KGS，每箱毛重 6.5KGS，纸箱尺寸 35CM×30CM×30CM
3. 货运代理公司：成都德诚国际货运代理有限公司 JHJ/CTU 统一社会信用代码 915101067022501009
4. 航班日期：2016 年 9 月 28 日
5. 航班号：CA875

操作要领

航空运单有正面条款和背面条款之分，不同的航空公司有自己的航空运单格式，不过基本都是借鉴 IATA[①]所推荐的标准格式，差别不大。

1. 货运单号码（The Air Waybill Number）：分别印在运单的左右上角及右下角。编号前三位是航空公司的 IATA 代码，后面的数字是货运单序号和检验号。本业务项下承运的航空公司是中国国际航空公司，代码为 999，货运单号码为 999-81045562。

① 国际航空运输协会（International Air Transport Association，简称 IATA）是一个由世界各国航空公司所组成的大型国际组织，其前身是 1919 年在海牙成立并在二战时解体的国际航空业务协会，总部设在加拿大的蒙特利尔，执行机构设在日内瓦。

2. 托运人名称和地址（Shipper's Name and Address）：本栏目填写托运人名称、地址、国家以及托运人电话、传真。信用证项下，此栏名称地址必须与受益人名称地址一致。

※本案例制单：

制单操作

Shipper's Name and Address	Shipper's Account Number
CHENGDU SHUXIN NATIVE PRODUCE IMP. & EXP. CORP. A-1502 YUNMAO MANSION NO.102 XIYULONG STREET QINGYANG DISTRICT, CHENGDU, CHINA TEL: 86-028-86632066 FAX: 86-028-86632065	

3. 发货人账号（Shipper's Account Number）：本栏目不需填写。

4. 收货人名称和地址（Consignee's Name and Address）：本栏目填写收货人名称、地址、所在国家以及收货人电话、传真。由于航空运单不是物权凭证且不可转让，该栏目不能做成指示抬头。

※本案例制单：

制单操作

Consignee's Name and Address	Consignee's Account Number
OLIVIER FOODS CO., LTD AUTOROUTE B26Y. 3 ST MAURICE-05700 PARIS FRANCE TEL：0033-1-47256094 FAX: 0033-1-47256095	

5. 收货人账号（Consignee's Account Number）：本栏目不需填写。

6. 承运人代理的名称和所在城市（Issuing Carrier's Agent Name and City）：若运单是由承运人的代理人签发，本栏目填写实际代理人的名称和城市名；若运单是由承运人直接签发，则本栏目留空不填。

※本案例制单：

制单操作

Issuing Carrier's Agent Name and City
JHJ/CTU

7. 代理人的 IATA 代号（Agent's IATA Code）：本栏目填写代理人的国际航协代号。

※本案例制单：

制单操作

Agent's IATA Code
08322360283

8. 代理人账号（Account Number）：本栏目一般不需填写。

9. 始发站机场及所要求的航线（Airport of Departure and Requested Routing）：本栏目填写 IATA 统一制定的始发站机场三字代码（如始发站机场名称不明，可以填写机场所在城市的 IATA 三字代码）。

※本案例制单：　　　　制单操作

Airport of Departure (Addr. of First Carrier) and Requested Routing
CTU CHENGDU

10. 运输路线和目的站（Routing and Destination）：

（1）至……第一承运人（To... By First Carrier）

To 栏目：如无转运，填写目的站机场名称，如需转运填写第一个转运点的 IATA 三字代码。

By First Carrier 栏目：填写第一承运人的 IATA 两字代码。

（2）至……第二承运人（To... By Second Carrier）

To 栏目：填写目的站机场或第二个转运点的 IATA 三字代码。

By Second Carrier 栏目：填写第二承运人的 IATA 两字代码。

以此类推。

※本案例制单：　　　　制单操作

To	By First Carrier Routing and Destination	To	By	To	By
CDG	**CA**				

11. 财务说明（Accounting Information）：本栏目填写与费用结算有关的事项，比如填写运费支付方式等。

※本案例制单：　　　　制单操作

Accounting Information
FREIGHT PREPAID

12. 货币和运费代码（Currency CHGS Code）：本栏目填写始发国的货币代码，运费代码一般不填。

※本案例制单：　　　　制单操作

Currency	CHGS Code
CNY	

13. 运费及声明价值费和其他费用（WT/VAL, weight charge/valuation charge, other）：本栏目的运费是根据货物计费重量乘以适用的运价得到的航空公司收取的运费。声明价值是指下面第 15 栏中向承运人申报价值时必须和运费一起交付声明价值费。其他费用是指在始发站的其他费用。若是预付，则在 PPD 栏目中打“×”符号，若是到付，则在 COLL 栏目中打“×”符号。

※本案例制单：　　　　制单操作

WT/VAL		Other	
PPD	COLL	PPD	COLL
×		×	

14. 供运输用声明价值（Declared Value for Carriage）：本栏目填写发货人要求的用于运输的声明价值，一般可以按照发票金额填写。如果发货人无要求，则填写“N.V.D.”（No Value Declared）。

※本案例制单：

制单操作

Declared Value for Carriage
N.V.D.

15. 海关声明价值（Declared Value for Customs）：本栏目填写的价值是提供给海关的征税依据。以出口货物报关单或商业发票作为征税标准，本栏目可以留空不填或填写“As Per INV”；如果货物为样品等数量较少且无商业价值，可填写“N.C.V.”（No Customs Valuation）。

※本案例制单：

制单操作

Declared Value for Customs
AS PER INV

16. 目的地机场（Airport of Destination）：本栏目填写目的地机场。注意需要填写机场所在城市名。

※本案例制单：

制单操作

Airport of Destination
PARIS (CDG)

17. 航班及日期（Flight/Date For Carrier Use Only）：本栏目一般由承运人填写航班号及航班日期。

※本案例制单：

制单操作

Flight/Date	For Carrier Use Only	Flight/Date
CA875 SEP. 28, 2016		

18. 保险金额（Amount of Insurance）：本栏目只有在航空公司提供代保险业务而客户有此需要时才填写，如没有则打“×××”符号。

※本案例制单：

制单操作

Amount of Insurance
×××

19. 处理注意事项（Handling Information）：本栏目填写需要注明的内容，如：

（1）被通知人

（2）飞机随带的有关商业单据名称

（3）包装情况

（4）唛头

（5）发货人对货物在途中的特别指示

（6）对第二承运人的要求

※本案例制单： 制单操作

Handling Information	
O.F. C-S185 PARIS NO./C 1-150	**COMMERCIAL INVOICE AND PACKING LIST ARE ATTACHED**

20. 货物件数和运价组合点（No. of Pieces RCP, Rate Combination Point）：本栏目填写货物包装件数。如 20 箱，填写“20”。如果使用非公布直达运价计算运费时，在件数下面填写运价组合点城市的 IATA 三字代码。

※本案例制单： 制单操作

No. of Pieces RCP
150

21. 毛重（Gross Weight）：本栏目填写适用于运价的货物实际毛重。

※本案例制单： 制单操作

Gross Weight
975

22. 重量单位（kg/lb）：以千克为单位的填写“K”，以磅为单位的填写“L”。

※本案例制单： 制单操作

kg / lb
K

23. 运价等级（Rate Class）：本栏目填写重量等级分界点运价的代码，针对不同的航空运价共有 10 种代码：

M——最低运费

N——45 千克以下货物使用的普通货物运价

Q——45 千克以上货物使用的普通货物运价

C——指定商品运价

R——等级货物附减运价

S——等级货物附加运价

U——集装化设备基本运费或运价

E——集装化设备附加运价

X——集装化设备附加说明

Y——集装化设备折扣

※本案例制单：

制单操作

Rate Class
Q

24. 商品代码（Commodity Item No.）：本栏目在使用特种运价时需要填写商品代码。如：使用指定商品运价时，填写商品品名代码；使用等级货物运价时，填写附加或附减的百分比；集装货物时，填写集装货物运价等级。本业务项下采用的是45千克以上的普通货物运价，所以本栏目可以留空不填。

25. 计费重量（Chargeable Weight）：本栏目填写航空公司据以计算运费的计费重量，可能是货物的实际毛重，也可能是货物的体积重量。

※本案例制单：

制单操作

Chargeable Weight
975

26. 运价（Rate/Charge）：本栏目填写该批货物适用的费率。

※本案例制单：

制单操作

Rate Charge
28.63

27. 运费总额（Total）：本栏目填写计收运费的总额，即为计费重量乘以适用的费率。

※本案例制单：

制单操作

Total
27,914.25

28. 货物品名、数量，含尺寸或体积（Nature and Quantity of Goods Incl. Dimensions or Volume）：本栏目填写货物的名称和货物的尺寸以及体积。尺寸的单位为厘米，体积的单位为立方米。

※本案例制单：

制单操作

Nature and Quantity of Goods (incl. Dimensions or Volume)
SALTED MATSUTAKE MUSHROOM **DIMS: 35CM×30CM×30CM** **V: 4.725M³**

29. 计重运费，预付或到付（Weight Charge, Prepaid/Collect）：本栏目在对应的“预付”或“到付”栏目中填写第 27 栏中的运费额。

※本案例制单：　　制单操作

Prepaid Weight Charge	Collect
27,914.25	

30. 其他费用（Other Charges）：本栏目填写除了运费和声明价值附加费以外的其他费用。其他费用以 IATA 规定的三字代码表示，并填写出具体的金额。三字代码中的前两个字母表示某项费用，第三个字母表示费用应支付给承运人（C）或代理人（A）。

※本案例制单：　　制单操作

Other Charges
AWC: 50.00 MYC: 490.75 SCC: 340.00

31. 声明价值费、税费（Valuation Charge, Tax）：本栏目在对应的“预付”或“到付”栏目中填写声明价值费和适用的税款。如无对应金额，本栏目留空不填。本业务项下不需填写。

32. 代理人收取的其他费用（Total Other Charges Due Agent）：本栏目在对应的“预付”或“到付”栏目中填写代理人收取的其他费用总额。本业务项下无代理人收取的其他费用，不需填写。

33. 承运人收取的其他费用（Total Other Charges Due Carrier）：本栏目在对应的“预付”或“到付”栏目中填写承运人收取的其他费用总额。本业务项下为第 30 栏其他费用的总额。

※本案例制单：　　制单操作

Total Other Charges Due Carrier	
880.75	

34. 承运人或其代理签字（Signature of Shipper or His Agent）：本栏目由承运人或其代理签字或盖章。

※本案例制单：　　制单操作

Shipper certifies that the particulars on the face hereof are correct and that **insofar as any part of the consignment contains dangerous goods, such part is properly described by name and is in proper condition for carriage by air according to the applicable Dangerous Goods Regulations.**
JHJ/CTU …………………………………… Signature of Shipper or his Agent

35. 承运人填写栏（For Carrier）：

（1）填开日期（Executed on Date）

本栏目所填日期为航空运单的签发日期，也就是本业务项下货物的装运日期。但如果信用证规定要注明实际起飞日期，则应该予以照办，并将所注明的实际起飞日期视为装运日期。

（2）填开地点（At Place）

本栏目填写城市的全称或缩写。

（3）承运人或其代理签字（Signature of Shipper or His Agent）

本栏目由承运人或其代理人签字，并需表明签字人的身份，如是承运人签字，则加注“As Carrier”；若是代理人签字，则注明“As Agent”。

※本案例制单： 制单操作

SEP. 28, 2016	CHENGDU	JHJCTU001
Executed on (date)	at (place)	Signature of Issuing Carrier or its Agent

附航空运单制单样例

999CTU81045562		999－81045562
Shipper's Name and Address	Shipper's Account Number	
CHENGDU SHUXIN NATIVE PRODUCE IMP. & EXP. CORP. **A-1502 YUNMAO MANSION NO.102 XIYULONG STREET QINGYANG DISTRICT, CHENGDU, CHINA** **TEL: 86-028-86632066 FAX: 86-028-86632065**		Copies 1, 2 and 3 of this Air Waybill are originals and have the same validity.
Consignee's Name and Address	Consignee's Account Number	It is agreed that the goods described herein are accepted for carriage in apparent good order And condition (except as noted) and SUBJECT TO THE CONDITIONS OF CONTRACT ON THE REVERSE HEREOF. ALL GOODS MAY BE CARRIED BY AND OTHER MEANS INCLUDING ROAD OR ANY OTHER CARRIER UNLESS SPECIFIC CONTRARY INSTRUCTIONS ARE GIVEN HEREON BY THE SHIPPER. THE SHIPPER'S ATTENTION IS DRAWN TO THE NOTICE CONCERNING CARRIER'S LIMITATION OF LIABILITY. Shipper may increase such limitation of liability by declaring a higher value for carriage and paying a supplemental charge if required.
OLIVIER FOODS CO., LTD **AUTOROUTE B26Y.3 ST MAURICE-05700 PARIS FRANCE** **TEL：0033-1-47256094 FAX: 0033-1-47256095**		
Issuing Carrier's Agent Name and City **JHJ/CTU**		Accounting Information **FREIGHT PREPAID**
Agent's IATA Code **08322360283**	Account No.	
Airport of Departure （Addr. of First Carrier） and Requested Routing		
CTU CHENGDU		

To	By First Carrier Routing and Destination	To	By	To	By	Currency	CHGS Code	WT/VAL PPD	WT/VAL COLL	Other PPD	Other COLL	Declared Value for Carriage	Declared Value for Customs
CDG	**CA**					**CNY**		×		×		**N.V.D.**	**AS PER INV**

Airport of Destination	Flight/Date	For Carrier Use Only	Flight/Date	Amount of Insurance	INSURANCE—If Carrier offers insurance, and such insurance is requested in accordance with the conditions thereof, indicate amount to be insured in figures in box marked "Amount of Insurance."
PARIS （CDG）	**CA875 SEP. 28, 2016**			×××	

Handling Information	
O.F. **C-S185** **PAIRS** **NO./C 1-150**	**COMMERCIAL INVOICE AND PACKING LIST ARE ATTACHED**

（续表）

No. of Pieces. RCP	Gross Weight	kg/lb	Rate Class	Commodity Item No.	Chargeable Weight	Rate Charge	Total	Nature and Quantity of Goods （incl. Dimensions or Volume）
150	975	K	Q		975	28.63	27,914.25	SALTED MATSUTAKE MUSHROOM DIMS: 35CM×30CM×30CM V: 4.725M^3
150	975						27,914.25	

Prepaid Weight Charge Collect		Other Charges		
27,914.25		AWC: 50.00 MYC: 490.75 SCC: 340.00		
Valuation Charge				
Tax				
Total Other Charges Due Agent		Shipper certifies that the particulars on the face hereof are correct and that **insofar as any part of the consignment contains dangerous goods, such part is properly described by name and is in proper condition for carriage by air according to the applicable Dangerous Goods Regulations.**		
Total Other Charges Due Carrier		JHJ/CTU		
880.75		Signature of Shipper or his Agent		
Total Prepaid	Total Collect	SEP. 28, 2016	CHENGDU	JHJCTU001
28,795.00				
Currency Conversion Rates	CC Charges in Dest. Currency			
		Executed on （date）	at（place）	Signature of Issuing Carrier or its Agent
For Carrier's Use only at Destination	Charges at Destination	Total Collect Charges		999—81045562

相关知识

一、运输单据的分类及性质

（一）海运提单（Ocean Bill of Lading）

由承运人、船长或代理人签发，用以证明货物已由承运人接收或装船以及承运人保证据此交付货物的单证。它具有货物收据、运输契约证明、物权凭证的性质和作用。凭正本结算和提货。

（二）海运单（Sea Waybill）

海上运输契约的证明和货物收据，但不是物权凭证，不能凭此海运单提货，收货人栏记实名和地址，不能背书转让。如若信用证没有表示可接受此类单据时，银行通常不接受此类单据。

（三）多式联运单据（Combined Transport Document）

至少两种或两种以上的运输方式且第一程不能是水上运输，由多式联运经营人收到货物后签发的运输单据，其性质和作用与海运提单完全相同。目前被国际商会认可的多式联运单据为“波罗的海国际航运公会[①]的联运单据”和“FIATA[②]联运单据”。该单据有两种：多式运输单据（Multi-modal Transport Document, MTD 或 M.T. B/L）和联合运输单据（Combined Transport Document, CTD 或 C.T. B/L）又称集装箱联运单据。

（四）航空运单（Air Waybill）

航空运输公司及其代理人签发给托运人表示已收妥货物并接受托运的货物收据，属于运输契约，可以用作结算单据。航空运单可以做为核收运费的依据和海关查验放行的基本单据，但是此类单据不是物权凭证，不能凭此提货，收货人一栏必须填写实名和地址，不能背书转让。

（五）铁路运输单据（Rail Transport Documents）

此类单据是铁路承运人或其代理人签发的供托运人用于结算的货运收据，此类单据仅仅表明承运人和托运人之间的运输契约关系，不是货权凭证，不能仅凭以提货，须附身份证明，收货人栏须填写实名和地址，不能背书转让。铁路运输单据分为两种：承运货物收据（Cargo Receipt）适用于对我国港澳地区的货物出口和国际铁路联运运单（International Through Rail Waybill），简称“铁路运单”（Rail Waybill）适用于国际货协成员国之间的铁路货物运输。

（六）公路或内陆水运运输单据（Documents for Land Transport and Internal On-water Transport）

此类单据是采用公路或内陆水运时，由承运人或其代理人签发的货运收据，此类单据仅表明承运人和托运人之间的运输契约关系，不是货权凭证，不能仅凭以提货，须附身份证明，不能背书转让。

（七）快递、邮包收据或投邮证明（Parcel Receipt or Post Certificate）

邮包收据或投邮证明是由快递公司或邮政机构签发给托运人的货运收据或证明，它是邮包递送人收到并运送货物的依据，可用作结算，但不是物权凭证，收货人栏必须填写实名和地址。

二、常见国际海运提单的种类

从不同的角度划分，海运提单有很多分类，这里重点说说以下几种。

---

① 波罗的海国际航运公会，英文全称为 The Baltic and International Maritime Council，简称 BIMCO，是一个具有 100 多年历史的国际航运组织。目前，BIMCO 已有 120 个成员国，2 500 多个会员，其中 955 个船东会员、1 413 家船舶代理和经纪会员、46 家保险公司和保赔协会会员和 94 家其他航运组织会员。BIMCO 的船东会员共拥有 1.4 万多艘船舶，5.25 亿载重吨的运力，约占世界海运业总运力的 65%，在全球航运业中具有举足轻重的地位。

② 国际货运代理协会联合会是一个非营利性国际货运代理的行业组织。该会于 1926 年 5 月 31 日在奥地利维也纳成立，总部设在瑞士苏黎士，并分别在欧洲、美洲、亚太、非洲和中东五个区域设立了地区办事处，任命有地区主席。其中亚洲和太平洋地区秘书处设在印度孟买。其目的是保障和提高国际货运代理在全球的利益。其成员包括世界各国的国际货运代理行业，拥有 76 个联盟会员，1 751 个个体会员，遍布 124 个国家和地区，包括 3 500 个国际货运代理公司。

（一）按货物是否已装船划分

已装船提单（On Board B/L）和收妥待运提单（Received for Shipment B/L）

1. 已装船提单：提单上预先印就“已装船”文字（如：Shipped on board the vessel named here in apparent good order and condition...）的提单通常就不必再另外加注“已装船”（On Board）批注了。

2. 收妥待运提单：该类提单上预先印就“Received in external apparent good order and condition...”且提单中没有任何“已装船”批注，或者提单上载有“预期船只”或类似的限定语，则这类提单为“收妥待运提单”，也称“备运提单”，银行不接受此类提单。若此类提单加注“已装船”批注后即变为已装船提单。

（二）按对货物外包装状况划分

清洁提单（Clean B/L）和不清洁提单（Unclean B/L）

1. 清洁提单：指货物装船时“表面状况良好”，提单上没有包装的不良加注，如短少、污渍或破损之类的批语。“清洁”一词不需要在提单上出现。

2. 不清洁提单：该类提单上承运人记录了托运的货物或包装外表有短少、污渍或破损等状况不良或存在缺陷的批语，银行不接受不清洁提单。但若承运人在提单上加注以下批语，不能认定该提单是不清洁提单：

（1）不明白表示货物或包装不能令人满意，如只批注：旧包装箱、旧桶等；

（2）强调承运人对于货物或包装性质所引起的风险不负责任；

（3）否认承运人知晓货物的内容、重量、容积、质量或技术规格；

（4）属于提单和贸易合同中规定的免责条款的批注。

（三）按收货人/抬头划分

记名提单（Straight B/L）、不记名提单（Open B/L）和指示提单（Order B/L）

此三种提单的收货人（Consignee）填写方法以及相关背书转让的格式以表格的形式予以具体说明（见表 11-1）。

表 11-1 提单抬头填写与背书要求

提单种类	收货人填写	背书格式	使用情况
记名提单	ABC Co., Ltd.	不能背书转让	较少使用
不记名提单	To Bearer 或空白不填	不需背书就可转让	风险大，很少使用
指示提单	To Order	由托运人空白背书，可以转让	广泛使用
	To Order of Shipper	由托运人背书，可以转让	广泛使用
	To Order of ××× Bank（这家银行一般是开证行）	托运人不需背书，背书由×××银行自行处理，可以转让	当开证申请人没有全额缴纳开证行规定的所需保证金，开证行会要求使用这类提单
	To Order of ××× Co.（这家公司一般是开证申请人）	托运人不需背书，背书事宜由×××公司自行处理，可以转让	使用少，遇此提单一般要求修改信用证

（四）其他种类

1. 倒签提单（Ante-dated B/L）：是指在货物装船完毕后，承运人或其代理人应托运人的要求，将提单上的签发日期提早于该批货物实际装船完毕的日期，以此满足信用证对装运期的规定。表面上倒签提单使得提单签发日期与信用证规定的装运期相吻合，方便了结汇，但它改变不了实际开航日期和抵达目的港的日期的真实情况，属于违法提单。如果这种情况事先没有征得收货人的同意，而引起收货人的异议，承运人要承担由此产生的一切风险和责任。

2. 预借提单（Advanced B/L）：由于信用证上规定的装运日期将到期而货物因故尚未装船，或尚未装船完毕，在此情况下，托运人为了顺利交单结汇而向承运人或其代理人提出预先签发并借到“已装船提单”。预借提单仍属违法提单，承运人承担的风险和责任比倒签提单更大。

3. 顺签提单（Post-dated B/L）：货物实际于信用证规定的最早装运期之前装船，但提单日期打在规定的最早装运期之后，便于出口方及早取得单据结算货款，属于违法提单。

4. 过期提单（Stale B/L）：一种情况下是指出口商取得提单后超过了银行规定的交单期限，未能及时交单到银行，此类提单一般习惯上又称为滞期提单。银行不接受滞期提单，除非收货人同意接受；另一种情况下是指货物先抵达目的港，而提单晚于货物到港时间到达进口人手中，这种情况会造成进口人无法及时清关提货，习惯上此类提单亦称为过期提单，这种情况在近海贸易中容易出现。

5. 电放提单（Telex Release B/L）：货物装船完毕后，承运人或其代理人已经签发了提单给托运人，应托运人的要求，承运人或其代理人收回全套正本提单，并以电传电报等方式通知其在目的港的代理将货物交给提单收货人。这种操作方式称之为“电放”，这类提单即为电放提单。具体操作为：承运人或其代理人凭托运人的电放申请，在正本提单上加盖“电放”（Surrendered 或 Telex Release）的印章，并发送给承运人在卸货港的船务代理人，凭以放货。

除此之外，还有直达提单（Direct B/L）、转船提单（Transshipment B/L）、联运提单（Through B/L）和多式联运提单（Combined Transport B/L）、班轮提单（Liner B/L）和租船合约提单（Charter Party B/L）、船公司提单（Carrier B/L）、代理人提单（Agent B/L）、全式提单（Long Form B/L）和简式提单（Short Form B/L）、正本提单（Original B/L）和副本提单（Copy B/L）等。

三、海运费的计算

海运货物一般以班轮运输为主，无论是整箱还是拼箱货物均按照班轮运价支付运费。班轮运价包括基本运费与附加运费两部分。在实际业务中，外贸公司通常是通过和国际货运代理公司进行议价并确定国际运费。

（一）拼箱装运费

要计算拼箱海运费，首先要明白班轮运费的计算标准，然后再根据不同计算标准核算具体的运费。班轮运费计算标准见表 11-2。

1. 计算标准

表 11-2　班轮运费计算标准

计算标准	缩写标注	内容解释
重量法	W	按照货物的毛重（重量吨）计算，以每公吨作为计算单位，精确到小数点后三位。
体积法	M	按照货物的体积（尺码吨）计算，以每立方米作为计算单位，精确到小数点后三位。
从价法	Ad.Val	按照货物 FOB 价值作为计算标准。
选择法	W/M	在重量法和体积法两者之间选择，承运人按照收费较高的一种计收运费。
	W Or Ad Val	在重量法和从价法两者之间选择，承运人按照收费较高的一种计收运费。
	M Or Ad Val	在体积法和从价法两者之间选择，承运人按照收费较高的一种计收运费。
	W/M Or Ad Val	在重量法、体积法和从价法三者之间选择，承运人按照收费较高的一种计收运费。
综合法	W & Ad Val	按照重量吨计费并加上从价运费。
	M & Ad Val	按照尺码吨计费并加上从价运费。
按件法	/	无法衡量重量和测量体积，按照件（头、只、辆）为单位计收运费。如活牲畜、汽车等货物。
临时议定法	/	对于大宗低值货物，采用船、货双方临时议定运价的方法。

2. 计算步骤和公式

（1）根据货物的英文名称从货物分级表中查出有关货物的计费等级和计算标准；

（2）从航线费率表中查出该货物的基本费率和各项附加费率；

（3）运费=基本运费+附加运费；

（4）根据计算标准乘以单位运价得到运费总额。

具体公式为：基本运价（1 + 各种附加费率）×每件包装运费吨×包装总件数

例如：出口苹果汁（Apple Juice）一批，计 100 箱，每箱毛重为 60 千克，每箱体积为 0.080 立方米，从上海装运出口到加拿大多伦多，计算该批货物的国际运费。

解答：第一步：根据货物的英文名称 Apple Juice 从货物分级表中查得该货物的等级为 8 级，计算标准为 M。

第二步：从航线等级费率表中查中国—加拿大航线，得到 8 级货物相应的基本运费率为 219.00 元/运费吨，燃油附加费 20%。

第三步：计算每一运费吨的单位运价：219.00+219.00×20%=262.80/运费吨

第四步：根据计算标准得到总运费额：0.080×100×262.80=2 102.40 元

（二）整箱装运费

基本采用包箱费率乘以箱数的方式计算运费。根据中国远洋运输公司使用的交通运输部《中国远洋货运运价本》，常见的包箱费率有以下三种：

1. FAK 包箱费率：对每一集装箱不分货类统一收取的费率。

2. FCS 包箱费率：按不同货物等级制定的包箱费率。货物等级也是 1~20 级，但级差较小。一般低价货费率高于传统运输费率，高价货则低于传统运输费率；同一等级货物，实重货运价高于体积货运价。

3. FCB 包箱费率：既按不同货物等级或货类，又按计算标准制定的费率。同一级费率因计算标准不同，费率也不同。

例如：中远班轮以 2 个 20 英尺集装箱装运盐渍松茸罐头 2 500 箱，以 CY/CY 为交货条件，目的港为瑞典斯德哥尔摩港（Stockholm），该货物等级为 8 级。经查中远运价表，该航线下，8—10 级货物对应的一个 20 英尺集装箱的运价为 USD1 850.00，则该批货物的总运费应为 USD1 850.00×2=USD3 700.00。

四、航空运费的计算

国际航空运价主要有普通货物运价、等级货物运价、指定货物运价和集装箱货物运价四类。在实际业务中主要以普通货物运价为主。每单货物的空运费根据货物所适用的运价和货物的计费重量计算而得。

航空运费=计费重量×运价

（一）计费重量

计费重量是指用以计算货物航空运费的重量。一般情况下，重货以实际毛重作为计费重量，轻泡货以体积重量作为计费重量。以 0.5kg 为最小计费单位，重量尾数不足 0.5kg 的，按 0.5kg 计算；0.5kg 以上不足 1kg 的，按 1kg 计算。两种以上的货物在一份运单上，按其总量比较，确定其计费重量。

（二）运价等级极差划分：

1. 5kg 及其以下的货物，用 M 表示；

2. 45kg 以下的货物，用 N 表示；

3. 45kg 及其以上的货物，用 Q 表示。

★ 级次越高，费率越低；计费重量越大，运费越低。

★ 应把同一目的地的多批货物集中发给到港的货运代理，由到达港的代理统一收货后，分交给不同的收货人。

（三）体积重量

根据国际航协的规定，将货物的体积按一定比例折算的重量称为体积重量。折算方法为：

体积重量（千克）= 货物体积（立方米）÷0.006（立方米/千克）

（四）普通货物航空运费的计算方法

1. 按照体积重量的公式将货物的体积折算成体积重量；
2. 体积重量与实际毛重比较，择其高者作为计费重量；
3. 航空运费=计费重量×运价=单件计费重量率×包装总件数×运价

例如：有一批货物，毛重 285 千克，体积 0.9 立方米，自成都空运到日本东京，运价每千克人民币 31.63 元，计算该批货物的航空运费。

解答：第一步：折算体积重量

0.9 立方米÷0.006（立方米/千克）=150 千克

第二步：比较实际毛重和体积重量的大小

毛重 285 千克＞体积重量 150 千克，所以应按照毛重计收运费。

第三步：根据航空运费的计算公式计算运费

航空运费=285 千克×31.63=9 014.55 元

操作能力训练

思考题

S11-1　海运提单为什么要背书？背书的原则是什么？

操作题

C11-1　根据附录 3.1 里提供的制单信用证 3-13-2（见本书第 230 页），用提单格式一，独立缮制符合要求的提单。

C11-2　讨论和评讲后，根据附录 3.1 里的其余制单信用证（见本书第 230 页），用提单格式二，逐一缮制符合要求的提单。

C11-3　探索学习下一项目，并根据附录 3.1 里的制单信用证 3-13-1（见本书第 230 页），缮制符合要求的受益人证明和装运通知。

项目十二

拟写各种证明和装运通知

学习目标

[知识目标] 了解证明文件的种类，了解通知的分类，掌握拟写证明和装运通知的要点。

[能力目标] 能按信用证要求，正确把握拟写证明的日期和文件名，正确拟写其语句，能完整拟写装运通知。

一、拟写受益人证明

受益人证明（Beneficiary’s Certificate）狭义是指受益人根据信用证要求拟写的证明文件，广义则是指由受益人向银行提交的信用证要求的所有证明文件。它属于其他单据类，但跟主要单据一样具有同等重要的价值。受益人只有完全满足了信用证的相关条款要求，并正确拟写了所要求的证明，才能顺利结算货款。

项目描述（案例情境描述）

山东希望土产进出口公司向马来西亚出口一批山东黑枣，进口方通过银行开来信用证。出口方经审核无误后，开始缮制来证要求提供的全套单据。本次业务为拟写受益人证明。

操作要领（拟写受益人证明的要求）

证明文件本无统一的或固定的格式要求，但又有一些共通的要素在拟写证明时应予以显示。

1. 信头或函头（Letter Head）：拟写证明文件必须在出具人的公司函头或信头下缮制证明内容。

※本案例制单：　　来证条款　　　　　　　　　　　　　　　　　　　　　　制单操作

来证条款：

BENEFICIARY: SHANDONG HOPE NATIVE PRODUCT I/E CORP.
62，GUANGXI ROAD, QINGDAO, CHINA

制单操作：

山东希望土产进出口公司
Shandong Hope Native Product I/E Corp.
No.62, Guangxi Road, Qingdao, China

2. 单据日期（Date of Issue）：单据日期应以运输单据日期为中轴。如果证明的事情应在货物装运前进行，则日期应在运输单据之前；反之，则应在运输单据日期之后。不仅如此，日期还须合理，不可违反惯例规定或常理太早或太晚。本例单据日期在 8 日或以前都可接受。

※本案例制单：　　来证条款　　　　　　　　　　　　　　　　　　　　　　制单操作

来证条款：

6) BENEFICIARY TO AIRMAIL DIRECTLY TO OPENER ONE SET OF NON-NEGOTIABLE DOCUMENTS IMMEDIATELY AFTER SHIPMENT AND A CERTIFICATE OF COMPLIANCE TO THIS EFFECT IS

制单操作：

Date: July 7, 2015

3. 参考号（Reference Numbers）：证明文件上应显示信用证号码和发票号码等参考文件号码，便于单据查阅和配套。如果信用证有明确反对，则应按开来的信用证要求拟写。本例没有相反规定的条款。

※本案例制单：　　来证条款　　　　　　　　　　　　　　　　　　　　　　制单操作

Re: L/C No.　　PGH000348DC
Invoice No.　　BP13SHS02INV1051

4. 文件名称（Title of Document）：拟写证明文件的单据名称必须与来证要求相符。文件名的词根须与证明语句中的谓语动词词根一致。譬如动词为 certify，则文件名须用 certificate；动词为 state，则文件名须用 statement；动词为 declare，则文件名须用 declaration；动词用 specify，则文件名可为 Beneficiary's Specifying Letter。

※本案例制单：　　来证条款　　　　　　　　　　　　　　　　　　　　　　制单操作

来证条款：

AND A CERTIFICATE OF COMPLIANCE TO THIS EFFECT

制单操作：

Beneficiary's Certificate

5. 文件内容（Contents）：证明的内容必须与信用证条款要求相符，有些文字须一致；必要时应改变谓语动词的时态，切勿照抄来证的不定式或 v-ing 形式。本例证明的语句时态须改变。

※本案例制单：　　来证条款　　　　　　　　　　　　　　　　　　　　　　制单操作

来证条款：

6) BENEFICIARY TO AIRMAIL DIRECTLY TO OPENER ONE SET OF NON-NEGOTIABLE DOCUMENTS IMMEDIATELY AFTER SHIPMENT AND A CERTIFICATE OF COMPLIANCE TO THIS EFFECT IS

制单操作：

We herein as beneficiary certify that one set of non-negotiable documents has been airmailed directly to the opener immediately after shipment.

6. 加注内容（Extra Notations）：在非信用证结算或如果信用证没有条款要求在单据上额外加注什么内容，该文件就可以用正式结束敬语完成了。但若来证要求额外显示什么，则须照办。本例在特别条款第 3 款和第 4 款对所有单据都有加注要求，须照办。

※本案例制单：　　来证条款　　　　　　　　　　　　　　　　　　　　　　制单操作

来证条款：

3) DOCUMENTS TO EVIDENCE THAT ALL PACKAGES BEAR SHIPPING MARKS: SHS/PENANG/1-UP
4) DOCUMENTS TO EVIDENCE THAT PACKING IS DONE AS FOLLOWS:
IN CARDBOARD CARTONS OF 25KGS NET OR 26.2KGS GROSS PER CARTON

制单操作：

It is evidenced that all packages bear shipping marks:
SHS/PENANG/1-UP and packing is done as follows:
In cardboard cartons of 25kgs net or 26.2kgs gross per carton.

7. 签署（Signature & Stamp）：证明文件都须签章，才能名副其实作为证明。

※本案例制单：　　来证条款　　　　　　　　　　　　　　　　　　　　制单操作

Yours faithfully,
XXX (stamped)

附受益人证明制单样例

山东希望土产进出口公司

Shandong Hope Native Product I/E Corp.

No.62, Guangxi Road, Qingdao, China

Date: July 7, 2015

Re：L/C No.　　PGH000348DC

Invoice No.　BP13SHS02INV1051

Beneficiary's Certificate

Dear Sirs:

We herein as beneficiary certify that one set of non-negotiable documents has been airmailed directly to the opener immediately after shipment.

It is evidenced that all packages bear shipping marks:
SHS/PENANG/1-UP and packing is done as follows:
In cardboard cartons of 25kgs net or 26.2kgs gross per carton.

Yours faithfully,
×××（stamped)

二、拟写装运通知

装运通知（Shipping Advice）是由受益人向信用证特定的对象用电文形式发出的货物装运情况通报，它仍属于受益人证明的范畴。

项目描述（案例情境描述）

山东希望土产进出口公司向马来西亚出口一批山东黑枣，进口方通过银行开来信用证。出口方经审核无误后，开始缮制来证要求提供的全套单据。本次业务为货物装运通知。

操作要领（拟写装运通知的要求）

1. 信头或函头（Letter Head）：拟写装运通知必须在出具人的公司函头或信头下缮制内容，以表明发件人。

※本案例制单：

来证条款	制单操作
BENEFICIARY: SHANDONG HOPE NATIVE PRODUCT I/E CORP. 62，GUANGXI ROAD, QINGDAO, CHINA	山东希望土产进出口公司 Shandong Hope Native Product I/E Corp. No.62, Guangxi Road, Qingdao, China

2. 传真头（Fax Head）：装运通知过去都是用电报（cable）或电传（telex）发出。20 世纪 90 年代中期传真机在我国商务中心普及后，通知就改用传真方式发送了。因此，通知应该有传真头，包括的信息有：日期、页码、收件人及其传真号码、发件人及其传真号码、联系人（attn）等。如果有必要，还应注明附件（amendment）和抄送（c.c.）。其中尤以日期和收件人联系号码最为重要。日期以运输单据日期为中轴，如果买方投保，则通知日期应在运输单据之前；反之，日期可在运输单据日期之后，但须在装运后 48 小时之内。除此之外，银行还须注意收件人是否符合信用证要求。本例运输和保险由卖方负责，通知日期在装运日后两天内可接受。

※本案例制单：

来证条款	制单操作
CIF PENANG INCO Shipped per m/v "Victoria" on July 5, 2015.	Date: July 7, 2015 # of Pages: 01 / 1 To: Soo Hup Seng Trading Co. SDN BHD. (Fax: x x x x x x x) From: Shandong Hope Native Product I/E Corp. (Fax: x x x x x) Attn : x x x

3. 文件名（Title of Document）：装运通知的文件名即单据的主题，可用的英文名有 Shipping /Shipment Advice, Shipping/Shipment Note 等，应与来证要求一致或相符。

※本案例制单：

来证条款	制单操作
5) BENEFICARY TO ADVISE OPENER BY TELEX / FAX ALL DETAILS OF SHIPMENT A	**Shipment Advice**

4. 开场段落（Opening Para.）：装运通知的首段需要简单说明相关货物的装运情况。

※本案例制单：

来证条款	制单操作
	Dear Sirs: We herein as beneficiary are taking pleasure in advising/informing you that shipment of the goods under your Order No. Soo-6378 has been effected with details as follows:

5. 装运细节（Details of Transport）：装运细节应能包括三方面的信息，尽到充分之责。① 商品信息：品名、数量（重要的是包装数量）和价值；② 运输信息：装运港、卸货港、船名航次、装运日期（信息极为重要）、唛头、集装箱编号、总毛重、总体积；③ 参考文件号：发票号、提单号、信用证号、合同号或订单号。

※本案例制单：　　来证条款　　　　　　　　　　　　　　　　　　　　　　　　制单操作

Commodity:	Shandong Black Dates	
Quantity:	5 m/t in 200 cardboard cartons	
Total Value:	HKD 46,150.00	
Port of Loading:	Qingdao	
Port of Destination:	Penang, Malaysia	
Vessel & Voyage:	Victoria	
On Board Date:	July 5, 2015	ETA：During mid July, 2015
Shipping Marks:	SHS/Penang/1-up	
Container:	EISU2628205	
Gross Weight:	5,240.00 kg	
Measurement:	14.850 M^3 (cubic meters)	
Invoice No.	BP13SHS02INV1051	
B/L No.	CCFASH1820960	
L/C No.	PGH000348DC	
S/C No.	×××××××	

6. 尾段（Ending Para）：由于装运通知通常是一笔交易结束的文件，有经验的业务员常在其尾段表达继续合作的愿望，使该笔业务起到承上启下的作用。

※本案例制单：　　来证条款　　　　　　　　　　　　　　　　　　　　　　　　制单操作

It is our desire that the shipment will reach you in good order and condition and will turn out to your entire satisfaction. We are quite pleased to have had a pleasant and successful cooperation with you and are looking forward to more opportunities for us to send our prompt and careful attention to your orders.

7. 加注内容（Extra Notations）：如果来证有加注要求，制单时应予以照办。以非信用证方式结算或信用证没有条款要求加注时，制单是不应该画蛇添足的。

※本案例制单：　　来证条款　　　　　　　　　　　　　　　　　　　　　　　　制单操作

来证条款	制单操作
3) DOCUMENTS TO EVIDENCE THAT ALL PACKAGES BEAR SHIPPING MARKS: SHS/PENANG/1-UP 4) DOCUMENTS TO EVIDENCE THAT PACKING IS DONE AS FOLLOWS: IN CARDBOARD CARTONS OF 25KGS NET OR 26.2KGS GROSS PER CARTON	It is evidenced that all packages bear shipping marks: SHS/PENANG/1-UP and packing is done as follows: In cardboard cartons of 25kgs net or 26.2kgs gross per carton.

附装运通知制单样例

山东希望土产进出口公司

Shandong Hope Native Product I/E Corp.

No.62, Guangxi Road, Qingdao, China

Date: July 7, 2015　　　　　　　　　　　　# of Pages: 01/1

To: Soo Hup Seng Trading Co. SDN BHD. (Fax:×××××)

From: Shandong Hope Native Product I/E Corp. (Fax:×××××)

Attn：×××

Shipment Advice

Dear Sirs:

We herein as beneficiary are taking pleasure in advising/informing you that shipment of the goods under your Order No. Soo-6378 has been effected with details as follows:

Commodity:　　Shandong Black Dates

Quantity:　　5 m/t in 200 cardboard cartons

（续表）

Total Value:	HKD 46,150.00	
Port of Loading:	Qingdao	
Port of Destination:	Penang, Malaysia	
Vessel & Voyage:	Victoria	
On Board Date:	July 5, 2015	ETA：During mid July, 2015
Shipping Marks:	SHS/Penang/1-up	
Container:	EISU2628205	
Gross Weight：	5,240.00 kg	
Measurement：	14.850 M^3 (cubic meters)	
Invoice No.	BP13SHS02INV1051	
B/L No.	CCFASH1820960	
L/C No.	PGH000348DC	
S/C No.	×××××××	

It is our desire that the shipment will reach you in good order and condition and will turn out to your entire satisfaction. We are quite pleased to have had a pleasant and successful cooperation with you and are looking forward to more opportunities for us to send our prompt and careful attention to your orders.

It is evidenced that all packages bear shipping marks:
SHS/PENANG/1-UP and packing is done as follows:
In cardboard cartons of 25kgs net or 26.2kgs gross per carton.

Yours faithfully,
××× (stamped)

相关知识

一、拟写受益人证明

（一）各种证明单据的分类

信用证项下的证明单据主要是用于证明受益人满足了信用证的相关条款。常见信用证要求受益人向银行提交的证明单据有：

1. 受益人证明/声明/申明（Beneficiary's Certificate/Statement/Declaration）：由受益人拟写证明文件，说明已按信用证要求按时向特定对象寄出单据或船样（Shipping Samples）。

2. 邮包收据和快邮/快递收据（Post Receipt/Speed Post Receipt/Couriers Receipt）：由邮局或快递公司签发，用于证明受益人已按时向特定对象寄出信用证要求的材料。常见的快递公司有 EMS（特快专递）和 DHL（信使专递）。

3. 包装、唛头、货品证明（Certificate of Packing or Shipping Marks or Quality）：由受益人拟写的证明货物装运状况良好，或唛头无误的文件。

4. 船东证明（Shipowner's Certificate），包括：

船籍和航程证明（Certificate of Registry/Itinerary）：属于政治条款单据，主要由阿拉伯国家开出的信用证里有这样的条款要求。

船级证明（Confirmation of Class）：要求证明运载船舶属于某一等级。不宜接受。

船龄证明（Certificate of Vessel Age）：要求证明货轮航行使用时间低于某一年份。

货装集装箱船证明（Certificate of Container Vessel）：证明按要求货已装上集装箱船。

船代运费证明（Freight Statement）：船方提供的证明运费付讫的文件。

船长或大副收据（Master's/Mate's Receipt, M/R）：由船长或大副签发的装船收据，证明装船货物是否完好无损，是提单是否清洁的原始单据。

（二）各种证明的一般内容和要求

1. 信用证要求的证明并无统一格式要求，一般在出具人公司函头纸上拟写即可。

2. 证明文件的日期以运输单据日期为中轴，或前或后，但必须符合逻辑并合理。凡是证明的内容应该在装运前发生的，则证明文件的日期须在运输单据日期前；凡证明的事情只能在货物装运后进行的，则单据日期须在运输单据日期后，且合理，一般三日内。

3. 如果信用证没有相反条款，证明文件应注明信用证号码和发票号码作为参考号。

4. 文件必须要有单据名称，且符合信用证要求。

5. 证明文件一般用正式格式，内容必须符合信用证要求，拟写的语句时态须符合实际情况。当来证用的是非谓语动词形式或命令语句时，切不可照搬。

6. 证明文件必须正式签署盖章。

二、拟写装运通知

（一）通知的分类

在国际贸易中，通知分为到船通知（Vessel Notice）或装运指示（Shipping Instruction），由买方向卖方发出；装运通知（Shipping Advice），由卖方向买方发出。

（二）装运通知的地位和作用

在 FOB，FAS 和 FCA 等交货条件下，买方或信用证申请人负责安排运输，须履行及时、充分的通知义务，及早通知卖方或信用证受益人有关运载船舶到达装运港的必要信息，以便卖方能够按时装运货物。否则，即便货物逾期尚未装上运载工具，被指定货物一旦受损，都由买方承担责任。同样，受益人或卖方也必须履行自己的及时、充分通知义务，以快捷的方式告知申请人或买方货物装运情况，以便进口方及时办理货运保险、清关、运输、仓储和分销等事项。如果未尽充分、及时的通知，对于已装上运载工具的货物，一旦出现损失，卖方仍要承担全部责任。

（三）装运通知的主要内容

无论是买方负责运输（FOB，FAS，FCA），或是买方负责货运保险（FOB，CFR，CPT 等），或是买方只负责接货清关（CIF，CIP），卖方的装运通知内容都要完整，才能尽到充分通知的义务。卖方的通知一般应包括三大板块的信息，即商品信息、运输信息和参考编号。总之，信息须满足进口方办理货运保险、清关、仓储、分销等业务活动目的。

（四）装运通知的操作

装运通知的信息必须完整充分，考虑到近洋运输的因素，发送日期最晚在装运后 48 小时内，但以买方办理货运保险的条件交货，通知发送日期应在货物装运前。考虑到远洋时差因素，通知应在货物装运前一天发出。考虑到文件传输的安全性，发送的方式一般以电传或传真为好。进口方为货物办理了预约保险的情况下，会要求出口方把装运通知同时发给指定的保险公司一份。

操作能力训练

思考题

S12-1 贸易术语通则中规定卖方有责任向买方发出及时、充分的通知是指什么？

操作题

C12-1 根据附录 3.1 里提供的制单信用证 3-13-2（见本书第 230 页），独立拟写符合要求的证明单据。

C12-2 讨论和评讲后，根据附录 3.1 里的其余制单信用证（见本书第 230 页），逐一拟写符合要求的证明单据。

C12-3 探索学习下一项目，并根据附录 3.1 里的制单信用证 3-13-1（见本书第 230 页），用汇票格式一独立尝试缮制符合要求的汇票。

C12-4 独立学习 ISBP（2013 最新版本）和 UCP600 中关于汇票的条款。

项目十三

缮制商业汇票

汇票的含义及作用

汇票是国际结算的三大结算工具之一，也是国际贸易中使用频率最高的一种金融单据。在采用信用证结算和托收结算方式的出口业务中，出口商必须出具汇票，连同其他货运单据一起按时向银行提交，才能获得货款。汇票通常在获取运输单据后缮制。无论是信用证方式还是托收方式，使用的汇票通常都是由出口商缮制的，属于商业汇票。

汇票究其本质是一种无条件支付的书面命令。但是作为信用证项下交单文件的组成部分，汇票所记载的内容也必须符合信用证的条款规定和UCP600及ISBP的相关条款的规定。

学习目标

［知识目标］掌握信用证项下和托收项下汇票的填制方法，了解相关票据法，了解三种国际结算工具及其在贸易中的运用，理解佣金和折扣的计算和支付方法。

［能力目标］能正确缮制信用证项下汇票和托收项下的汇票。

项目描述（案例情境描述）

山东希望土产进出口公司完成货物装船，并取得提单后，根据信用证要求缮制全套结汇单据，并准备于规定的期限内完成交单议付。本次业务为山东希望土产进出口公司业务员缮制商业汇票，相关信用证参阅项目四，其他的必要信息参阅前面相关项目。

操作要领

汇票本无固定或统一格式，但无论哪种格式，其基本内容或栏目都是相同的。我们分别就信用证和托收两种结算方式项下的汇票缮制，做如下讨论和操作演示。

一、信用证项下商业汇票的缮制要领

1. 汇票的名称（Title of Document）：必须写明“汇票”（Bill of Exchange 或 Draft）字样，否则汇票无效。

2. 汇票号码（Draft No.）：为了便于查阅和配套使用，本栏目填写的单据号码与商业发票的一致。

※本案例制单：　　商业发票相关条款　　　　制单操作

4.发票日期和发票号 Invoice Date and No.
BP15SHS02INV1051　JUNE 28, 2015

No.　BP15SHS02INV1051

3. 汇票小写金额（Amount in Figure）：汇票金额可以与发票金额相同或小于发票金额，但不得大于商业发票的金额，包括汇票的金额和币种两部分。小于发票金额的部分，可能是佣金（明佣或暗佣），可能是贸易的折扣，也可能是买方提前支付的预付款。本例金额应与发票金额一致。

※本案例制单：　　信用证条款　　　　制单操作

DRAFTS: AT SIGHT FOR FULL INVOICE VALUE OF GOODS DRAWN ON OURSELVES

For　HK46,150.00
(amount in figure)

4. 出票地点和出票日期：出票地点应在出口商所在地，一般已印就。出票日期即为银行寄单日期，应由议付行向开证行寄单时代为填写，现实中也有银行要求出票人自己填写的。该日期应晚于运输单据日期，UCP600 规定交单后银行有 5 个工作日。

※本案例制单：　　信用证条款　　　　制单操作

PERIOD FOR PRESENTATION: DOCUMENTS TO BE PRESENTED WITHIN 15 DAYS AFTER THE ISSUANCE OF THE SHIPPING DOCUMENTS BUT WITHIN THE VALIDITY OF THE CREDIT.

QINGDAO, CHINA
(place and date of issue)

5. 付款期限（Maturity Date）：填写来证规定的付款期限，在金额下找关键词 draft at。一般可分为即期付款和远期付款两类。即期付款只需在汇票固定格式栏内打上“at sight”。若已印有“at ____ sight”，应在 sight 前的横线上打一种符号占据，如“*****”，其目的主要是为了避免任何修改或添加。

远期付款一般有四种：

（1）见票后若干天付款。应填上“at ***×× days after sight”，即以付款人见票日第二天为起算日，受票人表示承兑后，在若干天后到期付款。

（2）出票后若干天付款。应填上“at ***×× days after date”或“... after draft”，即以汇票出票日第二天为起算日，若干天后到期付款。这时要在后面的 sight of 字面上打上××××或斜线，予以覆盖或划掉。

（3）提单日后若干天付款。应填上“at ***×× days from B/L”，即付款人以提单签

发日第二天为起算日，若干天后到期付款。此时要将汇票上“sight of”划掉，并在汇票上方空白处注明提单日期，即“B/L DATE: ××××”。

需要强调的是，无论用了 after 还是 from，银行付款的起算日期都以载明的日期次日算起。汇票上的付款日期前须用一种符号占据，以免被篡改。

（4）某指定日期付款。例如指定 2018 年 2 月 25 日为付款日，即在 At 后填上“25th Feb. 2018”，并将汇票上印就的“sight of”划掉。这种汇票称为“定期付款汇票”或“板期汇票”。

（5）远期信用证的汇票表示方法。如来证为远期付款，但有条款显示“Usance drafts are to be negotiated at sight basis and presented to drawee bank for discount at buyer’s cost.”，则汇票付款期限应按条款规定制作成相应的远期付款，同时在本栏上方或下方加上：“negotiable at sight basis and bank interest for drawee’s account”。

本案付款期限为见票即付或即期付款。

※本案例制单：　信用证条款	制单操作
DRAFTS: AT SIGHT FOR FULL	At ****** sight of this

6. 受款人（Payee）：本栏条款属于支付命令（Order of Honor），是出票人命令受票人无条件支付的条款。如果在此加上了支付条件，则该汇票失效。这一栏用来填受款人也称收款人或抬头，一般填出口地议付行，填写指定银行的名称和地址（分行或银行所在地即可），此时出票人不做背书。在实践中，也有的填写出票人，由出票人做记名背书交银行议付，即“Please pay to ×××Bank”，下面记录背书人信息。本例填写了议付行。

议付信用证分为限制议付和自由议付或公开议付两种。若信用证金额以下的“available with…”后有确定的银行，则本汇票交指定的银行议付；若“available with…”后没有确定的银行，或显示的是“any bank by negotiation”，则本汇票交出口地任何银行议付。

※本案例制单：　信用证条款	制单操作
AVAILABLE BY NEGOTIATION	Pay to BANK OF CHINA, QINGDAO BRANCH or order

7. 汇票金额大写（Amount in Words）：要求用文字表示大写金额。填写的货币用全称，不可用代码，其前面可写 Say，也可不写，其意思为中文的“即”，但金额的数目文字后必须写“only”，相当于中文的“整”字。例如，SAY UNITED STATES DOLLARS ONE THOUSAND TWO HUNDRED AND THIRTY FOUR ONLY。大写金额不得涂改，且须与小写金额相符。我国票据法规定大小写必须一致，但英国票据法规定以大写为准。若出现语法错误，被视为不符点；若出现拼写错误，只要不会引起歧义，将不被视为不符点。有小数的金额大写方法参见发票讲解。

※本案例制单：　商业发票相关条款	制单操作
15. 总值（用数字和文字表示）Total Amount (in figure and word) SAY H.K. DOLLARS FORTY-SIX THOUSAND ONE HUNDRED AND FIFTY ONLY.	H.K. DOLLARS FORTY-SIX THOUSAND ONE HUNDRED AND FIFTY ONLY (amount in words)

8. 收讫条款（Value Received）：该条款又称对价条款。信用证项下汇票不填此栏，仅

托收项下汇票此栏内才填写商品的包装件数和品名。本例为信用证结算，无须填写此栏。

※本案例制单：　商业发票相关条款　　制单操作

______ Of ______
(quantity)　(name of commodity)

9. 出票依据（Drawn Under）：此栏又称出票条款，一般填写开证行+信用证号码+开证日期，除非信用证另有规定。在信用证的上部获取相关信息。

※本案例制单：　信用证条款　　制单操作

DC. NUMBER: PGH000348DC
DATE OF ISSUE: 21 MAY2015

Drawn under THE HONG KONG AND SHANGHAI BANKING CORP LTD., PENANG
L/C No. PGH000348DC dated MAY 21, 2015

THE HONGKONG AND SHANGHAI BANKING CORP LTD., DOWNING STREET, PENANG
ISSUE OF AN IRREVOCABLE DOCUMENTARY CREDIT

10. 受票人（Drawee/Payer）：汇票的受票人又称付款人。信用证方式下付款人通常应为付款银行，应详细填写付款行的名称和地址。

根据UCP600规定，信用证方式的汇票以开证行或其指定银行为付款人，不应以申请人为汇票的付款人。如果信用证要求以申请人为汇票的付款人，银行将视该汇票为一份附加的单据；而如果信用证未规定付款人的名称，汇票付款人亦应填开证行名称。

在信用证业务中，汇票付款人是按信用证“draw on××”，或“draft on××”或“drawee××”来确定的。本例“draft(s)... drawn on ourselves”条款表明，付款人为开证行。

※本案例制单：　信用证条款　　制单操作

DRAFTS: AT SIGHT FOR FULL INVOICE VALUE OF GOODS DRAWN ON OURSELVES

To:
THE HONG KONG AND SHANGHAI BANKING CORP. LTD.
DOWNING STREET, PENANG　SHAN
MALAYSIA

11. 出票人（Drawer）：出票人为信用证的受益人，托收项下即为出口人，需在右下方签字栏盖签字章或填写受益人的英文名称，并由法人代表或其授权人签字。

※本案例制单：　信用证条款　　制单操作

For and on behalf of
LTD.
SHANDONG HOPE NATIVE PRODUCT I/E CORP.
×××
(signature)

12. 背书（Endorsement）：由于汇票可以议付或转让，就需要背书，一般是由收款人开始进行首次背书。背书大多是空白背书，即在票据背面仅签下背书人名称+签字+背书日期。如果是做记名背书或称特别背书，则还须在空白背书之上写下被背书人的名称，即“PLEASE PAY TO...”，具体方法参见保单和提单讲解。本例在支付命令中已明确收款人为议付行，出票人不做背书。

13. 份数（Copies）：汇票是金融单据或支付工具，并不属于装运单据。汇票一套为两份，采用“付一不付二，付二不付一”的原则。

附信用证项下商业汇票制单样例：

BILL OF EXCHANGE

No. BP15SHS02INV1051

For HK46,150.00　　　　QINGDAO, CHINA

(amount in figure)　　　　**(place and date of issue)**

At ****** **sight of this FIRST Bill of Exchange (SECOND being unpaid)**

Pay to BANK OF CHINA QINGDAO BRANCH **or order the sum of**

H.K. DOLLARS FORTY-SIX THOUSAND ONE HUNDRED AND FIFTY ONLY

(amount in words）

Value received for ________ **Of** ________

(quantity)　　　　**(name of commodity)**

Drawn under THE HONG KONG AND SHANGHAI BANKING CORP LTD., PENANG

L/C No. PGH000348DC **dated** MAY 21, 2015

To:　　　　**For and on behalf of**

THE HONG KONG AND SHANGHAI BANKING CORP. LTD.

DOWNING STREET, PENANG　　　　SHANDONG HOPE NATIVE PRODUCT I/E CORP.

MALAYSIA　　　　×××

(signature)

二、托收项下商业汇票的制作

托收结算方式项下商业汇票的制作和信用证结算方式下略有不同，在此针对区别于信用证项下商业汇票的不同的项目做介绍。

1. 出票日期（Date)：托收项下的汇票出票地点和日期可以由出票人交票时填写，也可请托收行在寄单时代为填写。该日期应晚于提单日期。

2. 付款期限（Maturity Date)：D/P 即期托收方式的汇票付款期限可以直接填“D/P at sight”，填写方法为在 At 前面加 D/P，即“D/P At ***×× sight”。

制单操作

D/P At ******* sight of this SECOND Bill of exchange(FIRST being unpaid)

3. 受款人（Payee)：托收项下汇票的收款人（受款人）一般是填写卖方的开户银行即托收行，此时出票人不做背书；实践中也有的填写出票人或债权人自己，由出票人做记名背书后交给托收行。银行收有货款后，通知出票人结汇。

制单操作

Pay to BANK OF CHINA, QINGDAO BRANCH or order

4. 出票依据或收讫条款（Drawn under/Value Received)：托收项下汇票的出票依据需填写商品的包装件数、品名或不会引起歧义的商品总名称、商业发票的号码及其日期，也可加上合同协议号。

制单操作

Against shipment of 200 CTN SHANDONG BLACK DATES

UNDER INV. NO. xxxxxx JUN. 28, 2015 AND ORDER NO. S00-6378

5. 付款人或受票人（Payer/Drawee）：托收项下汇票的付款人填进口商公司英文名称和地址。

制单操作

To:
SOO HUP SENG TRADING CO. SDN BHD.
165 1ST FLOOR, VICTORIA STREET,
10300 PENANG MALAYSIA

附托收项下商业汇票填制样例：

BILL OF EXCHANGE

No. BP15SHS02INV1051

For **HKD46,150.00** **QINGDAO, CHINA**

(amount in figure) **(place and date of issue)**

D/P At ****** sight of this SECOND Bill of exchange (FIRST being unpaid)**

Pay to BANK OF CHINA, QINGDAO BRANCH or order the sum of

H.K. DOLLARS FORTY-SIX THOUSAND ONE HUNDRED AND FIFTY ONLY.

(amount in words)

Against shipment of 200 CTN SHANDONG BLACK DATES

UNDER INV. NO. xxxxxx DATED JUN. 28, 2015 AND ORDER NO. S00-6378

To:
SOO HUP SENG TRADING CO. SDN BHD.
165 1ST FLOOR, VICTORIA STREET,
10300 PENANG, MALAYSIA

For and on behalf of
SHANDONG HOPE NATIVE PRODUCT I/E CORP.
×××
(signature)

相关知识

一、国际结算工具的分类

（一）汇票（Bill of Exchange, Draft）

1. 定义和性质

汇票是出票人签发，要求付款人在见票时或者在指定日期无条件支付确定的金额给收款人或者持票人的票据。汇票是最主要的国际贸易结算工具。

世界各国广泛引用的英国票据法对汇票的定义是:“汇票是由一人签发给另一人的无条件书面命令，要求受票人见票时或于未来某一规定的或可以确定的时间，将一定金额的款项支付给某一特定的人或其所指定的人或持票人。”

2. 汇票在国际贸易中的运用

汇票通常一式两份，采用“付一不付二”的原则，主要用于大额贸易的货款支付，其支付方式为信用证或托收。

（二）本票（Promissory Note）

1. 本票的含义和性质

本票是出票人经签名做出的在确定的时间内（即期或定期或在可以确定的将来时间）无条件支付一定金额给特定的人或其指定人或来人的书面承诺。

本票是自付证券，它是由出票人自己对收款人支付并承担绝对付款责任的票据，即使远期本票也需出票人自行承兑。这是本票和汇票、支票最重要的区别。在本票法律关系中，基本当事人只有出票人和收款人，债权债务关系相对简单。本票的出票人即是付款人。

2. 本票在国际贸易中的运用

本票是一张遗失不补的金融结算单据，主要用于小额贸易的货款支付，特别适合边境交货的贸易。另外，本票也适合用于收付贸易双方的费用。

（三）支票（Cheque, Check）

1. 支票的含义和性质

支票是出发票人签发的，委托受票人（办理支票存款业务的银行或者其他金融机构）在见票时无条件支付确定的金额给受款人或者持票人的票据。

支票一经背书即可流通转让，具有通货作用，成为替代货币发挥流通手段和支付手段职能的信用流通工具。

支票的付款期限为即期。多数国家的票据法规定：支票应见票即付，不得另订付款日期，禁止签发远期支票，以避免因付款期限过长而产生空头支票的后果。

2. 支票在国际贸易中的运用

在国际贸易中，支票主要用于对小额货款和各种费用的支付或结算。我国用于国际结算的支票通常为旅行支票。

二、佣金和折扣的计算

当信用证表示发票价含有佣金或应予折扣时，佣金或折扣须在汇票上予以扣除，即汇票上应填制实际所能收回的扣除了佣金或折扣的金额。此时，汇票金额小于发票金额。

（一）佣金及含佣价的计算

佣金（commission）又称手续费（brokerage），是介绍业务或代之买卖的中间商获得的服务报酬。佣金一般由卖方付给，但有时也可由买方付给。

佣金分为明佣和暗佣。价格中包含了佣金的为“含佣价”或“明佣价”。价格中不包含佣金的为“暗佣价”，一般由卖方在合同执行完后支付给中间人，不在发票等有关单据的价格中显示。如果有关价格未对佣金做出表示，而且双方又无任何其他约定，则应理解为不含佣价，或称净价。为了表明价格不含佣金，有时价格中需要做出说明。如：USD84.39/set CIF Sydney net。

佣金率的幅度一般在 1%～5%之间，用百分号表示。如：USD 87.00/set CIFC3（or CIFC3%）Sydney，或者 USD 87.00/set CIF Sydney, including 3% commission。

佣金的计算方法为：含佣价=净价/（1–佣金率），佣金=含佣价×佣金率。

（二）折扣的计算

折扣（discount, rebate, allowance）是卖方在原价的基础上给买方的价格优惠或减让，一般都在卖方收款或买方付款时执行，主要为了扩大销售。折扣也分为明扣和暗扣，在合同中表示出来的为明扣，一般用百分号表示。

折扣的幅度没有固定的幅度，往往根据业务需要再确定，有时折扣幅度是很大的。折扣的表示方法可用百分号，也可用绝对数表示，也可用文字表述。如：

USD150 Per M/T CIF Singapore Less 3% Discount，或 USD 87.00/set CIF Sydney, including 3% discount，或 USD 87.00/set CIF Sydney less discount USD5.00

折扣的计算方法为：折扣=发票金额（原价）×折扣率。例如，CIF 发票为 20 000 美元，折扣率为 4%，则应减折扣 800 美元。即，卖方净收入=原价×（1–折扣率）。

操作能力训练

思考题

S13-1　为什么信用证项下的汇票付款人不能写进口商呢？

操作题

C13-1　根据附录 3.1 里提供的制单信用证 3-13-2，用格式一独立缮制符合要求的汇票。

C13-2　讨论和评讲后，根据附录 3.1 里制单信用证 3-13-3 和 3-13-4，用格式三缮制符合要求的汇票。

C13-3　根据附录 3.1 里提供的托收制单材料，用格式四独立缮制符合要求的汇票。

C13-4　学习下一项目，根据审单信用证 C14-1 及其资料，尝试独立审核全套进口单据。

附录 3.1　制单信用证及其资料

制单操作能力训练 3-13-1

制单信用证 3-13-1

SENDER:	TRUST BANK COPENHAGEN DENMARK
RECEIVER:	BANK OF CHINA, DALIAN BRANCH
SEQUENCE OF TOTAL:	27: 1/1
FORM OF DOC. CREDIT:	40A: IRREVOCABLE
DOC. CREDIT NUMBER:	20: LC82H00114
DATE OF ISSUE	31C: 140115

EXPIRY :	31D: DATE 140228 PLACE CHINA
APPLICANT BANK	51A: TRUST BANK COPENHAGEN DENMARK
APPLICANT	50: SEMCO MARITIME CO. A/S SVENDBORGVEJ253, DK5260 DENMARK
BENEFICIARY	59: DALIAN INTERNATIONAL FREE TRADING CO., LTD. NO.28 CHANGCHUN ROAD E1, DALIAN, CHINA
AMOUNT	32B: EUR164,700.00
AVAILABLE WITH/BY	41D: ANY BANK BY NEGOTIATION
DRAFTS AT	42C: SIGHT
DRAWEE	42A: TRUST BANK COPENHAGEN DENMARK
PARTIAL SHIPMENTS	43P: NOT ALLOWED
TRANSSHIPMNET	43T: NOT ALLOWED
LOADING IN CHARGE	44E: DALIAN PORT
FOR TRANSPORT TO	44F: COPENHAGEN
LATEST DATE OF SHIP	44C: 140210
DESCRIPTION OF GOODS	45A:

COMMODITY: FIRE EXTINGUISHING SYSTEM
WZ-Q/T-Q4 1800 SETS AT EUR45.5 PER SET, WZ-Q/T-E3 1,800 SETS AT EUR46.0 PER SET IN CTNS OF 9 SETS EACH
TERMS OF DELIVERY: CIF COPENHAGEN (INCOTERMS 2010)

DOCUMENTS REQUIRED 46A:

+ SIGNED ORIGINAL COMMERCIAL INVOICE IN 2 COPIES SHOWING CONTRACT NO. AND INDICATING ALL THE GOODS ARE OF CHINA ORIGIN.

+ 3/3 OF CLEAN ON BOARD OCEAN BILLS OF LADING MADE OUT TO ORDER AND BLANK ENDORSED MARKED FREIGHT PREPAID NOTIFYING APPLICANT.

+ SIGNED ORIGINAL PACKING LIST IN 2 COPIES SHOWING NAME OF THE MANUFACTURER, QUANTITY, G.W. AND N.W. OF EACH CARTON.

+ SIGNED ORIGINAL CERTIFICATE OF QUALITY IN 2 COPIES ISSUED BY CIQ.

+ INSURANCE POLICY IN DUPLICATE COVERING ALL RISKS AS PER CIC OF PICC.

+ ORIGINAL GSP CERTIFICATE OF ORIGIN FORM A ISSUED BY AUTHORISED PARTY.

+ BENEFICIARY'S CERTIFIED COPY OF FAX DISPATCHED TO APPLICANT WITHIN 48 HOURS AFTER SHIPMENT INDICATING CONTRACT NO., NAME OF VESSEL AND DETAILS OF SHIPMENT.

+ BENEFICIARY'S CERTIFICATE CERTIFYING THAT ONE COPY OF INVOICE

AND ONE CERTIFICATE OF NON-WOODEN PACKING HAVE BEEN SENT TO THE APPLICANT BY DHL WITHIN 5 WORKING DAYS AFTER SHIPMENT.

ADDITIONAL COND 47A:

+ INVOICE MUST NOT BE SENT WITH GOODS TO NEW SHIPYARD.

+ ALL SHIPPING DOCUMENTS MUST SHOW L/C NO.

+ ALL ORIGINAL DOCUMENTS CALLED FOR UNDER THIS CREDIT MUST BE CLEARLY MARKED ORIGINAL ON THEIR FACES.

DETAILS OF CHARGES 71B:

+ ALL BANKING CHARGES OUTSIDE THE ISSUING BANK INCLUDING THOSE OF REIMBURSEMENT BANK ARE FOR ACCOUNT OF BENEFICIARY.

+ DISCREPANCY FEE OF USD50 WILL BE DEDUCTED FOR EACH DRAWING FROM PORCEEDS.

PRESENTATION PERIOD 48: DOCUMENTS TO BE PRESENTED WITHIN 15 DAYS AFTER ISSUANCE OF THE TRANSPORT DOCUMENTS BUT WITHIN THE VALIDITY OF THE CREDIT.

CONFIRMATION 49: WITHOUT

INSTRUCTIONS 78: ALL DOCUMENTS TO BE FORWARDED TO TRUST BANK COPENHAGEN DENMARK IN ONE COVER BY COURIER SERVICE UNLESS OTHERWISE STATED ABOVE. WE SHALL HONOR THE DRAFT UPON PRESENTATION.

THIS CREDIT IS SUBJECT TO UCP600.

制单操作能力训练 3-13-1 装运货物相关资料：

1. S/C NO.: DIFT14-03
2. INV NO: BP2633, DATE: JAN. 20, 2014
3. 唛头：SM/COPENHAGEN/C/NO.1-400
4. HS 编码：8424100000 通关单编号：210500215103414000 监管条件：B
5. 生产厂商：大连鑫宏消防器材设备有限责任公司
   DALIAN XINHONG FIRE-FIGHTING EQUIPMENT AND FACILITIES CO., LTD
   大连市人民路 36 号
   生产单位商检登记注册号：2100336546 3C 认证书号码：2100/8950
6. 出口商：大连国际自贸有限责任公司商检注册登记号：2100587702
   大连国际自贸有限责任公司海关注册登记号：1100556623
   单证业务员：陈琳琳 报关员：薛枫 授权对外签字人：张明光
7. 国际货运代理：大连锦程国际货运代理有限公司
8. 船名航次: EASTWIND VOY NO: 3008H

9. 集装箱号/封号：GATU859766/6620888　GATU859767/6620999　GATU859768/6620777

10. 大连到哥本哈根 40 英尺整柜运费率: USD600.00

11. B/L No.: SITGSHTYT11277B

12. 装船日期: FEB. 3, 2014，直达，不转船

13. @G.W: 29KGS/CTN　@N.W: 27KGS/CTN　@MEA: 70CM*70CM*75CM

14. 提单签发人：大连外轮代理公司 DALIAN OCEAN SHIPPING AGENCY CO. 王铁斌

15. 船代目的港代理：ASAHI LOGISTICS CO., LTD
15 TOM ST. COPENHAGEN, DENMARK
TEL: 0045-123456　FAX: 0045-123457

16. 保险公司目的港代理：MARITIME ENGLINEERS PTE. LTD
ROOM 25, 6th FLOOR, SHINKO BULILDING
NO.7, CAT ST. COPENHAGEN, DENMARK
TEL: 0045-223456　FAX: 0045-223457

17. 一切险保费率 1%

制单操作能力训练 3-13-2

制单信用证 3-13-2

OCBC Bank　　Original For Beneficiary

SINGAPORE　　**085181**

11 FL, SUNON PLAZA, SINGAPORE 078300

SINGAPORE

IRREVOCABLE DOCUMENTARY CREDIT NUMBER: PGM960441

DATE OF ISSUE: MARCH 15, 2016

BENEFICIARY: SHANGHAI MINGYU TRADING CORPORATION 1230 ZHONGSHAN ROAD N. 1 SHANGHAI 200437, CHINA	APPLICANT: TAN AZIZ & MUSTAFA TRADING 10 ANSON ROAD, #27-29 INTERNATIONAL PLAZA SINGAPORE 079903, SINGAPORE
ADVISING BANK: HK+SHANGHAI BANKING CORPORATION LTD SHANGHAI BRANCH 185 YUANMINGYUAN ROAD SHANGHAI 200002, CHINA	AMOUNT: USD142,800.00 0 PERCENT MORE OR LESS ALLOWED USD ONE HUNDRED AND FORTY TWO THOUSAND AND EIGHT HUNDRED ONLY CIF PENANG (INCOTERMS 2000)
PARTIAL SHIPMENTS: ALLOWED TRANSSHIPMENT: ALLOWED	DATE AND PLACE OF EXPIRY: MAY 15, 2016 IN CHINA
SHIPMENT FROM: SHANGHAI TO: PENANG	CREDIT AVAILABLE BY NEGOTIATION WITH ADVISING BANK ONLY
LATEST BY: APRIL 30, 2016	

DEAR SIRS,

WE HEREBY ISSUE THIS IRREVOCABLE DOCUMENTARY CREDIT IN YOUR FAVOUR WHICH IS AVAILABLE BY NEGOTIATION OF YOUR DRAFT(S) AT 30 DAYS AFTER B/L DRAWN ON THE ISSUING BANK BEARING THE NUMBER AND DATE OF THIS DOCUMENTARY CREDIT AS WELL AS THE NAME OF ISSUING BANK FOR 97% INVOICE VALUE OF GOODS ACCOMPANIED BY THE FOLLOWING DOCUMENTS WITH EACH IN DUPLICATE IF NOT STATED OTHERWISE:

+ COMMERCIAL INVOICES SHOWING THE BREAKDOWN OR SPLIT OF AMOUNT AS FOLLOWS: FOB VALUE…FREIGHT…(IN CASE OF CFR) AND FOB VALUE…FREIGHT…INSURANCE PREMIUM…(IN CASE OF CIF) AND TOTAL (CFR/CIF) VALUE.

+ FULL SET OF ORIGINAL CLEAN ON BOARD MARINE BILLS OF LADING PLUS ONE COPY MADE OUT TO SHIPPER'S ORDER ENDORSED IN BLANK, MARKED "FREIGHT PAID" AND SHOWING FREIGHT AND NOTIFY US AND HUP WAT SDN BHD, 6 CAMPBELL STREET, 10100 PENANG, MALAYSIA.

+ MARINE INSURANCE POLICY OR CERTIFICATE FROM CHINA PACIFIC INSURANCE COMPANY LIMITED IN ASSIGNABLE FORM TO OUR ORDER FOR FULL CIF VALUE PLUS TEN PERCENT SHOWING THE PREMIUM PAID AND COVERING ALL RISKS AS PER OCEAN MARINE CARGO CLAUSES (1/1/1981) OF THE PEOPLE'S INSURANCE COMPANY OF CHINA (ABBREVIATED AS C.I.C.–ALL RISKS) AND INDICATING WAREHOUSE TO WAREHOUSE IS INCLUDED WITH CLAIMS, IF ANY, PAYABLE TO US PAYING BANK ON APPLICANT'S BEHALF IN MALAYSIA.

+ CERTIFICATE OF CHINESE ORIGIN ISSUED OR ATTESTED BY C.C.P.I.T. STATING THE NAME AND ADDRESS OF MANUFACTURERS OR PRODUCERS AND STATING THAT GOODS EXPORTED ARE WHOLLY OF DOMESTIC ORIGIN.

+ SIGNED DETAILED PACKING LIST SHOWING GROSS WEIGHT, NET WEIGHT AND MEASUREMENTS OF EACH ARTICLE NO./TYPE/COLOUR/DESIGN.

+ THE GOODS TO BE SHIPPED MUST BE IN GOOD ORDER AND A STATEMENT TO THIS EFFECT IS REQUIRED.

GOODS: COVERING 120,000M OF THREE-WIRE RAINBOW LIGHTING IN FOUR COLOURS. ALL OTHER DETAILS ARE AS PER SALES CONTRACT NO.HWSBSC0306 OF MARCH 6, 2016

ADDITIONAL CONDITIONS:

+ A FEE OF USD50.00 SHOULD BE DEDUCTED FROM THE REIMBURSEMENT CLAIM FOR EACH PRESENTATION OF DISCREPANT DOCUMENTS UNDER THIS DOCUMENTARY CREDIT. IF NOT STATED TO THE CONTRARY, THESE CHARGES SHALL BE FOR THE ACCOUNT OF

BENEFICIARY.

+ SHIPMENT TO BE EFFECTED ON FCL BASIS AND BILLS OF LADING TO EVIDENCE THIS.

+ ALL ORIGINAL SHIPPING DOCUMENTS CALLED FOR UNDER THIS CREDIT MUST BE CLEARLY MARKED ORIGINAL ON THEIR FACES.

+ SHIPPING MARKS: HUP S/B
SALES CONTRACT NO.
PENANG
C/NO. 1-UP

（AS EVIDENCED ON B/L AND INSURANCE POLICY/CERTIFICATE）

PERIOD FOR PRESENTATION: WITHIN TEN DAYS AFTER DATE OF SHIPMENT BUT WITHIN THE VALIDITY OF THE CREDIT.

CONFIRMATION INSTRUCTION: WITHOUT

BANK TO BANK INSTRUCTION:

+ ALL BANKING CHARGES OUTSIDE MALAYSIA INCLUDING ADVISING AND NEGOTIATING COMMISSIONS, AND OUR TELEX CHARGES ARE FOR THE ACCOUNT OF BENEFICIARY.

+ PLEASE DEDUCT FROM THE PAYMENT AGENT COMMISSION 3% PAYABLE TO THE OPENER.

INFORMATION TO PRESENTING BANK:

+ DOCUMENTS TO BE DISPATCHED TO OCBC BANK, SINGAPORE 11 FL, SUNON PLAZA, SINGAPORE 078300 SINGAPORE BY COURIER SERVICE IN ONE LOT.

+ THE AMOUNT OF EACH NEGOTIATION MUST BE ENDORSED ON THE CREDIT.

+ ON RECEIPT OF DOCUMENTS CONFORMING TO THE TERMS OF THIS DOCUMENTARY CREDIT, WE UNDERTAKE TO REIMBURSE YOU IN THE CURRENCY OF THIS DOCUMENTARY CREDIT IN ACCORDANCE WITH YOUR INSTRUCTIONS. NEGOTIATING BANK'S DISCOUNT AND OR INTEREST, IF ANY PRIOR TO REIMBURSEMENT BY US ARE FOR THE ACCOUNT OF BENEFICIARY.

+ EXCEPT SO FAR AS OTHERWISE EXPRESSLY STATED, THIS DOCUMENTARY CREDIT IS SUBJECT TO UNIFORM CUSTOMS AND PRACTICE FOR DOCUMENTARY CREDIT (1993 REVISION), INTERNATIONAL CHAMBER OF COMMERCE PUBLICATION NUMBER 500.

YOURS FAITHFULLY,

OCBC Bank, Singapore

Vicky Lee

制单操作能力训练 3-13-2 装运货物相关资料：

颜色	数量	计量单位	单价（USD）	包装种类	装箱方式	毛重（kg）	净重（kg）	长（cm）	宽（cm）	高（cm）
红色	40 000	米	1.17	纸箱	80	15	14	35	35	23
黄色	32 000	米	1.19	纸箱	80	15	14	35	35	23
蓝色	16 000	米	1.20	纸箱	80	15	14	35	35	23
绿色	32 000	米	1.21	纸箱	80	15	14	35	35	23

发票日期	发票号码	产地证号码	税则号	保单号码	保险费率
2016 年 3 月 29 日	HWSB0306	CS01424	9405.4090	PSH-04384	0.80%

装船日期	提单号码	船名航次	海运费
2016 年 4 月 22 日	COS8492023	Qi Ming V.288	USD737.50/20'

保险代理：Investigators Legal Advisers & Surveyors

1118 Doriwalan Road, Nasim Building, 10100 Penang, Malaysia

制单操作能力训练 3-13-3

制单信用证 3-13-3

FIN/Session/ISN:	F01 4062	352006
Own Address:	COMMHKHHXXXX	BANK OF COMMUNICATIONS HONG KONG BRANCH HONG KONG
Input Message Type:	700	ISSUE OF A DOCUMENTARY CREDIT
Sent to:	COMMCNSHASHI	BANK OF COMMUNICATIONS SHANGHAI （SHANGHAI BRANCH）
Input Time:	1502	
DATE OF ISSUE:	JAN-27-2015	
Priority:	Normal	
MUR:	SHI	

27: SEQUENCE OF TOTAL 1/1

40A: FORM OF DOCUMENTARY CREDIT
IRREVOCABLE

20: DOCUMENTARY CREDIT NUMBER
LCB00020078

31D: DATE AND PLACE OF EXPIRY
MAR, 7, 2015 IN HONG KONG CHINA

50: APPLICANT
SLC TECHNOLOGIES ASIA PACIFIC LTD.

SUITE 606 ISLAND PLACE TOWER, 510 KING'S ROAD, NORTH POINT, HONG KONG, CHINA

59: BENEFICIARY

CHINA HUAYUAN ENTERPRISE CORPORATION

17/F. NO.525 JIANGUO WEST ROAD, SHANGHAI, CHINA

32B: CURRENCY CODE AMOUNT

USD141,775.00

41D: AVAILABLE WITH…BY…—NAME/ADDR.

ADVISING BANK BY NEGOTIATION

42C: DRAFTS AT…

AT 45 DAYS AFTER DATE FOR 100 PERCENT INVOICE VALUE

42D: DRAWEE—NAME AND ADDRESS

BANK OF COMMUNICATIONS HONG KONG BRANCH

10F ANTOON BUILDING, 200 STANLIE RD., HONG KONG, CHINA

43P: PARTIAL SHIPMENTS

NOT ALLOWED

43T: TRANSSHIPMENT

ALLOWED

44A: ON BOARD/DISP/TAKING CHARGE

SHANGHAI

44B: FOR TRANSPORTATION TO

BARCELONA

44C: LATEST DATE OF SHIPMENT

FEB-21-2015

45A: DESCP OF GOODS AND/OR SERVICES

SPARE PARTS FOR ALARM SYSTEM

DETAILS ARE AS PER BUYER'S ORDER NO. SLCTJ-PO9975

CIF BARCELONA INCOTERMS 2010

SHIPPING MARKS: S. L. C./SLCTJ-SC9975/BARCELONA/C/NO 1-UP

46A: DOCUMENTS REQUIRED

++ COMMERCIAL INVOICE IN 3 COPIES CERTIFYING THAT THE GOODS ARE MADE OF HIGH QUALITY ELECTRONIC ELEMENTS.

++ 3/3 SET OF "CLEAN ON BOARD" OCEAN BILLS OF LADING MADE OUT TO THE ORDER AND IN FAVOR OF ISSUING BANK, MARKED FREIGHT PREPAID NOTIFYING APPLICANT AND US.

++ PACKING NOTE/WEIGHT LIST IN 3 COPIES INDICATING QUANTITY/GROSS AND NET WEIGHTS OF EACH PACKAGE AND CERTIFYING THAT THE GOODS ARE PACKED IN STRONG EXPORT CARTONS.

++ BENEFICIARY'S LETTER DECLARING THAT ONE SET OF NON-NEGOTIABLE SHIPPING DOCUMENTS INCLUDING INVOICE AND PACKING LIST HAVE BEEN

SENT TO APPLICANT BY UPS IMMEDIATELY AFTER SHIPMENT.

++ INSURANCE CERTIFICATE IN DUPLICATE ISSUED BY NEW CHINA INSURANCE CO., LTD. BLANK ENDORSED FOR 115 PERCENT OF THE INVOICE VALUE SHOWING CLAIMS PAYABLE AT DESTINATION IN CURRENCY OF THE CREDIT COVERING INSTITUTE CARGO CLAUSES(A) AND INSTITUTE WAR CLAUSES(CARGO).

++ CERTIFICATE OF ORIGIN GSP FORM A IN 3 FOLDS ISSUED BY AUTHORITIES.

47A: ADDITIONAL CONDITIONS.

++ A DISCREPANT DOCUMENT FEE OF USD 55.00 WILL BE DEDUCTED FROM PROCEEDS OF DOCUMENTS PRESENTED WITH DESCREPANCY(IES).

++ THE BILL OF LADING MUST SHOW THE SHIPPING COMPANY'S AGENT AT THE DESTINATION PORT WITH ITS DETAILED NAME AND ADDRESS.

++ ALL DOCUMENTS MUST INDICATE THE CREDIT NUMBER, DATE AND NAME OF THE ISSUING BANK.

++ TOTAL AMOUNT IN WORDS, TOTAL GROSS WEIGHT, TOTAL NUMBER OF PACKAGE MUST APPEAR ON THE INVOICE.

++ ANY FREIGHT CHARGES MUST NOT APPEAR ON THE TRANSPORT DOCUMENTS.

++ THE INSURANCE DOCUMENT MUST INDICATE THE INSURANCE AGENT AT THE PORT OF DESTINATION WITH FULL NAME AND ADDRESS.

++ TWO ADDITIONAL COPIES OF INVOICE, BILL OF LADING AND INSURANCE CERTIFICATE MUST BE SENT TO APPLICANT THROUGH THE ISSUING BANK.

71B: ALL BANKING CHARGES OUTSIDE OPENING BANK ARE FOR BENEFICIARY'S AC.

48: PERIOD FOR PRESENTATION： WITHIN 15 DAYS AFTER THE DATE OF SHIPMENT

78: INSTRUCTS TO PAY/ACCPT/NEGOT BANK: ALL DOCUMENTS TO BE DESPATCHED TO ISSUING BANK IN ONE LOT BY FIRST AVAILABLE AIRMAIL.

THIS CREDIT IS SUBJECT TO UCP 600.

MAC: Authentication Code 198378B

CHK: Check Sum

制单操作能力训练 3-13-3 装运货物相关资料：

货号	数量（SET）	单价（USD）	包装	包装种类	毛重（kg）	净重（kg）	尺码（cm）
TJEX2352	750	72.50	5	CTN	11	8.5	40×35×35
TJEX3352	500	81.30	5	CTN	11	8.5	40×35×35
TJEX3355	850	55.00	5	CTN	11	8.5	40×35×35

合同号	合同日期	发票号码	发票日期	提单号	提单日期
SLCTJ-SC9975	2014.12.28	HY-99FP375	2015.2.10	PO4708	2015.2.21

船名航次：LIAN HE V.34　　船代信息：Safee Forwarding Company Limited

香港转船　　出口方签字人：刘伟恭　　P.O. Box 455, Singapore

制单操作能力训练 3-13-4

制单信用证 3-13-4

Emirates Bank International Limited

P.O. Box 2925
Dubai
United Arab Emirates

Telefax: 09714-264986
Cable: EMIRATESBK
Telex: 46455 EBIDB EM
Date of Issue: 25th January, 2016

Irrevocable Documentary Credit	Credit No. ELC–TFS–201679
Advising Bank Bank of China, Henan Branch 16 Huayuan Road, Zhengzhou, China	Applicant BDE Company P.O. Box 2002, Dubai, U.A.E.
Beneficiary Henan FT I/E Corporation No. 92 Wenhua Road, Zhengzhou, China	Amount in Words and Figures USD16,128.00 (United States Dollars Sixteen Thousand One Hundred and Twenty Eight Only) CFR DUBAI Incoterms 2010
Available in China Expiry until 15th April, 2016	
Dear Sirs, We hereby issue this Irrevocable Documentary Credit in your favour which is available with any bank by negotiation of your drafts at 45 days from sight drawn on ourselves for full invoice value of goods and marked "Drawn under Emirates Bank International Limited Credit No. ELC-TFS-201679 Dated 25th January, 2016" accompanied by the following Documents: * Signed Commercial Invoices in 6 Copies indicating the freight and FOB value, stating the Name and Address of the Manufacturer and certifying the Origin of Goods and Contents to be true and correct. * Full Set of "Clean" on Board Marine Bills of Lading made out to order of issuing bank and marked Freight Prepaid, notifying Applicant. * Certificate of Origin issued by Chamber of Commerce and certifying the Goods to be of China Origin, Stating the full Name and Address of the Manufacturer of Goods. Covering Shipment of the following Goods: 21,800 Dozen Pairs of Men's Printed Nylon Stretch Socks Size: 26×27CM Standard, Colours: 6 Colours Equally Assorted, Brand: Golden Pine Made in Shanghai, China, Design No. N3004-D33 and N3004-D92 Each10,900 Dozen Pairs @ USD2.304 Per Dozen Pair CFR Dubai/Sharjah Shipping Marks: BDE/DUBAI/Nos. 1-436 Dispatch/Shipment from China to Dubai or Sharjah latest 25th March, 2016 Partial Shipment is allowed. Transshipment is allowed at Hong Kong only.	
We hereby engage with Drawers or Bona Fide Holders that Drafts drawn in conformity with the Terms of this Credit will be duly honoured on Presentation.	
Directions to Advising Bank We have issued this Documentary Credit as detailed above. We request you to notify the Credit to the Beneficiary.	
Other Documents required: * Insurance covered by Buyer. Shipment Advice quoting Name of Carrying Vessel, Date of Shipment, Shipping Marks, Amount and Name & Address with Telephone Number of the Carrying Vessel's Agent in Dubai should be sent to ALLIANCE INSURANCE(P.S.C.) P.O. Box 5501, Dubai, UAE by Telex over their Telex No. 46048 ALNCE EM or by Fax No. (09714) 225129 Dubai and the carbon copy to Applicant and the covering Telex/Fax Copy must accompany the Documents. * Packing List in 6 Copies under Separate Sets. * One Copy each of Invoices, Certificate of Origin and Transport Documents along with Shipment Samples must be sent to Applicant by Speed post. A compliance Certificate to this effect issued by Beneficiary together with the relevant Speed post Receipt	

（续表）

must accompany the Documents. * Certificate issued by the Ship owner or Agent certifying that the Carrying Vessel is allowed by Arab Authorities to call at Arabian Ports and is not scheduled to call at any Israeli Ports during its Voyage to the United Arab Emirates. In case of Shipment by United Arab Shipping Co. Line Vessels, such certificate is not required.
SPECIAL INSTRUCTIONS: 1. Invoices must certify that the goods shipped and all details are as per Order No. 6533/95 of M/S. ALHELO TRADING COMPANY, DUBAI, U.A.E. and Beneficiary's Sales Note No. 95No.1-16. 2. Shipment Advice giving full details must be sent to M/S. ALHELO TRADING COMPANY, U.A.E. by Telex over their Telex No. 46692 ALHELO EM or by Cable over their Cable Address ALHELO, DUBAI within 1 day after shipment and a copy of the relevant transmitted Telex/Cable Advice must accompany the documents. 3. Combined transport (Land and Sea) Bills of Lading are acceptable. 4. The Negotiating Bank must deduct from the payment to the Beneficiary Agent's Commission @ 1% off 100% of the CFR Invoice Value Payable to M/S. ALHELO TRADING COMPANY, P.O. BOX 5365, DUBAI, U.A.E. and claim reimbursement for the net amount only after such deduction which must be confirmed on their negotiation schedule. 5. Shipment must be effected by CIMC Line and/or Maersk Line and/or Untied Arab Shipping Company Line Vessels and Bills of Lading must be issued by these Lines only. 6. Packing: Each pair in a printed polybag, 1 dozen pairs of equally assorted colours in a printed box then finally 50 dozen pairs per Export Carton and Packing List must evidence compliance. 7. This credit number must be only shown on drafts and invoices. 8. If possible Invoices is to indicate HARMONIZED SYSTEM COMMODITY CODE NUMBER (H.S.CODE NUMBER). The Department of Ports & Customs, U.A.E. warns suppliers that failure to quote the relevant HARMONIZED SYSTEM (H.S.) COMMODITY CODE NUMBER on the Commercial Invoices will result in unnecessary delay in clearance.
FURTHER DIRECTIONS TO ADVISING/NEGOTIATING BANK: * The amount of each drawing must be endorsed on reverse of Page 1 of this Credit. * Documents must be couriered/dispatched by registered Airmail in one cover. * All Banking Charges outside the country of issuance of this Credit are for beneficiary's account. In Reimbursement, the Negotiating Bank is authorized to draw on our account with CHEMICAL BANK, 15th FLOOR, 55 WATER STREET, NEW YORK, N.Y. 10014-0199. U.S.A. Authorized Signature

制单操作能力训练 3-13-4　装运货物相关资料：

发票号码：XH-005　　发票日期：2016 年 3 月 15 日

提单号码：ML21816　　提单日期：2016 年 3 月 23 日

船名航次：Red Star　V.506　　海运费：USD 1 153.00

总毛重：9 000.00kgs　　总净重：8 720.00kgs

总体积：48.069CBM（50×49×45CM）

制单操作能力训练 3-13-5

制单合同 3-13-5

形 式 发 票

PROFORMA INVOICE

编号 NO. : 2017CTHS02108

日期 DATE: APR.3, 2017

卖方 THE SELLERS:　JIANGXI TEXTILES IMPORT & EXPORT COTTON
YARN & PIECE-GOODS COMPANY LTD.
8/F, JIANGXI TEXTILES MANSION, 168 XIAOBEI ROAD, NANCHANG, CHINA
买方 THE BUYER: SPEEDWELL LIMITED
PLOT NO. M-4/2, ROAD NO. -7, SECTION-7,
MIRPUR, DHAKA-1216, BANGLADESH
双方确认对本形式发票订立的下列条款达成了一致意见，并照此交易。
The undersigned Seller and Buyer confirm having reached agreement with the terms and conditions set forth below in this Proforma Invoice and will do business in accordance with then.

品名及规格 DESCRIPTION	数量 QUANTITY	单价 UNIT PRICE	金额 AMOUNT
FABRICS FOR 100PCT EXPORT ORIENTED READYMADE GARMENTS INDUSTRY 98/2 COTTON/SPANDEX CANVAS CONST: 21+12×16+16+70D 140×62 WIDTH 50/52 INCH	45,000YDS	CIF CHITTAGONG USD1.70/YD	INCOTERMS 2010 USD76,500.00

总值 TOTAL VALUE:　US DOLLARS SEVENTY-SIX THOUSAND FIVE HUNDRED ONLY
包装 PACKING:　PACKED IN 22 BALES
装运期 TIME OF SHIPMENT:　BEFORE MAY 31, 2017 BY SEA
装运口岸和目的地 LOADING PORT AND DESTINATION:　FROM SHANGHAI TO CHITTAGONG
保险 INSURANCE:　COVERING ALL RISKS AND WAR RISK FOR 10% OVER INVOICE VALUE
付款条件 TERMS OF PAYMENT: D/P AT SIGHT
装运标记 SHIPPING MARKS: AT THE SELLER'S OPTION
备注 REMARKS: 5 % MORE OR LESS IN QUANTITY AND VALUE ALLOWED AT SELLERS' OPTION.

附 ATTACHMENT: SHIPPING DOCUMENTS REQUIRED AS BELOW:
COMMERCIAL INVOICE IN DUPLICATE WITH DETAILS AS PER P/I NO. 2017CTHS02108
DETAILED PACKING LIST IN DUPLICATE
CERTIFICATE OF CHINA ORIGIN ISSUED BY AUTHORITIES
CERTIFICATE TO THE EFFECT THAT SELLER HAS COMPLIED ALL TERMS AND CONDITIONS OF P/I NO. 2017CTHS02108 DT. MAR.3, 2017
SHIPPING ADVICE WITH DETAILS OF SHIPMENT TO BE EFFECTED
3/3 CLEAN ON BOARD OCEAN B/L MADE OUT TO ORDER MARKED FREIGHT PAID NOTIFYING BUYER
2/2 INSURANCE POLICY FROM PROPERTY INSURANCE CO. OF CHINA

买方 THE BUYER ×××	卖方 THE SELLER ×××

制单操作能力训练 3-13-5 装运货物相关资料：

INV. NO.: 24HS024018
INV.DATE: MAY 25, 2017
B/L NO.: FYPX0403335CHI
B/L DATE: MAY 30, 2017
PORT OF LOADING: SHANGHAI PORT
H.S.CODE: 5211.3200
NAME OF VESSEL: MOL MAAS V.571 W
TOTAL QUANTITY: 44,914 YDS
PACKAGES: 22 BALES
WEIGHT: N.W.: @75.0KGS/BALE
MEASUREMENT:@0.1364CBMS (68.2×50×40 CM)
G.W.: 77.3KGS/BALE
SELLER'S BANKER: BANK OF CHINA, JIANGXI BRANCH

制单操作能力训练 3-13-6

制单合同 3-13-6

庆丰酿造食品有限责任公司

QINGFENG BREWING FOODS CO., LTD.

NO.18, HUANCHENG ROAD PIDU DISTRICT, CHENGDU, CHINA

TEL: (86-028)82201345　　FAX: (86-028)82201346

成交确认书
SALES CONFIRMATION

编号 NO. SCCG00-C-S166

日期 DATE: JULY 5 2016 IN CHENGDU

买方：

Buyer: TANGKU FOOD TRADING CO., LTD.

Add: 3-38-20 SOGA, CHUO-KU, TOKYO, JAPAN

兹经买卖双方同意成交下列商品订立条款如下：

The undersigned seller and buyer have agreed to close the following transactions according to the terms and conditions stipulated below:

唛头 Marks & No.	品名规格 Description of Goods	数量 Quantity	单价 Unit Price	总价 Amount
T.K. C-S166 TOKYO C/NO. 1-UP	Sichuan Flavor Seasoning	3,000 Boxes	FCA Chengdu Airport Incoterms 2010	
			USD1.95/box	USD5,850.00
合约总值 Total Value	SAY US DOLLARS FIVE THOUSAND EIGHT HUNDRED AND FIFTY ONLY			

1. 包装：每盒装两袋，每袋 50 克，30 盒装一个纸箱，共计 100 箱

Packing: Goods are to be packed in boxes of 50g/bag×2 bags each, 30 boxes to a carton, total in 100 ctn.

2. 装运：于 2016 年 8 月从中国成都空运至日本东京

Delivery: During Aug. 2016 from Chengdu, China to Tokyo, Japan by Air

3. 付款条件：买方应于发货前 5 天将全部货款以电汇方式预付至卖方的账户

Terms of Payment: The buyer shall pay 100% of the sales proceeds in advance by T/T 5 days before the date of delivery into seller's A/C No. 1088639534105 with Bank of China, Pixian Branch.

4. 单据要求 Documents Required:

+ 商业发票 Commercial Invoice

+ 装箱单 Packing List

+ 品质证书 Quality Certificate

检测项目： 苯甲酸，山梨酸，TBHQ

Items of Inspection: Sorbic acid, Benzoic acid, TBHQ

+ 普惠制原产地证书 GSP Form A

This sales confirmation is made in two original copies and becomes valid after signature, one copy to be held by each party.

Signed by: ZOI

买方 The Buyer	卖方 The Seller
	庆丰酿造食品有限责任公司
TANGKU FOOD TRADING CO., LTD.	QINGFENG BREWING FOODS CO., LTD.
YAMA TOSHIYA	张成江
________________	________________

制单操作能力训练 3-13-6 装运货物相关资料：

1. 商品名称：四川风味调味料
2. 商品 HS 编码：2103909000
3. 包装方式：每袋 50G，两袋装一盒，30 盒装一个纸箱
   纸箱尺码：45CM×30CM×20CM，每箱净重：3KGS，每箱毛重：4KGS
4. 出口商海关注册登记号：2170036980
5. 出口商商检注册登记号：5100945003
6. 出口商食品卫生许可证号：5100/18056
7. 出口商统一社会信用代码：91510106099766 38F
8. 航空公司/航班号：CA1406
9. 航班日期：2016 年 8 月 2 日
10. 空运单号码：86057793
11. 报关公司：成都逸程报关代理有限责任公司
    统一社会信用代码 915101065062311020

模块四

进口单据综合审核

审核单据（checking documents）是指根据合同（非信用证结算）或信用证（信用证结算）对进出口贸易的货运或装运单据（shipping documents）进行全面复核和审查。审单工作分为出口审单（由出口方内部审单）和进口审单（由开证行和进口方付汇审单）。出口审单的主要目的是顺利地收汇，进口审单的主要目的是保证顺利清关和分销，及时付汇。

项目十四

综合审核进口单据

学习目标

［知识目标］了解 UCP600 和 ISBP 有关单据的条款，了解审单的分类和作用，掌握审核全套单据的原则、方法和要点，了解单据中存在的常见的不符点。

［能力目标］能正确区分出口审单和进口审单，能准确熟练审核信用证项下全套装运单据。

项目描述（案例情境描述）

审核单据是缮制单据的逆向操作，也是单证工作的一个必要环节或步骤。在扎实地学习了缮制单据后，请学习者根据下面介绍的审单要点（Checklist），独立操作能力训练里的单据审核工作。审单项目，因信用证而异，但基本条款及其需要掌握的原则大致相同。银行通常首先审核汇票，进出口商也可以按单据管理顺序后审汇票。在此学习审核信用证项下全套进口单据。

操作要领

下表总结了不同类型单据的审核要点。

国际贸易装运单据的审核要点

单据种类	审核要点
汇票 Draft/Bill of Exchange	（1）单据号码是否与发票相同，一般采用发票号码或由银行自编。 （2）出票依据信息须准确，开证行名称、信用证号码和日期正确。

续表

单据种类	审核要点
汇票 Draft/Bill of Exchange	托收项下的汇票出票依据应填写发票号码。 （3）出票地点应在出口地，须载明汇票日期，即议付行打上的寄单日期。当然，如果是出口方送交银行前审单，该栏则暂无日期。 （4）金额小写的币种正确，金额等于或小于发票金额且不超过信用证金额，保留两位小数。若来证在总金额前有“about”字样，按10%容差掌握。 （5）金额大写须与小写一致，正确、规范，最后须有“only”一词。 （6）付款期限须与信用证条款一致，查找 draft at 后面的要求。托收项下的汇票须在 At 前面注明 D/P 或 D/A。 （7）受款人即收款人（Pay to）须符合条款要求，查找“available”一词所在条款的规定。若无指定交单银行，则可为出口人当地的任何一家银行。 （8）受票人或付款人须与信用证规定一致，须注明地址并正确，查找“drawn on”或“drawee”一词。托收项下的付款人应是进口人。 （9）出票人应为受益人，注意名称和签字。托收项下为出口人。 （10）审核汇票是否背书以及背书是否符合要求和正确。一般若由银行做背书，出口审单则无此项。 （11）检查份数是否符合要求，一般一式两份。 （12）汇票的收讫条款（Value received）仅在托收项下填写，包装件数和品名须正确，跟发票一致。
商业发票 Commercial Invoice	（1）单据名称须与信用证要求相符，不得为临时发票或形式发票。 （2）出具人应与汇票的出票人相同，绝大多数情况下也是信用证的受益人，除非信用证另有规定。审核名称和地址与来证相符。 （3）抬头人应为信用证申请人，审核名称和地址与来证一致。 （4）运输详情应有具体港口和运输方式或运载工具，且正确。 （5）注意发票日期，信用证有无明确规定不接受早于开证日的单据。 （6）显示的合同号和信用证号码是正确的。 （7）应显示支付条款，且与信用证规定一致。 （8）唛头应与来证或货物包装一致，注意参考号和包装种类和件数正确。 （9）货物描述须与来证相符，品名、货号须正确，未遗漏应有的文字。 （10）货物数量和单位须正确，与来证和出仓单一致。 （11）单价和币种须正确，价格术语完整，若来证有术语来源，应照显示。 （12）各品种的金额和总金额须正确，符合允许的容差，大写应无误。 （13）正确显示包装方法，包装件数大小写正确，大写数字须有“only”。 （14）以重量为数量单位的货物应显示正确的以千克为单位的总毛净重。以面积、体积、容积为数量单位的货物，显示的总尺码须正确。 （15）审核是否有原产地说明，应显示原产地国名。 （16）若来证的单据条款和附加条款里对发票有附加内容要求，审核加注内容是否无遗漏且与来证条款相符。 （17）签署应符合来证要求，证实发票须签署。交单正副本份数须满足来证条款要求。
包装单据 Packing Documents	（1）单据名称和交单正副本份数必须与来证要求一致。 （2）单据日期和编号及其他参考号应与发票一致。 （3）品名、规格、数量、唛头须与发票一致，或互为补充，不得矛盾。 （4）包装序号、件数、各重量和体积的小计须准确，与仓单一致。 （5）应有详细包装方法和各品种每个包装的毛净重和体积，且正确。 （6）须显示包装件数的大小写，且与发票一致。

续表

单据种类	审核要点
包装单据 Packing Documents	(7) 若来证有加注要求，加注内容须完整、正确。 (8) 若来证有签署要求，签署须正确，无遗漏。
商检证书 Inspection Certificate	(1) 单据种类、名称和交单正副本份数必须与来证要求一致。 (2) 商品信息须与发票一致。 (3) 证书文字内容须与来证要求相符。 (4) 单据日期正确且须等于或晚于发票，等于或早于提单。 (5) 出证机构和签署须与来证要求相符。 (6) 证书内容若有更改，须有授权人签字并加盖“更改章”。
原产地证明 Certificate of Origin	(1) 单据名称、种类和交单正副本份数须与来证要求一致。 (2) 出口商和收货人名称地址须正确且与发票一致。须确定收货人为最终进口商，进口国为最终销售国别或地区。 (3) 所载明的运输详情、唛头、品名和包装件数大小写等内容须正确，且不与发票或其他单据相矛盾。 (4) 原产地说明或引用，或商品协调编码须准确无误。 (5) 数量须为商品的正常数量且正确，与发票一致。 (6) 若货物描述栏尚有添加余地，出口审单应注意隔断符号是否已打。 (7) 若来证有加注要求，其加注内容须正确，与来证要求相符。 (8) 申明栏信息须完整且正确，其日期须在发票和签发日期之间且合理。 (9) 签发栏机构须正确，符合来证要求。签字不得被盖章压住。签发地点应与申明地点一致，在出口地。签发日期须等于或早于运输单据。
保险单据 Insurance Documents	(1) 单据名称和交单正副本份数须与信用证要求一致。 (2) 保险单据的抬头或被保险人或保单受益人须符合信用证要求。 (3) 保单所载明的发票号、唛头、包装件数大小写、品名须与发票一致。 (4) 显示的投保金额或保险金额须与来证要求投保加成的计算相符，币别无误，大小写相符，大写后有“only”一词。 (5) 单据载明的运输细节和装运日期须与发票和运输单据相符或一致。 (6) 投保险别须与来证要求相符，须注明投保依据或适用的保险条款。注意保险条款的名称和版本日期须正确。 (7) 注意保单上须载明目的地赔付代理人的名称和详细地址。 (8) 赔付地点须为具体港口，描述符合来证要求。 (9) 若来证有加注要求，其加注内容须与信用证要求相符。 (10) 保单签发日期须等于或早于运输单据。 (11) 保单签发机构须符合惯例规定，须明确签发人为保险公司或承保人或其授权的代理人，且须有被授权人签字。 (12) 保单一般应为可转让形式，其背书须符合信用证要求，日期须早于或等于最晚交单期限。
运输单据 Transport Documents	(1) 单据种类、名称和交单正副本份数须与信用证要求相符。 (2) 发货人或货主的名称和地址应与来证要求相符且正确。 (3) 收货人和被通知人须与信用证规定一致且正确。 (4) 装运细节和运载工具须与发票互为一致。 (5) 唛头、品名、毛重和体积须与发票一致且正确。 (6) 若来证有加注要求，其加注内容须与信用证要求相符。 (7) 提单表面无装运不良记录，譬如短装、破损、污渍等。

续表

单据种类	审核要点
运输单据 Transport Documents	（8）外包装件数须大小写相符，且与发票记载一致。 （9）运费支付状况应与交货条件或贸易术语规定的责任义务相符，预付或到付地点须为具体港口且正确。预付金额填写须符合来证要求。 （10）海运提单须注明装船信息（on board the vessel）且正确，装运日期须不晚于来证规定的最晚装运日期，且有装船方签署。 （11）正本份数须大小写且符合信用证要求。 （12）签发地点须在装运港，签发日期须早于汇票日期。 （13）提单的签署须符合惯例规定，签署人或为船公司或其代理人，或为船长或其授权人，须注明签署人的名称、身份和被授权人签字。 （14）海运提单一般为可转让形式，背书必须符合来证要求，日期须早于或等于最晚交单期限。
其他单据 Other Documents	（1）单据种类、名称和交单正副本份数须与信用证要求一致。 （2）单据的日期须合理，以运输单据日期为中轴，或早于或晚于。 （3）应有必要的参考号且正确。 （4）证明内容和文句须符合信用证条款要求且正确。 （5）证明须有正确签署。

相关知识

一、审单的性质、作用和分类

审单是指对全套货运单据进行复核和审查，跟制单一样，同是国际贸易单证工作的主体工作部分，它直接关系到进出口双方能否顺利实现贸易结算。审单通常分为信用证项下审单和非信用证结算审单；出口审单和进口审单。

二、审单的原则、依据和方法

1. 信用证项下审单的原则是单证相符、单单一致，审单的主要依据是“一证三惯例”，即信用证、国际商会的《跟单信用证统一惯例》第600号出版物（简称UCP600）、国际商会《关于审核跟单信用证项下单据的国际标准银行实务》第681号出版物（简称ISBP ICC681）和国际商会《跟单信用证项下银行间偿付统一规则》第725号出版物（URR725）。按“相符交单”原则处理单据。

2. 非信用证结算的单据审核原则是单货一致、单约一致和单单一致，其依据主要是买卖合约和装运的货物。

3. 出口审单是指出口方制单结束后的自我审核和送交银行前的审单员最后复审，其原则仍是单货一致、单证相符或单约一致、单单一致。审单的主要方法是“纵向审核”，做到“单证相符”或“单约一致”；然后是“横向审核”，以商业发票为中心，做到“单单一致”。

应该说明的是，出口审单并不是简单地核对文字和数字，而要从安全收汇和顺利履约的角度出发，既要考虑单据本身要正确，又要顾及更改单据后可能牵涉到的一系列具体问题。例如审单发现唛头有误，则首先要通知有关部门检查并重刷包装唛头。

4. 议付行审单可以属于广义的出口审单。议付行或托收行仅负责对出口方提交的单据按信用证所要求的单据种类和份数或托收委托书所列单据进行清点和核对，并不负责对单据的不符点进行审核。即便议付行出于自身利益的考虑，对单据做了不符点审核，也不对此负责。

5. 进口审单是指进口方收到出口方（汇付方式项下）或出口方银行（信用证或托收项下）提交的全套货运单据后进行审核工作，它包括了进口人审核、开证行审核和申请人审核。

以汇付和托收方式结算的贸易，由进口人审核出口方或银行送达的货运单据，其依据和原则是单货一致、单约一致和单单一致。以信用证方式结算的贸易，由开证行和申请人对议付行提交的单据进行审核。尽管按照国际惯例规定，开证行承担独立审单的义务，不以开证申请人的意见为转移。但在实际操作中，开证行为了更好地服务于客户，同时也为了降低自身的风险，往往在实施付款前，都会充分考虑开证申请人的意见，把单据复印给进口方，供他们审核。何况银行对单据是否伪造、单货是否相符等问题并不负责，须由赎单人自行确定。

如果进口方审单无误并决定付款赎单，应在银行规定的时间内（UCP600 规定开证行仅有 5 个工作日）向银行提交对外付款/承兑通知书；如果审单认为有不符点（discrepancy），应在信用证到单通知上明确表示拒付，列出单据的不符点并加盖财务专用章或约定的其他印鉴，在规定的时间内交还给银行。进口人应视不符点的性质、国际惯例、贸易关系和自身业务需要等因素，确定是否接受不符点单据。

三、审单的具体操作方法

1. 核对信用证，制单是否与信用证要求或文字一致或相符（与信用证比对）；
2. 制单是否满足了信用证条款的要求，特别是加注要求（检查有无遗漏）；
3. 制单是否显示了能发挥本单据功能而本身应有的所有信息（检查是否有遗漏）；
4. 本单据显示的信息是否与其他单据一致（与其他单据对比）；
5. 在信用证有文字拼写错误的情况下，制单是否照写，并在其后加括号显示出正确拼写。

四、不符点单据的处理

若受益人提交的单据种类、内容和份数与信用证条款规定不一致或单据之间彼此矛盾，即被认为单证不符。开证行有权对不符点单据拒绝付款。

单据不符可分为无关紧要的单据不符和名副其实的单据不符。对于无关紧要的单据不符，银行并不能以此作为拒付的理由，否则就构成了不当拒付，会面临受益人的追诉。名副其实的单据不符可以作为银行拒付的理由，因为此类不符直接违背了“单证相符”的标准或原则。然而在实践中，银行在对单据的不符点进行评估时，由于缺乏统一的操作标准，很难明确界定“无关紧要”和“名符其实”，常常陷于两难境地。

1. 议付行的处理方法

（1）退单修改：若议付行在审单时发现了不符点，且这些不符点单据是来得及更换或修改的，一般应将全套单据退还给受益人进行修改、更换、补齐后再提交议付。

（2）凭保议付：对于一些轻微的不符点单据，由受益人向议付行出具付款保证书，承认并列明单据的不符点，并声明如果开证行拒付，受益人将偿还议付行所垫付的款项和费用。同时，受益人电请开证人授权开证行付款。对此，议付行可以做“凭保议付”。必须说明两点：保证书是受益人与议付行之间的协议，对开证行没有约束力；开证人同意接受不符点单据并不能代表或意味着开证行接受。

（3）表提：议付行把不符点开列在银行寄单函上，寄给开证行并征求其意见，得到同意付款的肯定答复后即行议付。

（4）电提：议付行暂不把不符点单据寄给开证行，而是将单据的不符点用电传（telex）的方式通知开证行。若开证行同意付款，再行议付并寄单；若不同意，受益人则可早日收回单据，设法改正或另作处理。

（5）有证托收：遇有严重不符点的单据或无法更改的单据，或信用证的有效期已过，议付行可接受受益人的委托，向开证行寄单并注明“信用证项下单据作托收处理”。这种改信用证结算为跟单托收结算的做法被称作“有证托收”；而正常的托收则为“无证托收”。

2. 开证行的处理方法

开证行收到议付行寄来的单据后，应仔细审核。发现有不符点需要拒付时，应在收到单据后第二天起算的五个工作日内做出拒付通知（Notice of Dishonor/Protest）。通知书上应一次性列明全部不符点，并说明是退回单据还是暂为代管听候处置，以电讯方式通知议付行。否则，银行将失去拒付的权利，使得拒付无效。

3. 申请人的处理方法

（1）更正单据或拒付：当进口单据出现的不符点将给进口方造成损失时，在时间允许的情况下，申请人可以要求受益人更换单据；若条件不允许，进口方可以要求银行拒绝接受单据。同样应在银行规定的时间内一次性提出全部拒付理由，并明确处理单据的方式。

（2）放弃不符点：如果单据出现的不符点无损于进口方的利益，比如声明文句的拼写错误，申请人可以放弃不符点，即接受不符点单据。同样应在三日内向银行做出答复。

4. 受益人的处理方法

遇到单据有不符点，对于来得及更换的单据，应尽全力在规定的交单期前处理后重新提交银行；对于无法更换的不符点单据，应及时跟开证申请人沟通，争取对方接受不符点单据，并授权开证行付款。只有通过信用证原渠道收到的开证行的改证通知书，才对开证行有约束力。受益人对改证通知书中两个及以上的不符点修改条款，要么全部接受，要么全部拒绝，不能部分接受，部分拒绝。

操作能力训练

思考题：

S14-1　为什么单据中出现拼写错误而不会引起歧义时，不作为不符点审核呢？

S14-2　想一想出口审单与进口审单有哪些不同之处。

操作题：

C14-1　综合审单操作能力训练一。根据下列信用证及货物实际装运情况，独立审核全套装运单据。

审单信用证 C14-1

UNITED ARAB BANK
Public Joint Stock Company
(Affiliated to Societe Genetele, France)

SHARJAH BRANCH

April 20th, 2016

BANK OF CHINA
Anhui Branch
313, Changjiang Middle Road
Hefei 230061, Anhui
CHINA, Telex 90026 BOCHF CN
Fax (0551)2641012

Dear Sirs,

Please advise **M/s. AHCOF INTERNATIONAL DEVELOPMENT CO., LTD.** Sunon Plaza, 389-399, Jinzhai Road, Hefei, China, Tel. 0086-551-2881126/2881013, Fax 0086-551-2831057/8, of our opening in their favour an Irrevocable Documentary Credit **No. 21/01/1111 for USD 6,970.00** (U.S Dollars Six Thousand Nine Hundred and Seventy Only) CFR DUBAI valid in China until **10th June, 2016** covering supply of:

CO-OP BRAND FOUL MEDAMES
Total quantity-1,700 Master cartons, each of 24 Cans × 397g
At the rate of USD 4.10 per master carton, CFR Dubai or Sharjah (Incoterms 2000)

Shipment from China to Dubai or Sharjah in 1 × 20 feet container, latest by **31st May, 2016** Partial shipments **not allowed,** Transshipment **not allowed.**

Applicant -CONSUMER OPERATIVE U.A.E.
P.O.BOX7039, SHARJAH, UNITED ARAB EMIRATES
FAX NO. 9716 6670339/6670363

This documentary credit is available with any Bank by negotiation against the documents detailed herein and beneficiary's draft **at 45 days from the date of bill of lading,** drawn on **L/C issuing Bank** for full invoice value of goods accompanied by the following documents.

1. Signed Commercial Invoice in 3 copies (1+2), bearing the following clauses. We hereby certify that:
   (a) This invoice is authentic.
   (b) It is the only invoice issued by us for the goods described herein.
   (c) It shows their exact value without deduction of any discount.
   (d) Their origin is China.

2. Full set of "Clean Shipped on Board" Bill(s) of Lading bearing this L/C number, the name, address and telephone number of carrying vessel's agent in the port of destination, drawn to the order of United Arab Bank, Sharjah branch and showing freight prepaid and marked notify United Arab Bank, Sharjah branch and applicant. Other than the date of issue bill(s) of lading must show the date of on board of goods.

3. Bill(s) of lading must evidence carrying vessel is not Israeli and not calling at Israeli ports except for vessels owned and operated by United Arab Shipping Company. Alternatively shipping company's or their agents certificate to this effect will be acceptable which accompany the shipping documents.

4. Insurance arranged by applicant. Shipment under this credit must be advised by telefax by the beneficiary within 7 working days after shipment direct to Sharjah Insurance and Reinsurance Co., P. O. Box 792, Sharjah, U.A.E. Fax+9716-5352545, and applicant referring their policy No.
HMR/2016/000635, giving full details of shipment. A copy of such advice to accompany the documents.

5. Certificate of origin issued in English stating that the goods are of Chinese origin, duly approved by China Chamber of International Commerce.

6. Packing list in three copies.

7. Certificate of weight in three copies.

8. Certificate issued by shipping company or their agent certifying that:

(a) The carrying vessel is conference line vessel.

(b) Age of carrying vessel dose not exceed 15 years.

9. Quality Certificate issued by the Beneficiary.

The Beneficiary must issue a Certificate of Quality (which shall be a part and partial of the negotiating documents) stating as under:

We do hereby certify and confirm that the product shipped under L/C No.21/01/1111 dated 20/04/2016 is tested under strict quality control before packing and sealing and found that the same conforms the exact requirements of qualitative aspects suggested and agreed between the Applicant and Beneficiary as per their business contract. Any deviation on this effect on quality shall be under the risk and responsibility of the beneficiary only. Also, it is certified and confirmed that the product so shipped conforms strictly in accordance with the health requirements of the Ministry of Health in the U.A.E and its Emirates, and that deviations resulting to any consequential problems shall be under the risk and responsibility of the beneficiary only, product liability in all sense are undertaken herewith.

10. Packing.

The Beneficiary shall issue a letter specifying therewith that the packing for export of the goods under this L/C is done in proper order, so as to avoid leakage and breakage, the tins are properly labeled and the master carton boxes used for packing are printed properly with product descriptions and other relevant required information.

SPECIAL CONDITIONS

1. Documents to be presented within 10 days after the date of issuance of transport documents but within the validity of the credit.

2. The number, the date of the credit and the name of our bank must be quoted on all documents required.

3. If all credit terms and conditions are not complied with or documents sent on collection basis or documents sent having discrepancies but not advised and during our scrutiny discrepancies were observed, in either case we shall deduct 0.125% (minimum USD 60/–) from the bill amount being our discrepancies handing fees as well as any other charges.

4. Negotiation under reserve or guarantee not allowed.

5. One one-negotiable copy of bill of lading to be sent with original set of documents.

6. Bill of lading set must consist of three originals.

7. Bill of lading must mention container numbers.

8. Transport documents bearing a date of issuance prior to the date of this credit are not acceptable.

9. Transport documents bearing reference by stamp or otherwise to costs additional to the freight charges, such as costs of, or disbursement incurred in connection with loading, unloading or similar operations are not acceptable.

10. Quality.

The quality of the product under this L/C must be exactly in accordance with the Sample submitted and as per specifications furnished by the beneficiary in the agreement dated 11th July, 2005 and invoice must certify the same.

11. The goods shipped under this L/C must be with latest production date with maximum shelf life, but as per the existing health regulations of the Ministry of Health in U.A.E. and its Emirates only. Invoice must certify the same.

12. Production and expiry dates with batch Number to be mentioned on Tins, Packing List and Health Certificate.

13. Harmonized system code number should be mentioned on Commercial Invoices for the goods shipped.

14. Shipping marks-CCU/313, P.O. BOX No.7039, SHARJAN. U.A.E. (Shipping documents must evidence the same).

15. Non-negotiable documents.

A complete set of non-negotiable documents evidencing therewith that the goods are shipped exactly in accordance with the terms and conditions laid down in this L/C must be sent by courier service to the Applicant by the Beneficiary within three (3) days from the date of shipment of goods. A certificate to this effect from Beneficiary must accompany original set of documents.

16. In case documents are not legalized by U.A.E. Embassy, legation or Consulate, legalization cost will be deducted from the proceeds payable to beneficiary and negotiating bank must confirm the same.

DIRECTIONS TO ADVISING BANK

1. All charges outside U.A.E. are on account of beneficiary.

2. Please advice this L/C to beneficiary without adding your confirmation.

DIRECTIONS TO NEGOTIATING BANK

All charges outside U.A.E. are on account of beneficiary.

Upon receipt of documents complying strictly with the terms of this credit, we will remit the proceeds to your nominated Bank on due date, if documents are found in order. Amount of each drawing must be endorsed on the L/C. All documents are to be dispatched by negotiating Bank to United Arab Bank, P. O. Box 881, Sharjah, U.A.E., in two lots (original by courier services at beneficiary's cost and duplicate by registered airmail).

Except so far as otherwise expressly stated, this documentary credit is subject to the Uniform Customs and Practice for Documentary Credit (1993 revision, International Chamber of Commerce, Paris, France, Publication No. 500).

Mohammed Ata Zeinuddin　　Khawaja H assan Zafarullah

B-9　　A-34

UNITED ARAB BANK

P.O. Box 881, SHARJAH

14-1　装运货物相关资料：

发票号：	AFLA01041-3
装运港：	NANTONG CHINA
目的港：	DUBAI
装运日期：	2016 年 5 月 25 日
B/L NO.:	UGMUI145207010265
VESSEL AND VOYAGE NO.:	ANHUA1#V.2221E
CONTAINER NUMBER:	GVDU2041118/212814
PRODUCTION DATE:	2016 年 5 月
BATCH NUMBER:	081
健康证书编号：	R321100202020575

原产地证书编号： 7681243
HARMONIZED SYSTEM CODE NO.: 2005.9020

综合审单操作全套货运单据 C14-1

1

凭
drawn under UNITED ARAB BANK
信用证或购买证第 号
L/C or A/P No. 21/01/1111
日期 年 月 日
dated April 20, 2006
按 息 % 付 款
Payable with interest @ % per annul
号码 汇票金额 中国合肥 年 月 日
No. AFLA01041—3 **Exchange** for USD6,970.00 Hefei, China 20
见票 日 后 （本汇票之副本未付）
At 45 DAYS after Sight of this **FIRST** of Exchange (Second of exchange being unpaid)
交付 或其指定人
Pay to the order of **BANK OF CHINA, ANHUI BRANCH**
金额
The sum of SAY US DOLLARS SIX THOUSAND NINE HUNDRED AND SEVENTY ONLY
收讫价值 数量 商品
Value received for ____ of ____
(quantity) (commodity)

此致 谨代表
To CONSUMER OPERATIVE U.A.E. For and on behalf of
P.O. BOX 7039, SHARJAH, AHCOF INTERNATIONAL DEVELOPMENT CO., LTD.
UNITED ARAB EMIRATES

× × ×

....
(Authorized Signature)

<table>
<tr><td>Issuer
AHCOF INTERNATIONAL DEVELOPMENT CO., LTD. SUNON PLAZA 389-399 JINZHAI ROAD HEFEI, CHINA
TEL: 0086-551-2881126/2881013
FAX: 0086-551-2831057/8</td><td colspan="2">商 业 发 票
COMMERCIAL INVOICE</td></tr>
<tr><td>To
CONSUMER OPERATIVE U.A.E.
P.O. COX 7039, SHARJAH, UNITED ARAB EMIRATES FAX NO.9716-6670339/6670363</td><td>No.
AFLA01041-3</td><td>Date
May 25, 2016</td></tr>
<tr><td rowspan="2">Transport Details

FROM NANTONG, CHINA TO DUBAI BY SEAFREIGHT</td><td>S/C No.</td><td>L/C No.
21/01/1111</td></tr>
<tr><td colspan="2">Terms of Payment
L/C 45 DAYS FROM THE DATE OF BILL OF LADING</td></tr>
</table>

Marks and No.	Number and Kind of Packages Description of Goods	Quantity	Unit Price	Amount
		CARTONS	PER MASTER CARTON	
CCU/313 P.O. BOX NO.7039 SHARJAH U.A.E.	CO-OP BRAND FOUL MEDAMES QUANTITY-1,700 MASTER CARTONS, EACH OF 24 CANS × 397G IN 1×20 FEET FCL CONTAINER	1,700	USD4.10	USD6,970.00

WE HEREBY CERTIFY THAT:
A) THIS INVOICE IS AUTHENTIC.
B) IT IS THE ONLY INVOICE ISSUED BY US FOR THE GOODS DESCRIBED HEREIN.
C) IT SHOWS THEIR EXACT VALUE WITHOUT DEDUCTION OF ANY DISCOUNT.
D) THEIR ORIGIN IS CHINA.
-THE NUMBER, THE DATE OF THE CREDIT:
21/01/1111 April 20, 2016
-THE NAME OF ISSUING BANK:
UNITED ARAB BANK
-THE QUALITY OF THE PRODUCT UNDER THIS L/C IS EXACTLY IN ACCORDANCE WITH THE SAMPLE SUBMITTED AND AS PER SPECIFICATIONS FURNISHED BY THE BENEFICIARY IN THE AGREEMENT DATED 11TH JULY 2005.
- THE GOODS SHIPPED UNDER THIS L/C IS WITH LATEST PRODUCTION DATE WITH MAXIMUM SHELF LIFE. BUT AS PER THE EXISTING HEALTH REGULATIONS OF THE MINISTRY OF HEALTH IN U.A.E. AND ITS EMIRATES ONLY.

× × ×

AHCOF INTERNATIONAL DEVELOPMENT CO., LTD.

Issuer AHCOF INTERNATIONAL DEVELOPMENT CO., LTD. SUNON PLAZA 389-399 JINZHAI ROAD HEFEI, CHINA	装 箱 单 **PACKING LIST**	
To CONSUMER OPERATIVE U.E.A. P. O. BOX 7039, SHARJAH, UNITED ARAB EMIRATES	Invoice No. AFLA01041	Date May 25th, 2016

Marks and Numbers.	Description of Goods	Quantity	GR. WT(@, Total)	NT. WT(@, Total)
CCU/313 P.O. BOX NO.7039 SHARJAH U.A.E	CO-OP BRAND FOUL CARTONS MEDAMES QUANTITY—1,700 MASTER CARTONS, EACH OF 24 CANS × 397G IN 1 × 20 FEET FCL CONTAINER -THE NUMBER, THE DATE OF THE CREDIT: 21/01/1111 April 20, 2016 -THE NAME OF ISSUING BANK: UNITED ARAB BANK -PRODUCTION DATE: 05. 2016 EXPIRY DATE: 10th June, 2016 BATCH NUMBER: 081	1,700	@11.00KGS/18,700.00KGS	@9.528KGS/16,197.60KGS

AHCOF INTERNATIONAL DEVELOPMENT CO., LTD.

× × ×

Issuer AHCOF INTERNATIONAL DEVELOPMENT CO., LTD. SUNON PLAZA 389-399 JINZHAI ROAD HEFEI, CHINA	重 量 单 **CERTIFICATE OF WEIGHT**	
To CONSUMER OPERATIVE U.A.E. P.O. BOX 7039, SHARJAH, UNITED ARAB EMIRATES	Invoice No. AFLA01041—3	Date May 25th, 2016

Marks and Numbers.	Description of Goods	Quantity	GR. WT(@, Total)	NT. WT(@, Total)
CCU/313 P.O. BOX NO. 7039 SHARJAH U.A.E	CO-OP BRAND FOUL CARTONS MEDAMES QUANTITY—1,700 MASTER CARTONS, EACH OF 24 CANS × 397G IN 1 × 20 FEET FCL CONTAINER -THE NUMBER, THE DATE OF THE CREDIT: 21/01/1111 April 20, 2016 -THE NAME OF ISSUING BANK: UNITED ARAB BANK -PRODUCTION DATE: 05. 2016 EXPIRY DATE: 10th June, 2016	1,700	@11.00KGS/18700.00KGS	@9.528KGS/16197.00KGS

AHCOF INTERNATIONAL DEVELOPMENT CO., LTD.

× × ×

<table>
<tr><td>1. Exporter
AHCOF INTERNATIONAL DEVELOPMENT CO., LTD.
SUNON PLAZA 389-399 JINZHAI ROAD, HEFEI, CHINA
TEL: 0086-551-2881126/2881013, FAX: 0086-551-2831057/58</td><td rowspan="2">Certificate No. 7681243
CERTIFICATE OF ORIGIN
OF
THE PEOPLE'S REPUBLIC
OF CHINA</td></tr>
<tr><td>2. Consignee
CONSUMER OPERATIVE U.A.E.
P.O. BOX 7039, SHARJAH, UNTTED ARAB EMIRATES
FAX NO.9716-6670339/6670363</td></tr>
<tr><td>3. Means of Transport and Route
FROM NANTONG CHINA TO DUBAI
BY SEAFREIGHT</td><td rowspan="2">5. For certifying authority use only
CHINA COUNCIL FOR THE PROMOTION OF INTERNATIONAL TRADE IS CHINA CHAMBER OF INTERNATIONAL COMMERCE</td></tr>
<tr><td>4. Country/Region of Destination
UAE</td></tr>
</table>

<table>
<tr><td>6. Marks and Numbers

CCU/313
P. O. BOX NO. 7039
SHARJAH V.A.E.</td><td>7. Number and Kind of Packages; Description of Goods

FOUL MEDAMMES (BROAD BEANS)
QUANTITY—17,700 MASTER CARTONS.
EACH OF 24 CANS × 397G
IN 1 × 20 FEET FCL CONTAINER
- THE NUMBER, THE DATE OF THE CREDIT:
21/01/1111 April 20, 2016
- THE NAME OF ISSUING BANK:
UNITED ARAB BANK
- WE STATE THAT THE GOODS ARE OF CHINESE ORIGIN
- NAME AND ADDRESS OF MANUFAC-TURER
AHCOF INTERNATIONAL DEVELOPMENT CO., LTD. SUNON PLAZA 389-399 JINZHAI ROAD HEFEI, CHINA
(SAY TOTAL ONE THOUSAND SEVEN HUNDRED CARTONS ONLY)</td><td>8. H. S. Code

2005.
9020</td><td>9. Quantity

1,700
CANS</td><td>10. Number and Date of Invoices

AFLA01041-3
MAY 25th, 2016</td></tr>
</table>

<table>
<tr><td>11. Declaration by the exporter
The undersigned hereby declares that the above details and statements are correct, that all the goods were produced in China and that they comply with the Rules of Origin of the People's Republic of China.

安徽安粮国际发展股份有限公司
AHCOF INTERNATIONAL DEVELOPMENT CO., LTD.

HEFEI CHINA MAY 25th, 2016 佳小勇

Place and date, signature and stamp of authorized signatory</td><td>12. Certification
It is hereby certified that the declaration by the exporter is correct.

HEFEI CHINA MAY 24, 2016

Place and date, signature and stamp of certifying authority</td></tr>
</table>

CERTIFICATE

DATE: MAY 25, 2016
B/L NO. UGMUI145207010265
VESSEL/VOY: ANHUA1 # V.2221E

WE HEREBY CERTIFY THAT
(A) THE CARRYING VESSEL IS CONFERENCE LINE VESSEL.
(B) AGE OF CARRYING VESSEL DOES NOT EXCEED 15 YEARS.
— THE NUMBER, THE DATE OF THE CREDIT:
21/01/1111　　　　April 20th, 2016
— THE NAME OF ISSUING BANK:
UNITED ARAB BANK
— SHIPPING MARKS: CCU/313
P. O. BOX NO. 7039
SHARJAH, U.A.E.

中国船务代理公司江苏南通公司
CHINA MARINE SHIPPING AGENCY
JIANGSU NANTONG CORPORATION（2）

CHINA JIE
GENERAL MANAGER
AS AGENT ACTING ON BEHALF OF THE CARRIER

AHCOF INTERNATIONAL DEVELOPMENT CO., LTD.

SUNON PLAZA, NO. 389-399 JINZHAI ROAD, HEFEI, CHINA
TEL: 0086-551-2831126/2881013　　FAX: 0086-551-2881057/8
E-MAIL: Dep10@ ahcof. com

QUALITY CERTIFICATE

INV. NO. AFLA01041-3
DATE: MAY 25, 2016
SHIPPING MARKS: CCU/313
P. O. BOX NO. 7039
SHARJAH, U.A.E.
THE NUMBER, THE DATE OF THE CREDIT:
21/01/1111　　　　April 20, 2016
THE NAME OF ISSUING BANK: UNITED ARAB BANK

WE DO HEREBY CERTIFY AND CONFIRM THAT THE PRODUCT SHIPPED UNDER L/C NO. 21/01/1111 DATED 20/04/2016 IS TESTED UNDER STRICT QUALITY CONTROL BEFORE PACKING AND SEALING AND FOUND THAT THE SAME CONFORMS THE EXACT REQUIREMENTS OF QUALITATIVE ASPECTS SUGGESTED AND AGREED BETWEEN THE APPLICANT AND BENEFICIARY AS PER THEIR BUSINESS CONTRACT. ANY DEVIATION ON THIS EFFECT ON QUALITY SHALL BE UNDER THE RISK AND RESPONSIBILITY OF THE BENEFICIARY ONLY. ALSO, IT IS CERTIFIED AND CONFIRMED THAT THE PRODUCT SO SHIPPED CONFORMS STRICTLY IN ACCORDANCE WITH THE HEALTH REQUIREMENTS OF THE MINISTRY OF HEALTH IN THE U.A.E. AND ITS EMIRATES, AND THAT DEVIATIONS RESULTING TO ANY CONSEQUENTIAL PROBLEMS SHALL BE UNDER THE RISK AND RESPONSIBILITY OF THE BENEFICIARY ONLY, PRODUCT LIABILITY IN ALL SENSE ARE UNDERTAKEN HEREWITH.

× × ×
AHOOF INTERNATIONAL DEVELOPMENT CO., LTD.

AHCOF INTERNATIONAL DEVELOPMENT CO., LTD.

SUNON PLAZA, NO. 389-399 JINZHAI ROAD, HEFEI, CHINA
TEL: 0086-551-2881126/2881013 FAX: 0086-551-2831057/8
E-MAIL: Dep10@ ahcof. com

TO: CONSUMER OPERATIVE U.A.E. DATE: May 25, 2016

DEAR SIRS,
WE SPECIFY THAT THE PACKING FOR EXPORT OF THE GOODS UNDER THIS L/C IS DONE IN PROPER ORDERS, SO AS TO AVOID LEAKAGE AND BREAKAGE. THE TINS ARE PROPERLY LABELED AND THE MASTER CARTON BOXES USED FOR PACKING ARE PRINTED PROPERLY WITH PRODUCT DESCRIPTIONS AND OTHER RELEVANT REQUIRED INFORMATION.

THE NUMBER, THE DATE OF THE CREDIT:
21/01/1111 April 20, 2016
THE NAME OF ISSUING BANK: UNITED ARAB BANK.
SHIPPING MARKS: CCU/313
P. O. BOX NO. 7039
SHARJAH, U.A.E.

× × ×
AHOOF INTERNATIONAL DEVELOPMENT CO., LTD.

AHCOF INTERNATIONAL DEVELOPMENT CO., LTD.

SUNON PLAZA, NO. 389-399 JINZHAI ROAD, HEFEI, CHINA
TEL: 0086-551-2881126/2881013 FAX: 0086-551-2831057/8
E-MAIL: Dep10@ ahcof. com

DATE: MAY 29, 2016

TO: CONSUMER OPERATIVE U.A.E.
P.O. BOX 7039, SHARJAH, UNITED ARAB EMIRATES
FAX NO. 9716-667039/6670363
REFERRING TO YOUR POLICY NO. HMR/2016/000635

DEAR SIRS,
THIS IS TO INFORM YOU THAT THE SHIPMENT UNDER YOUR ABOVE POLICY NUMBER HAS BEEN EFFECTED.
FULL DETAILS OF SHIPMENT:
1,700 MASTER CARTONS, EACH OF 24 CANS × 397G CO-OP BRAND FOUL MEDAMES
VALUE: USD6,970.00
B/L NO. UGMU145207010265
VESSEL AND VOYAGE NO.: ANHUA1 # V. 2221E
CONTAINER NUMBER: GVDU2041118/212814
FROM NANTONG, CHINA TO DUBAI ON MAY 25, 2016
THE NUMBER, THE DATE OF THE CREDIT:
21/01/1111 April 20, 2016
THE NAME OF ISSUING BANK: UNITED ARAB BANK.
SHIPPING MARKS: CCU/313
P.O. BOX NO. 7039
SHARJAH, U.A.E.

AHCOF INTERNATIONAL DEVELOPMENT CO., LTD.
× × ×

AHCOF INTERNATIONAL DEVELOPMENT CO., LTD.

SUNON PLAZA, NO. 389-399 JINZHAI ROAD, HEFEI, CHINA
TEL: 0086-551-2881126/2881013　　FAX: 0086-551-2831057/8
E-MAIL: Dep10@ ahcof. com

DATE: MAY 29, 2016

TO: SHARJAH INSURANCE AND REINSURANCE CO.
P.O. BOX 792, SHARJAH, U.A.E.
FAX 9716-5352545
REFERRING TO YOUR POLICY NO. HMR/2016/000635

DEAR SIRS,
THIS IS TO INFORM YOU THAT THE SHIPMENT UNDER YOUR ABOVE POLICY NUMBER HAS BEEN EFFECTED.
FULL DETAILS OF SHIPMENT:
1,700 MASTER CARTONS, EACH OF 24 CANS × 397G CO-OP BRAND FOUL MEDAMES
VALUE: USD6,970.00
B/L NO. UGMU145207010265
VESSEL AND VOYAGE NO.: ANHUA1 # V. 2221E
CONTAINER NUMBER: GVDU2041118/212814
FROM NANTONG, CHINA TO DUBAI ON MAY 25, 2016
THE NUMBER, THE DATE OF THE CREDIT:
21/01/1111　　　April 20, 2016
THE NAME OF ISSUING BANK: UNITED ARAB BANK.
SHIPPING MARKS: CCU/313
P.O. BOX NO. 7039
SHARJAH, U.A.E.

AHCOF INTERNATIONAL DEVELOPMENT CO., LTD.
× × ×

AHCOF INTERNATIONAL DEVELOPMENT CO., LTD.

SUNON PLAZA, NO. 389-399 JINZHAI ROAD, HEFEI, CHINA
TEL: 0086-551-2831126/2881013　　FAX: 0086-551-2881057/8
E-MAIL: Dep10@ ahcof. com

BENEFICIARY'S　CERTIFICATE

INV. NO. AFLA01041-3
DATE: MAY 24, 2016
SHIPPING MARKS: CCU/313
P.O. BOX NO. 7039
SHARJAH, U.A.E.
THE NUMBER, THE DATE OF THE CREDIT:
21/01/1111　　　　April 20, 2016
THE NAME OF ISSUING BANK: UNITED ARAB BANK

DEAR SIRS:

WE DO HEREBY CERTIFY THAT A COMPLETE SET OF NON-NEGOTIABLE DOCUMENTS EVIDENCING THEREWITH THAT THE GOODS ARE SHIPPED EXACTLY IN ACCORDANCE WITH THE TERMS AND CONDITIONS LAID DOWN IN THIS L/C HAS BEEN SENT BY COURIER SERVICE TO THE APPLICANT BY BENEFICIARY WITHIN THREE (3) DAYS FROM THE DATE OF SHIPMENT OF GOODS.

YOURS TRULY,

AHOOF INTERNATIONAL DEVELOPMENT CO., LTD.
× × ×

中华人民共和国出入境检验检疫

ENTRY-EXIT INSPECTION AND QUARANTINE OF
THE PEOPLE'S REPUBLIC OF CHINA

健康证书　　编号 NO. R321100202020575

HEALTH CERTIFICATE

发货人名称及地址
Name and Address of Consignor　AHCOF INTERNATIONAL DEVELOPMENT CO., LTD.
11/14FL SUNON PLAZA NO. 389-399, JINZHAI ROAD, HEFEI, CHINA

收货人名称及地址
Name and Address of Consignee　* * *

品名
Description of Goods　CO-OP BRAND FOUL MEDAMES

		标记及号码 Marks & No.
加工种类或状态 State or Type of Processing	CANNED FOOD	CCU/313, P.O. BOX NO.7039 SHARJAH, U.A.E.
报检数量/重量 Quantify/Weight Declared	–16,197.6KG–	
包装种类及数量 Number and Type of Packages	–1,700– CARTONS	
贮藏和运输温度 Temperature during Storage and Transport	* * *	

加工厂名称、地址及编号（如果适用）NANTONG CANNED FOOD FACTORY OF JIANGSU PROVINCE
Name Address and Approval No. of the　95 RENMIN ROAD WEST, NANTONG CITY, JIANGSU, CHINA
Approved Establishment (if applicable)　ESTABLISHMENT NO. : 3200/01004

启运地
Place of Despatch　NANTONG, CHINA

到达国家及地点
Country and Place of Destination　DUBAI, U.A.E.

运输工具
Means of Conveyance　BY SEA

发货日期
Date of Despatch　MAY 24, 2016

检验结果
RESULTS OF INSPECTION

THE GOODS ARE FIT FOR HUMAN CONSUMPTION

* * * * * * * *

REMARKS: L/C NO. 21/01/1111，April 20, 2016, UNITED ARAB BANK
PRODUCTION DATE May, 2016
EXPIRY DATE June 10, 2016
BATCH NUMBER 081

签证地点 Place of Issue　NANTONG　　签证日期 Date of Issue MAY 24, 2016

授权签字人 Authorized Officer　HUYUPENG　　签　名 Signature　×　×　×

中华人民共和国出入境检验检疫机关及其官员或代表不承担签发证书的任何财产责任。

No financial liability with respect to this certificate shall attach to the entry-exit inspection and quarantine authorities of the P. R. of China or to any of its officers or representatives.

UNIGLORY **BILL OF LADING**

UNIGLORY MARINE CORPORATION

<table>
<tr><td colspan="2">(1) Shipper/Exporter
AHCOF INTERNATIONAL DEVELOPMENT CO., LTD.
SUNON PLAZA 389-399 JINZHAI ROAD HEFEI CHINA
TEL: 0086-551-2881126/2881013
FAX: 0086-551-2831057/8
Shipper code</td><td colspan="2">(4) Document No. FIRST ORIGINAL</td></tr>
<tr><td colspan="2">(2) Consignee (complete name and address) (unless Provided otherwise a consignment "TO Order" means To Order of Shipper.)
TO ORDER</td><td colspan="2">(5) Forwarding Agent-References
CARRYING VESSEL'S AGNET AT THE PORT OF DESTINATION:
UNIGLORY (U.A.E.) L.L.C.
5FL., SHIPPING TOWER, AL MINAA RD.,
P. O. BOX, 34984 DUBAI U.A.E.
TEL: 971-4-3934999(11 LINES)
FAX: 971-4-3938261/3938264</td></tr>
<tr><td colspan="2">(3) Notify Party (complete name and address)
UNITED ARAB BANK, SHARJAH BRANCH
Notify code</td><td colspan="2">(6) Also Notify Party (complete name and address)</td></tr>
<tr><td>(8) Pre-carriaged by</td><td>(9) Place of Receipt/Date</td><td colspan="2" rowspan="2">In Witness Whereof, the undersigned, on behalf of Uniglory Marine Corporation, the Master and the Owner of the vessel, has signed the number of Bill(s) of lading stated below, all of this tenor and date, one which being accomplished, the others to stand void.</td></tr>
<tr><td>(10) Ocean Vessel/Voy No.
ANHUA1# V2221E</td><td>(11) Port of Lading
NANTONG, CHINA</td></tr>
<tr><td>(12) Port of Discharge
DUBAI</td><td>(13) Place of Delivery</td><td colspan="2">(7) Onward Inland Routing/Export Instructions (for the Merchant's reference only)</td></tr>
<tr><td colspan="4">Particulars furnished by the Merchant</td></tr>
<tr><td>(14) Container No. And SEAL No. Marks & No.

CCU/313
P.O. BOX NO. 7039
SHARJAH, U.A.E.

GVDU2041118/212814 20'

(17) TOTAL NUMBER OF CONTAINERS OR PACKAGES
(in words)</td><td>(14) Quantity and Kind of Package

1
CONTAINER</td><td>(15) Description of Goods
SHIPPER'S LOAD COUNT & SEAL
SAID TO CONTAIN: 1,700 CARTONS
CO-OP BRAND FOUL MEDAMES
QUANTITY—1,700 MASTER CARTONS,
EACH OF 24 CANS × 397G
IN 1 × 20 FEET FCL CONTAINER
— THE NUMBER, THE DATE OF THE CREDIT 21/01/1111 April 20th, 2016
—THE NAME OF ISSUING BANK:
UNITED ARAB BANK
THE CARRYING VESSEL IS NOT ISRAELI AND NOT CALLING AT ISRAELI PORTS
SAY ONE CONTAINER ONLY</td><td>(16) Measurement (M3)
Gross Weight (KGS)

18,700 KGS 24 M3

(18) Declared Value $__ and pays the applicable ad. valorem tariff rate. Carrier's package limitation shall not apply</td></tr>
<tr><td>(19) FREIGHT & CHARGES</td><td colspan="2">Revenue Tons Rate Per
AS ARRANGED

中国船务代理公司江苏南通公司
CHINA MARINE SHIPPING AGENCY JIANGSU NANTONG CORPORATION (2)</td><td>Prepaid Collect

中国船务代理公司江苏南通公司
CHINA MARINE SHIPPING AGENCY JIANGSU NANTONG CORPORATION(2)</td></tr>
<tr><td rowspan="2">(20) B/L NO.
UGMU145207010265
AVLA0041</td><td colspan="2">(21) Number of Original B(s)/L
3</td><td>(22) Prepaid at
NANTONG | (23) Collect at</td></tr>
<tr><td colspan="2">(24) Place of B(s)/L Issue Date
May 25th, 2016 NANTONG</td><td>(25) Exchange Rate | (26) Exchange Rate</td></tr>
<tr><td>(27) Service Type Mode

FCL/FCL 0/0</td><td colspan="3">(28) Laden on Board the Vessel
SHIPPED ON BOARD
CHEN JIE
GENERAL MANAGER
AS AGENT ACTING ON BEHALF THE CARRIER

CHEN JIE
GENERAL MANAGER
AS AGENT ACTING ON BEHALF OF THE OF CARRIER

By________________________

AS AGENTS FOR THE CARRIER UNIGLORY MARINE CORPORATION</td></tr>
</table>

C14-2　综合审单操作能力训练二　根据以下信用证和相关资料，独立审核货运单据。

审单信用证 C14-2

******MESSAGE HARDCOPY*****　　12.04.06　　PAGE NO.9178

Status: DISPOSED TO THE TDVQ

Station: 1　　BEGINNING OF MESSAGE

....

FIN/Session/ISN:	FO1　　.SS.　　.SEQ.,
Own Address:	DLXBINBBAKPM DHANALAKSHMI BANK LTD., THE BANGALORE
Input Message Type:	700　ISSUE OF A DOCUMENTARY CREDIT
Sent to:	BCITCNSHX X X X　　INTESABCI S.P.A SHANGHAI (SHANGHAI BRANCH)
Input Time:	
MIR:	
Priority/Obso1 period:	Normal/100 Minutes

....

SEQUENCE OF TOTAL	27:	1/1
FORM OF DOCUMENTARY CREDIT	40A:	IRREVOCABLE
DOCUMENTARY CREDIT NUMBER	20:	LCBLR0100371
DATE OF ISSUE	31C:	160507
DATE AND PLACE OF EXPIRY	31D:	160617 CHINA
APPLICANT BANK－BIC	51A:	DLXBINBBKPM DHANALAKSHMI BANK LTD, THE BANGALORE
APPLICANT	50:	AMRIT BANASPATI CO., LTD. D.H. ROAD, FATEPUR, 24PGSOUTH, W.B-743513, INDIA
BENEFICIARY	59:	JIANGXI ZHAOHUI CHEMICALS CO. LTD. NO.291 TIANXIANG ROAD, NANCHANG CHINA
CURRENCY CODE AMOUNT	32B:	USD48,000.00
PERCENTAGE CREDIT AMT TOLERANCE	39A:	10/10
AVAILABLE WITH...BY-NAME & ADDR:	41D:	ANY BANK IN CHINA BY NEGOTIATION
DRAFTS AT...	42C:	30 DAYS AFTER B/L DATE FOR 70 PERCENT OF THE INVOICE VALUE
DRAWEE－BIC	42A:	DHANALAKSHMI BANK LTD. THE AYARKUNNAM

PARTIAL SHIPMENTS	43P:	NOT ALLOWED
TRANSSHIPMENT	43T:	ALLOWED
ON BOARD/DISP/TAKING CHARGE AT/FM	44A:	TIANJIN, CHINA
FOR TRANSPORTATION TO	44B:	AYARKUNNAM, INDIA.
LATEST DATE OF SHIPMENT	44C:	160527
DESCRIPTION OF GOODS OR SERVICES:	45A:	ANTIOXIDANT BHT (GRANULAR) AS PURCHASE ORDER NO. IMP/012/2015-16 DATED 20 MAR. 2016 AT CIF USD3,000/MT AYARKUNNAM, INDIA INCOTERMS 2010
DOCUMENTS REQUIRED	46A:	ALL IN ENGLISH AND IN DUPLICATE UNLESS OTHERWISE SPECIFIED. (1) SIGNED COMMERCIAL INVOICE IN ORIGILNAL AND SEVEN COPIES QUOTING (A) PURCHASE ORDER NO.IMP/012/2015-16 DATED 20 MAR, 2016 (B) HS CODE 38123010. (2) FULL SET OF CLEAN ON BOARD OCEAN BILLS OF LADING OF A REGULAR LINER VESSEL MARKED FREIGHT PREPAID DRAWN ON OR ENDORSED/CONSIGNED TO ORDER AND NOTIFY (A) THE OPENING BANK AND (B) THE APPLICANT. (3) PACKING LIST. (4) INSURANCE CERTIFICATE IN TRIPLICATE BY PICC, BLANK ENDORSED, DATE NOT LATER THAN THE TRANSPORT DOCUMENT MARKED PREMIUM PAID, FOR AT LEAST 120 PERCENT OF INVOICE VALUE COVERING INSTITUTE CARGO CLAUSE (A), INSTITUTE WAR CLAUSE (CARGO), INSTITUTE STRIKE CLAUSE (CARGO), WAREHOUSE TO WAREHOUSE CLAUSE, INCLUDING TRANSSHIPMENT RISK, CLAIMS PAYABLE IN INDIA AND IN CURRENCY OF CREDIT QUOTING CLAIM SETTLING AGENTS NAME

		AND ADDRESS IN INDIA.
ADDITIONAL CONDITIONS	47A:	(1) ALL DOCUMENTS SHOULD QUOTE THE CREDIT NUMBER, DATE AND NAME OF ISSUING BANK. (2) DOCUMENTS DATED PRIOR TO THE DATE OF CREDIT ARE NOT ACCEPTABLE. (3) ALL CHARGES OUTSIDE INDIA ARE FOR BENEFICIARY'S ACCOUNT. (4) DOCUMENTS SHOULD BE NEGOTIATED WITHIN 21 DAYS FROM THE DATE OF BILL OF LADING BUT WITHIN THE VALIDITY OF THE CREDIT.
CONFIRMATION INSTRUCTIONS	49:	WITHOUT
INSTR TO PAYG/ACCPTG/NEGOTG BANK	78:	(1) DOCUMENTS ARE TO BE SENT TO US IN TWO CONSECUTIVE SETS, FIRST BY COURIER AND SECOND BY COURIER/ REGISTERED POST. (2) ON NEGOTIATION OF CREDIT CONFORMING DOCUMENTS, WE WILL REMIT THE PROCEEDS, AS PER NEGOTIATING BANK'S INSTRUCTION. (3) THIS DOCUMENTARY CREDIT IS SUBJECT TO UCP DC (1993 REV) ICC PUB NO.500. (4) THIS IS AN OPERATIVE INSTRUMENT AND NO MAIL CONFIRMATION TO FOLLOW.

14-2　装运货物相关资料

(1) 货物总净重：16 000.00KG

(2) 货物总毛重：18 144.00KG

(3) 体积：25CBM

(4) 货物总件数：640 袋

(5) 唛头：A&B

AYARKUNNAM

1-640

MADE IN CHINA

综合审单操作全套货运单据 C14-2

江西进出口公司

JIANGXI ZHAOHUI CHEMICALS CO., LTD.

NO.291 Tianxiang Road, Nanchang, Jiangxi, China

INVOICE

To: AMRIT BANASPATI CO., LTD.
D.H. ROAD, FATPUR, 24PGSOUTH, W.B-73513, INDIA

Invoice No: JXZH060517
Date: May 6, 2016

Marks & No.	Quantities & Description	Unit Price	Amount
A&B AYARKUNNAM 1-640 MADE IN CHINA	16 MT ANTIOXIDANT BHT (GRANULAR) AS PURCHASE ORDER NO.IMP/012/2015-16 DATED: MAR. 20, 2016	CIP AYARKUNNAM USD3,000/MT	USD48,000.00

中国太平洋保险公司

CHINA PACIFIC INSURANCE COMPANY LIMITED

保 险 单　　　　号码

INSURANCE POLICY　　NO.：222000113066

中国太平洋保险公司（以下称承保人）根据被保险人的要求，在被保险人向承保人缴付约定的保险费后，按照本保险单承保险别和背面所载条款与下列特款承保下述货物运输保险，特立本保险单。

This Policy of insurance witnesses that China Pacific Insurance Company Limited (hereinafter called "The Underwriter") at the request of the Insured named here under and in consideration of the agreed premium paid to the Underwriter by the Insured, undertakes to insure the undermentioned goods in transportation subject to the conditions of this Policy as per the Clauses printed overleaf and other special clauses attached hereon.

被保险人

Insured: JIANGXI ZHAOHUI CHEMICALS CO., LTD.
NO. 291 TIANXIANG ROAD, NANCHANG, CHINA

标记 Marks & No.	包装及数量 Quantity	保险货物项目 Description of Goods	保险金额 Amount Insured
As per Invoice No. JXZH060515	640 BAGS 16,000.00KGS	ANTIOXIDANT BHT	USD57,600.00

总保险金额

Total Amount Insured: U.S. DOLLARS FIFTY SEVEN THOUSAND SIX HUNDRED ONLY.

保费　　　　　费率　　　　　装载运输工具

Premium: as arranged　Rate: as arranged　Per conveyance S.S: CSCL SHANGHAI V.012W

开行日期　　　　　自　　　　　至

Slg.on or abt: MAY 17, 2016　From: TIANJIN　TO BOMBAY

承保险别

Conditions: COVERING INSTITUTE CARGO CLAUSE(A), INSTITUTE WAR CLAUSE (CARGO).
INSTITUTE STRIKE CLAUSE(CARGO)

所保货物，如遇出险，本公司凭本保险单及其他有关证件给付赔款。所保货物，如发生本保险单项下负责赔偿的损失或事故，应立即通知本公司下述代理人查勘。

Claims if any, payable on surrender of this policy together with other relevant documents. In the event of accident whereby loss or damage may result in a claim under this Policy immediate notice applying, for survey must be given to the Company's Agent as mentioned hereunder.

中国太平洋保险公司南昌分公司 CHINA PACIFIC INSURANCE COMPANY LIMITED NANCHANG BRANCH 李明诚 GENERAL MANAGER

赔款赔付地点

Claims payable at INDIA IN USD

日期

Date: MAY 17, 2016

<table>
<tr>
<td colspan="2">Shipper
JIANGXI ZHAOHUI CHEMICALS CO., LTD.
NO., 291 TIANXIANG ROAD,
NANCHANG, CHINA</td>
<td colspan="4" rowspan="6">B/L NO. 8RUFL07N0223CLB

中国对外贸易运输总公司
CHINA NATIONAL FOREIGN TRADE TRANSPORTATION CORP.
COMBINED TRANSPORT BILL OF LADING
SHIPPED on board in apparent good order and conditions (unless otherwise indicated) the goods or packages specified herein and to be discharged at the mentioned port of discharge or as near thereto as the vessel may safely get and be always afloat.
The shipper, Consignee and the Holder of the Bill of Lading hereby expressly accept and agree to all printed, written or stamped provisions, exceptions and conditions of this Bill of Lading, including those on the back hereof.
The weight, measure, marks and numbers, quantity, contents and value, being particularly finished by the Shipper, are not checked by the Carrier on lading.
IN WITNESS whereof the number of original Bills of Lading stated below have been signed, one of which being accomplished, the other(s) to be void.</td>
</tr>
<tr>
<td colspan="2">Consignee or Order
TO ORDER</td>
</tr>
<tr>
<td colspan="2">Notify Address
DHANALAKSHMI BANK LTD.
THE BANGALORE</td>
</tr>
<tr>
<td>Pre-carriage by</td>
<td>Port of Loading
TIANJIN</td>
</tr>
<tr>
<td>Vessel & Voyage
CSCL
SHANGHAI
V.0120W</td>
<td>Port of Transshipment
BOMBAY</td>
</tr>
<tr>
<td>Port of Discharge
AYARKUNNAM</td>
<td>Final Destination</td>
</tr>
<tr>
<td>Container/Seal No. or Marks and No.
A & B
AYARKUNAM
1-640
MADE IN
CHINA

CCLU2530830
B87384
CY/CY 20GP</td>
<td colspan="3">Number and kind of packages Description of goods

640 BAGS OF ANTIOXIDANT BHT</td>
<td>Gross Weight

18,000.00KG</td>
<td>Measurement

$27.00M^3$</td>
</tr>
<tr>
<td colspan="3">Freight and Charges
FREIGHT PREPAID</td>
<td colspan="3">REGARDING TRANSSHIPMENT INFORMATION PLEASE CONTACT</td>
</tr>
<tr>
<td rowspan="2">EX. Rate</td>
<td>Prepaid at
TIANJIN</td>
<td>Freight Payable at</td>
<td colspan="3">Place and Date of Issue
TIANJIN CHINA 15 MAY, 2016</td>
</tr>
<tr>
<td>Total Prepaid</td>
<td>Number of Original B/L

THREE (3)</td>
<td colspan="3">Signed for or on behalf of the carrier:
CHINA NATIONAL FOREIGN TRADE TRANSPORTATION CORP.
王立
AS CARRIER</td>
</tr>
</table>

Bill of Exchange

凭　　　　　　　　　　　　　　　　　　　　　　　　　　　　信用证
Drawn under DHANALAKSHMI BANK LTD. THE BANGALORE　　L/C NO.LCBLR0100371

日期　　　　　　　　　　　　支取按____息_____
Dated: 2016/05/07　　　　payable with interest@______ %______ per annul

号码　　　　汇票金额　　　　　　　　中国南昌　　　　年　月　日
No. JXZH060517　Exchange for USD48,000.00　Nanchang, China

见票　　　　　日后　　　　　　（本汇票之正本未付）
At ********** sight of this **SECOND** of Exchange (First of Exchange being unpaid)

付交
pay to the order of BANK OF CHINA, JIANGXI BRANCH

金额
the sum of U.S. DOLLARS FORTY EIGHT THOUSAND ONLY.

收讫价值
Value received for

此致　　　　　　　　　　　　　　　　　　　　谨代表
To　DHANALAKSHMI BANK LTD.　　　　　　For and on behalf of
THE AYARKUNNAM　　　　　　　　　　JIANGXI ZHAOHUI CHEMICALS CO., LTD.

王丰
(Authorized Signature)

C14-3　综合审单操作能力训练三　根据以下信用证和相关资料，独立审核全套货运单据。

审单信用证 C14-3

中国银行　　　　　　　　新加坡分行
BANK OF CHINA　　　　　　SINGAPORE BRANCH
4 BATIERY ROAD # 01-00 BANK OF CHINA BUILDING, SINGAPORE 049908
TEL:4398333 CABLE:CHUNGKUO TELEX:23047BKCHINA FAX:3458792 SWIFT: BKCHSGSG

ADVISING BANK:　　BANK OF CHINA, SHANGHAI
IRREVOCABLE DOCUMENTARY CREDIT NO. 123456 DATED: APRIL 15, 2016
DATE AND PLACE OF EXPIRY: 31 MAY 2016 IN BENEFICIARY'S COUNTRY
BENEFICIARY: SHANGHAI JINHAI IMP. & EXP. GROUP GARMENTS BRANCH
NO. 50 LANE 424 YAOHUA ROAD

SHANGHAI CHINA
APPLICANT: ANTAK DEVELOPMENT PTE LTD.
101 KIT CHENER ROAD
JALAN PLAZA, SINGAPORE
TEL NO. 3423457 FAX NO. 4723457
AMOUNT: USD56,300.00 CIF SINGAPORE (INCOTERMS 2010)
(UNITED STATES DOLLARS FIFTY SIX THOUSAND THREE HUNDRED ONLY)
PARTIAL SHIPMENTS: NOT ALLOWED
TRANSSHIPMENT: NOT ALLOWED
SHIPMENT FROM CHINA PORT TO SINGAPORE
LATEST SHIPMENT DATE: 25 MAY, 2016
THIS CREDIT IS AVAILABLE WITH THE ADVISING BANK BY NEGOTIATION AGAINST PRESENTATION OF THE DOCUMENTS DETAILED HEREIN AND BENEFICIARY'S DRAFT(S) AT SIGHT DRAWN ON ISSUING BANK FOR FULL INVOICE VALUE.
DOCUMENTS REQUIRED (IN TWO FOLDS UNLESS OTHERWISE STIPULATED):
1. SIGNED COMMERCIAL INVOICE
2. SIGNED WEIGHT/PACKING LIST
3. CERTIFICATE OF CHINESE ORIGIN
4. INSURANCE POLICY/CERTIFICATE ENDORSED IN BLANK FOR 110% CIF VALUE COVERING WAR RISK AND ALL RISKS
5. FULL SET PLUS ONE PHOTOCOPY OF CLEAN ON BOARD OCEAN BILLS OF LADING MADE OUT TO ORDER OF BANK OF CHINA, SINGAPORE MARKED FREIGHT PREPAID AND NOTIFY APPLICANT
EVIDENCING SHIPMENT OF:
700 DOZENS MEN COTTON WOVEN LABOURER SHIPTS (USD 19,180.00)
800 DOZENS MEN COTTON WOVEN SHIRTS (USD 31,680.00)
160 DOZENS MEN COTTON WOVEN SHIRTS (USD 5,440.00)
S/C NO. 00SHGM3178B
SHIPPING MARKS:
K. K. G. T.
73718
SINGAPORE
NO. 1-190

OTHER TERMS AND CONDITIONS:
1. ALL BANK CHARGES INCLUDING REIMBURSEMENT CHARGES OUTSIDE SINGAPORE ARE FOR ACCOUNT OF BENEFICIARY.

2. THE NUMBER AND DATE OF THIS CREDIT AND THE NAME OF ISSUING BANK MUST BE QUOTED ON ALL DOCUMENTS.

3. A FEE OF USD 40.00 (OR ITS EQUIVALENT) TO BE DEDUCTED FROM THE PROCEEDS UPON EACH PRESENTATION OF DISCREPANT DOCUMENTS EVEN IF THE CREDIT INDICATES THAT ALL BANKING CHARGES ARE FOR THE ACCOUNT OF APPLICANT AND ACCEPTANCE OF SUCH DOCUMENTS DOES NOT IN ANY WAY ALTER THE TERMS AND CONDITIONS OF THIS CREDIT.

4. THE WHOLE CONSIGNMENT TO BE UNDER ONE BILL OF LADING.

5. BENEFICIARY'S CERTIFICATE TO CERTIFY THE FOLLOWINGS IS REQUIRED:

(A) INVOICE, WEIGHT/PACKING LIST AND NON-NEGOTIABLE BILL OF LADING MUST BE AIRMAILED TO THE APPLICANT IMMEDIATELY AFTER SHIPMENT.

(B) COPIES OF INVOICE AND BILLS OF LADING HAVE BEEN FAXED TO APPLICANT IMMEDIATELY AFTER SHIPMENT.

6. INSURANCE POLICY OR CERTIFICATE MUST SHOW CLAIMS SETTLING AGENT AS: "CHINA INSURANCE CO., LTD. SINGAPORE."

7. BILLS OF LADING TO EVIDENCE THE FOLLOWINGS:

(A) SHIPMENT EFFECTED INTO 20 FEET CONTAINER LOAD (CY-CY).

(B) SHIPMENT EFFECTED BY CONTAINERISED VESSEL ONLY.

(C) SHOWING APPLICANT ADDRESS, TELEPHONE NO. AND FAX NO.

(D) SHOWING CARRIER/CARRIER'S AGENT AS: "CHINA OCEAN SHIPPING (GROUP) CO."

(E) SHOWING CONTAINER NUMBER.

8. SHIPMENT OF THE WHOLE CONSIGNMENT EFFECTED INTO LOOSE CARGO LOAD IS NOT ACCEPTABLE.

9. PACKING: GOODS MUST BE PACKED IN STRONG CARTONS AND STRAPPED WITH STRONG NYLON STRAPS. WEIGHT/PACKING LIST TO SHOW THIS EFFECT IS REQUIRED.

10. IT IS ALLOWED TO INCREASE OR DECREASE THE QUANTITY AND AMOUNT BY 5%.

INSTRUCTIONS TO THE NEGOTIATING BANK:

THE AMOUNT AND DATE OF EACH NEGOTIATION MUST BE ENDORSED ON THE REVERSE OF THE ORIGINAL CREDIT BY THE NEGOTIATING BANK.

ALL DOCUMENTS ARE TO BE SENT TO ISSUING BANK IN ONE LOT UPON RECEIPT OF DOCUMENTS IN CONFORMITY WITH THE TERM AND CONDITIONS OF THIS CREDIT, WE SHALL CREDIT OUR HEAD OFFICE ACCOUNT WITH US.

THIS CREDIT IS ISSUED SUBJECT TO UNIFORM CUSTOMS AND PRACTICE FOR DOCUMENTARY CREDITS (1993 REVISION) ICC PUBLICATION NO. 500.

BANK OF CHINA, SINGAPORE

AUTHORIZED SIGNATURES

14-3 装运货物相关资料：
发票号码：SHGM7056
发票日期：2016 年 5 月 4 日
各品种货物每件包装毛重、净重及尺码：

货号/规格	装运数量及单位	毛/净重（件）	尺码
1094L	700DOZ	33KGS/31KGS	68×46×45 cm
286G	800DOZ	45KGS/43KGS	72×47×49 cm
666	160DOZ	33KGS/31KGS	68×46×45 cm

包装情况：
一件一塑料袋装，6 件一牛皮纸包，8 打或 10 打一外箱。
尺码搭配：

	M	L	XL
① 1094L:	M	L	XL
	3	3	4 = 10 打/箱
② 286G:	M	L	XL
	1.5	3	3.5 = 8 打/箱
③ 666:	M	L	XL
	1.5	3.5	3 = 8 打/箱

提单号码：COSC---503
承运船名及航次：ZHONGHE V. 040
集装箱号：COSU------257289
B/L DATE：2016 年 5 月 15 日
装运港：上海
保险单号码：SZDB 331　　日期：2016 年 5 月 13 日
保险代理：CHINA INSURANCE CO., LTD. SINGAPORE
4 BATIERY ROAD #08---0018th FLOOR, BANK OF CHINA BUILDING, SINGAPORE 0104
产地证编号：7681249
商品编号：6211.3200

综合审单操作全套货运单据 C14-3

<table>
<tr><td rowspan="2">Issuer
SHANGHAI JINHAI IMP. & EXP. GROUP
GARMENTS BRANCH
NO. 50 LANE 424 YAOHUA ROAD
SHANGHAI CHINA</td><td colspan="2">商 业 发 票
COMMERCIAL INVOICE</td></tr>
<tr></tr>
<tr><td>To
ANTAK DEVELOPMENT PTE LTD.
101 KIT CHENER ROAD
JALAN PLAZA, SINGAPORE</td><td>No. SHGM 7056</td><td>Date: May 4, 2016</td></tr>
<tr><td rowspan="2">Transport Details

FROM SHANGHAI CHINA TO SINGAPORE BY SEA</td><td>S/C NO. 00SHGM3178</td><td>L/C NO. 123456</td></tr>
<tr><td colspan="2">Terms of Payment
L/C AT SIGHT</td></tr>
</table>

Marks and Numbers	Number and Kind of Packages; Description of Goods	Quantity	Unit Price	Amount
	SHIRTS		CIF SINGAPORE	
	MEN COTTON WOVEN LABOURER SHIPTS			
K. K. G. T.	ART NO.1094I	700 DOZENS	USD27.40/DOZ	USD19,180.00
73178	MEN COTTON WOVEN SHIRTS			
SINGAPORE	ART NO.286G	800 DOZENS	USD39.60/DOZ	USD31,680.00
NO.1-190	MEN COTTON WOVEN SHIRTS			
	ART NO.666	160 DOZENS	USD34.00/DOZ	USD 5,440.00
				USD56,300.00

PACKED IN 190 CTNS ONLY

SHANGHAI JINHAI IMP. & EXP. GROUP GARMENTS BRANCH

× × ×

Issuer SHANGHAI JINHAI IMP. & EXP. GROUP GARMENTS BRANCH NO.50 LANE 424 YAOHUA ROAD SHANGHAI CHINA	装 箱 单 **PACKING LIST**
To ANTAK DEVELOPMENT PTE LTD. 101 KIT CHENER ROAD JALAN PLAZA SINGAPORE	Invoice No. SHGM 7056 / Date May 4, 2016

Marks and Numbers	Numbers and Kind of Packages; Description of Goods	Quantity	G.W.(KGS)	N.W.(KGS)	MEAS.(M^3)
	SHIRTS				
K. K. G. T.	MEN COTTON WOVEN LABOURER SHIRTS	70CTNS	33	31	0.141
73718	MEN COTTON WOVEN SHIRTS	100CTNS	45	43	0.166
SINGAPORE	MEN COTTON WOVEN SHIRTS	20CTNS	33	31	0.141
NO. 1-190	TOTAL:	190CTNS	7,470.00	7,090.00	29.290

SHANGHAI JINHAI IMP. & EXP. GROUP GARMENTS BRANCH

× × ×

交单份数：2 份

1. Exporter SHANGHAI JINHAI IMP. & EXP. GROUP GARMENTS BRANCH NO. 50 LANE 424 YAOHUA ROAD SHANGHAI CHINA	Certificate NO. 7681249 **CERTIFICATION OF ORIGIN** **OF** **THE PEOPLE'S REPUBLIC OF CHINA**
2. Consignee ANTAK DEVELOPMENT PTD LTD. 101 KIT CHENER ROAD JALAN PLAZA SINGAPORE	
3. Means of Transport and Route FROM SHANGHAI CHINA TO SINGAPORE BY SEA	5. For certifying authority use only
4. Country/Region of Destination	

6. Marks and Numbers	7. Number and Kind of Packages; Description of Goods	8. H.S. Code	9. Quantity	10.Number and Date of Invoice
K. K. G. T. 73718 SINGAPORE NO. 1-190	MEN COTTON WOVEN LABOURER SHIPTS (SHIRTS) ART. 1094L MEN COTTON WOVEN SHIRTS ART. NO. 286G MEN COTTON WOVEN SHIRITS ART. NO. 666	6211.3200	1,660 DOZS	SHGM7056 MAY 4, 2016

11. Declaration by the exporter The undersigned hereby declares that the above details and statements are correct, that all the goods were produced in China and that they comply with the rules of Origin of the People's Republic of China. Place and date, signature and stamp of authorized signatory	12. Certification It is hereby certified that the declaration by the exporter is correct. Place and date, signature and stamp of certifying authority

中 国 人 民 保 险 公 司

THE PEOPLE'S INSURANCE COMPANY OF CHINA

总公司设于北京　一九四九年创立

HEAD OFFICE: BEIJING　ESTABLISHED IN 1949

发票号码_____　　保 险 单　　保险单号次____

INVOICE NO. SHAM 7056_　　**INSURANCE POLICY**　　POLICY NO. _SZDB331

中 国 人 民 保 险 公 司 （ 以 下 简 称 本 公 司 ）

THIS POLICY OF INSURANCE WITNESSES THAT THE PEOPLE'S INSURANCE COMPANY OF CHINA (HEREINAFTER CALLED "THE COMPANY")

根　据

AT THE REQUEST OF　SHANGHAI JINHAI IMP. & EXP. GROUP GARMENTS BRANCH

(以下简称被保险人)的要求，由被保险人向本公司缴付约定的保险费，按照本保险单承保险别和背面所载

(HEREINAFTER CALLED THE "INSURED") AND IN CONSIDERATION OF THE AGREED PREMIUM PAID TO THE COMPANY BY THE INSURED, UNDERTAKES TO INSURE THE UNDERMENTIONED GOODS IN TRANSPORTATION

条款与下列条款承保下述货物运输保险，特立本保险单。

SUBJECT TO THE CONDITIONS OF THIS POLICY AS PER THE CLAUSES PRINTED OVERLEAF AND OTHER SPECIAL CLAUSES ATTACHED HEREON.

标记 MARKS & NO.	包装数量 QUANTITY	保险货物项目 DESCRIPTION OF GOODS	保险金额 AMOUNT INSURED
AS PER INV. NO. SHAM7056	190CTNS	SHIRTS	USD56,300.00

总保险金额：

TOTAL AMOUNT INSURED: SAY U.S. DOLLARS FIFTY SIX THOUSAND THREE HUNDRED ONLY

保费　　费率　　装载运输工具

PREMIUM AS ARRANGED　　RATE AS ARRANGED　　PER CONVEYANCE S.S. ZHONGHE 040

开航日期　　自　　至

SLG.ON OR ABT. AS PER B/L　　FROM　SHANGHAI　TO SINGAPORE

承保险别：

CONDITIONS　　WAR RISK AND ALL RISKS

所 保 货 物 ， 如 遇 出 险 ， 本 公 司 凭 本 保 险 单 及 其 他 有 关 证 件 给 付 赔 款 。

CLAIMS, IF ANY, PAYABLE ON SURRENDER OF THIS POLICY WITH OTHER RELEVENT DOCUMENTS.

所 保 货 物 ， 如 发 生 保 险 单 项 下 负 责 赔 偿 的 损 失 或 事 故，

IN THE EVENT OF ACCIDENT WHEREBY LOSS OR DAMAGE MAY RESULT IN A CLAIM UNDER THIS POLICY

应 立 即 通 知 本 公 司 下 述 代 理 人 查 勘。

IMMEDIATE NOTICE APPLYING FOR SURVEY MUST BE GIVEN TO THE COMPANY'S AGENT AS MENTIONED HEREUNDER.

CHINA INSURANCE CO., LTD.
4 BATIERY ROAD #08 -0018th FLOOR
BANK OF CHINA BUILDING SHANGHAI 0104

中 国 人 民 保 险 公 司
THE PEOPLE'S INSURANCE CO. OF CHINA
马国华

赔款偿付地点

CLAIM PAYABLE AT SHANGHAI IN USD

出 单 公 司 地 区

ADDRESS OF ISSUING OFFICE______

23 ZHONGSHAN DONG YI LU SHANGHAI, CHINA

日期

DATE MAY 13, 2016_____

Shipper
SHANGHAI JINHAI IMP. & EXP. GROUP
GARMENTS BRANCH NO.50 LANE 424
YAOHUA ROAD SHANGHAI CHINA

B/L NO.
COSC-503

中国远洋运输（集团）总公司
CHINA OCEAN SHIPPING (GROUP) CO.
CABLE: COSCO BEIJING
TLX: 210740 CRC CN

Consignee
TO ORDER

Notify Party
ANTAK DEVELOPMENT PTE LTD.
101 KIT CHENER ROAD
JALAN PLAZA SINGAPORE
TEL. NO. 3423457 FAX NO. 4723456

ORIGINAL

Combined Transport BILL OF LADING

RECEIVED in apparent good order and condition except as otherwise noted the total number of containers or other packages or units enumerated below for transportation from the place of receipt to the place of delivery subject to the terms and conditions hereof. One of the bills of lading must be surrendered duly endorsed to the Carrier by or on behalf of the Holder of the Bill of Lading, the rights and liabilities arising in accordance with the terms, and conditions hereof shall, without prejudice to any rule of common law or stature rendering them binding on the Merchant, become binding in all respects between the Carrier and the Holder of the Bill of Lading as though the contract evidenced hereby had been made between them. IN WITNESS Whereof the number of original Bills of Lading stated under have been signed, all of this tenor and date, one of which being accomplished, the other(s) to be void.

Pre-carriage by	Place of Receipt
Ocean Vessel Vov. No. ZHONGHE 040	Port of Loading SHANGHAI

Port of Discharge	Place of Delivery	Final Destinations (of the goods-not the ship)
SINGAPORE		See Article 7 paragraph (2)

Marks & No. Container/Seal No.	No. of Containers or P'kgs	Kind of Packages; Description of Goods	Gross Weight kg	Measurement M^3
K. K. G. T. 71387 SINGAPORE NO.1-190	190CTNS	SHIRTS SHIPMENT EFFECTED INTO 20 FEET CONTAINER LOAD (CY-CY) SHIPMENT EFFECTED BY CONTAINERISED VESSEL ONLY CONTAINER NUMBER: COSU257289	7,470KGS	26.744 M^3

TOTAL NO. OF CONTAINERS OR PACKAGES (IN WORDS)	SAY ONE HUNDRED AND NINETY CARTONS ONLY

FREIGHT & CHARGES	Revenue Tons	Rate	Per	Prepaid	Collect

Ex. Rate:	Prepaid at	Payable at	Place and date of Issue SHANGHAI MAY 15, 2006
	Total Prepaid	No. of Original B(s)/L ONE (1)	Signed for the Carrier CHINA OCEAN SHIPPING (GROUP) CO.　李翔

LADEN ON BOARD THE VESSEL

DATE　　　　By______________　（TERMS CONTINUED ON BACK HEREOF）

（COSCO STANDARD FORM 11）　CHINA OCEAN SHIPPING (GROUP) CO.　　　PRINTED IN 1999

李翔

凭

Drawn under BANK OF CHINA SINGAPORE BRANCH

信用证第　　号　　　日期　　　年　月　日　按　　　息　　　　　　　付　　款

L/C No. 123456　　Dated 26 MAY, 2016　　Payable with interest @ ______% per annul

号码　　　　　　　　汇票金额　　　　　　　中国上海　　　　　年　月　日

No. SHGM 7066　　Exchange for USD 56,300.00　　Shanghai, China　Date:

见票　　　　　　　　日后　　　　　　　　（本票之第二联未付）

At 30 DAYS AFTER　sight of this First of **Exchange** (Second of exchange being unpaid)

付　或其指定人

Pay to the order of BANK OF CHINA, SHANGHAI

金　额

The sum of UNITED STATES DOLLARS FIFTY SIX THOUSAND THREE HUNDRED ONLY

收讫价值

Against shipment of ______

此致

To : ANTAK DEVELOPMENT PTE LTD.

101 KIT CHENER ROAD

JALAN PLAZA SINGAPORE

For and on behalf of

SHANGHAI JINHAI IMP. & EXP.

GROUP GARMENTS BRANCH

×××

(Authorized signature)

1

C14-4　综合审单操作能力训练四　根据下列信用证及货物实际装运情况，独立审核全套装运单据。

审单信用证 C14-4

Emirates Bank International PJSC　　PAGE NO. 1

TRADE FINANCE SERVICES, P.O. BOX 2923, DUBAI, U.A.E. DATE OF ISSUE: 19 FEB., 2014

IRREVOCABLE DOCUMENTARY CREDIT	DOCUMENTARY CREDIT NO.: ELC-TFS-001600
ADVISING BANK BANK OF CHINA, SHANGHAI BRANCH CHINA	APPLICANT: LOYAL TRADER P.O. BOX 6058, DUBAI, U.A.E. TEL: 3535177　FAX:3535133
BENEFICIARY: SHANGHAI VIM IMPORT & EXPORT CO., LTD. 350 WU ZHONG ROAD SHANGHAI 200331, CHINA TEL NO.65268894　FAX NO. 65268895	AMOUNT IN WORDS AND FIGURES: USD 245,882.80 (US DOLLARS TWO HUNDRED FORTY FIVE THOUSAND EIGHT HUNDRED EIGHTY TWO AND EIGHTY CENTS ONLY) AVAILABLE WITH: ANY BANK IN CHINA FOR PRESENTATION EXPIRY UNTIL 3 APR., 2014

DEAR SIRS:

WE HEREBY ISSUE THIS IRREVOCABLE DOCUMENTARY CREDIT IN YOUR FAVOUR WHICH IS AVAILABLE BY PAYMENT IN DUBAI OF YOUR DRAFTS AT SIGHT DRAWN ON US FOR FULL INVOICE VALUE OF GOODS AND MARKED “DRAWN UNDER EMIRATES BANK INTERNATIONAL PJSC CREDIT NUMBER ELC-TFS-001600” ACCOMPANIED BY THE FOLLOWING DOCUMENTS:

1. COMMERCIAL INVOICE IN 4 COPIES STATING THE NAME AND ADDRESS OF MANUFACTURER OR PROCESSOR, FOB VALUE AND INSURANCE PREMIUM, CERTIFYING THE ORIGIN OF GOODS AND CONTENTS TO BE TRUE AND CORRECT.
2. FULL SET (3/3) OF CLEAN “ON BOARD” MARINE BILLS OF LADING PLUS ONE NON-NEGOTIABLE COPY ISSUED TO THE ORDER OF EMIRATES BANK INTERNATIONAL PJSC MARKED FREIGHT PREPAID AND NOTIFY APPLICANT. THE BILL OF LADING MUST STATE NAME, ADDRESS AND NAME OF CONTACT PERSON OF THE CARRYING VESSEL’S AGENT IN DUBAI.
3. CERTIFICATE OF ORIGIN IN DUPLICATE ISSUED BY CHINA COUNCIL FOR THE PROMOTION OF INTERNATIONAL TRADE AND CERTIFYING THE GOODS TO BE OF MANUFACTURER OR PROCESSOR AND EXPORTER OF GOODS AND NAME OF THE EXPORTING COUNTRY.
4. (2/2) INSURANCE POLICY/CERTIFICATE ISSUED IN NEGOTIABLE FORM FOR CIF INVOICE VALUE PLUS 20 PCT COVERING ICC (A) & ICC WAR, SHOWING THE NUMBER OF ORIGINALS ISSUED, CLAIMS PAYABLE IN DUBAI, AND NAME AND ADDRESS OF THE COMPANY IN UAE TO APPLY TO FOR CLAIMS.

COVERING SHIPMENT OF THE FOLLOWING GOODS:

PAGE NO. 2

ATTACHED TO AND FORMING PART OF DOCUMENTARY CREDIT NO. ELC-TFS-001600 DATED 19 FEB., 2014
DOUBLE HORSE BRAND SPORTING SHOES AS PER S/C NO. VIM-UAE021 DATED 2014 FEB. 1. FOR DETAILS OF MERCHANDISE REFER PAGE NO.3 SHIPPING MARKS: 00LT07060/LOYAL/DUBAI/NO. 1-UP (TO BE STATED IN PACKING LIST AND BILL OF LADING) ADDITIONAL DOCUMENTS REQUIRED ARE LISTED ON THE COUNTINUATION SHEET ATTACHED.
DESPATCH/SHIPMENT FROM: ANY CHINESE PORT TO PORT RASHID, DUBAI LATEST 19 MARCH, 2014 PARTIAL SHIPMENT: ALLOWED TRANSSHIPMENT: ALLOWED
WE HEREBY ENGAGE WITH DRAWERS OR BONA FIDE HOLDERS THAT DRAFTS DRAWN IN CONFORMITY WITH THE TERMS OF THIS CREDIT WILL BE DULY HONOURED ON PRESENTATION AND DRAFTS ACCEPTED WITHIN THE TERMS OF THIS CREDIT WILL BE DULY HONOURED AT MATURITY.

DIRECTIONS TO ADVISING BANK:	ADVISING BANK'S NOTIFICATION
WE HAVE ISSUED THIS DOCUMENTARY CREDIT AS DETAILED ABOVE. WE REQUEST YOU TO NOTIFY THE CREDIT TO THE BENEFICIARY WITHOUT ADDING YOUR CONFIRMATION.	

OTHER DOCUMENTS REQUIRED: 5. SHIPMENT ADVICE QUOTING THE NAME OF THE CARRYING VESSEL, DATE OF SHIPMENT, NUMBER OF PACKAGES, MARKS, AMOUNT, LC NUMBER MUST BE MADE OUT TO APPLICANT AND ISSUING BANK BY FAX WITHIN 2 DAYS FROM THE DATE OF SHIPMENT. COPIES OF TRANSMITTED SHIPMENT ADVICES ACCOMPANIED BY TRANSMISSION REPORTS. 6. PACKING LIST IN TRIPLICATE SHOWING NET WEIGHT, GROSS WEIGHT AND MEASUREMENT OF EACH PACKAGE. 7. SHIPMENT MUST BE EFFECTED BY CONFERENCE LINE AND/OR REGULAR LINE VESSELS, WHICH ARE COVERED UNDER INSTITUTE CLASSIFICATION CLAUSE AND ARE NOT MORE THAN 15 YEARS OF AGE AND A CERTIFICATE TO THIS EFFECT ISSUED BY THE SHIPPING COMPANY OR THEIR AGENTS MUST ACCOMPANY THE DOCUMENTS. 8. CERTIFICATE ISSUED BY THE CARRIER/MASTER OR THEIR AGENT CERTIFYING THAT THE CARRYING VESSEL IS ALLOWED BY ARAB AUTHORITIES TO CALL AT ARABIAN PORTS AND IS NOT SCHEDULED TO CALL AT ANY ISRAELI PORT DURING ITS VOYAGE TO THE UNITED ARAB EMIRATES. IN CASE OF SHIPMENT BY UNITED ARAB SHIPPING CO. LINE VESSELS, SUCH CERTIFICATE IS NOT REQUIRED. 9. INSPECTION CERTIFICATE IN TWO COPIES ISSUED AT THE LOADING PORT. SPECIAL INSTRUCTIONS: 1. ANTE DATED DOCUMENTS ARE NOT ACCEPTABLE AND ALL DOCUMENTS TO BE DATED.

PAGE NO. 3

ATTACHED TO AND FORMING PART OF DOCUMENTARY CREDIT NO. ELC-TFS-001600
DATED 19 FEBRUARY, 2014

2. BILLS OF LADING ISSUED BY FREIGHT FORWARDERS ARE NOT ACCEPTABLE.
3. BILL OF LADING MUST NOT SHOW ANY CORRECTION/ALTERATION AND\OR DELETION EVEN WITH THE AUTHENTICATION FROM THE SHIPPING COMPANY OR THEIR AGENTS.
4. CHATER PARTY BILL OF LADING IS ACCEPTABLE.
5. ALL DOCUMENTS MUST QUOTE ISSUING BANK'S NAME, LETTER OF CREDIT NUMBER AND DATE OF ISSUE.
6. ALL DOCUMENTS MUST BE ISSUED IN ENGLISH LANGUAGE.
7. IF POSSIBLE INVOICES TO INDICATE HARMONIZED SYSTEM COMMODITY CODE NUMBER (H.S. CODE NUMBER). THE DEPARTMENT OF PORTS & CUSTOMS UAE WARNS SUPPLIERS THAT FAILURE TO QUOTE THE RELEVANT HARMONIZED SYSTEM (H.S.) COMMODITY CODE NUMBER ON THE COMMERCIAL INVOICE WILL RESULT IN UNNECESSARY DELAY IN CLEARANCE.
8. SHIPMENT MUST BE EFFECTED IN CONTAINER ON FCL BASIS AND BE INDICATED IN B/L.

DETAILS OF MERCHANDISE:
SPORTING SHOES

(1) V04-A-02/05/07	USD15.60	PER PAIR
(2) V04-B-01/06/09	USD18.50	PER PAIR
(3) V04-AG-02/05/09	USD20.20	PER PAIR
(4) V04-C-02/05/09	USD24.40	PER PAIR

BRAND: DOUBLE HORSE

PACKING: IN STRONG CARTONS AND INVOICE TO CERTIFY THE SAME
CIF RASHID, DUBAI INCOTERMS 2000

ALL OTHER DETAILS ARE AS PER INDENT NO. 00LT07060 OF M/S LOYAL TRADER, DUBAI, UAE AND INVOICE TO CERTIFY THE SAME.

FURTHER DIRECTIONS TO ADVISING/PRESENTING BANK:
* THE AMOUNT OF EACH DRAWING MUST BE ENDORSED ON REVERSE OF PAGE 1 OF THIS LC.
* DOCUMENTS MUST BE COURIERED TO US IN TWO LOTS.
* A DISCREPANCY HANDLING FEE OF USD50.00 OR ITS EQUIVALENT WILL BE DEDUCTED BY US TO BENEFICIARY FOR EACH SET OF DOCUMENTS PRESENTED WITH DISCREPANCY.
* ALL BANKING CHARGES OUTSIDE THE COUNTRY OF ISSUANCE OF THIS CREDIT ARE FOR BENEFICIARY'S ACCOUNT INCLUDING ADVISING AND PRESENTING BANK CHARGES.

PAGE NO. 4

ATTACHED TO AND FORMING PART OF DOCUMENTARY CREDIT NO. ELC-TFS-001600
DATED 19 FEB., 2014

*IF DOCUMENTS ARE PRESENTED BY ANY BANK OTHER THAN THE ADVISING BANK, THE PRESENTING BANK MUST CONFIRM ON THEIR COVERING SCHEDULE THAT ALL CHARGES OF ADVISING BANK HAVE BEEN PAID.

*PLEASE QUOTE OUR ABOVE LC REFERENCE NUMBER IN ALL YOUR COMMUNICATION AND CORRESPONDENCE TO OURSELVES.

*IN REIMBURSEMENT, PLEASE CLAIM ON OUR ACCOUNT WITH OUR NEW YORK BRANCH PROVIDED DOCUMENTS IN COMPLIANCE WITH THE CREDIT TERMS UNDER YOUR AUTHENTICATED SWIFT/TESTED TELEX TO US AND OUR FUNDS DEPT. IN PORT RASHID ADVISING THE DETAILS OF NEGOTIATION, SHIPMENT DATE, B/L NUMBER, NAME OF VESSEL, AND NUMBER OF COURIER RECEIPT FOR SENDING DOCUMENTS TO US BEFORE 3 DAYS FOR YOUR CLAIM.

------------------END OF THIS DOCUMENTARY CREDIT ---------------------

MR. C. ALUDAL. SLRA
AUTHORIZED SIGNATURE

14-4 装运货物相关资料：

货号	数量	计量单位	单价 (US$)	包装种类	装箱方式	毛重 (KG)	净重 (KG)	长 (CM)	宽 (CM)	高 (CM)
V04-A-02/05/07	3,328	PAIR	15.60	CTN	16	28	26	60	50	40
V04-B-01/06/09	3,500	PAIR	18.50	CTN	14	25	23	50	50	40
V04-AG-02/05/09	2,976	PAIR	20.20	CTN	12	24	22	43	45	52
V04-C-02/05/09	2,832	PAIR	24.40	CTN	12	24	22	40	60	44

承运船名和航次： FEI LONG V.230
装船日期： MAR.5, 2014
海运包箱费率： USD1,800.00

发票号码： VIMINV256
发票日期： FEB.8, 2014
保险费率： 0.80%
税则号： 6403.2000

综合审单操作全套货运单据 C14-4

上海维姆进出口有限责任公司

SHANGHAI VIM IMPORT & EXPORT CO., LTD.

350 WUZHONG ROAD, SHANGHAI 200331, CHINA

TEL NO.: 65268894　　FAX NO.: 65268895

COMMERCIAL　INVOICE

TO: LOYAL TRADING, P.O. BOX 6058,　　编号 No.：VIMINV256
DUBAI, U.A.E.　　日期 Date：2014/2/8
TEL NO.: 3535177　FAX NO.: 3535133

装船口岸　　目的地　　运输方式
From SHANGHAI　　To PORT RASHID, DUBAI　　By FEI LONG V. 230

信用证号数　　合同/订单号　　支付方式
L/C No. ELC-TFS-001600　S/C No. VIM-UAE021　Payment Term: L/C AT SIGHT

唛头 Marks and Numbers	品名 Description of Goods	数量 Quantity	包装件数 No. of Packages	单价 Unit Price	总金额 Amount
				CFR RASHID, DUBAI	
00LT07060 LOYAL DUBAI NO.1-942	DOUBLE HORSE BRAND SPORTING SHOES AS PER S/C NO. VIM-UAE012　DATED 2004 FEB.1.				
	V04-A-02/05/07	3,328		US$15.60	US$51,916.70
	V04-B-01/06/09	3,500		US$18.50	US$64,750.00
	V04-AG-02/05/09	2,976		US$20.20	US$60,115.20
	V04-C-02/05/09	2,832		US$24.40	US$69,100.80
	TOTAL:				USD245,882.80
TOTAL VALUE					

WE CERTIFY THE ORIGIN OF GOODS AND CONTENTS ARE TRUE AND CORRECT.

E. & O. E.

上海维姆进出口有限责任公司

SHANGHAI VIM IMPORT & EXPORT CO., LTD.

× × ×

（交单份数：一正三副）

PACKING NOTE

1) TO	2) INVOICE NO.	3) INVOICE DATE
LOYAL TRADER, P.O. BOX 6058, DUBAI, U.A.E. TEL NO.: 3535177 FAX NO.: 3535133	VIMINV256	FEB. 8, 2014
	4) MARKS & NO. 00LT07060 LOYAL RASHID NO.1-942	

5) NOS.	6) NOS. & KINDS OF PKGS	7) ITEM	8)QTY	9) G.W.(kg)	10) N.W.(kg)	11) MEAS(m3)
		DOUBLE HORSE BRAND SPORTING SHOES				
1-280	208CTN	V04-A-02/05/07	3,328PC	5,824.00	5,408.00	24.960
281-458	250CTN	V04-B-02/06/09	3,500PC	6,250.00	5,750.00	25.000
459-707	248CTN	V04-AG-02/05/09	2,976PC	5,952.00	5,456.00	24.954
708-942	236CTN	V04-C-02/05/09	2,832PC	5,646.00	5,192.00	24.921
TTL	942CTN		12,636PC	23,690.00	21,806.00	99.835

SAY NINE HUNDRED AND FORTY TWO CARTONS.

ISSUED BY

SIGNATURE

交单份数：1 正 2 副

1. Exporter (full name and address) SHANGHAI VIM IMPORT & EXPORT CO., LTD. 305 WUZHONG ROAD, SHANGHAI 200331, CHINA TEL NO.65268894　FAX NO.65268895	Certificate No.　VIMORI122 **CERTIFICATE OF ORIGIN** **OF** **THE PEOPLE'S REPUBLIC OF CHINA**
2. Consignee (full name, address, country) LOYAL TRADER P.O. BOX 6058, DUBAI, U.A.E. TEL NO.: 3535177　FAX NO.: 3535133	
3. Means of transport and route FROM SHANGHAI TO PORT RASHID, DUBAI BY SEA	5. For certifying authority use only
4. COUNTRY/REGION OF DESTINATION PORT RASHID, DUBAI	

6. Marks and Numbers of Packages	7. Description of Goods; Number and Kind of Packages	8. H.S. Code	9. Quantity or Weight	10. Number and Date of Invoice
00LT007060 LOYAL DUBAI NO.1-942	SPORTING SHOES 942 CASES (SAY NINE HUNDRED AND FORTY ONLY)	6,403.2000	23,690KG	VIMINV256 8 FEB., 2014

11. **Declaration by the exporter** The undersigned hereby declares that the above details and statements are true and correct; that all the goods were produced in China and that they comply with the Rules of Origin of the People's Republic of China. SHANGHAI VIM IMPORT & EXPORT CO., LTD.　×××　（盖章） SHANGHAI　2004/3/9 Place and date. signature and stamp of authorized authority	12. **Certification** It is hereby certified that the declaration by the exporter is true and correct. （沪） CHINA COUNCIL FOR THE PROMOTION OF INTERNATIONAL TRADE （SHANGHAI） 陶绍延 SHANGHAI　7 MAR., 2014 Place and date. signature and stamp of certifying authority

中保（财产）保险有限公司 上海 分公司

The People's Insurance (Property) Company of China, Ltd., Shanghai Branch

发票号码
Invoice No.

保险单号次
Policy No. VIMINS124

海 洋 货 物 运 输 保 险 单

MARINE CARGO TRANSPORTATION INSURANCE POLICY

被保险人:
The Insured: SHANGHAI VIM IMPORT & EXPORT CO., LTD.

中保财产保险有限公司（以下简称本公司）根据被保险人的要求，及其所缴付约定的保险费，按照本保险单承担的险别和背面所载条款与下列特别条款承保下列货物运输保险，特签发本保险单。

This policy of Insurance witnesses that The People's Insurance (Property) Company of China, Ltd. (hereinafter called "The Company"), at the request of the Insured and consideration of the premium paid by the Insurers, undertakes to insure the under-mentioned goods in transportation subject to the condition of this Policy as per the Clauses printed overleaf and other special clauses attached hereon.

保险货物项目 Descriptions of Goods	包装 单位 数量 Parking Unit Quantity	保险金额 Amount Insured
SPORTING SHOES	942 CTNS	USD 245,882.80

承保险别
Condition COVERING ICC (A) & ICC WAR

货物标记
Marks of Goods AS PER INVOICE NO. VIMINV256

总保险金额：
Total Amount Insured: U.S. DOLLARS TWO HUNDRED FORTY FIVE THOUSAND EIGHT HUNDRED EIGHTY TWO AND 80/100 ONLY

保费
Premium AS ARRANGED

运输工具
Per conveyance S. S FEI LONG

开航日期
Slg. on or abt AS PER B/L NO. VIMBL142

起运港
From SHANGHAI

目的港
To PORT RASHID, DUBAI

所保货物，如发生本保险单项下可能引起索赔的损失或损坏，应立即通知本公司下述代理人查勘。如有索赔，应向本公司提交保险单正本（本保险单共有　份正本）及有关文件。如一份正本已用于索赔，其余正本则自动失效。

In the event of loss or damage which may result in a claim under this Policy, immediate notice must be given to the Company's Agent as mentioned hereunder. Claims, if any, one of the Original Policy which has been issued in　Original (s) together with the relevant documents shall be surrendered to the Company. If one of the Original Policy has been accomplished, the others to be void.

ENOC Complex, Sheikh Rashid Road
P.O. Box 6442, Dubai, UAE
Tel: 3374400 Fax: 3134202

ORIGINAL

中保财产保险有限公司 上海 分公司
THE PEOPLE'S INSURANCE (PROPERTY) COMPANY OF CHINA, LTD.
SHANGHAI BRANCH

赔款偿付地点
Claim payable at / in RASHID, DUBAI

General Manager:

The People's Insurance (Property) Company of China, Ltd

日期
Date 2014/3/7

在
at SHANGHAI

地址：中国上海中山东一路 23 号 TEL:3234305 3217466-44 Telex:33128 PICCS CN.
Address: 23 Zhongshan Dong Yi Lu Shanghai, China. Cable: 42001 Shanghai

Shipper SHANGHAI VIM IMPORT & EXPORT CO., LTD. 305 WUZHONG ROAD, SHANGHAI 200331, CHINA TEL NO. 65268894　FAX NO. 65268895	B/L NO.　VIMBL124 **COSCO** 中国远洋运输（集团）总公司 **CHINA OCEAN SHIPPING (GROUP) CO.** **CABLE: COSCO BEIJING** **TELEX: 210740 CPC CN** ORIGINAL Combined Transport B/L
Consignee TO THE ORDER OF SHIPPER	
Notify LOYAL TRADER P.O. BOX 6085, DUBAI, U.A.E. TEL NO.: 3535177　FAX NO.: 3535133	

Pre-carriage by	Place of Receipt	
Ocean Vessel Voy. No. FEI LONG V. 230	Port of Loading SHANGHAI	
Port of Discharge PORT RASHID, DUBAI	Place of Delivery	*Final Destination　via

Container No.	Seal No. Marks & No.	No. & Kind of Packages; Description of Goods	Gross Weight	Measurement
	AS PER INVOICE NO.VIMINV265	942 CTNS OF SPORTING SHOES	23,690KG	98.835M³

TOTAL NUMBER OF CONTAINERS OR PACKAGES (IN WORDS)　SAY NINE HUNDRED FORTY TWO CARTONS

Freight & Charges	Revenue Tons	Rate	Per	Prepaid	Collect

Ex. Rate	Prepaid at:	Payable at	Place and Date of Issue: SHANGHAI　8 FEB., 2014
	Total Prepaid	No. of Original B/L THREE　(3)	Signed as the Carrier above/as the Agent for the Carrier above

LADEN ON BOARD OF THE VESSEL Date　By __COSCO______ 8 FEB., 2014　邢建伟 COSCO STANDARD FORM11　(TERMS CONTINUED ON BACK HEREOF)	COSCO AS CARRIER ABOVE 邢建伟

背书：SHANGHAI VIM IMPORT & EXPORT CO., LTD.　　交单：3 份

×　×　×

上海维姆进出口有限责任公司

SHANGHAI VIM IMPORT & EXPORT CO., LTD.

350 WUZHONG ROAD, SHANGHAI 200331, CHINA

TEL NO.:65268894 FAX NO.:65268895

SHIPPING ADVICE

Date: MAR. 8, 2014 # of pages: 01/1

To: LOYAL TRADER (FAX NO.: 3553133)

From: SHANGHAI VIM IMPORT & EXPORT CO., LTD. (FAX NO.:65268895)

Attn:

Dear Sirs:

Re: Shipment of DOUBLE HORSE BRAND SPORTING SHOES

Under Covering Note/Open Policy No.

Letter of Credit No. ELC-TFS-001600

In compliance with your requirement for insurance purpose as set forth in the said credit, we wish to advise you that the captioned shipment has been effected. The details of the shipment are as follows:

Commodity:	DOUBLE HORSE BRAND SPORTING SHOES
Quantity:	12636PC
Total Value:	USD 245,882.80
Port of Loading:	SHANGHAI
Port of Destination:	PORT RASHID, DUBAI
Gross Weight:	23,690KG
Measurement:	$98.835M^3$
Contract No./Order No.	VIM-UAE021
Bill of Lading No.	VIMBL124

We hope that the shipment will reach you in a good condition and we are expecting more opportunities for us to cooperate with you.

Yours faithfully,

SHANGHAI VIM IMPORT & EXPORT CO., LTD.

× × ×

BILL OF EXCHANGE

No. VIMINV256

For HKD 245,882.80　　　　　　　　　　DUBAI　2004/3/8

(amount in figure)　　　　　　　　　　(place and date of issue)

At 30 DAYS sight of this FIRST Bill of Exchange (SECOND being unpaid)

Pay to LOYAL TRADER, P.O. BOX 6058, DUBAI, U.A.E. or order

the sum of U.S. DOLLARS TWO HUNDRED FORTY FIVE THOUSAND EIGHT HUNDRED EIGHTY TWO AND EIGHTY CENTS ONLY

(amount in words)

Value received for ____________ of ____________

(quantity)　　　　(name of commodity)

Drawn under EMIRATES BANK INTERNATIONAL PJSC

L/C No. ELC-TFS-006100 dated FEB. 19, 2014

To:

EMIRATES BANK INTERNATIONAL PJSC

TRADE FINANCE SERVICES

For and on behalf of

____

(signature)

C14-5　探索学习开立与审核信用证项目，并根据操作 C3-1 的资料，尝试填写开立信用证申请书。

C14-6　探索学习开立与审核信用证项目，并根据附录 2 里操作题 C3-2 的资料，尝试审核相关信用证，并记录不符点，提出修改意见。

模块五

合同价格和盈亏核算

在国际贸易单证工作中有很多费用的计算，需要计算运费、保险金额和保险费、佣金、折扣、利息或贴现息、两种以上货币汇价的换算、不同贸易术语的价格换算，以及核算合同价格、盈亏额和盈亏率等。

价格核算是出口业务的关键一环，也是单证业务的实际需要。它直接关系到交易磋商成败和签约双方的经济利益。事实上，核算合同价格和盈亏情况，是在国际贸易的对外报价环节和签约环节进行的。

上述各种计算的操作，大多已在前面各个项目里介绍和学习过了。本项目仅对核算出口合同价格和出口合同盈亏进行介绍和学习。

项目十五

核算合同价格和盈亏

学习目标

［知识目标］掌握核算出口合同价格的方法，掌握核算出口合同盈亏成本的方法。
［能力目标］能熟练、准确核算出口合同价格，能熟练、准确核算出口合同盈亏成本。

一、核算合同价格

项目描述（案例情境描述）

为加强经济核算，提高准确合理报价的计算能力和效率，有必要对出口价格核算进行扎实地学习和训练。现以一则实例进行价格核算操作演示。

例题 15-1

某公司拟与客户签约，出口一批货物到阿根廷布宜诺斯艾利斯港。请根据下列资料核算 CIF 美元单价。
品名：旋风牌足球（“Tiger” Football）　货号：SWB32S　报价数量：一个 20’集装箱
包装：24 只/纸箱　尺码：58×42×41cm　毛重/净重：14kg/12kg
工厂供货价格：165 元/只　增值税率：17%　出口退税率：8%
国内费用：包装费每箱 20 元；每个 20’集装箱货物所需支付的其他费用有：仓储费 125 元，国内运杂费 250 元，商检费 100 元，报关费 50 元，港口费 200 元，业务费 1 000 元，其他 400 元。
海运费：一个 20 英尺集装箱从上海至 BUENOS AIRES 的包箱费率为 3 600 美元。
保险为发票金额加成 10%投保一切险，费率为 0.9%。
报价预期利润率为 15%，报价中需包括 5%的佣金。
人民币兑美元汇率为 8.25:1（注意计算过程保留四位小数，结果保留两位小数）

操作要领（出口报价核算讲解）

1. 出口商品价格的构成

众所周知，以 CIF 交货条件为例，国际贸易价格的表示方法为 EUR 24.00 per set CIF Hamburg，它表明了这个单价里包含了卖方的成本以及到目的港的保险费和海运费，同时也说明了一般价格里包含的要素有成本（cost）、费用（expenses）和利润（profit）。

2. 成本的核算

同世界其他许多国家实行退税政策一样，为了避免外国消费者既为出口国政府纳税，又为其本国政府纳税这种双重纳税的情况出现，我国政府在出口环节实行了退税政策和举措。在这种制度下，出口方在对外核价时，往往都将政府的退税额按公布的退税率预先算出并从采购成本中予以扣除。因此，我们的出口成本就有采购成本（增值税发票价成本或出厂价）与实际成本（扣除退税额的成本）的概念之分。公式推导和计算方法如下：

由于，采购成本 = 含税成本（发票款）
= 生产成本 + 增值税额 = 生产成本 + 生产成本 × 增值税率（17%）
= 生产成本（1 + 增值税率 17%）

则，生产成本 = 含税成本（发票款）÷（1 + 增值税率）

又，出口退税收入 = 生产成本 × 退税率
= 含税成本（发票款）× 退税率 ÷（1 + 增值税率）

则，实际成本 = 含税成本 − 退税收入
（退税后） = 含税成本 − 含税成本 × 退税率 ÷（1 + 增值税率）
= 含税成本 ×〔1 − 退税率 ÷（1 + 增值税率）〕

或 $$= \frac{\text{含税成本（1+增值税率）}}{\text{1+增值税率}} - \frac{\text{含税成本×退税率}}{\text{1+增值税率}}$$

$$= \frac{\text{含税成本×（1+增值税率 − 退税率）}}{\text{1+增值税率}}$$

※ 本案例操作：

货号：SWB32S

实际成本=165 −165 × 8% ÷ 1.17 = 165（1 − 8% ÷ 1.17）= 153.717 9 元

3. 各种费用的核算

进出口价格里含有各种费用，包括关税、国内费用和国外费用。

（1）关税额：各国海关对进出口货物征收的税额。我国海关计征进出口关税额均以完税价为计算基数。完税价以元为单位，采用进位取整的方法，关税额保留两位小数，具体公式如下：

进口关税额 = CIF 合同价 × 汇率中间价 × 进口关税率

（FOB 和 CFR 价须换算成 CIF 价）

出口关税额 = FOB 离岸价 × 汇率中间价 × 出口关税率/（1 + 出口关税率）

我国仅对极少数出口商品计征出口关税。因此，绝大多数商品出口关税率为零。

（2）国内费用：为了清晰概念，方便计算，我们通常把本币支出的费用称为国内费用，涉及包装费、仓储费、国内运输费、港区港杂费、认证费、商检费、报关费、关税、垫款利息、差旅费、通讯费、接待费、其他费用等四大板块的费用，即仓储运杂费、证书费、银行利息和业务费用。计算方法如下（务必分清总体费用和单独费用）：

1）每个单位商品的包装费用分摊：单个包装费 ÷ 包装方法

2）各项费用相加之和，再分摊到单个商品：总费用额 ÷ 总订货量

3）定额费用：含税采购价 × 定额费用率（以收购价为基数测算出相对稳定的费用比率。事实上，这种计算费用的方法更适应业务的需要，被更广泛地使用）

4）资金利息：含税采购价 × 年利率 × 资金占用天数÷360（这是使用资金的成本）

5）进口增值税：（关税完税价格 + 关税）÷（1–消费税率）× 增值税率（进口计算才用）

（3）国外费用：相应地，凡是用外币支付的费用都被称作国外费用，包括了主运费、保险费、客户佣金、银行手续费等。

1）主运费的分摊：海运费（或空运费）÷总订货量

2）保险费：CIF 成交价 ×（1 + 投保加成率）× 保险费率

3）客户佣金：含佣价（成交合同价）× 佣金率

4）银行手续费：银行手续费总额 ÷ 总订货量，或 CIF 成交价 × 银行费用率（这是银行提供服务而收取的劳务费用，小额交易才予计算，大额贸易往往忽略不计）

（4）确定起订量的方法

由于核算价格需要把费用分摊到单一单位的商品上，这就需要预先计算出起订量（Minimum Quantity）。国际贸易中常用的最小规格货柜为 20 英尺集装箱，通常是以此货柜整箱装（FCL）的数量作为起订量或装货总量。核算起订量的具体方法如下（全部计算过程保留四位小数，结果保留两位小数）：

1）计算出每件包装的重量吨和尺码吨（毛重单位为公吨 MT，尺码单位为体积 m^3）

2）比较两者的大小，以确定运费吨（按 W/M 计费标准，重量和体积从高计收）

3）计算一个 20 英尺货柜（集装箱）整箱所能装的包装件数（去掉小数位，取整）

常见集装箱有效装载：常见集装箱规格	有效装载体积	有效装载重量
1A 型（40 英尺）：8’ × 8’ × 40’	$55m^3$	24.5MT
1C 型（20 英尺）：8’ × 8’ × 20’	$25m^3$	17.5MT

例 1　某商品的外包装毛重 24kg，尺码 60 × 50 × 40cm，计算 20’货柜的装柜量：

24÷1 000 = 0.024MT，0.6 × 0.5 × 0.4 = $0.12m^3$，尺码＞毛重，取尺码计算，即

25÷0.12 = 208.333 3 件外包装，去位取整得 208 件外包装。

例 2 某商品的外包装毛重 60kg，尺码 40 × 40 × 30cm，计算 20’货柜的装柜量：

60 ÷ 1 000 = 0.06MT，0.4 × 0.4 × 0.3 = 0.048m^3，毛重＞尺码，取重量计算，即

17.5 ÷ 0.06 = 291.666 6 件外包装，去位取整得 291 件外包装。

4）根据装箱方法，计算装柜的货物总数量：装箱方法 × 装柜的包装件数

※本案例操作：

货号：SWB32S

① 一个 20’的集装箱能装运的货物数量：

尺码 0.58 × 0.42 × 0.41 = 0.099 88m^3，毛重 14 ÷ 1 000 = 0.014，尺码＞毛重，取体积。

25 ÷ 0.099 88 = 250.30 箱，去位取整，得 250 箱。24 × 250 = 6 000 只

② 国内费用：（20 × 250 + 250 + 100 + 50 + 200 + 125 + 1 000 + 400）÷ 6 000 = 7125÷6 000

= 1.187 5 元

③ 出口运费：3 600 ÷ 6 000 = 0.6 美元，或 3 600 × 8.25 ÷ 6 000 = 4.950 0 元

4. 预期利润的核算

利润是出口价格包含的三大因素之一，预期利润的大小由出口企业自行决定。利润可以用某一固定的数额表示，也可用利润率表示。用利润率表示时，应当注意计算的基数，既可以用某一成本作计算基数，也可用销售价格作为计算的基数。

生产成本利润额：生产成本 × 利润率　　　　（生产部门使用）

出口成本利润额：出口总成本 × 利润率　　　　（财务部门使用）

销售收入利润额：出口报价（CIF 价）× 利润率　（业务部门常用）

5. 核算出口价格的公式推导和计算方法

推导一个投保加成 10%的 CIFC3 的出口价格核算公式，为方便起见，设 CIFC3 为 X。

X =（出厂价或收购价−出口退税额 + 国内费用）÷ 汇率 + 主运费 + 佣金%X + 预期利润%X + 1.1 × 保险费%X + 银行费%X

X−佣金%X−预期利润%X−1.1 × 保险费%X−银行费%X =（退税后成本 + 国内运杂费）÷ 汇率 + 主运费

X*（1−佣金% − 预期利润% − 1.1 × 保险费% − 银行费%）=（退税后成本 + 国内运杂费）÷ 汇率 + 主运费

$$X=\frac{（退税后成本+国内运杂费）\div 汇率+主运费}{1-佣金\%-预期利润\%-1.1\times 保险费\%-银行费\%}$$ 即

$$CIFC3=\frac{[出厂价\times（1-退税率\div 1.17）+国内费用]\div 汇率+主运费}{1-（佣金\%+预期利润\%+1.1\times 保险费\%+银行手续费\%）}$$

需要说明的是：这是一个通用公式，也可以用来计算 CFR 价格和 FOB 价格。当银行手续费为具体金额时，应放在分子跟主运费相加。增值税率较为固定为 17%，投保加成通常为 10%。

※本案例操作：

货号：SWB32S

$$\text{CIFC5}=\frac{(153.7179+1.1875)\div8.25+0.60}{1-(5\%+15\%+1.1\times0.9\%)}=\frac{154.9054\div8.25+0.60}{1-(5+15+1.1\times0.9)\div100}$$

$$=19.3764\div0.7901=\text{USD}24.52$$

答：对外出口货物 CIF 含佣 5%的价格应为每只足球 24.52 美元。

相关知识

在价格磋商过程中，卖方报价后买方通常会还价。如果买方的还盘无法再提高，卖方又想保持一定的利润率，卖方应该考虑怎么核算新的收购价去跟国内的供应商进行价格谈判。现介绍根据报价核算公式推导变形得到的核算国内收购价公式：

$$\text{国内收购价}=\frac{[\text{卖价}(1-\text{利润率}-\text{佣金率}-1.1\times\text{保费率})-\text{主运费}]\times\text{汇率}-\text{国内各项费用之和}}{1-\text{退税率}/(1+\text{增值税率})}$$

即

$$\text{国内收购价}=\frac{(\text{卖价}-\text{各种国外费用})\times\text{汇率}-\text{利润}-\text{国内各项费用之和}}{1-\text{退税率}/(1+\text{增值税率})}$$ 即

$$\text{国内收购价}=\frac{\text{人民币净收入}-\text{利润}-\text{国内各项费用之和}}{1-\text{退税率}/(1+\text{增值税率})}$$

在国内的一些外贸公司里经常使用一张成本核算表格，清楚地列出各项核算内容。现介绍如下：

出口成交核算表

编号__________　　日期___________

商品名称及规格______________　　出口国家/地区__________

供货单位______________________　　成交价格_______________

买方__________________________　　汇率___________________

成交数量______________________

装卸口岸/地点：从__________至__________经由___________

成本	1. 进货成本（含税成本）： 增值税率：______% 消费税率：_______% 2. 出口退税收入： 退税率：______% 3. 实际采购成本：
费用	1. 出口运费（外币/本币）： 包装： 毛重： 尺码： 计算标准和费率： 2. 出口保险费（外币/本币）： 投保险别及相应保险费率： 加____成投保金额： 3. 客户佣金（外币/本币）： 4. 佣金率：______% 5. 国内费用（外币/本币）： 包装费： 仓储费： 经营管理费： 商检费： 运杂费： 报关费： 其他费用：
利润	利润额（外币/本币）： 利润率______%

操作能力训练

思考题：S15-1 为什么计算出口报价过程中要保留四位小数，结果只保留两位小数呢？

S15-2 如果主运费是以美元计收的，出口报价需要以其他币别核算，怎么计算才能既清楚又快捷呢？

操作题：C15-1 根据本项目附录 4（见本书第 311 页）里提供的其余出口报价计算题，独立逐一计算出口报价。

C15-2 探索学习盈亏核算，根据本项目附录 4（见本书第 311 页）里提供的盈亏题 15-3，尝试核算合同的盈亏。

二、核算合同盈亏

项目描述（案例情境描述）

出口成本核算或出口合同盈亏核算是指对拟成交或已成交的盈亏额和盈亏率进行核算，是出口业务的一项十分重要的工作，也是加强业务管理极为重要的一环，符合单证业务的实际需要，有利于及时总结交易情况。出口签约前要做到心中有数，必须做好成本核算工作。

盈亏核算现在主要采用两个重要的衡量指标：出口换汇成本和出口盈亏率。为加强经济核算，提高准确进行出口合同盈亏核算的计算能力，有必要对出口成交的盈亏核算进行扎实的学习和训练。现以一则实例进行盈亏核算操作演示。

例题 15-2

某公司拟与客户签约，出口一批货物 14 250 双，签约总额为 75 817 美元 CIF 大阪。该批商品购进价为 574 980 元（含增值税 17%），费用定额率为 6%，出口退税率为 9%，保险费为 1 015 美元，海运费为 2 840 美元，当时银行汇价的美元买入价为 8.30 元人民币。

请根据上述资料核算该笔业务出口盈亏率。

（注意计算过程保留四位小数，结果保留两位小数）

操作要领（合同盈亏核算讲解，盈亏率和换汇成本）

（一）核算出口盈亏率

核算出口合同的盈亏情况，通常是根据拟成交价或已成交价核算盈亏额和盈亏率，以求掌握执行该笔业务的前景。

1. 核算出口盈亏涉及的几个概念

盈亏率：如前所述，出口盈亏率实际上分为出口销售盈亏率和出口成本盈亏率。其区别就在于，以销售收入（即出口成交金额）为基数作分母的为销售盈亏率；以成本支出（即出口总成本）为基数作分母的即为成本盈亏率。业务部门通常用销售盈亏率进行业务管理。

出口总成本：出口总成本实为出口实际总成本，它是外贸企业采购价（生产企业出厂价）+国内费用（关税额、包装费、运杂费、业务费、证书费、资金利息等）–出口退税额，即

出口总成本=商品进货价+国内费用–出口退税收入，或实际成本+各项国内费用之和

出口外汇净收入：外汇毛收入（拟成交总额）扣除各项外汇支出（海运费、保险费、佣金、银行手续费）等国外费用，即

外汇净收入＝外汇毛收入–外汇总支出

出口人民币净收入：出口外汇净收入按当时银行外汇牌价买入价折算的人民币总额，即

人民币净收入＝外汇净收入×银行汇率（买入价）

出口人民币毛收入：出口外汇毛收入按当时银行外汇牌价买入价折算的人民币总额（出口人民币总收入），即

人民币毛收入＝外汇毛收入×银行汇率（买入价）

2. 出口盈亏额和盈亏率的计算方法

我们知道，盈亏率分为出口销售盈亏率和出口成本盈亏率，核算盈亏率都跟盈亏额有关。因此，核算盈亏率应先计算出盈亏额，即收入－支出。其结果为正数即盈利；负数为亏损。

在此基础上，以总收入为基数作分母，计算结果则为销售盈亏率；若以出口总成本作为分母，计算结果则为成本盈亏率。

（1）出口销售盈亏率

根据出口价格核算公式，可推导出口销售盈亏率核算公式：

$$\text{CIFC} = \frac{(\text{实际成本}+\text{国内费用})\div\text{汇率}+\text{海运费}}{1-\text{利润率}-\text{佣金率}-1.1\times\text{保费率}}$$

〔CIFC（1–利润率–佣金率–1.1×保费率）–海运费〕×汇率

＝实际成本＋国内费用

〔CIFC（1–佣金率–1.1×保费率）–CIFC×利润率–海运费〕×汇率

＝实际成本＋国内费用

〔CIFC（1–佣金率–1.1×保费率）–海运费〕×汇率–CIFC×利润率×汇率

＝实际成本＋国内费用

〔CIFC（1–佣金率–1.1×保费率）–海运费〕×汇率–（实际成本＋国内费用）

＝CIFC×利润率×汇率

$$\text{利润率}=\frac{[\text{CIFC}(1-\text{佣金率}-1.1\times\text{保费率})-\text{海运费}]\times\text{汇率}-(\text{实际成本}+\text{国内费用})}{\text{CIFC}\times\text{汇率}\times 100\%}$$

即，$\text{利润率}=\dfrac{\text{外汇净收入}\times\text{汇率}-\text{出口实际总成本}}{\text{外汇毛收入}\times\text{汇率}}\times 100\%$

因此，$\text{出口销售盈亏率}=\dfrac{\text{亏额（人民币净收入}-\text{出口总成本）}}{\text{出口总收入（人民币毛收入）}}\times 100\%$

（2）出口成本盈亏率

将上述公式的分母改为出口总成本，即为出口成本盈亏率公式。

$$即，出口成本盈亏率=\frac{盈亏额（人民币净收入-出口总成本）}{出口总成本}\times 100\%$$

※本案例操作：

解题 1：出口销售盈亏率

出口销售人民币净收入＝外汇净收入×汇率＝（75 817–1 015–2 840）×8.30
＝597 284.60 元

出口总成本＝574 980（1–0.09/1.17）＋574 980×6%＝530 750.81＋34 498.80
＝565 249.61 元

或　＝574 980×（1＋6%）–574 980×0.09/1.17＝609 478.80–44 229.23
＝565 249.57 元

人民币毛收入（出口外汇总额×汇率）＝75 817×8.30＝629 281.10 元

盈亏额＝597 284.60–565 249.61＝32 034.99 元，或 597 284.60–565 249.57
＝32 035.03 元

当然，也可以用收支两条线的思路核算盈亏额，即

人民币净收入＋退税收入–出口成本＝597 284.60＋44 229.23–609 478.80
＝32 035.03 元

$$出口销售盈亏率=\frac{32\ 035}{629\ 281.10}\times 100\% = 5.09\%$$

答：该笔业务销售利润率为 5.09%。

解题 2：出口成本盈亏率

$$出口成本盈亏率=\frac{人民币净收入-出口实际总成本}{出口实际总成本}\times 100\%$$

$$=\frac{597\ 284.60-565\ 249.57}{565\ 249.57}\times 100\% =5.67\%$$

答：该笔业务出口成本利润率为 5.67%。

（二）计算出口换汇成本

出口换汇成本是指出口商品净收入一个单位外汇所需的人民币成本，即用多少元人民币换回一美元或一个单位其他货币。它是一项衡量外贸企业和进出口业务盈亏的重要指标。

1. 核算换汇成本涉及的几个概念

出口总成本：或称出口实际总成本，它是所有本币支出减除退税额后的所得。

外汇净收入：如前所学，它是对外签约金额减去所有外币支出的所得。

2. 出口换汇成本的计算方法

首先需要计算出人民币出口总成本，然后计算出外汇净收入，两项相除。要求比值结果保留四位小数。当换汇率＜银行牌价时，表示盈利；反之，则表示亏损。计算公式如下：

$$出口换汇成本=\frac{出口总成本（人民币）}{出口销售外汇净收入（外币）}\quad 即$$

$$=\frac{退税后实际成本+各项国内费用}{拟成交额-海运费-保险费-佣金-银行手续费}$$

※本案例操作：

出口总成本 = 574 980 ×（1 + 6%）−574 980 × 0.09/1.17 = 609 478.80−44 229.23
=565 249.57 元

或　574 980（1−0.09/1.17）+ 574 980 × 6% =530 750.81 + 34 498.80 = 565 249.61 元

出口销售外汇净收入 = 75 817−1 015−2 840 = 71 962.00 美元

$$出口换汇成本=\frac{56\ 5249.57}{71\ 962.00}=7.854\ 8$$

（三）用换汇成本核算盈亏率

同样的，核算盈亏率必然先核算盈亏额。

1. 核算盈亏率涉及的几个概念

外汇净收入：前面已做介绍，它是签约金额减去所有外币支出的所得。

人民币毛收入：如前所学，它是对外签约外币金额乘以银行买入价汇率所得。

2. 出口换汇成本核算盈亏的计算方法

（1）盈亏额

用银行外汇汇率买入价作为收入，减去换汇成本，再乘以外汇净收入即得到盈亏额。

盈亏额=（银行外汇汇率买入价−换汇成本）× 外汇净收入

※本案例操作：

出口利润额=（8.30−7.854 8）× 71 962 = 32 037.48 元

（2）出口销售盈亏率

用计算获得的盈亏额这个结果除以人民币毛收入，即可得到销售盈亏率。即

$$出口销售盈亏率=\frac{（银行外汇汇率买入价-换汇成本）\times 外汇净收入}{人民币毛收入\times 100\%}$$

※本案例操作：

人民币毛收入 = 出口外汇毛收入 × 汇率买入价 = 75 817 × 8.30 = 629 281.10 元

出口销售利润率 = 32 037.48/75 817 × 8.30 × 100% = 5.09%

（3）出口成本盈亏率

用银行外汇汇率买入价作为收入，减去换汇成本得到盈亏额，再除以换汇成本。即

$$出口成本盈亏率=\frac{（银行外汇汇率买入价-换汇成本）}{换汇成本\times 100\%}$$

※本案例操作：

出口成本利润率 = （8.30−7.854 8）/ 7.854 8 × 100% = 5.67%

答：该笔业务换汇成本为 7.854 8，销售利润率为 5.09%，成本利润率为 5.67%。

至此，可以肯定，经两种方法验算，本案例核算的销售利润率和成本利润率都是正确的。

实际上，用换汇成本核算盈亏率跟前面介绍的盈亏率核算方法道理是相通的。在实践中，这两种方法可以互为验证或检验。

操作能力训练

思考题： S15-3　为什么计算换汇成本要保留四位小数呢？

S15-4　想一想用换汇成本核算盈亏额和盈亏率的道理。

操作题： C15-3　根据本项目附录 4 里提供的其余盈亏核算题，独立核算合同盈亏。

附录 4　合同核算计算题

题 15-1　卡拉奇（KARACH）某客户对上海奇乐公司的“飞跃”牌缝纫机表示极大兴趣，首次订单量为 1 × 20’FCL。产品具体资料如下：（增值税为 17%，退税率为 9%）

型号	包装方式	供货价格	尺码（cm）	毛/净重（kg）
GN800	1 台/箱	260（元/台）	43 × 35 × 35	9.17/7.0

费用：出口定额费率为 4%；垫款 30 天，垫款利率为 8%（一年按 360 天计）；海洋运费为 1 900 美元/20’集装箱；货物按 CIFC3 价格的 110%投保一切险和战争险（费率分别是 0.85%和 0.5%）；预期客户要求的佣金率是 3%。公司报价利润率为 10%；美元兑人民币汇率为 1:7.25。

请计算奇乐公司向该客户报出的 FOB、CFR、CIF 价格。

题 15-2 信梁公司欲出口一批不锈钢厨具至开普敦，3 个货号各装一个 20’货柜

货　号	包装方式	长 CM	宽 CM	高 CM	毛重 KG	购货成本
3SA1012	2 套/纸箱	24	15	25	11	180 元
3SA1013	2 套/纸箱	61.5	30.5	74	22	144 元
3SA1004	8 套/纸箱	63	35.5	25	14	55 元

已知上海至开普敦 20 英尺 FCL 海运费为 2 200 美元，增值税率为 17%，退税率为 9%。加一成投保一切险加战争险，保险费率分别是 0.8%和 0.3%。这批货包装费每箱 2 元，国内定额费用率为 3.4%，银行贷款年利率为 5.3%（一年按 360 天计算），公司垫款 50 天。如果公司预期利润率为成交金额的 12%，银行手续费 300 美元，客户要求 3%的佣金。请报出第三个货号的 CIFC3 CAPETOWN 价格。（人民币兑美元汇率为 6.67:1）

题 15-3 我方向泰国某公司出口一批货号为 BY200234 的高压电缆。

包装方式为 55 米/箱，尺码为 50×40×24cm，毛重为 66 公斤。

供货价：60 元/米，增值税：17%，退税率：13%

国内费用：包装费 15 元/箱；一个 20’集装箱费用如下：

仓储费 500 元，国内运杂费 800 元，商检费 150 元，报关费 50 元，港口费用 400 元，业务费用 1 200 元，其他费用 2 100 元，证书费为整批货采购价的 0.2%。

保险：按发票金额加成 10%，投保一切险和战争险，费率分别为 0.9%和 0.3%

海运费：从上海到曼谷港一个 20’集装箱运费为 750 美元

汇率：6.45 元人民币/美元，公司预期利润：10%。

（1）请根据上述条件，试报该产品的 CIFC5 每米单价（起订量为一个 20’货柜）；

（2）对方还盘 CIFC5 价格为 9.67 美元，计算我方销售利润额和利润率是多少；

（3）按对方还盘价，同时保持 8%的利润，则国内供货价应为多少？

题 15-4 盛大有限公司收到曼彻斯特（Manchester）的 F.B.B. IMP & EXP CO., LTD. 传真，表示对其经营的陶瓷器皿感兴趣，并对其中的汤碟（SOUP PLATE）询盘。

品名：汤碟（Soup Plate），货号：S4314-4326

包装方式：8 套/纸箱，毛/净重：10 千克/8 千克，尺码：54.5×35×24cm

供货价：95 元/套，退税率：8%，增值税率：17%

费用：包装费每箱 8 元，定额费用率（国内运杂费为供货价的）1.205%，银行手续费为成交金额的 0.5%。银行贷款年利率为 5.3%（一年按 360 天计算），公司垫款 50 天。

保险：按发票金额的 110%投保海运一切险和战争险，费率分别是 0.8%和 0.5%

海运费：上海至曼彻斯特 20’集装箱包箱费率是 2 230 美元。

预期利润：10%，汇率：美元兑人民币汇率为 1:6.7611，英镑兑人民币为 1:8.8478。

（1）根据外方公司要求，报出每套汤碟的 CIF 含佣 5%的英镑价格；

（2）不久对方来电，出价每套 GBP12.45/set CIFC5 Manchester，订一个 20’集装箱的货。若按此价格成交，盛大公司销售盈亏率是多少？

（3）最后以每套 12.57 英镑成交。若盛大公司想保持 9%的利润，则国内供货价应为多少？

题 15-5 某出口商品 1 000 件，每件 17.30 美元 CIF 纽约，总价为 17 300 美元。其

中运费 2 160 美元，保险费 112 美元。进货价每件 117 元人民币（含 VAT17%），定额费用率为 10%，出口退税率为 9%，当时银行的美元买入价为 8.28 元人民币。

（1）求该笔业务的出口换汇成本和盈亏额。

（2）试用换汇成本方法求该笔业务的出口收汇盈亏率和成本盈亏率。

题 15-6 上海中兴毛纺厂与新加坡莱恩斯贸易有限公司达成一笔出口 1 000 套化纤羽绒服的交易，以 CIF 价成交，每套 55 美元。外商订购一个 20 英尺的集装箱货物。

经了解，羽绒服的国内购货成本为每套 420 元（人民币，下同）；一个 20’集装箱的海运费为 1 100 美元；该批服装的出口仓储费为 650 元，国内报关费为 350 元，包装费为 1 000 元，港口装船费为 900 元，中兴公司业务费为 2 500 元，国内段运杂费为 2 000 元，商检费按购货成本的 0.1%计；海运保险费按 CIF 成交价加一成投保一切险，费率为 1%；羽绒服出口有 9%退税（以购货成本计算），增值税率为 17%。中兴公司承诺给外方公司总成交金额 5%的佣金。（美元兑人民币汇率为 1:7.60）

求中兴公司达成该笔交易的出口换汇成本、盈亏额和销售盈亏率和成本盈亏率（用两种方法计算，进行验证）是多少？

题 15-7 中国五矿进出口公司向泰国五金贸易有限公司出口一批黄铜圆丝，货号分别是 SWG36 和 SWG39，采用散货装。每公吨圆丝的国内收购价分别为 22 000 元和 22 500 元（人民币，下同）。泰国公司将以每公吨 2 850 美元 CIFC3 Bangkok 价购买 6 公吨 SWG36 黄铜和 8 公吨 SWG39 黄铜。每公吨黄铜的海洋运费为 47 美元。出口该批货物的国内包干费用为 3 200 元，保险按成交价加一成投保一切险，费率为 0.98%。退税为 9%，增值税为 17%，美元兑人民币汇率为 1:7.60。

求达成该笔交易五矿公司的换汇成本、盈亏额和销售盈亏率和成本盈亏率（用两种方法计算，进行验证）。